AutoCAD® 2002: A Building Approach

Book 1
Learning the Basics

AutoCAD® 2002: A Building Approach

Book 1
Learning the Basics

Terry D. Metz

Marion Technical College

Upper Saddle River, New Jersey
Columbus, Ohio

Library of Congress Cataloging-in-Publication Data

Metz, Terry D.
  AutoCAD 2002 : a building approach / Terry D. Metz.
    p. cm.
  Contents: bk. 1. Learning the basics -- bk. 2. Taking command -- bk. 3. From concept to application.
    ISBN 0-13-048058-4 (bk. 1) -- ISBN 0-13-048050-9 (bk. 2) -- ISBN 0-13-048061-4 (bk. 3)
  1. Computer graphics. 2. AutoCAD. I. Title.
T385 .M48 2003
620'.0042'02855369--dc21   2002007060

Editor in Chief: Stephen Helba
Executive Editor: Debbie Yarnell
Editorial Assistant: Sam Goffinet
Media Development Editor: Michelle Churma
Production Editor: Louise N. Sette
Production Supervision: Karen Fortgang, bookworks
Design Coordinator: Diane Ernsberger
Text Designer: STELLARViSIONs
Cover Designer: Jason Moore
Cover art: Terry D. Metz
Production Manager: Brian Fox
Marketing Manager: Jimmy Stephens

This book was set in Adobe Caslon and Futura by STELLARViSIONs. It was printed and bound by Courier Kendallville, Inc. The cover was printed by Phoenix Color Corp.

Screen representations used with permission from and under the copyright of Autodesk Inc. ©2002 Autodesk Inc.

Pearson Education Ltd.
Pearson Education Australia Pty. Limited
Pearson Education Singapore Pte. Ltd.
Pearson Education North Asia Ltd.
Pearson Education Canada, Ltd.
Pearson Educación de Mexico, S. A. de C.V.
Pearson Education—Japan
Pearson Education Malaysia Pte. Ltd.
Pearson Education, *Upper Saddle River, New Jersey*

Copyright © 2003 by Pearson Education, Inc., Upper Saddle River, New Jersey 07458. All rights reserved. Printed in the United States of America. This publication is protected by Copyright and permission should be obtained from the publisher prior to any prohibited reproduction, storage in a retrieval system, or transmission in any form or by any means, electronic, mechanical, photocopying, recording, or likewise. For information regarding permission(s), write to: Rights and Permissions Department.

10 9 8 7 6 5 4 3 2 1

ISBN: 0-13-048058-4

Dedication

I wish to dedicate this book to my wife Becky. Her patience, love, and support gave me strength to complete this work, and her editing skills greatly improved its readability. I also wish to dedicate it to the memory of my parents, Leonard and Mary Metz, who provided me with the freedom, opportunity, and resources to explore and develop the talents that led me to the field of engineering.

Preface

The purpose of this book and its companions, *AutoCAD® 2002: A Building Approach, Book 2: Taking Command* and *AutoCAD® 2002: A Building Approach, Book 3: From Concept to Application,* is to teach the fundamentals of using AutoCAD 2002 so that you can make simple, but professional engineering drawings.

This book takes you from opening the AutoCAD program for the very first time to being able to efficiently use the basic commands to set up, draw, and print drawings. It covers different techniques for putting lines on a drawing and drawing specific shapes such as rectangles, circles, arcs, and ellipses. You will also learn about the different types of engineering units and their use in engineering. As part of the activities in this book, you will make and save your own personalized drawing template, add text to your template, and use it for making drawings in this and the companion books. To give you "real-world" practice, there are *Applying the Concepts* exercises at the end of most of the modules, and a *Final Project* at the end of the book. Sections in Appendix A cover the use of combination and architect's scales for those who are not familiar with, or who need to review, these topics.

Instead of showing you the myriad commands available in AutoCAD 2002, this book teaches you the most efficient methods of using the AutoCAD program. When learning a new computer program, it is easy to be overwhelmed with all that the program can do, and it can be confusing when many methods to do the same thing are introduced at the same time. It is far better to learn one method well and then, after becoming proficient in this method, look for other ways to accomplish the same tasks. Therefore, this book generally focuses on using the toolbars to access most of the drawing and editing tools. By learning to identify and use the buttons on the toolbars, you will find yourself quickly becoming proficient at making simple drawings.

To the student

The step-by-step approach used in this book guides you through the learning process and teaches you how to use the AutoCAD program. But you must be careful when using this learning method. It is very easy to fall into the habit of doing the "mechanical" steps as outlined without engaging your brain so that you learn from the steps you are doing. You always must know both *what* you are doing in each step and *why*. As you progress through each step, check it off; and as you check it off, ask yourself whether you understand why you did what you did. If not, figure out why. When checking the boxes, use a pencil so you can erase and do the step over if you do not truly understand the "why."

If you get lost in a section, back up to the beginning of that section and try again. I have always felt that the most important button on any software program is the UNDO button. It allows you to back up one step at a time and correct your mistakes without starting over entirely. The person who developed this button understood that mistakes will be made, and that deleting everything and starting at the very beginning is not very efficient. You will learn about this button early in the book, so don't be afraid to use it to back up a few steps and do them over again so that you learn from the experience.

This book does not provide you with information on every single feature in AutoCAD. I recommend that you purchase a small reference guide to the software and keep it handy to look up other ways of doing things or new things that you would like to do. AutoCAD also provides you with immediate help, from *Help* buttons inside dialog boxes that describe the features of that box to selecting the *F1* function key to open AutoCAD 2002's extensive user documentation that will help you with every facet of the program.

I also encourage you to "play" with the software. Try to learn things on your own. Explore new ways to speed up your work. CAD operators in industry are paid both for applying their technical knowledge to engineering design and on how productive they are at using the program. As with most learned skills, the more you practice the better you become. This book is not intended to teach engineering design; however, it will teach you the basics of AutoCAD to enable you to become proficient at using this software. You can then build on the basic foundation these books provide.

To the instructor

Although this is a first edition, it is far from being an untested text. The methods used in this book have been used for years in various educational settings. The modules in this book have been classroom tested with good success over the past two years by me and other regular and adjunct faculty at Marion Technical College.

The methods of step-by-step learning work well for teaching software programs, since students progress at different rates. During a lecture students who fall behind can become frustrated and may give up listening, hoping to figure it out later. Students who pick up things quickly may start exploring other features or jump ahead; and although exploration is an excellent way to learn, these students may tune out the instructor and miss some important point the instructor is trying to make. The other students who are following the instructor are busy refocusing their attention from the instructor to the computer, to the instructor, and back to the computer over and over again. This is a very inefficient way to learn something as complicated as a software program.

Students are often forced to purchase textbooks with lengthy discussions on sometimes trivial topics that they quickly forget as soon as the course or exam is over. But most students do not read the assigned portions of their textbooks. Instead, they tend to learn by looking at the examples in the book or figuring out how to do things or how to solve problems on their own. In short, students learn best by doing.

Moreover, you cannot learn to operate a software program by simply reading a book. Often I have taken along a text or manual while traveling without computer access, hoping to learn how to operate a particular new software program. It was a waste of time. Without hands-on interaction with the computer, learning does not take place.

This is why I decided to try the step-by-step approach in my classes. All the students read the book; they have to because it is the only way they know what to do next. I usually give a short introductory lecture at the start of each class with the computers off so I have the students' attention. Then, the students start working on their own, and I offer help when someone is having problems. If someone finishes work early, I challenge him or her with additional tasks. I always encourage students to "play" with the program and try to discover other features or ways of doing things on their own. I never allow students to rush through a module or assignment as there is a chance that they only did the "mechanical" steps; they did not learn the "why." So this text does not eliminate the instructor; instead, it frees the instructor to spend time helping those students who need help.

In addition to its use in the classroom, this text is also appropriate for distance learning. Students can purchase the student edition of AutoCAD, install it on a personal computer, and complete the activities at home or work. Drawings can then be transferred through e-mail between student and instructor. If your school does not currently have a distance learning course in AutoCAD, this may be an excellent and cost-efficient way to get one started.

This book, along with its companions, also provides flexibility by using a modular format. No textbook is perfectly laid out the way an instructor would like to teach the material. The modularized approach allows you to assign modules or activities in the order you prefer. It can also be used for business and industry training. Companies can determine what skills their employees need and then use the modules and activities to provide training in those particular areas.

About the Instructor's Manual

I have included assignments with the activities in this book. They provide a good basic foundation for someone learning AutoCAD because they allow students to practice the skills they learn in the modules and activities. In my classes I always supplement these assignments with additional assignments that I hand out on a weekly basis. This allows me to control the pace of the class and keep students from rushing ahead. I usually require students to pass a quiz on the previous module before they get the next set of assignments. This allows me to adjust the number of additional assignments for a particular class, since some classes just seem to progress slower than others, while maximizing the number of assignments the students complete. I have included the additional assignments I use on the CD-ROM that is provided with the instructor's manual. You can print these supplemental assignments and use them in your class as you wish.

The CD-ROM provided with the instructor's manual also contains keys to all the assigned drawings, in both the book and the supplemental assignments in the instructor's manual, in *.dwg* format. You can plot these drawings and use them to check student assignments. I usually make transparencies of these drawings so I can overlay them on students' drawings to check for mistakes and to verify that they are to scale.

The manual also contains syllabi for both quarter and semester systems.

To all users of this book

I welcome all comments and suggestions that will improve these books. As a teacher, I am always looking for new ways to help students learn. Therefore, any suggestions that can help students will be included in future releases.

Acknowledgments

I would like to acknowledge those who made this book possible. Without their help, I could never have completed it.

Thank you to all the CAD students and their instructors at Marion Technical College who tested these materials, pointed out problems, and suggested improvements. Their comments and suggestions helped refine the material to make it more student-friendly.

Thank you to Tom Cole, Director of Engineering, Eagle Crusher Company, Inc., for his review and testing of these modules. Many of his suggestions are included in these books.

Thank you to Cindi Meier, Account Manager-Education, IMAGINiT Technologies, for providing me timely releases of AutoCAD 2002 that allowed me to update the modules to the latest version.

I would like to thank the reviewers of this text: Alex Devereux, ITT Technical Institute (AZ); Jerry M. Gray, West Georgia Technical College; Steve Rosbert, Gloucester County College (NJ); and Judith D. Wooderson, Ph.D., San Juan College (NM).

Contents

Module 1

Basics of the AutoCAD Program   1

Activity 1   Starting, Maximizing, Minimizing, and Closing AutoCAD   1
Activity 2   AutoCAD's Screen Layout   6
Activity 3   Personalizing the Screen Layout to Work for You   10
Activity 4   Opening an AutoCAD Drawing   16
Activity 5   Working with Multiple Drawings   24
Activity 6   Saving an AutoCAD Drawing   26
Activity 7   Printing a Drawing   29
              Module 1 Review Questions   32

Module 2

Putting Lines on a Drawing   35

Activity 1   Linear Units   35
Activity 2   Angular Units   41
Activity 3   The Cartesian Coordinate System   45
Activity 4   Drawing Lines Using Absolute Coordinates   54
Activity 5   Drawing Lines Using Relative Coordinates   61
Activity 6   Drawing Lines Using Polar Coordinates   66
              Applying the Concepts   72
              Module 2 Review Questions   74

Module 3

Modifying Objects on a Drawing 77

- Activity 1   Erasing   77
- Activity 2   Trim, Extend, Move, and Copy   85
  - Applying the Concepts   97
  - Module 3 Review Questions   98

Module 4

Drawing Regular-Shaped Objects 101

- Activity 1   Drawing Rectangles   101
- Activity 2   Drawing Polygons   111
- Activity 3   Drawing Chamfers   116
  - Applying the Concepts   124
  - Module 4 Review Questions   126

Module 5

Getting in Close and Moving Around a Drawing 129

- Activity 1   Zooming In and Out   129
- Activity 2   Panning   135
  - Module 5 Review Questions   139

Module 6

Drawing Curved Shapes 141

- Activity 1   Drawing Circles   141
- Activity 2   Drawing Arcs   153
- Activity 3   Drawing Ellipses   165
- Activity 4   Drawing Donuts and Solid Circles   175
- Activity 5   Drawing Fillets   180
  - Applying the Concepts   187
  - Module 6 Review Questions   189

Module 7
Putting Text on a Drawing 191

Activity 1 Dynamic Text 191
Activity 2 Multiline Text 205
Applying the Concepts 215
Module 7 Review Questions 217

Module 8
Using a Template and Setting a Drawing's Parameters 219

Activity 1 Starting a New Drawing Using a Template 219
Activity 2 Setting the Units and Limits of the Drawing Area 226
Module 8 Review Questions 229

Module 9
Final Project 231

Appendix A
Using Engineering Scales 235

Activity 1 Using a Combination Scale 235
Activity 2 Using an Architect's Scale 246
Appendix A Review Questions 255

Appendix B
Answers to End-of-Module Questions 257

Index 259

AutoCAD® 2002: A Building Approach

Book 1
Learning the Basics

Module 1

Basics of the AutoCAD Program

Activity 1

Starting, Maximizing, Minimizing, and Closing AutoCAD

Objectives: After completing this activity, you should be able to do the following:

- Open and close the AutoCAD 2002 program.
- Maximize and minimize the program window.
- Resize the program window.

Procedure: ☑ Check each box as you complete that item.

☐ Locate the *AutoCAD 2002* icon, shown in Figure 1-1, on the Windows desktop. Place the mouse pointer over the icon and double-click the left mouse button to open the program. If you perform this operation correctly, you will see a small hourglass next to the mouse pointer, indicating that the program is loading in the background.

Figure 1-1
Double-click the *Auto-CAD 2002* icon to open AutoCAD.

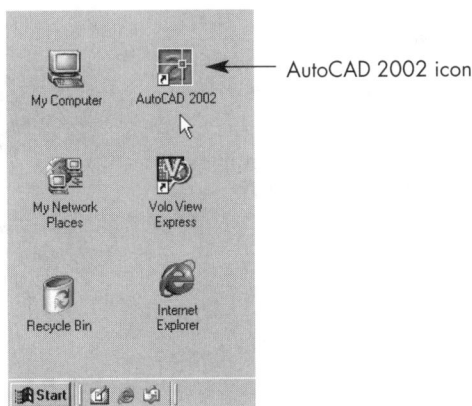

1

2   Module 1

If you are having trouble double-clicking fast enough to open the program, try saying "click-click" while you click the button. You will find that your finger follows your words.

If the AutoCAD 2002 icon is not on your desktop, you can still open the program by clicking the *Start* button, sliding the mouse pointer to the *Programs* menu item, and holding it there until the cascading *Programs* menu appears. Then slide the pointer to the right and down the *Programs* menu to highlight the *AutoCAD 2002* folder. Another cascading menu containing AutoCAD items will open. Slide the mouse pointer to the right and over the *AutoCAD 2002* item to highlight it. Click the left mouse button once to open the program. This sequence is shown in Figure 1-2.

The *Start* button is located on the Windows taskbar that is usually located at the bottom of the screen. To provide more work area, Windows can be set to automatically hide the taskbar. To make a hidden taskbar visible, move the mouse pointer all the way to the bottom of the screen, as if you are trying to drag it off the screen, and the taskbar will appear. If it does not, it may be hidden along the top or one of the sides of the screen.

☐   After a few seconds the program window will appear and after a few more seconds either the *AutoCAD 2002 Today* dialog box, Figure 1-3, or the *Startup* dialog box, Figure 1-4, will appear in the center of the screen. You will not be using either dialog box until a later activity, so close it by clicking once on the "X" button in the upper right-hand corner of the dialog box. This button is noted in each of the figures. The box will close and the program will continue to load. This may take some time, so be patient. (If neither dialog box appears, there is no problem. Allow the program to load and continue with the next step.)

☐   For this activity you will work with the three buttons located in the upper right corner of the program window. Depending on how the drawing window is configured, these buttons may appear as a single set, as seen in Figure 1-5a, or as a double set, as seen in Figure 1-5b. The buttons at the very top are for the AutoCAD program and are the ones you will be working with. Locate these buttons and make sure you use *only* these buttons in this activity.

☐   The *Minimize* button is the left one of the three buttons. Clicking this button will reduce the program window to a single button on the Windows taskbar, as shown in Figure 1-6. This button is used when you need to go back to the Windows desktop to open or work on another program. Clicking on the *AutoCAD 2002* taskbar button will restore and reactivate the program window. Try minimizing and restoring the program a few times. You will be required to do this in future activities.

Figure 1-2
Click on the *AutoCAD 2002* item from the *Programs* menu to open AutoCAD.

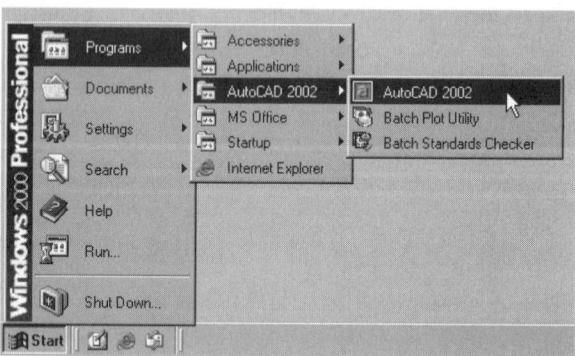

Figure 1-3
Click on the button in the corner of the *AutoCAD 2002 Today* dialog box to close it.

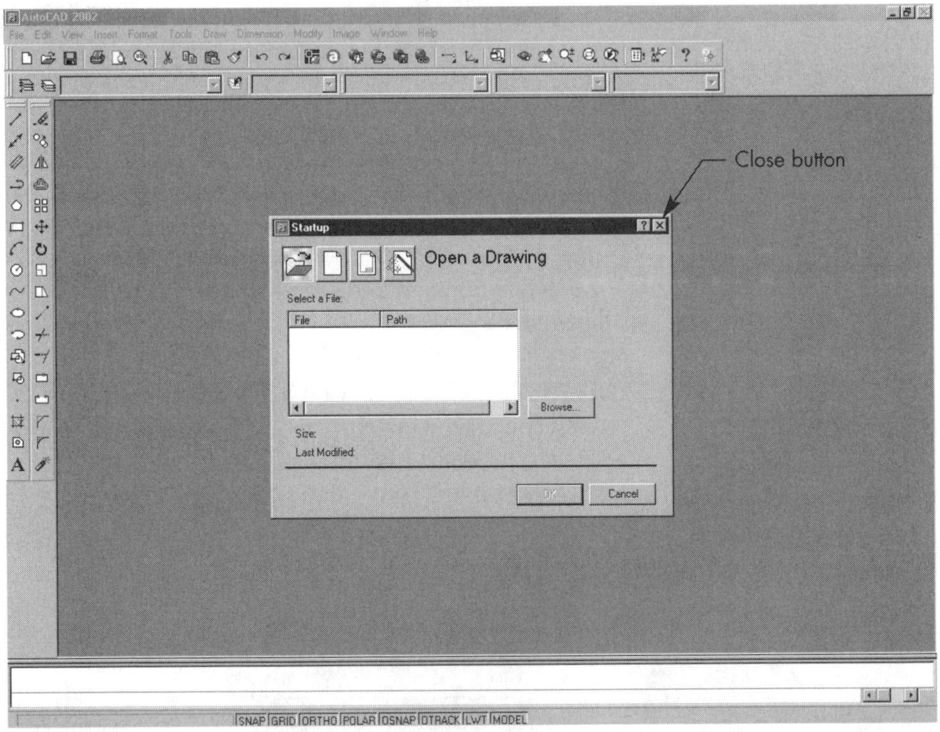

Figure 1-4
Click on the button in the corner of the *Startup* dialog box to close it.

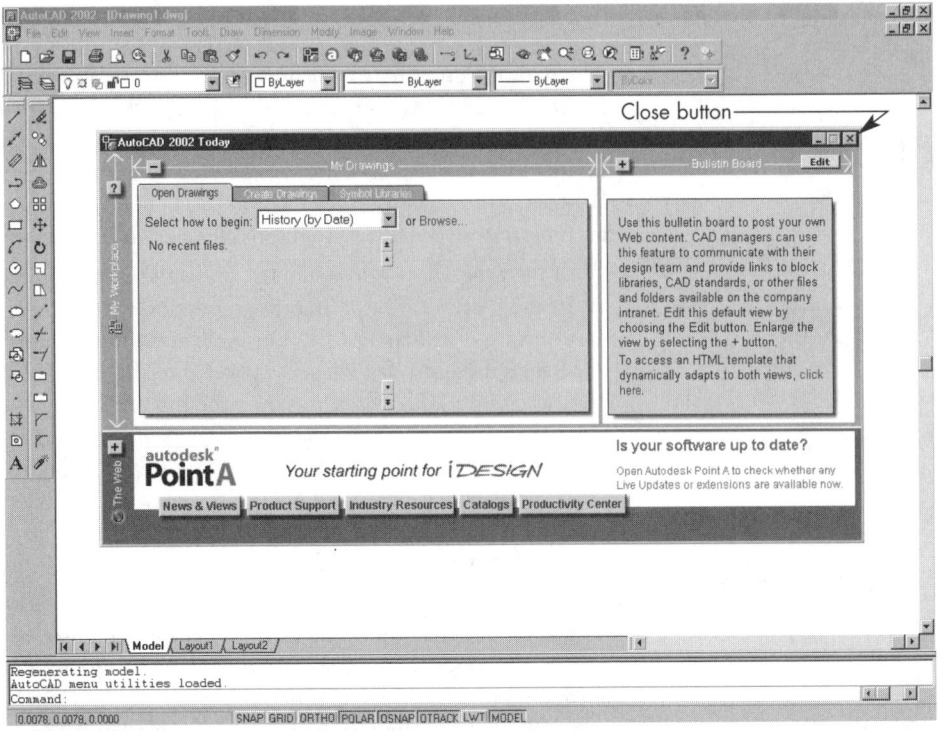

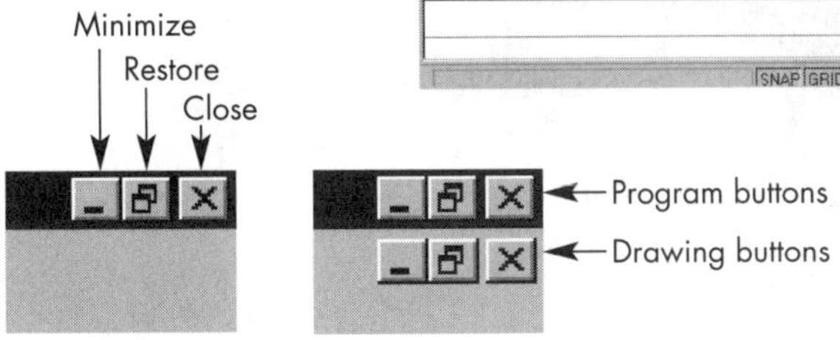

Figure 1-5
Minimize, Restore, and *Close* buttons (a) for AutoCAD program only or (b) for both program and drawing windows

Figure 1-6
Click on the *AutoCAD 2002* button on the Windows taskbar to restore and reactivate the program window.

3

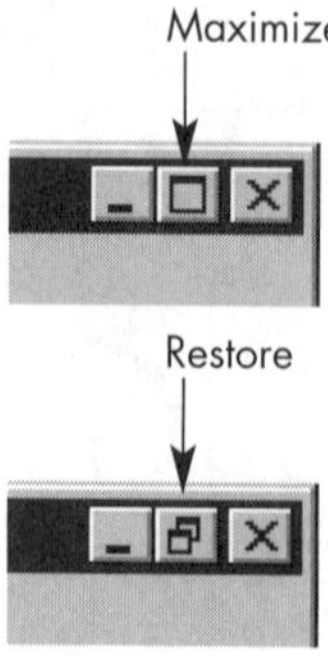

4 Module 1

Figure 1-7
The *Maximize* button makes the window fill the screen and the *Restore* button returns it to its previous size.

☐ The middle button may appear as either a *Maximize* or a *Restore* button, as shown in Figure 1-7. The *Maximize* button will make the program window fill the screen. The *Restore* button will return the program window to its previously set size, usually smaller than full screen. Click on the middle button several times and observe the changes in the buttons and window size. When you understand the function of these buttons, restore the screen to its smaller size so the *Maximize* button is showing.

☐ With the program window smaller, move the mouse pointer across the outside edges of the program window. When the mouse pointer is directly over one of the window's edges, it will change from a single arrow to a double arrow. The line will be horizontal, Figure 1-8a, when it is over the left and right sides of the window and vertical, Figure 1-8b, when it is over the top and bottom edges of the window. If you move the pointer to one of the four corners of the window, the line will be angled, Figure 1-8c. Move the pointer around the edges of the window, making sure you can produce the effects described above. You may not be able to see all four edges of the program window because part of it is off the screen. This is not a problem. Practice on the edges you have available.

☐ When the mouse pointer is shaped as a double arrow, that edge of the window can be resized in the direction of the arrows. Place the mouse pointer over the right (or left) edge of the program window so the arrowheads appear, and press and hold down the left mouse button. Move the mouse left and right, while holding the button down. You will see the outline of the edge of the window move as you move the mouse. Move the mouse so the outline is near the middle of the screen and release the mouse button. The program window will be resized to this new location. Repeat the above procedure and move the edge back to its original position.

Note: If part of the program window is off the computer screen, you can move the entire window by placing the mouse pointer in the colored area to the left of the Minimize button. Then press and hold the left mouse button and drag the program window to a new location. As you work on this activity, you may want to relocate the window occasionally to access other parts of the window.

☐ Try resizing the program window by moving each of the four sides and the corners. You may also want to switch between *Maximize* and *Restore* after each resize to see that the program window returns to the size you just set. When you understand how to resize the window, maximize the program window so the *Restore* button is showing.

☐ The third button is used to close the program and return to the Windows desktop. Click on the *Close* button to exit AutoCAD.

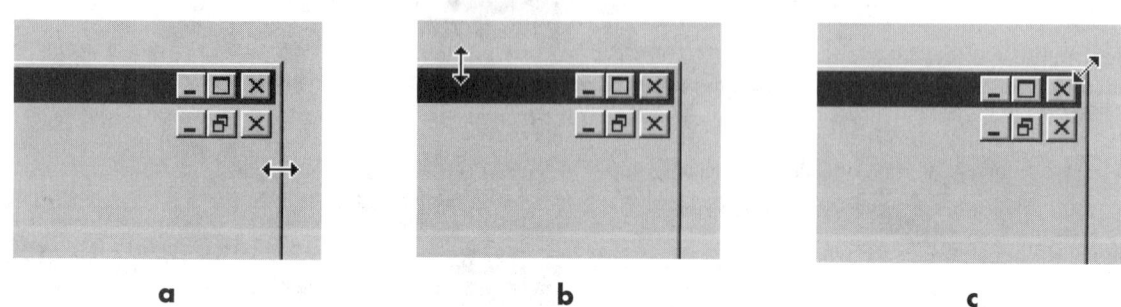

a   b   c

Figure 1-8
Pick on the edge of the window to resize it (a) horizontally, (b) vertically, or (c) angled from the corner.

To prevent losing any drawing information, AutoCAD will ask if you want to save the changes you have made to the drawing. In this activity you did not make any changes to the drawing, and you should not receive this prompt. If you do get the prompt, answer *No* and the program will close.

There are two additional ways of closing AutoCAD. You can click on the *File* pull-down menu and select *Exit* from the bottom of the list, or you can type **QUIT** next to COMMAND: in the command window and hit the *Enter* key.

☐ This is the end of Activity 1. You may want to try opening, closing, and resizing the AutoCAD program and window to make sure you fully understand these functions since they will be used often throughout the course.

Activity 2

AutoCAD's Screen Layout

Objectives: After completing this activity, you should be able to identify the following Auto-CAD screen features:

- Program window title bar
- Pull-down menus
- Standard toolbar
- Object properties toolbar
- Drawing area
- Model and Layout tabs
- Command window
- Status bar buttons

This activity will introduce you to the features of the AutoCAD program screen. It is important that you learn the names and locations of these features because you will be using them in future activities. As each feature is introduced, you will be given a brief description of its purpose or use. Each of the items will be covered in detail in future activities.

The locations of many of the features described in this activity can be changed. This allows CAD operators to place drawing tools in convenient locations to improve their productivity. After you open the program, your display may not look exactly like the one in Figure 1-9. It is important that you locate each feature listed in this activity so that you are familiar with its appearance, not its exact location. In the next activity you will learn to customize the screen layout to meet your needs.

Procedure: ☑ Check each box as you complete that item.

☐ Double-click on the *AutoCAD 2002* icon to open the program.

☐ When the *AutoCAD 2002 Today* or *Startup* dialog box appears, click on the *Close* button in its upper right corner to close the dialog box and continue loading the program. (If neither dialog box appears, there is no problem. Allow the program to load and continue with the next step.)

The program window should now look similar to the one shown in Figure 1-9. The one exception is that the drawing area on your screen is probably black. The drawing area in the figure has been changed to white for clarity. This will be the standard appearance in this and future activities.

☐ **Locate the program window title bar (a).** The program window *title bar* is located across the top of the AutoCAD window. It provides information about the program and the active drawing. When you start a new drawing, AutoCAD assigns it a generic name (Drawing1, Drawing2, etc.). The first time you save a drawing you are asked to give it a name. From then on, this new name will appear in the title bar. Since AutoCAD allows you to have several drawings open at the same time, it is important to refer to this bar from time to time to make sure you are working on the correct drawing.

Basics of the AutoCAD Program   7

Figure 1-9
AutoCAD's screen layout

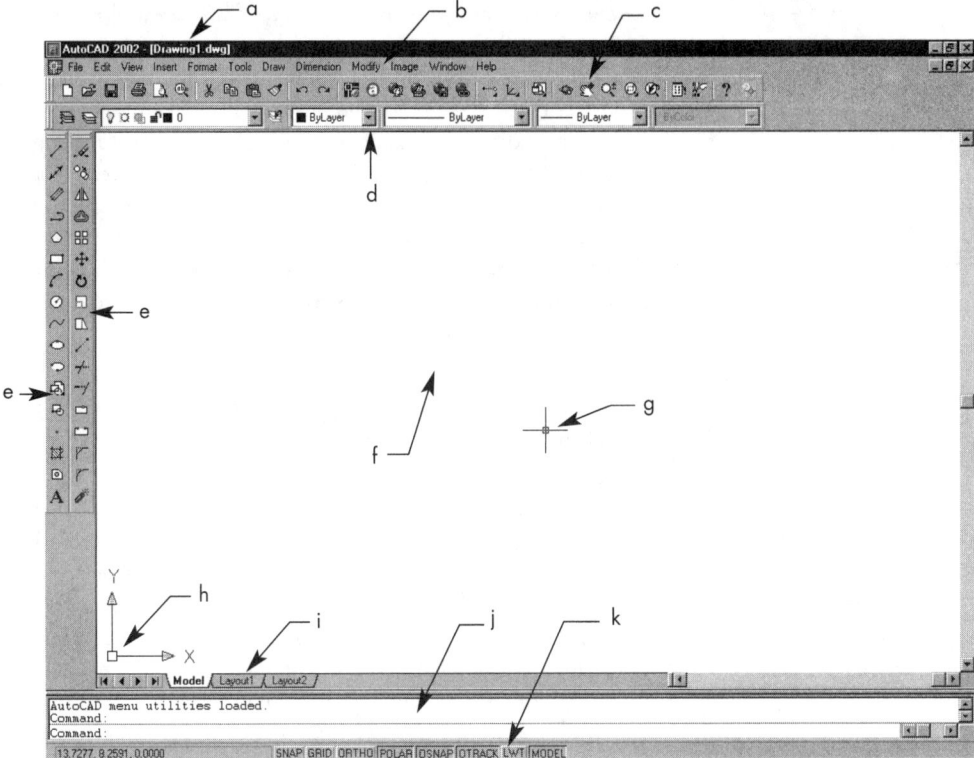

☐ **Locate the menu bar (b).** The *menu bar* is located beneath the title bar. Most Windows programs have a menu bar. Some of the menu names on this bar are common to all Windows programs, and others are unique to AutoCAD. Clicking on a menu name will cause a list of items to appear. Because this list comes down from the top of the screen, it is commonly referred to as a *pull-down menu*. Sliding the cursor down the menu allows you to highlight and select the item you want. You may want to spend some time looking at each of the pull-down menus. Menu items with an arrow on the right have an additional cascading menu that contains more items. To open a cascading menu, slide the mouse pointer to highlight the menu item and after a short pause the cascading menu will appear. To select items on the cascading menu, slide the mouse pointer to the right onto the new menu and down to the item you want. A pull-down menu and a cascading menu are shown in Figure 1-10.

Figure 1-10
Items with an arrow on pull-down menus have additional cascading menus.

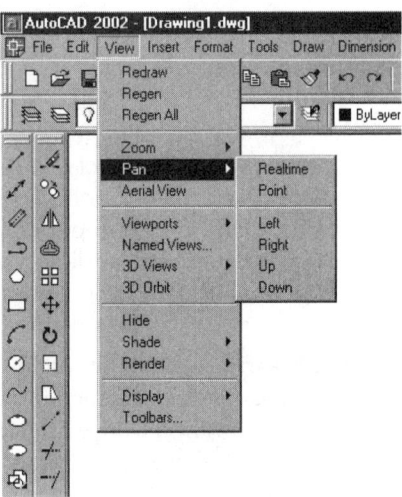

8 Module 1

- ☐ **Locate the Standard toolbar (c).** The *Standard* toolbar contains some items that are common to all Windows programs and some that are unique to AutoCAD. A toolbar is made up of buttons that perform certain operations. When you place the mouse pointer over one of the buttons, it takes on a "raised" appearance to let you know your pointer is in a position to select that button. If you have worked with other Windows programs, you may recognize the *New, Open,* and *Save* buttons on this toolbar. The picture on each button is there to remind you of the button's operation. If you forget what a button does, you can hold the mouse pointer over that button for a second and a small box called a "tooltip" will be displayed that gives you the button's function. The buttons on this and all other toolbars will be described in detail in future activities.

- ☐ **Locate the Object Properties toolbar (d).** The *Object Properties* toolbar is usually located below the standard toolbar. This toolbar is used to set the properties of objects in the drawing.

- ☐ **Locate the general drawing toolbars (e).** Two general drawing toolbars are shown in Figure 1-9. The number, type, and location of these toolbars vary, so you may have more than the two shown here or they may be in different locations. These toolbars are used to perform certain drawing operations. Using toolbar buttons to perform operations is usually faster than using either pull-down menus or typing in commands. This course will emphasize the use of toolbars to perform most drawing operations. In the next activity, you will learn to open, close, and relocate the general drawing toolbars to meet your drawing needs.

- ☐ **Locate the drawing area (f).** The drawing area is where you will actually make your drawing. This area is shown in white on the reference picture, but it will be probably be black on your screen.

- ☐ **Locate the graphics cursor (g).** The graphics cursor is a set of crosshairs with a square box at the center. This cursor appears when you are over the drawing window and is used to perform various drawing operations. If you move the cursor to areas other than the drawing area, its shape changes to a regular Windows pointer.

- ☐ **Locate the coordinate system icon (h).** The coordinate system icon identifies the location of the "x" and "y" axes. Sometimes it is easier to relocate or to rotate the axes to make drawing operations easier. The system icon will help remind you of the orientation of these axes.

- ☐ **Locate the Model and Layout tabs (i).** The *Model* and *Layout* tabs are at the bottom of the drawing window. They are used to select either model space, where you do the drawing, or layout space (sometimes called paper space), where you prepare your drawing for printing. When the *Model* tab is selected, the screen is usually black. When the *Layout* tab is selected, you see a white rectangular area that represents the piece of paper you will be printing on. In the future, you will work on drawings where the layout area includes the drawing border complete with company name and the drawing title block area.

Note: If you decide to select one of the layout tabs to see what paper space looks like, you will get a *Page Setup* dialog box as the program moves from model space to paper space. Click the *Close* button in the upper right corner and the dialog box will close. When you are done looking at paper space, click on the *Model* tab to return to model space.

- ☐ **Locate the Command window (j).** The *Command* window's location varies, so you may have to look around for this one. Some people prefer working with the command window below the drawing area, some like it above, and some use it as a floating window in the drawing area. In the next activity you will learn to change its position to a location that best suits your needs. The command window is very important because it is the place where you input information to the program, like dimensions, quantities, or commands, and it is where AutoCAD communicates with you, requesting needed information or describing what the program is currently doing.

- [ ] **Locate the Status bar (k).** The *Status bar* is located at the bottom of the program window. It contains a set of buttons that deal with drawing control functions. These buttons will be described in detail in future activities. It also contains the coordinate display, at the far left end, that shows the current location of the graphics cursor (g). Move the cursor around the drawing area and you should see the coordinates change. If they are not changing, it is because they are turned off. To turn them on, place the mouse pointer over the display numbers and click the left mouse button. They will now be active.

- [ ] This completes Activity 2. You may want to spend some time reviewing all the features described above. You should now be able to locate and name each feature without having to look it up.

- [ ] Click on the *Close* button to exit AutoCAD. If you are asked if you want to save the drawing, select *No*.

Activity 3

Personalizing the Screen Layout to Work for You

Objectives: After completing this activity, you should be able to do the following:

- Move and dock the command window.
- Change the number of text lines visible in the command window.
- Open and close the text window.
- Move and dock the toolbars.
- Show and hide toolbars.

Procedure: ☑ Check each box as you complete that item.

- ☐ Double-click on the *AutoCAD 2002* icon to open the program.
- ☐ When the *AutoCAD 2002 Today* or *Startup* dialog box appears, click on the *Close* button to close the dialog box and continue loading the program. (If neither box appears, there is no problem. Allow the program to load and continue with the next step.)

Moving and Docking the Command Window

In this section you will learn to move the command window to various locations. This allows you to place it at a location that is most convenient for you.

- ☐ Locate the *Command* window. It will probably be either above or below the drawing window.
- ☐ Move your mouse pointer around both the white and gray areas of the command window and observe how the pointer changes. When it is over the white areas, it has an "I" shape and when it is over the gray areas, it is an arrow.
- ☐ Locate the gray, square-shaped area that is below and to the right of the two scroll bars in the lower right corner of the command window. (See Figure 1-11.)
- ☐ Place the mouse pointer in this area, press and hold the left mouse button, drag the pointer to the middle of the drawing area, and release the button. The command window will come along for the ride. The command window is now "floating" in the drawing area. Floating means that it is not attached to any of the sides of the program window, but is in its own window that can be easily moved around the drawing area. The floating command window is shown in Figure 1-12. Note that it now has its own title bar.
- ☐ Place the mouse pointer in the same gray, square-shaped area of the command window, press and hold the left mouse button, and move the command window to a different location *in* the drawing window. Do this several times until you are comfortable with this operation.
- ☐ An alternative method of moving a floating window is to "grab" it in the window's title bar area. Place your mouse pointer in the command window's title bar area, press and hold the left mouse button, and drag it to a new location *in* the drawing area. Do this several times until you are comfortable with this operation.
- ☐ You are now going to "dock" the command window along the top of the program window above the drawing area. Place the mouse pointer in the command window's

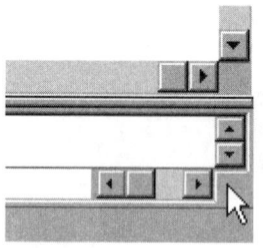

Figure 1-11
"Grab" the *Command* window in its gray area to relocate it.

Basics of the AutoCAD Program   11

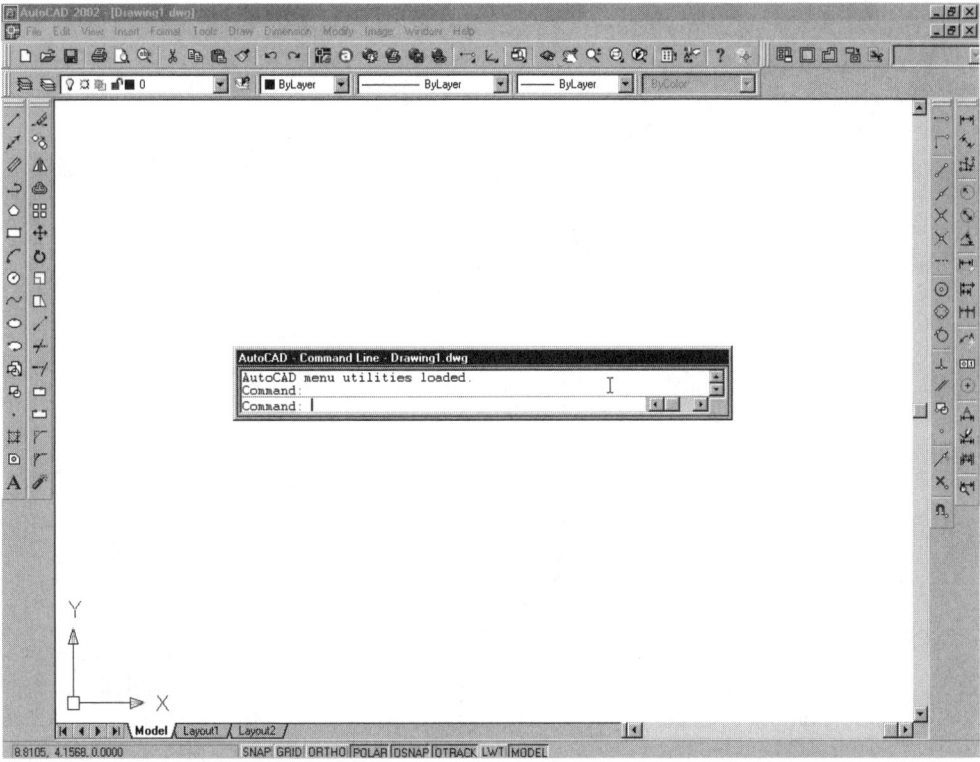

Figure 1-12
Floating *Command* window in drawing area

title bar, press and hold the left mouse button, and drag the window toward the top of the screen. As it reaches the edge of the drawing area, the shape of the outline of the command window will change from narrow to long. This is an indication that the window is over a docking area. Release the mouse button and the window will be docked at that location.

☐ The "docked" command window will be located either below, between, or above the standard and object properties toolbars. You can change the location by again grabbing the toolbar in the square gray area at its lower right corner and dragging it to a different location relative to these toolbars. Try this now. It may take some practice, but you should be able to place it above, between, and below the two toolbars.

☐ Using the procedures described above, you should also be able to move and dock the command window at the bottom of the program window below the drawing area. Do it now.

☐ Continue to practice moving the command window until you feel comfortable with this operation. When you are done practicing, relocate the command window to the bottom of the screen below the drawing area. Leave it there for the remainder of this activity.

Changing the Number of Lines of Text

In this section you will learn to change the number of lines of text in the command window to meet your needs.

☐ Place the mouse pointer somewhere near the middle of the command window. The cursor will be "I" shaped.

Figure 1-13
Pick the edge of the *Command* window to resize it for additional lines of text.

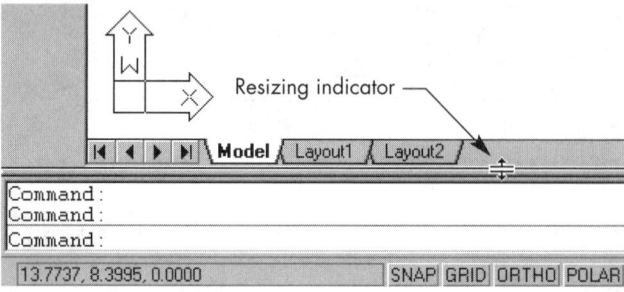

- *Slowly* move the cursor up toward the drawing area. As the pointer moves over the gray area of the command window, it will change into a standard arrow-shaped pointer.
- Continue to *slowly* move the pointer upward. As it reaches the edge of the command window, it will change into a pair of horizontal lines with two short vertical arrows. This is shown in Figure 1-13. It may take some practice to position the pointer exactly over the edge of the window.
- With the pointer over the edge, press and hold the left mouse button, and drag the pointer up a short way into the drawing area. A dark line, stretching across the program window, will indicate the location of the edge of the new window. Release the mouse button. The command window is now resized to view more lines of text. Since you have not completed any commands, the window is mostly empty. In the future, you will find that expanding the command window is a quick way of looking back at your previous commands.
- Place the pointer over the upper edge of the window, and when the cursor changes into double lines, press and hold the left mouse button. Drag the pointer all the way to the bottom of the screen and release the mouse button. Notice that the command window did not disappear, but instead contains only one line.
- Repeat the above procedures and change the number of lines in the command window to three (3). This is the *minimum* number of lines you should have showing when working in AutoCAD. If you try working with fewer than three, you may miss important information that AutoCAD is providing while you are making drawings. On the other hand, having too many lines in the command window wastes valuable drawing space.

Opening and Closing the Text Window

Sometimes three command lines are not enough, or you may want to check a command you did several steps earlier. This section will show you how to open a text window that will display every command line since you started the AutoCAD program.

- Press the *F2* function key located at the top of your keyboard and the text window, shown in Figure 1-14, will appear atop the program window. This window can be maximized, resized, and closed using the procedures learned in Module 1–Activity 1, to meet your needs. Since you have not done many operations, there will not be many lines of text. In the future as you work on drawings, you will find that this window is full, and it will have scroll bars that allow you to go back and check any previous operation done since the start of your drawing session.
- Press *F2* again and the window will close. Press *F2* several times to practice opening and closing the text window.

Basics of the AutoCAD Program   13

Figure 1-14
AutoCAD's text window

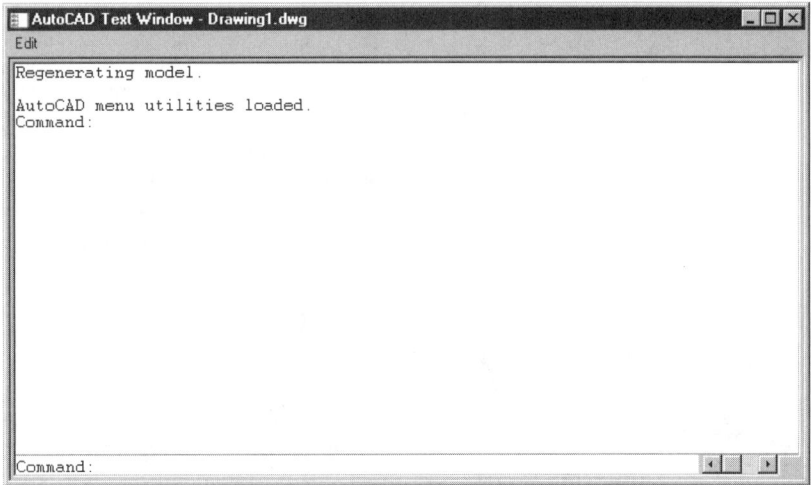

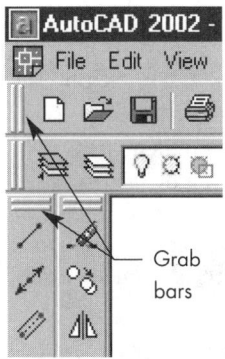

Figure 1-15
Use the grab bars at the end of the toolbars to move them.

Moving and Docking Toolbars

Like the command window, toolbars can be moved to new locations on the screen. In this exercise you will learn to move, float, and dock toolbars.

☐ Docked toolbars are moved by using grab bars. Grab bars, shown in Figure 1-15, appear as two raised lines located at the end of the toolbar. On vertical toolbars, the grab bars are located at the top, and on horizontal toolbars, they are located on the left end.

☐ Locate the grab bars on one of the *vertical* toolbars. Place your mouse pointer over the grab bars, press and hold the left mouse button, drag the toolbar to the center of the drawing area, and release the mouse button. The toolbar now becomes a floating window. This window can be reshaped using the methods discussed in Module 1–Activity 1. Some drafters use this method to make a floating tool palette so they can place the tools right next to their work.

☐ When the toolbar becomes a floating window, the grab bars disappear. The toolbar can now be "grabbed" using the title bar area. Place the mouse pointer in the title bar area, press and hold the left mouse button, drag the toolbar back to its original docked location, and release the mouse button. The toolbar is now docked.

Note

When the toolbar is about to be docked it will change to a tall vertical outline indicating the new shape of the toolbar. If the outline is horizontal, you are too close to the top or bottom of the drawing window. Move up or down until you get a vertical outline.

☐ The location of the docked toolbar will be determined by where the outline is when you release the mouse button. It is possible to place it on either side or below an existing docked toolbar. Practice moving the vertical toolbars by placing them in different locations inside, outside, and below other toolbars until you are comfortable with the procedure.

☐ The vertical toolbars can also be docked along the top or bottom of the drawing window. When you move the toolbar to the top or bottom of the screen, its outline will become horizontal and it can be docked in that location. Practice moving and docking the vertical bars to horizontal positions. When you are done practicing, move them back to their original positions. (See Figure 1-9 in Module 1–Activity 2 if you cannot remember where the original positions were.)

☐ The horizontal toolbars are moved using the same procedure. Practice moving and docking the object properties and standard toolbars. When you dock these, make sure the outline is horizontal before releasing the mouse button. Also make sure you can place the horizontal toolbars in different locations relative to other toolbars. When you are done practicing, move them back to their original positions. (See Figure 1-9 in Module 1–Activity 2 if you cannot remember where the original positions were.)

Showing and Hiding Toolbars

There are 26 toolbars available in AutoCAD 2002, as well as the availability of making additional custom toolbars. If all of these toolbars were turned on at once, there would be little room to draw, so you will want to work with only a few of them visible. In this part of the activity, you will learn how to show and hide toolbars.

☐ Place the mouse pointer over any of the visible toolbars and click the *right* mouse button. The toolbar menu shown in Figure 1-16 will appear with a list of all available toolbars. The ones that have a checkmark beside them are turned on (visible) and the others are turned off. There are usually four checked by default.

☐ Move the mouse pointer up and down the list and observe that each menu item is highlighted as the pointer passes over it. Move the pointer to highlight *Inquiry* and click the left mouse button. The menu will disappear and the *Inquiry* toolbar will appear as a floating window in the drawing area. If you wished, you could now dock the toolbar for future use. However, there is no need to do this because you are now going to turn it off in the next step.

☐ Place the mouse pointer over any toolbar (even the newly opened *Inquiry* toolbar), and click the *right* mouse button. Slide the mouse pointer to the *Inquiry* menu item and click the left mouse button. The menu and the *Inquiry* toolbar will disappear.

☐ Place the mouse pointer over any of the visible toolbars and click the *right* mouse button to open the *Toolbar* menu. Select *Dimension* from the menu and click the left mouse button. Using the procedures learned earlier in this activity, dock the *Dimension* toolbar along the right side of the drawing window.

☐ Repeat the above step, selecting the *Object Snap* toolbar from the list. Dock this toolbar beside and to the left of the *Dimension* toolbar.

☐ Repeat the above step, selecting the *Viewports* toolbar from the list. Dock this toolbar horizontally to the right of the *Standard* toolbar near the top of the screen.

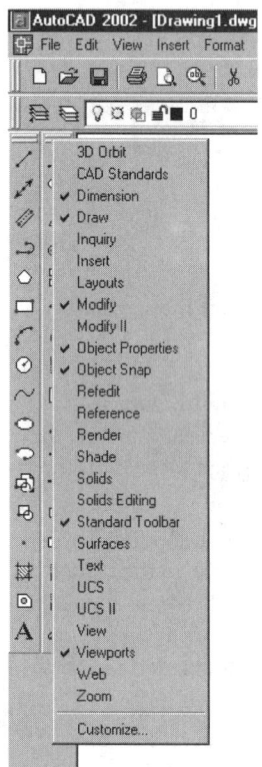

Figure 1-16
Right-click over any toolbar to open the toolbar menu.

Note

Sometimes a toolbar that is turned on is not visible on the screen. This can happen when another toolbar has "pushed" that toolbar off the screen. You may need to move a couple of the toolbars to find the one that is not visible.

The above method can be used to turn on and off any of the toolbars. For most activities, you will only use the seven toolbars listed below. Figure 1-17 shows the standard layout, with the seven toolbars, that will be used in most activities. You should now be able to locate and name each of the following toolbars without having to look it up. You can use this standard layout or make up your own.

- Dimension
- Draw

Basics of the AutoCAD Program 15

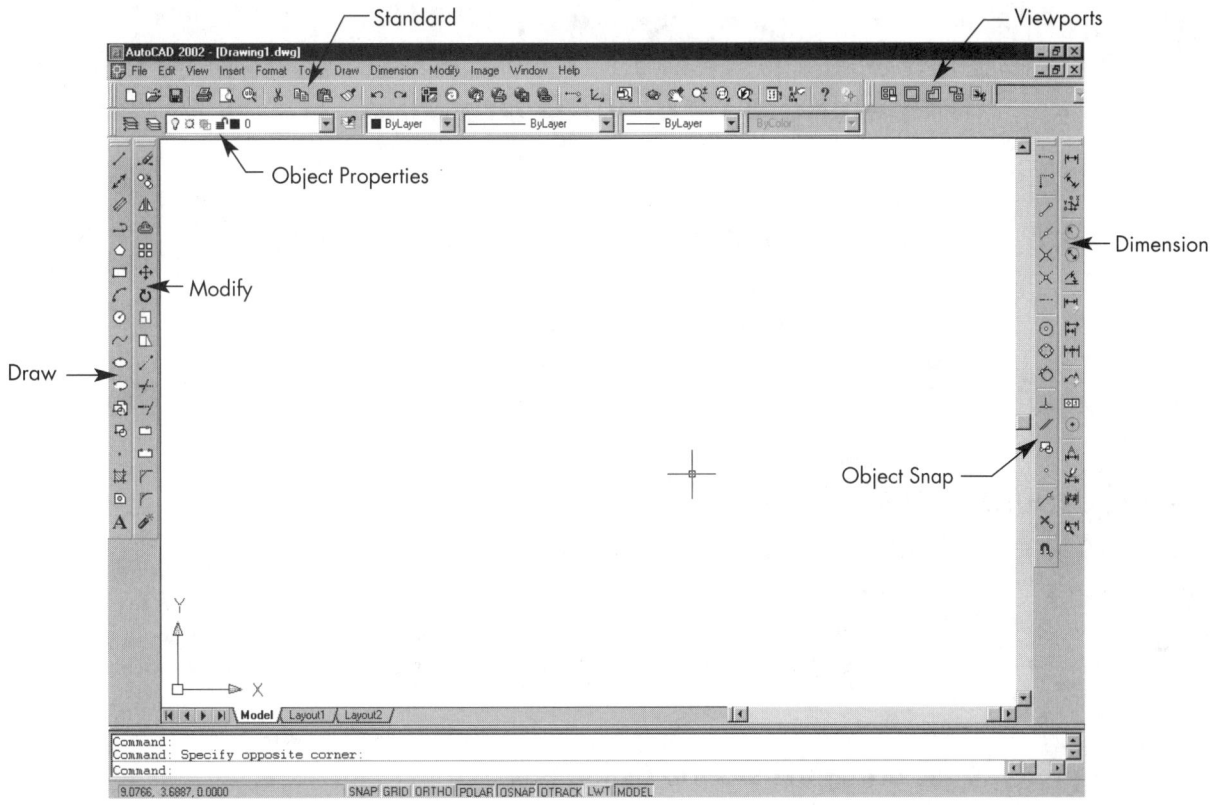

Figure 1-17
Standard layout showing the seven toolbars

- Modify
- Object Properties
- Object Snap
- Standard
- Viewports

If other people use your computer, they may turn toolbars on and off or resize the command window. Each time you start an activity, you should check to make sure that the seven toolbars are visible and ready to use. Where you place the toolbars around the screen is not important. The purpose of this activity is to give you the ability to customize the screen layout to meet your individual needs.

☐ This completes Activity 3. You may want to spend some time reviewing the procedures for moving, docking, and resizing program toolbars and windows.

☐ Click on the *Close* button to exit AutoCAD. If you are asked if you want to save the drawing, select *No*.

Activity 4

Opening an AutoCAD Drawing

Objectives: After completing this activity, you should be able to do the following:

- Locate and select the *Open* button on the *Standard* toolbar.
- Use the *Select File* dialog box to open an existing drawing.
- Use the Windows directory structure to locate files and folders.
- Open an existing drawing using the *AutoCAD 2002 Today* dialog box.

Procedure: ☑ Check each box as you complete that item.

☐ Double-click on the *AutoCAD 2002* icon to open the program.

☐ When the *AutoCAD 2002 Today* or *Startup* dialog box appears, click on the *Close* button to close the dialog box and continue loading the program. (If neither box appears, there is no problem. Allow the program to load and continue with the next step.)

Selecting the *Startup* Dialog Box

In this section you will learn how to specify which dialog box appears when the AutoCAD 2002 program opens.

☐ Wait for the program to completely load and *Command:* to appear in the command window.

☐ Click on the *Tools* pull-down menu and slide the pointer down to the bottom of the menu to highlight the *Options* selection. Click the left mouse button and the *Options* dialog box, shown in Figure 1-18, will open.

☐ You will see a set of seven tabs across the top of the dialog box. Click on the *System* tab.

☐ On the right-hand side, near the bottom of the *General Options* area, you will see *Startup:* and a white text box with a button containing a downward pointing arrowhead. Click on this button and a list of items will appear. This method of presenting a list of options is called a drop-down list and is used extensively in AutoCAD and most Windows programs. (See Figure 1-18.) This drop-down list contains only three items, but some lists are so extensive that you must use a scroll bar to see all the items. The following gives a brief description of each option on the Startup list.

Show TODAY startup dialog—The Today startup was introduced with the release of AutoCAD 2000i and provides additional functions for the CAD operator. Of these, there are three major functions. The first is a Bulletin Board that can be used to communicate information between computers inside a company using the company's intranet. The second function provides Internet access to AutoDesk's Point A, which allows downloading of program updates, industry news, and other helpful features and tips. Point A also allows placement of drawings on the Internet so that they can be accessed by others. Note: if your computer is not connected to the Internet, these functions will not be available to you. Finally, Today allows you to locate and open drawings, and to start new drawings from templates. In this activity you will learn how to open drawings using AutoCAD 2002 Today.

Basics of the AutoCAD Program   17

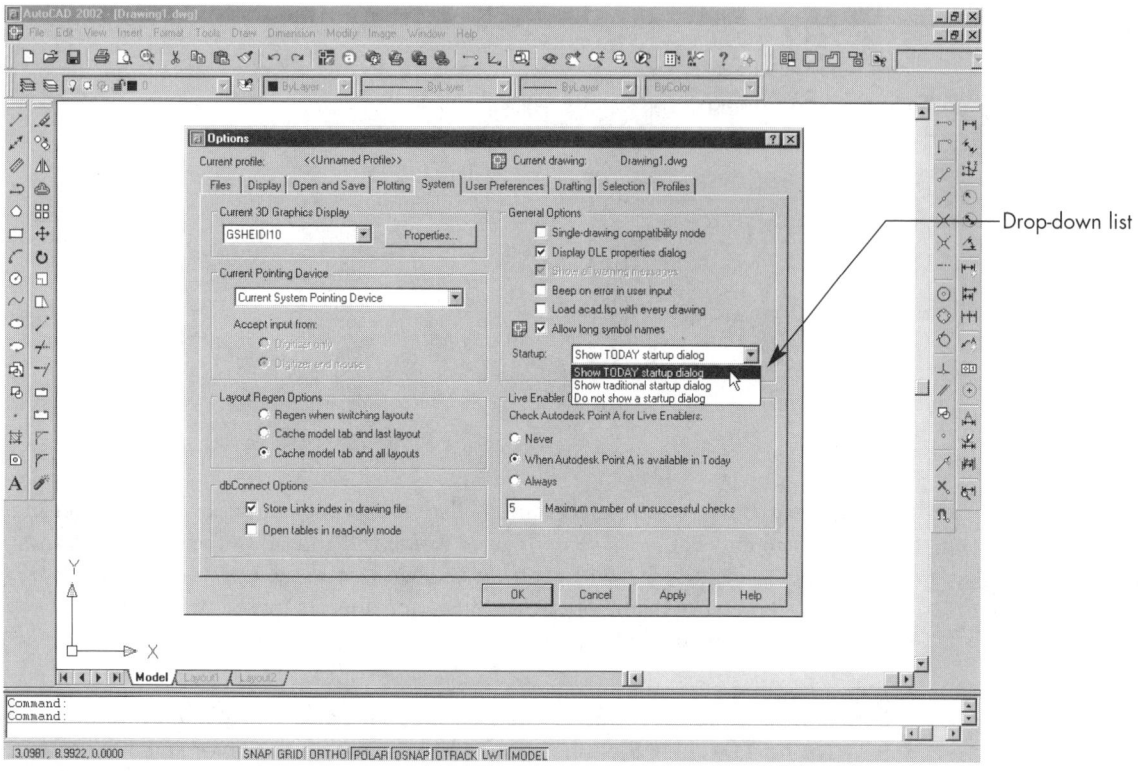

Figure 1-18
Select the *Show TODAY startup dialog* from the drop-down list.

> **Show traditional startup dialog**—Earlier versions of AutoCAD used this dialog box to open, start, and set up a drawing. It does not provide Internet access or the Bulletin Board features found in Today. AutoCAD provides this option for companies who do not use these functions and prefer to work with the traditional dialog box.
>
> **Do not show a dialog**—This option takes you directly to the drawing editor as AutoCAD opens. It automatically opens AutoCAD's default template. New drawings can then be set up, or an existing drawing opened from within AutoCAD.

☐ Click on the *Show TODAY setup dialog* option, the list will close, and the *Show TODAY setup dialog* will appear in the window.

☐ Click on the *Apply* button at the bottom of the dialog box, and then click on the *OK* button. This will close the dialog box and ensure that the *TODAY* box appears the next time you start AutoCAD.

Locating and Selecting the *Open* Button

In this section you will learn how to locate and select the *Open* button on the *Standard* toolbar. This is the first step in opening a drawing.

☐ Locate the *Standard* toolbar. It is usually located along the top of the screen below the pull-down menus. Since you learned how to move toolbars in the last activity, you or someone else may have placed it in another location, so you may have to look around to locate it.

☐ The second button from the left end of the *Standard* toolbar is the *Open* button. (See Figure 1-19.) It is easy to identify because it looks like an open file folder. If you are

Figure 1-19
Click on the *Open* button to open an existing drawing.

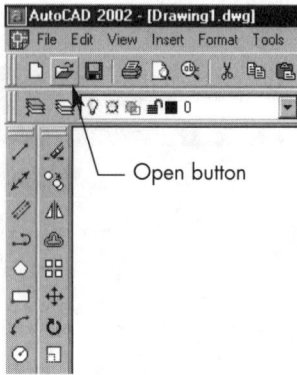

unsure that you have the correct button, place the mouse pointer over the button and hold it there for a couple of seconds and a *tooltip* will appear. In the future you can use *tooltips* to identify any button on any toolbar. Locate the *Open* button and place the mouse pointer over it. Notice that the button appears "raised" to indicate that you are over that particular button.

If the tooltip option has been turned off on your computer, you can restore it by typing **TOOLTIPS** on the command line, hitting the *Enter* key, typing **1** as the new value, and hitting the *Enter* key. This method is called setting the system variable and will be covered in more detail in a later activity. For the TOOLTIPS system variable 0 = off and 1 = on. By entering 1, you turned tooltips on.

☐ Make sure your mouse pointer is over the *Open* button and click the left button. After a few seconds the *Select File* dialog box, shown in Figure 1-20, will appear.

There are two additional ways of opening a drawing. You can click on the *File* pull-down menu and select *Open* from the list by clicking on it, or you can type **OPEN** next to *Command:* in the *Command* window and hit the *Enter* key. Both methods will open the *Select File* dialog box.

Using the *Select File* Dialog Box to Open an Existing Drawing

In this section you will learn how to open and close an existing drawing.

The procedures in this section are based on opening drawings from the CD provided with this book. If you or your school has installed the CD files on the computer's hard drive, you will need to look in the appropriate subdirectories on the C: drive. When the files are copied from the CD to a hard drive, they become *read-only* files and when you try to open them you will get an *AutoCAD Alert* asking if you want to open this *read-only* drawing. Select the *Yes* button and allow the drawing to load. *Read-only* does not mean that you cannot make changes to the drawing, only that you cannot save any changes to the original file. Companies often make their standard drawings *read-only* to protect them from accidental changes, but allow their employees to open, change, and save them with different names.

Basics of the AutoCAD Program   19

Figure 1-20
Locate and click on the CD-ROM drive [D:] in the *Select File* dialog box.

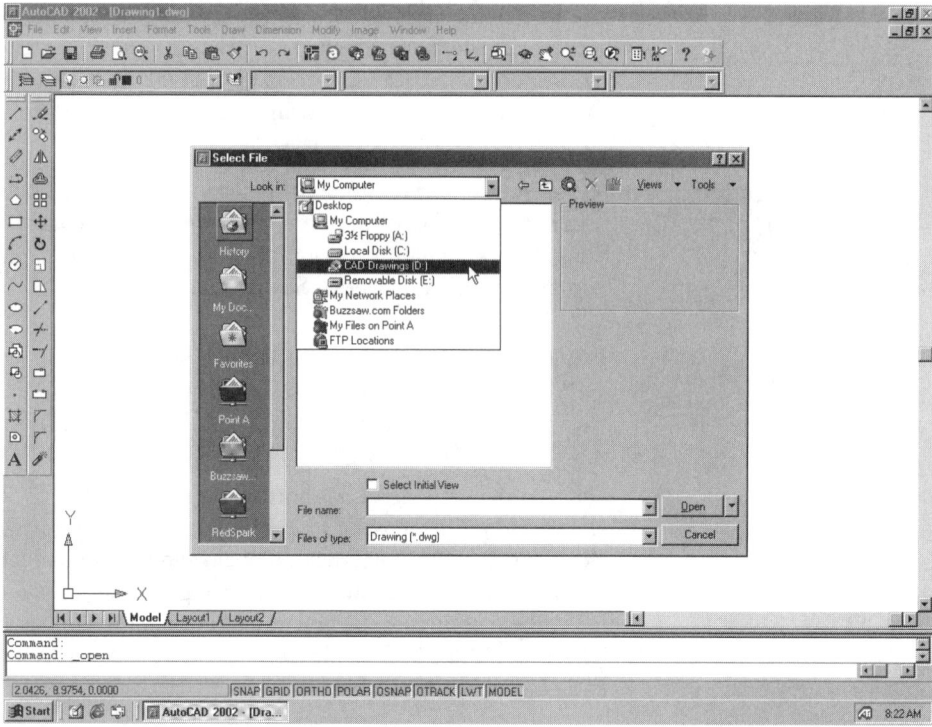

☐ At the top of the dialog box you will see a drop-down list labeled *Look In*. Click on the down arrow button to open the list. (See Figure 1-20.) Depending on the configuration and devices on your computer, your list may look slightly different.

☐ Locate the CD-ROM drive that contains this book's CD, probably drive D. Slide the mouse to highlight that item and click the left mouse button. The list will close and a list of the subdirectories on the CD will appear in the white area in the center of the dialog box. (See Figure 1-21.)

☐ Locate the *Module01* subdirectory on the list. Place the mouse pointer over the file folder next to the name and double-click the left mouse button. The subdirectory will open and a list of drawings in that subdirectory will appear. (See Figure 1-22.)

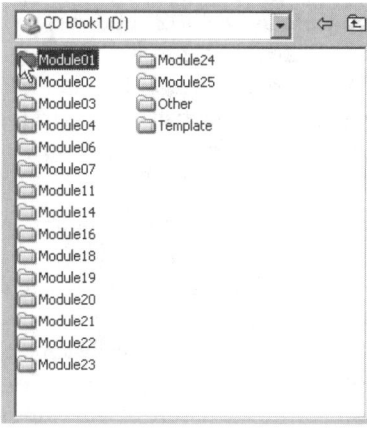

Figure 1-21
Double-click on *Module01* to open this subdirectory.

Figure 1-22
Click on the drawing file *M01A04-1.dwg* to highlight it.

20　Module 1

- [ ] Locate the drawing *M01A04-1.dwg* as shown. Depending on how your computer is configured, you may or may not see the *.dwg* extension after the file name. Place the mouse pointer over the icon to the left of the file name and click the left mouse button once to highlight the drawing file.

> **Note:** When selecting a file or subdirectory, it is always better to click on the icon and not on the file or subdirectory name. Sometimes when you click on the name you will enter the *edit name* mode and you might change something you don't want to change. So get in the habit of only clicking the icon.

- [ ] When the drawing is highlighted, click on the *Open* button. The dialog box will close and the drawing will open. You should see the message "Congratulations! You must have followed the directions perfectly." If you open any other file, you will not see this message.

- [ ] Click on the drawing's *Close* button. Be careful not to click the AutoCAD program close button. The drawing's *Close* button is below AutoCAD's. The drawing will close, but AutoCAD will remain open, and the original template drawing, Drawing1.dwg, will become the active drawing. Click the *Close* button to close this drawing without saving it. You will note that the program has taken on a different look. This is how AutoCAD looks with no drawings open. You only have the *Open*, *Close*, and *Help* buttons available.

Finding Files and Folders in Windows

In this section you will learn how to locate and open drawings located in other folders and on other drives.

- [ ] Click on the *Open* button and the *Select File* dialog box will appear. The program remembers the last folder you opened and returns you to that location.

- [ ] Open the *Look in* drop-down list and select the computer's hard drive [C:] by highlighting it and then clicking the left mouse button. A list of the files and folders on the C: drive will appear. Locate the *Program Files* subdirectory from the list and double-click on the file folder next to its name. Locate and double-click on the folder icon next to the *AutoCAD 2002* subdirectory.

> **Note:** If you cannot locate the AutoCAD 2002 subdirectory, look for a directory named MDT6. If AutoCAD 2002 was installed along with Mechanical Desktop 6, the AutoCAD program files will be in that directory. If your computer has the MDT6 directory, substitute MDT6 for AutoCAD 2002 in the remainder of this activity and in future activities.

- [ ] Locate the folder titled *Sample*. Place the mouse button over the icon for this folder and double-click the left mouse button to open it. You should see lots of drawings, indicated by the blue colored icon, listed along with several subdirectories. Move the slider at the bottom of the list to see all the drawings listed. Click on the icon of any drawing and a preview of that drawing will usually appear in the *Preview* window to the right of the list. The preview feature gives you an idea of which drawing you are opening. This is handy when you are unsure of a drawing's name, but can recognize what the drawing looks like.

- [ ] Locate and double-click on the icon next to the *1st Floor* drawing. The drawing will open. Double-clicking on a drawing file is the same as selecting it and then hitting the *Open* button.

Figure 1-23
Directory structure for the drawings in the *Sample* subdirectory

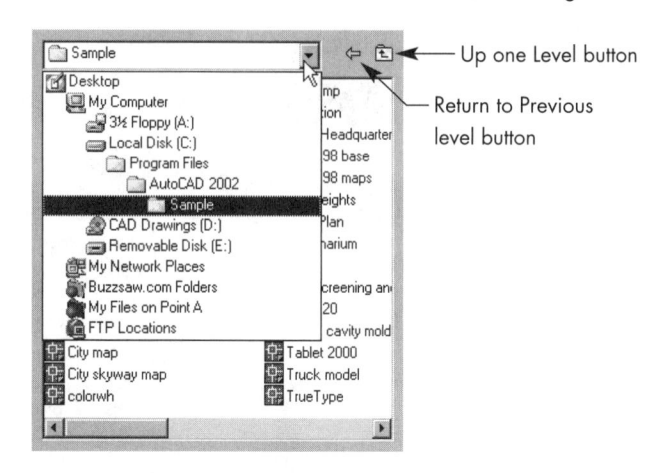

- Click on the *Close* box to close the *1st Floor* drawing. Be careful not to close AutoCAD.
- Click on the *Open* button.
- Open the *Look in* drop-down list. You should see a directory structure similar to Figure 1-23. This indicates that *Sample* is a subdirectory in *AutoCAD 2002*, and *AutoCAD 2002* is a subdirectory in *Program Files*. The *Program Files* folder is below hard drive C:, indicating that it is one of the primary folders on the hard drive.
- Click on the *AutoCAD 2002* file folder icon. This will take you up one folder in the directory structure, making *AutoCAD 2002* the current directory.
- Click on the button to the right of the drop-down list that has an icon of a yellow folder with an arrow. This is the *Up One Level* button that allows you to move up through the file structure. (See Figure 1-23.) This will take you up one folder level in the directory structure, making *Program Files* the current directory.
- Click on the button to the right of the drop-down list that has an icon of a blue arrow. This is the *Return to the Previous Level* button that takes you down through the file structure to the folders you came from. (See Figure 1-23.) This will take you back down one folder level in the directory structure, again making *AutoCAD 2002* the current directory.
- Click on the *Up One Level* button twice to return to the *C:* drive. This will take you to the top of the structure and show all the subdirectories on the hard drive.
- Click on the *Up One Level* button again. You will now see a list of all the drives available on your computer. You will probably have a 3 1/2 floppy drive [A:] and possibly a removable disk drive [E:]. You should be able to access these drives, when there is a disk in them, to open drawings using the same procedures you used to access drawings on the C: and D: drives in this activity. You may want to spend a few minutes going up and down the directory list and looking in different folders until you are comfortable with the procedures.
- Once you have completed this part, click the *Cancel* button to close the *Select File* dialog box. In the next section you will learn how to find and open a drawing during the AutoCAD startup, so click the AutoCAD *Close* button and close AutoCAD completely so you can restart it for the next section.

Using the *AutoCAD 2002 Today* Dialog Box to Open a Drawing

In this section you will learn how to open a drawing during the AutoCAD program startup.

- Double-click on the *AutoCAD 2002* icon to start the program. As the program opens, the *AutoCAD 2002 Today* dialog box will appear. (See Figure 1-24.)

22 Module 1

Figure 1-24
AutoCAD 2002 Today dialog box

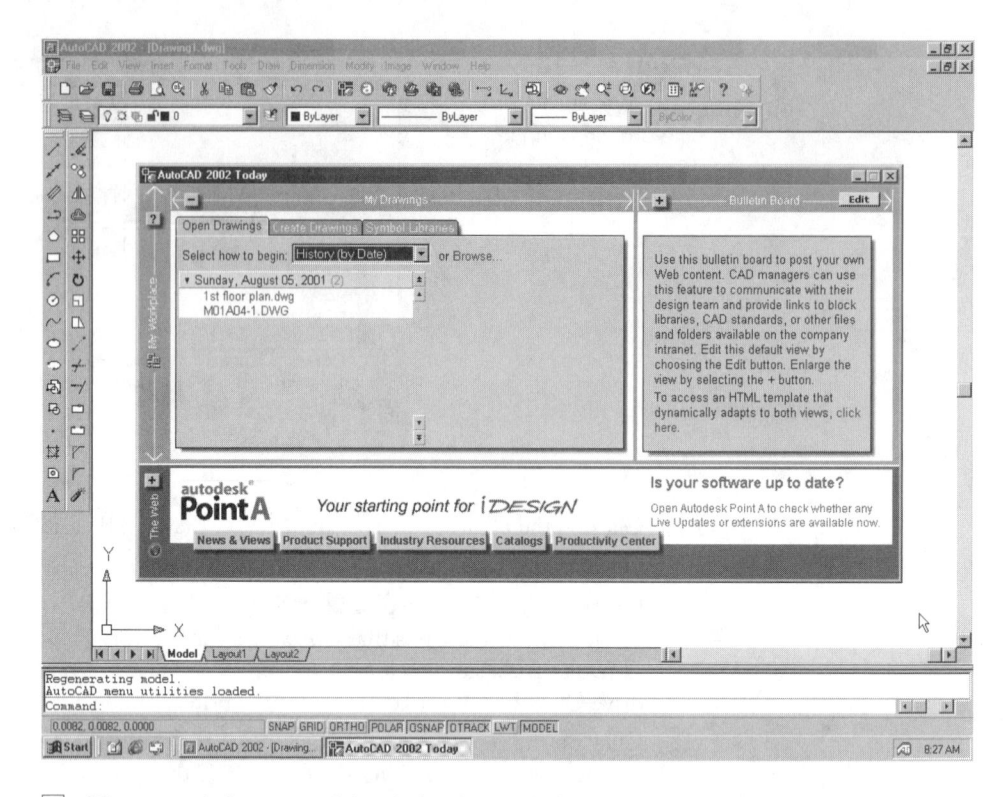

☐ The upper left corner of this dialog box, titled *My Drawings,* is where you open existing drawings and create new ones. If the *Open Drawings* tab is not selected, indicated by a light gray color, click on it to activate it. Your screen should look similar to Figure 1-24.

☐ Click on the *Select how to begin* drop-down list. (See Figure 1-25.) The following gives a brief description of each option. Click on each item to select it from the list before you read the description. This will let you see the arrangement of each option.

Most Recently Used—This option lists up to nine of the most recent drawings that were opened or worked on with the latest at the top of the list. You should see the *1st Floor* drawing at the top of the list, unless you opened other drawings later while practicing with the directory structure.

History (by Date)—This option sorts the drawings that were opened by date, with the most recent first. Drawings are listed by day during the current week, and by week for drawings prior to the current week. You can open and close a date's list by clicking on the arrowhead to the left of the date. The scroll bars to the right can be used to move up and down the list.

Figure 1-25
Four *Select how to begin:* options are available in the *AutoCAD 2002 Today* dialog box.

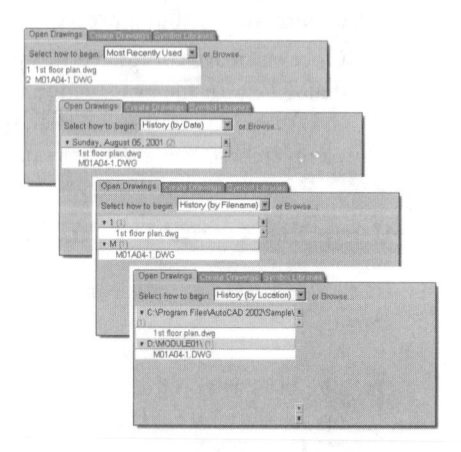

Basics of the AutoCAD Program   23

- **History (by Filename)**—This option sorts the drawings by their file name, based on the first character, number, or letter, in numeric or alphabetical order. You can open and close each character's list by clicking on the arrowhead to the left. The number listed in parentheses gives the number of drawings in that character's list.
- **History (by Location)**—This option sorts the drawings by the folder name where the drawing was saved. The list is sorted first by the drive letter where the folder exists. So if you are looking for a drawing you opened from the CD, you would start with the lists that begin with D:\, or the letter of the CD-ROM drive on your computer, and then look for the subdirectory where the drawing was stored. As in the other lists, the arrowhead opens and closes each list and the scroll bars can be used to access different parts of the list.

☐ If it is not selected, open the drop-down list and select *History (by Date)* by clicking on it. You are not going to use it now, but *History (by Date)* will be open the next time *AutoCAD 2002 Today* opens. The last function used becomes the default for the next time the dialog box opens.

☐ Next to the drop-down list you will see *or Browse…* The blue word "Browse" is a hyperlink that takes you directly to the *Select File* dialog box that you used earlier in this activity.

☐ Move the mouse pointer over the word "Browse." The cursor changes from the standard Windows pointer to a hand with a pointing finger. Click the left mouse button and *AutoCAD 2002 Today* will close and the *Select File* dialog box will open.

☐ Using the methods you learned earlier in this activity, locate *M01A04-1.dwg* on the Module Drawings CD, and open it. You now know how to find and open existing CAD drawings.

☐ Click on the close program button to close AutoCAD. If you get a dialog box that asks if you want to save the drawing, select *No* and let the program close.

Note: If you receive an AutoCAD alert stating that "AutoCAD cannot close Drawing1.dwg, because there is a command still active.", use the following steps to exit the program.

☐ Click the *OK* button to close the alert box.
☐ Click the *Close* button on the current drawing you have open. This will make *Drawing1* the active drawing.
☐ Hit the *Esc* key to cancel the active command associated with *Drawing1*.
☐ Click on AutoCAD's *Close* button to exit the program.

You may need to use this procedure whenever you close an AutoCAD drawing that was opened or created using the *Browse* hyperlink button in *AutoCAD Today*.

This completes this activity. In future activities you will be asked to open drawings using both the *AutoCAD 2002 Today* dialog box and the *Open* drawing button on the *Standard* toolbar. You may want to refer to this activity in the future if you forget how to open a drawing using either of these methods.

Activity 5

Working with Multiple Drawings

Objectives: After completing this activity, you should be able to do the following:

- Open two or more drawings and make each active.
- Cascade the drawings windows.
- Tile drawing windows horizontally and vertically.
- Close one or more drawing windows while leaving the others open.

Procedure: ☑ Check each box as you complete that item.

☐ Double-click on the *AutoCAD 2002* icon to open the program.

☐ When the *AutoCAD 2002 Today* dialog box appears, click the close button and allow the program to continue to load. It is important that you start this activity with the drawing maximized. If the default drawing appears in a window, maximize it now.

Open Two or More Drawings and Make Each Active

In this section you will open three drawings and switch between them, making each active.

☐ Click on the *Open* button on the *Standard* toolbar. When the *Select File* dialog box appears, click on the drop-down list, and locate and click on the CD-ROM drive. Double-click on the *Module01* file folder.

☐ Locate *M01A05-1.dwg*. (Remember, .dwg may not appear on your computer.) Double-click on its icon to open it. Note that when a drawing is open, its name appears in AutoCAD's title bar. (See Figure 1-26.)

☐ Using the same method, open *M01A05-2.dwg* next, and then *M01A05-3.dwg*.

☐ Move the mouse pointer to the *Window* pull-down menu and click the left mouse button. The bottom part of this menu shows the three drawings you have opened. (See Figure 1-27.) The active drawing, the one you can work on, has a checkmark next to it.

☐ Move the mouse pointer down the list, highlight *M01A05- 2.dwg*, and click the left mouse button. The list will close and Drawing 2 will become active.

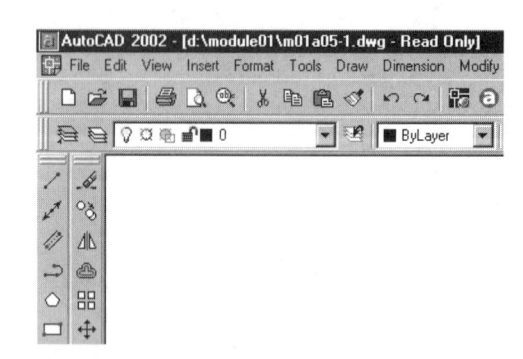

Figure 1-26
The program title bar shows the name and location of the active open drawing.

Figure 1-27
The *Windows* pull-down menu shows all open drawings.

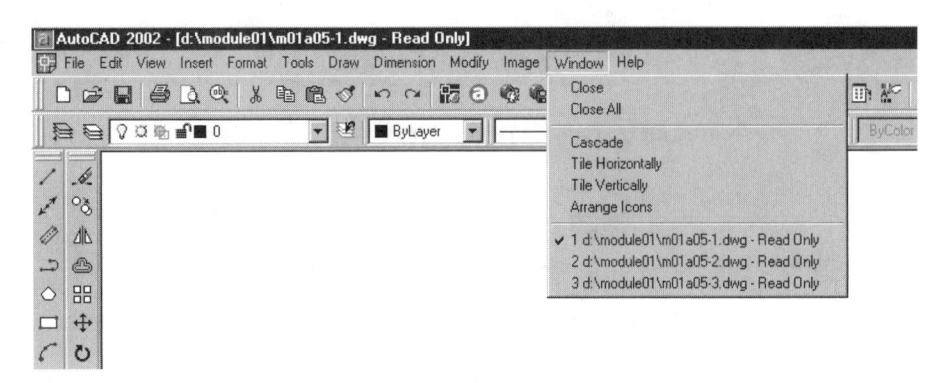

- Click on the *Window* pull-down menu and you will see that Drawing 2 is now checked.
- Make *M01A05-1.dwg* the active drawing by repeating the above procedure. If you did this correctly, you should see "This is Drawing 1" on your screen.

Cascading, Tiling, and Closing Drawings

In this section you will learn how to arrange the drawings in different ways to make it easier to move from one active drawing to another. You will also learn how to close one or more of the open drawings.

- Click on the *Window* pull-down menu. Slide the mouse pointer down to highlight the *Cascade* option and click the left mouse button. The three open drawings now appear in the drawing area, each in a window, stacked in a way that allows you to see each window's title bar.
- Two of the title bars are gray, indicating that they are not currently active, and the other title bar is in color, indicating that it is the active drawing. Place your mouse pointer over the title bar of Drawing 2 and click. That drawing becomes active and moves to the front of the stack. Repeat the procedure, to make Drawing 3 active.
- You will notice that the title bars of the other two drawings are now hidden. To make one of them active, you have two options. First, you can go to the *Window* menu and highlight and click on the drawing you want to make active. Try that now, making Drawing 2 active. The second method requires selecting *Cascade* from the *Window* menu. This will restack the drawings so you can see each of their title bars. You can then click on the title bar of the drawing you want to make active. Do this now, making Drawing 1 active.
- Click *Cascade* one more time so you can see the three title bars.
- The only drawing that you can work on is the active drawing. You are now going to close Drawing 3. Click on the title bar of Drawing 3 to make it active, and then click the *Close* button in its upper right corner. If you get a *Save changes to* message, click the *No* button. You should now have only Drawings 1 and 2 open.
- Another way of displaying more than one open drawing is by tiling. Go to the *Window* pull-down menu and select *Tile Horizontally*. The two drawings should now appear stacked (tiled). Go back to the *Window* menu and select *Tile Vertically*, and the two drawings will appear side by side. You can make either drawing active by clicking in its title bar.
- Close the active drawing by clicking on its *Close* button. If you get a *Save changes to* message, click the *No* button. Click on the *Maximize* button so the last drawing is no longer in a window, and then close that drawing and the AutoCAD program by clicking on their *Close* buttons.

Activity 6

Saving an AutoCAD Drawing

Objectives: After completing this activity, you should be able to do the following:

- Use the FILEDIA variable to show or hide the *Save Drawing As* dialog box.
- Save a drawing using the *Save As* command.
- Use the *Save Drawing As* dialog box to name and save a drawing to a specific drive.
- Locate and use the *Save* button on the *Standard* toolbar.

Procedure: ☑ Check each box as you complete that item.

- ☐ Double-click on the *AutoCAD 2002* icon to open the program. When the *AutoCAD 2002 Today* dialog box appears, select the *Open Drawings* tab if it is not already selected.
- ☐ As you did in a previous activity, use the *Browse* hyperlink to open the *Select File* dialog box. Go to the *Module01* subdirectory on the CD-ROM, and open the *M01A06-1.dwg* drawing file.
- ☐ When the drawing opens, you will see a view from an architectural drawing showing the front elevation of a house. If you don't, you have opened the wrong drawing. Close it and try again.

Setting AutoCAD to Show the *Save Drawing As* Dialog Box

The following steps are included here to ensure that AutoCAD displays the *Save Drawing As* dialog box. Saving can be done using the *Command line* prompts; but it is far easier to use the dialog box.

- ☐ Using the keyboard, type **FILEDIA**. It will appear next to *Command:* in the *Command* window. Hit the *Enter* key. (When you type commands in AutoCAD you have to be very careful; spelling does count.)
- ☐ The command line will now read "Enter new value for FILEDIA <1>". (You may have <0> instead of <1>.) For this and other dialog boxes to appear, the value must be set to "1". ("0" means do not show box.) Type "1" and press the *Enter* key.

Save a Drawing Using the *Save As* Command

In the following section you will rename and save a drawing.

Note: Most computers have several locations for saving drawings. The hard drive [C:] is the most common. In the past, the 3 1/2 floppy drive [A:] was used to save drawings to a disk so that files could be transported to other computers or locations. Because files are now much larger, most computers have other methods of saving and transporting files. Zip™ disk, SuperDisk™, and CD-RW drives are common types. These activities are written based on saving files to a *Removable Disk* drive [E:]. If you are saving to a different location, like a 3 1/2 floppy disk or a CD-RW, you will have to adjust the following procedure to save to that particular drive.

Figure 1-28
Select *Save As* from the *File* pull-down menu.

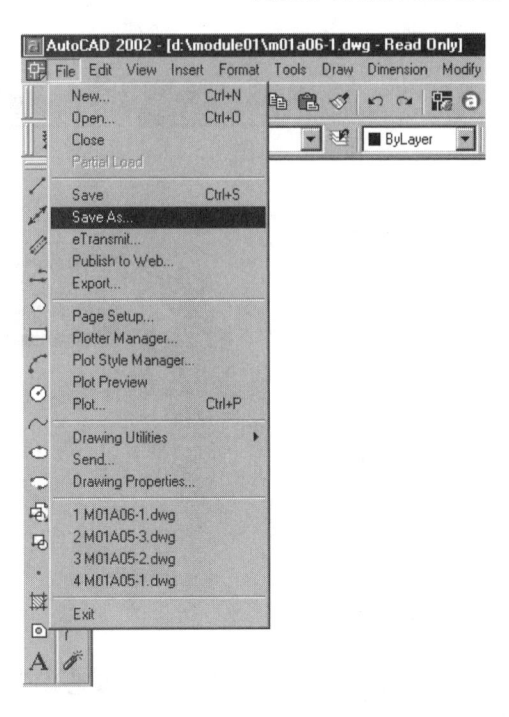

☐ For this activity you will save a drawing to your *Removable Disk*. Insert your disk into the proper drive before doing the next step.

☐ Click on the *File* pull-down menu, slide the mouse pointer down the list to highlight *Save As*, and click the mouse button. (See Figure 1-28.) The *Save Drawing As* dialog box will appear. This dialog box is similar to the *Select File* box from the last activity.

☐ Click on the arrow beside the *Save In:* drop-down list and slide the mouse pointer down the list to highlight *Removable Disk [E:]*. (See Figure 1-29.) Depending on your computer, the drive letter may be different, but it should still be identified as the *Removable Disk*. Click the left mouse button to make the *Removable Disk* drive the active directory.

☐ To rename the drawing, place the mouse pointer in the white box next to *File name:* and click the mouse button. Erase *M01A06-1.dwg* by using either the *Delete* or *Backspace* keys. Type **MY FIRST SAVE** in the box and click on the *Save* button. You will probably see the *Removable Disk* drive's light come on as the drawing is saved. The dialog box will close.

☐ Click on the *Window* pull-down menu and note that the default drawing Drawing1.dwg and MY FIRST SAVE.dwg are the only drawings listed. The drawing *M01A06-1* is no longer there.

Using the *Save* Button on the *Standard* Toolbar

In this section you will learn how to use the *Save* button to save the drawing you are working on.

☐ Locate the *Save* button on the *Standard* toolbar; it looks like a computer disk. (See Figure 1-30.) Every time you click on this button, you will save any changes made to the drawing. Click on the *Save* button now.

28   Module 1

Figure 1-29
Select the *Removable Disk* drive from the drop-down list in the *Save Drawing As* dialog box.

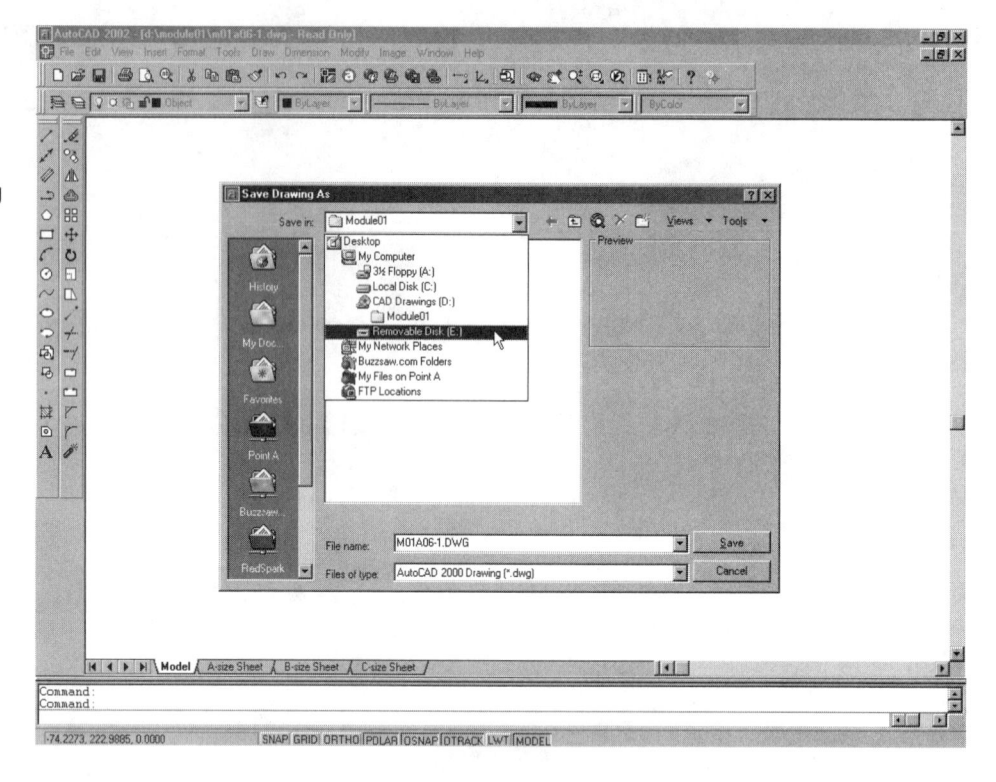

Figure 1-30
Click on the *Save* button to save a drawing.

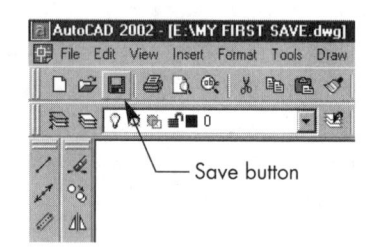

alternate method

There are two additional ways of saving a drawing. You can click on the *File* pull-down menu and select *Save* from the list by clicking on it, or you can type **SAVE** next to *Command:* in the *Command* window and hit the *Enter* key.

Note

Saving is very important in AutoCAD. A power failure or computer problem can occur at any time. If you have not saved recently, you will lose everything you have done since your last save. If you save only once an hour, you may lose an hour's work; save every 15 minutes and you may lose 15 minutes work; save every five minutes and, you may lose five minutes work, so use the *Save* button on the *Standard* toolbar and save often!

☐ This completes this activity. Click on the *Close* button to close the AutoCAD program.

Activity 7

Printing a Drawing

Objectives: After completing this activity, you should be able to do the following:

- Describe the difference between *Model* and *Paper* space.
- Change between *Model* and *Paper* space.
- Print a drawing from *Paper* space.

This activity is designed to give you a basic understanding of printing. It is intended to show you how to print your drawings on an A-size (8½ × 11) sheet of paper. A future activity will cover printing in more detail.

Procedure: ☑ Check each box as you complete that item.

☐ Double-click on the *AutoCAD 2002* icon to open the program.

☐ When the *AutoCAD 2002 Today* dialog box appears, select the *Open a Drawing* tab, and use the *Browse* hyperlink to locate the drawing *M01A07-1.dwg* in the *Module01* subdirectory on the CD.

Model Space

☐ When the drawing has finished opening, the screen will appear black with a drawing showing the front elevation of a house. The drawing has opened in *Model space*. You can verify that you are in *Model space* by looking at the tabs at the bottom of the drawing area. When you are in *Model space*, that tab will be black and the other tab(s) will be gray.

Model space is where all drawing work is done. Everything drawn in *Model space* is full size; e.g., a 2″ object is drawn 2″ long and a 5-mile object is drawn 5 miles long. The house that you are looking at is 50′-0″ wide and 27′-0″ high. As you will learn in a future activity, AutoCAD allows you to zoom in and out on a drawing so you can see everything on your small computer screen.

Drawing in *Model space* is easy since everything is full size. While you are making the drawing you do not have to worry what size paper you are going to print on. In mechanical "paper and pencil" drawing, you had to know what scale to draw in to ensure everything would fit on the piece of paper. Drawing at full size has another advantage: Any distances measured in *Model space* will be exact, and you will not have to make any calculations to convert them to a different scale.

Paper Space

☐ Click on the *Paper Space* tab at the bottom of the drawing area. The screen has changed from black to gray with a representation of a piece of paper, in white, in the middle. You can also verify that you are in *Paper space* because the *Model* tab at the bottom of the drawing area is now gray and the *Paper Space* tab is now white. The name on the tab can be changed. It has been given the name *Paper Space* on this drawing so you can easily identify it. In future activities you will see other names like *Layout1* and *A-size Sheet* on this tab.

Paper space is where you prepare a drawing for printing, not for doing drawing. You should get in the habit of drawing and making changes only in *Model space*. On your screen you will see the drawing of a house that was drawn in *Model space* plus the borders and title block of the finished drawing. *Paper space* gives you a representation of the finished product. The drawing of the house is inside a blue rectangle called a *Viewport*. Viewports are used to size objects so they fit on a piece of paper. In this case, the 50'-0" by 27'-0" house fits on the 8½" × 11" sheet of paper. In future activities you will learn how to use viewports to correctly size objects so they always print to scale.

Printing or Plotting

☐ Printing and plotting mean the same thing. Plotting is the term used when you make a paper copy of a drawing; but either word can be used, so feel free to use the term printing. If you are familiar with Windows programs, you will probably recognize the *Print* button on the *Standard* toolbar. (See Figure 1-31.) Locate this button, place the mouse pointer over it, and click the left mouse button. The *Plot* dialog box will appear.

All the features of this dialog box will be covered in greater detail in a future activity. Only the information needed for you to make an A-size print will be described here.

☐ If it is not currently active, click on the *Plot Device* tab. (See Figure 1-32.) This screen enables you to select a printer that you will plot to.

☐ In the *Plotter configuration* area, locate the *Name* drop-down list and select the letter size printer connected to your computer by clicking on its name. The printer in Figure 1-32 is a Lexmark™ printer, but yours will probably be a different model.

Figure 1-31
Click on the *Print* button to access the *Plot* dialog box.

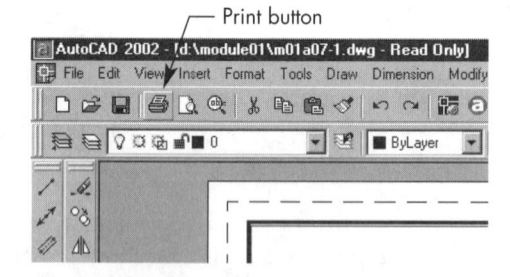

Figure 1-32
Select the *Plot Device* tab in the *Plot* dialog box to select the printer.

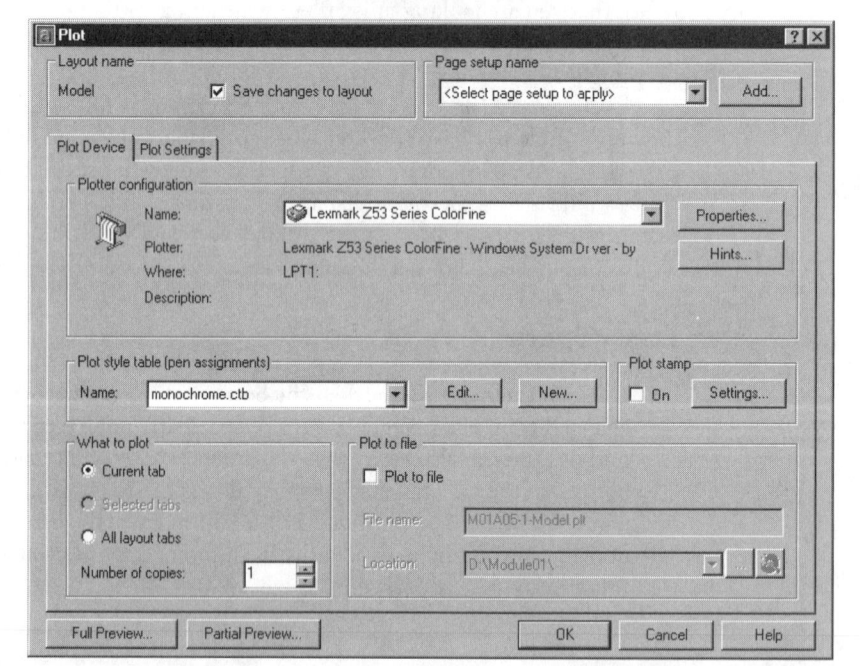

Basics of the AutoCAD Program   31

☐ In the *Plot style table (pen assignments)* area, locate the *Name* drop-down list and verify that *monochrome.ctb* appears in the window. If not, open the drop-down list and select it by clicking on it. This plot style maps all the colors on a drawing to print in black. This selection eliminates the high cost of color cartridges, and provides an easier to read print as some colors, like yellow, do not show well on white paper.

☐ Select the *Plot Settings* tab. (See Figure 1-33.) This page allows you to set paper size, plot area, and plot scale.

☐ In the *Paper size and paper units* area, locate the *Paper size* and verify that it is set to *Letter 8.5 x 11 in*. If not, use the drop-down list to change it.

☐ In the *Drawing orientation* area, verify that the button next to *Landscape* is selected. If not, select it by clicking on it.

☐ In the *Plot area*, verify that *Extents* is selected. If not, change it.

☐ In the *Plot scale* area, verify that the *scale* is 1:1. If not, use the drop-down list to change it.

☐ In the *Plot offset* area, verify that the *Center the plot* check box is checked. If not, click on the box to check it.

All other settings on this page should stay the same. Do not change any of them.

☐ Before printing, it is always a good idea to preview the finished drawing so that you can make any needed changes before wasting a piece of paper. Click on the *Full preview* button and you will see what the printout will look like.

☐ If everything looks OK, hit the *Enter* key on the keyboard and it will take you back to the *Plot* dialog box.

☐ Since you know everything is ready for printing, click on the *OK* button and your drawing will be sent to the printer. The dialog box will close and the screen will return to paper space.

☐ Retrieve the finished drawing from your printer.

This completes this activity. You should refer to this activity from time to time until you feel comfortable with the print operation.

☐ Click on the *Close* button to close the AutoCAD program.

Figure 1-33
Select the *Plot Settings* tab in the *Plot* dialog box to set the paper size and orientation.

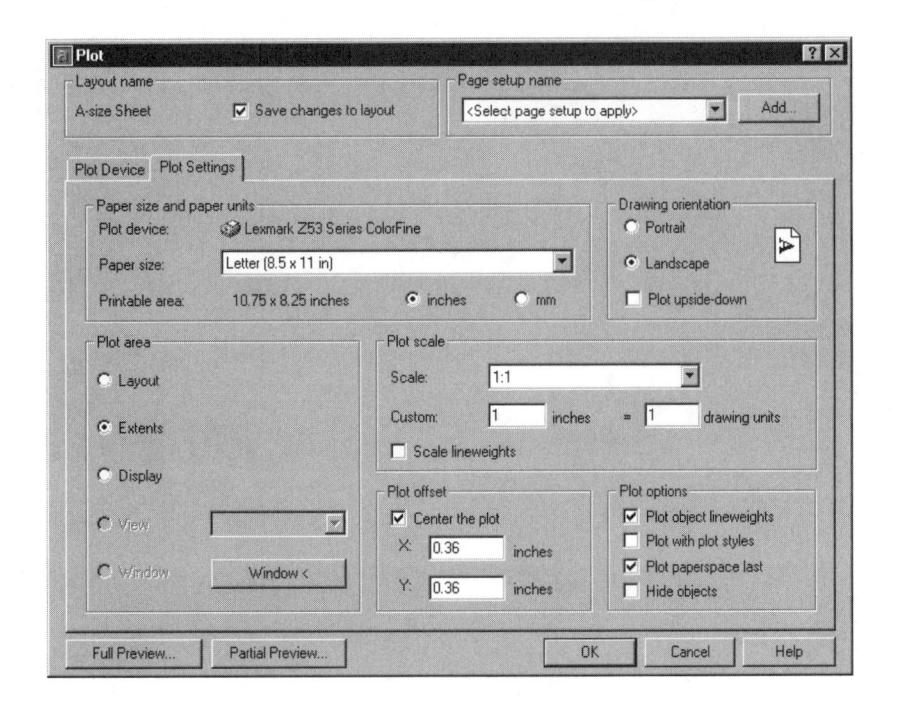

Module 1 Review Questions

These questions are provided to help you review the topics and concepts covered in this module.

True or False

Determine whether the statement is true or false. Place your answer, either T or F, in the blank.

_____ 1. AutoCAD's toolbars can be resized and placed next to the area of the drawing where you are working.

_____ 2. The *Open* button, located on the *Standard* toolbar, allows you to access and open drawings from the computer's hard drive and/or other storage devices like a floppy disk.

_____ 3. You can only have one drawing open at a time.

_____ 4. When printing a drawing, you should make sure the *Model* tab is active.

_____ 5. When selecting a drawing to open, you should always click on the drawing's icon and not its name.

_____ 6. Drawings can be opened by double-clicking on the drawing's icon.

_____ 7. The *Restore* button returns the drawing to its previously saved condition. It removes any changes, such as drawing or erasing objects, which you made since the last save.

_____ 8. The location of the *Command* window is fixed at the bottom of the screen.

_____ 9. Having too many toolbars open can reduce the amount of drawing space available on the screen.

_____ 10. It is a good idea to have only one *Command* line showing so you can maximize the drawing space available on the screen.

_____ 11. The *Text* window is accessed by hitting the *F2* function key on the keyboard.

_____ 12. It is normally easier and quicker to access commands from the toolbars than to access them from the pull-down menu.

_____ 13. It is easy to find and open a drawing as they are all saved in the same subdirectory.

_____ 14. Using *AutoCAD 2002 Today* lets you access recently opened drawings without having to search through the directory structure.

_____ 15. The *Window* pull-down menu is the only way to switch between drawings when you have more than one drawing open.

_____ 16. It is a good idea to save your drawing often in case of a computer malfunction or power outage.

Basics of the AutoCAD Program   33

Multiple-choice

Place the letter of the best answer in the blank.

1. This button is used to ____.
   a. close a drawing
   b. open a drawing
   c. save a drawing
   d. print a drawing

2. This button is used to ____.
   a. maximize a window
   b. minimize a window
   c. restore a window
   d. close a window

3. This button is used to ____.
   a. maximize a window
   b. minimize a window
   c. restore a window
   d. close a window

4. This button is used to ____.
   a. close a drawing
   b. open a drawing
   c. save a drawing
   d. print a drawing

5. This button is used to ____.
   a. maximize a window
   b. minimize a window
   c. restore a window
   d. close a window

6. This button is used to ____.
   a. close a drawing
   b. open a drawing
   c. save a drawing
   d. print a drawing

7. This button is used to ____.
   a. maximize a window
   b. minimize a window
   c. restore a window
   d. close a window

Matching

Match the number of the item shown in the figure with its name. Place the letter associated with the name in the blank.

1. ____
2. ____
3. ____
4. ____
5. ____
6. ____
7. ____
8. ____
9. ____
10. ____
11. ____
12. ____
13. ____

a. Object Properties toolbar
b. Command window
c. Drawing area
d. Status bar buttons
e. Program window title bar
f. Edit toolbar
g. Object Snap toolbar
h. Pull-down menu bar
i. Draw toolbar
j. Standard toolbar
k. Model and Layout tabs
l. Viewports toolbar
m. Dimension toolbar

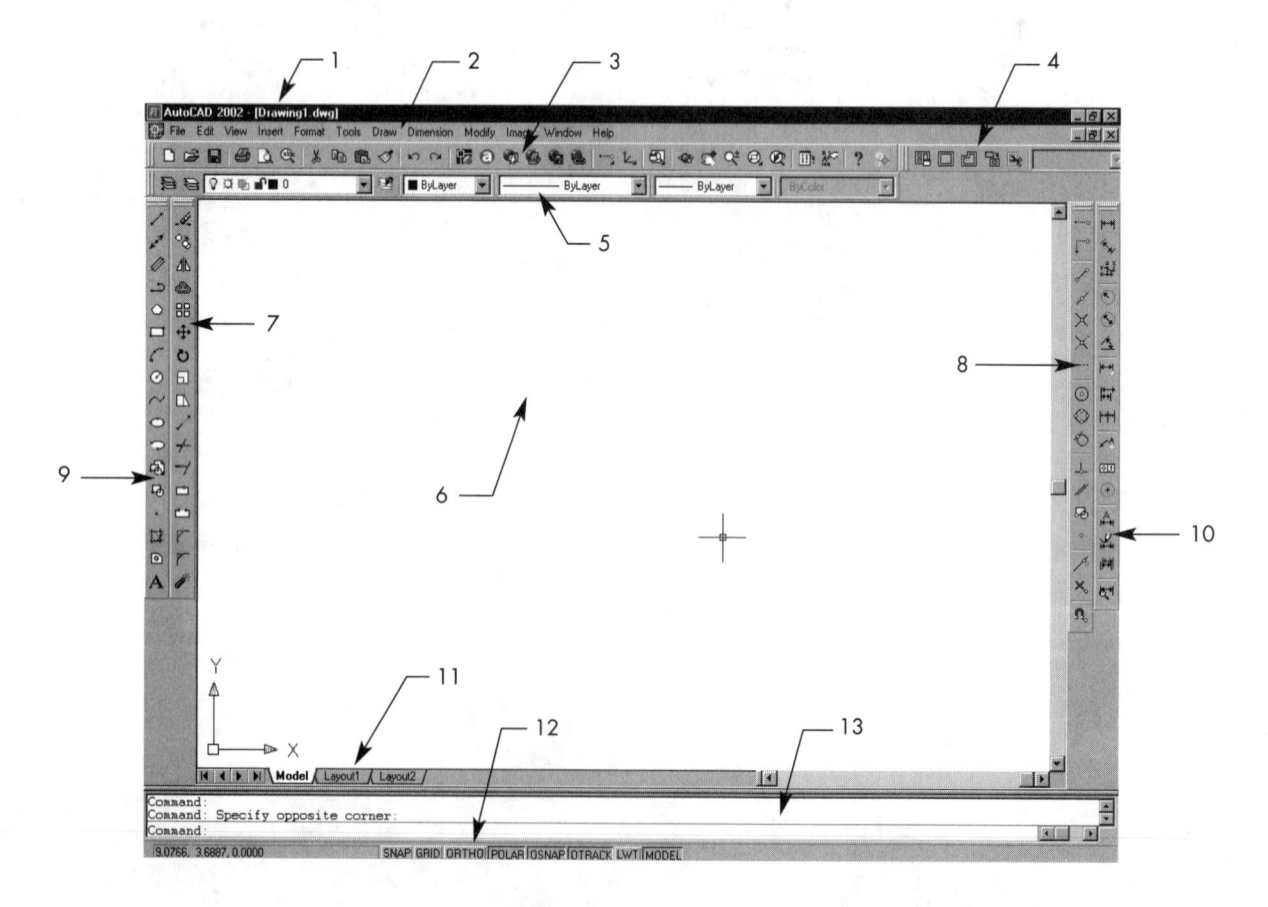

Module 2

Putting Lines on a Drawing

Activity 1

Linear Units

Objectives: After completing this activity, you should be able to do the following:

- Identify and use *Decimal* units.
- Identify and use *Fractional* units.
- Identify and use *Engineering* units.
- Identify and use *Architectural* units.
- Identify and use *Metric* units.
- Set the precision for all the above units.
- Locate and use the *Drawing Units* dialog box to set the linear units of a drawing.

Before you can start putting lines on a drawing you need to know about various types of units and how to input them into AutoCAD so that the program produces the output you desire. In AutoCAD there are five different formats (units) for describing linear distances. They are *Architectural, Decimal, Engineering, Fractional,* and *Scientific.* In this activity, you will learn how to identify and set the precision of all of these except scientific. Scientific units are used for very large or very small distances. Because they are used for very special applications, they will not be covered here.

The type of units used on a drawing depend on three major factors: (1) the size of the objects on the drawing, (2) the manufacturing processes that will be used to produce the objects on the drawings, and (3) the industry standard for the company that is producing or using the drawing. For the first factor, larger objects like buildings or steel structures tend to use architectural or engineering units that use a combination of feet and inches. Smaller objects tend to use either fractional or decimal units. Metric drawings only use decimal units. For the second factor, objects that require machining or more precision tend to use decimal units, whereas less precise manufacturing processes like welding or bolting use fractional or architectural units. Engineering units might be used in either case. For the third factor, most industries and/or companies have standards that specify the type of units to be used. Naturally architectural units would be used by most architectural firms. But they are also the standard for many other industries such as those who produce large welded structures like trusses or bridges.

36   Module 2

It is important that you understand units because one of the first things you do when starting a new drawing is set the units. In future activities, you will be expected to identify each of these types of units, set their precision, and know how to correctly enter them from the keyboard.

Procedure: ☑ Check each box as you complete that item.

☐ Double-click on the *AutoCAD 2002* icon to open the program.

☐ When the *AutoCAD 2002 Today* dialog box appears, select the *Open a Drawing* tab, and use the *Browse* hyperlink to locate and open the drawing *M02A01-1.dwg* from the *Module02* subdirectory on the CD.

☐ After the drawing opens, click on the *Format* pull-down menu and select *Units* from the list by clicking on it. (See Figure 2-1.)

☐ The *Drawing Units* dialog box will open. (See Figure 2-2.)

☐ For this activity, you will use the *Length* area of this dialog box. Before reading the description of each type of unit you will select that unit type from the drop-down list. You can then see an example of how each type of unit will appear on a drawing by looking at the first line in the *Sample Output* area located near the bottom of the dialog box.

Decimal Units

Decimal units are normally used on drawings that have smaller parts requiring machining or close tolerances. 15.5, 0.6250, and 60.0000 are examples of decimal units. Figure 2-3a shows how a decimal unit would appear as a dimension on a drawing. Open the *Type* drop-down list and select *Decimal* by clicking on it.

Precision is an indication of the exactness of a measurement. Clicking on the *Precision* drop-down list (Figure 2-3b) shows that AutoCAD offers a precision from 0 to 8 decimal places. The precision is an indication of how close the finished part must be to the given dimension. Unless there is a different tolerance given, it is assumed that the part must be made to ±1/2 the last decimal place (known as the uncertain digit). There is a big difference between 15.5 and 15.5000. You can make something 15.5″ long using a cheap

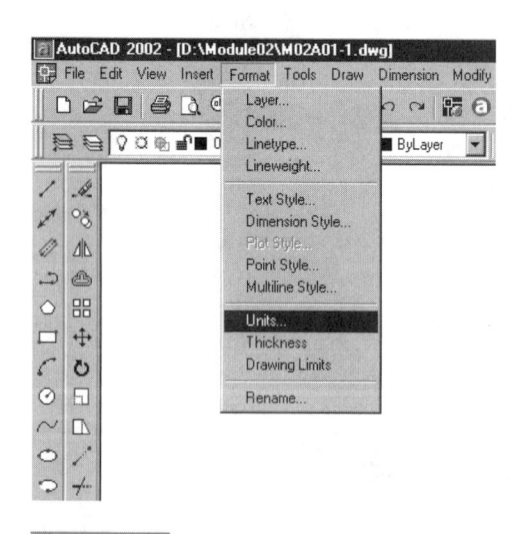

Figure 2-1
Select *Units* from the *Format* pull-down menu.

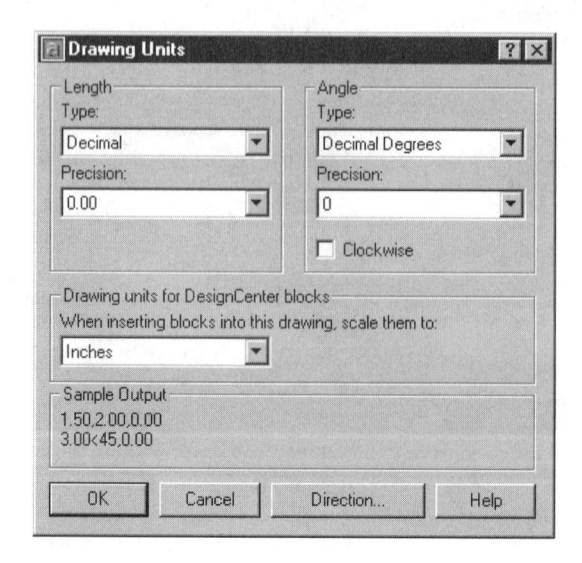

Figure 2-2
Drawing Units dialog box

Figure 2-3
Decimal units

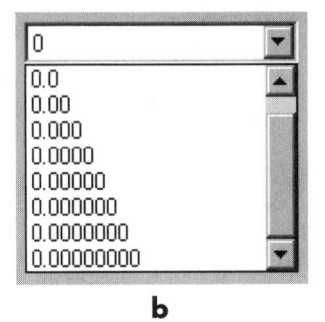

a   b

ruler and a saw, but to make it 15.5000″ requires special measuring tools and a machining or grinding operation.

AutoCAD rounds values based on where you set the precision. To get a good feel of precision, choose 0 precision (no decimal places) from the drop-down list and then close the *Units* dialog box by clicking the *OK* button. Move the mouse pointer *slowly* around the drawing area and observe how the coordinates of the cursor, on the left end of the *Status* bar, change. Notice that you have to move some distance before either the "x" or "y" coordinate value changes. These numbers do not give you an exact location of the pointer, and therefore you do not know with very much precision where the cursor is located.

Now go back to the *Units* dialog box and set the precision to 0.000 (three decimal places). Close the dialog box and move the pointer around the drawing area to see how the numbers change. You now have a little more knowledge of the precise location of the cursor. The higher you set the precision, the closer you come to knowing the exact location of the cursor. But no matter how high the precision, you will never know the exact location because the last decimal place is always rounded (uncertain). When you are done, select *Units* from the *Format* pull-down menu to return to the *Drawing Units* dialog box.

Note: When entering decimal units for a drawing, type the number as it appears using the keyboard. Do not include inch (″) marks or trailing zeros to the right of the decimal point. AutoCAD will always round everything to the precision you set. 15.5, 0.6250, and 60.0000, for example, would be entered as 15.5, .625, and 60.

Metric Units

When making a metric drawing, you will also use *Decimal* units. AutoCAD does not know the difference between inches and millimeters. When you are doing a metric drawing and enter 2, you will be entering 2 millimeters; and when you are working on a US Standard drawing and enter 2, you will be entering 2 inches. All the rules for entering decimal units apply to metric units. How to set up and use metric units will be covered in more detail in a future activity.

Fractional Units

Fractional units are usually used on drawings that have parts that are produced by cutting and welding operations. Fractions are commonly used in the US Customary system and are never used with the metric system of measurements. 15 1/2, 5/8, and 60 are examples of fractional units. Figure 2-4a shows how a fractional unit would appear as a dimension on a drawing. Open the *Type* drop-down list and select *Fractional* by clicking on it.

Clicking on the *Precision* drop-down list (Figure 2-4b) shows that AutoCAD offers a fractional precision from 0 (rounded to the whole inch) to 1/256″. The display on the *Status* bar will be in *Fractional* units and rounded to the precision you set. Choose 1/4 from

Figure 2-4
Fractional units

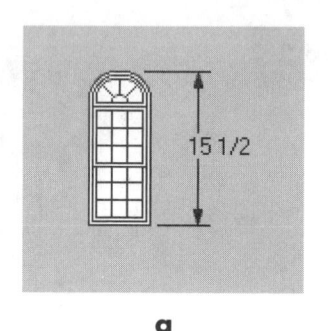

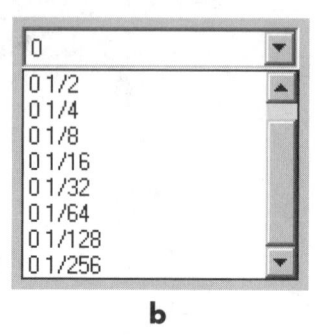

the *Precision* drop-down list and click *OK* to close the *Units* dialog box. Move the cursor around the screen to see how the numbers on the *Status* bar change. When you are done, select *Units* from the *Format* pull-down menu to return to the *Drawing Units* dialog box.

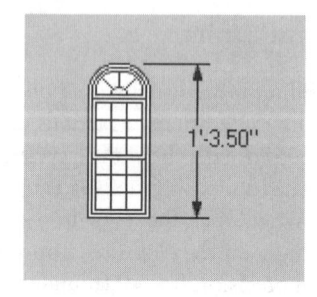

AutoCAD gives you two options for entering fractional units. The following shows examples of how you would enter the numbers 15 1/2, 5/8, and 60 into AutoCAD.

Option 1: Enter the number as a fraction. Notice that you have to place a dash (-) between the whole and fractional part of the number. Regardless of the method you use to enter a number, AutoCAD will always display it on the drawing in the format you choose from the *Drawing Units* dialog box.

15-1/2   5/8   60

Option 2: Enter the number as a decimal.

15.5   .625   60

Engineering Units

Engineering units are used on drawings that have parts that require feet and inch measure, but still require a higher level of precision. 1'-3.50", 0'-0.625", and 5'-0.000" are examples of engineering units. Figure 2-5a shows how an engineering unit would appear as a dimension on a drawing. Open the *Type* drop-down list and select *Engineering* by clicking on it.

Clicking on the *Precision* drop-down list (Figure 2-5b) shows that AutoCAD offers a precision from 0 to 8 decimal places on the part of the dimension that represents inches. The display on the *Status* bar will be in *Engineering* units and rounded to the set precision. Choose 0'-0.00" from the *Precision* drop-down list and click *OK* to close the *Units* dialog box. Move the cursor around the screen to see how the numbers on the *Status* bar change. When you are done, select *Units* from the *Format* pull-down menu to return to the *Drawing Units* dialog box.

Figure 2-5
Engineering units

AutoCAD gives you four options for entering engineering units. The following shows how 1'-3.50", 0'-0.625", and 5'-0.000" can be entered into AutoCAD. Regardless of the method you use to enter a number, AutoCAD will always display it on the drawing in the format you choose from the *Drawing Units* dialog box.

Option 1: Enter the number as a combination of feet and inches, using decimal inches. Notice that you must have the feet mark (') after the foot part of the number. For mixed feet and inch units, use the feet mark followed by the inches or parts of an inch. You do not place a space between the feet and inches.

    1'3.5   .625   5'

Option 2: Enter the number as a combination of feet and inches, using fractional inches. Notice that you have to put a dash (-) between the whole and fractional parts of the number.

    1' 3-1/2   5/8   5'

Option 3: Enter the number in inches (no feet) as a fraction. Notice that you have to put a dash (-) between the whole and fractional parts of the number.

    15-1/2   5/8   60

Option 4: Enter the number in inches (no feet) as a decimal.

    15.5   .625   60

Architectural Units

Architectural units are used on drawings that have larger parts, requiring feet and inch measurements, and with fractional inches. 1'-3 1/2", 0'-0 5/8", and 5'-0" are examples of architectural units. Figure 2-6a shows how an architectural unit would appear as a dimension on a drawing. Open the *Type* drop-down list and select *Architectural* by clicking on it.

Clicking on the *Precision* drop-down list (Figure 2-6b) shows that AutoCAD offers a precision from 0 (rounded to the whole inch) to 1/256". The display on the *Status* bar will be in *Architectural* units and rounded to the set precision. Choose 0'-0 1/2" from the *Precision* drop-down list and click *OK* to close the *Units* dialog box. Move the cursor around the screen to see how the numbers on the *Status* bar change. When you are done, select *Units* from the *Format* pull-down menu to return to the *Drawing Units* dialog box.

AutoCAD gives you four options for entering architectural units. The following section shows examples for the three values shown above. Regardless of the method you use

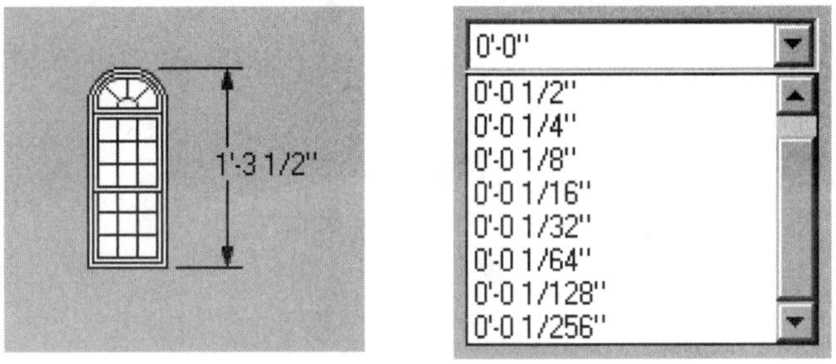

Figure 2-6
Architectural units

a   b

to enter a number, AutoCAD will always display it on the drawing in the format you choose from the *Drawing Units* dialog box.

Option 1: Enter the number as a combination of feet and inches, using decimal inches. Notice that you must have the feet mark (') after the foot part of the number. For mixed units, use the feet mark followed directly (no space) by the inches or parts of an inch.

1'3.5   .625   5'

Option 2: Enter the number as a combination of feet and inches, using fractional inches.

1' 3-1/2   5/8   5'

Option 3: Enter the number in inches (no feet) as a fraction. Notice that you have to put a dash (-) between the whole and fractional parts of the number.

15-1/2   5/8   60

Option 4: Enter the number in inches (no feet) as a decimal.

15.5   .625   60

☐ This completes this activity. You may want to spend some time selecting the various units and precisions, moving the cursor around the drawing area, and observing the effect on the display in the *Status* bar. When you are done, close the AutoCAD program by clicking the *Close* button.

Activity 2

Angular Units

Objectives: After completing this activity, you should be able to do the following:

- Identify and use *Decimal Degree* units.
- Identify and use *Deg/Min/Sec* units.
- Identify and use *Gradient* units.
- Identify and use *Radian* units.
- Identify and use *Surveyor* units.
- Set the precision of each of the above units.
- Locate and use the *Drawing Units* dialog box to set the angular units of a drawing.

Procedure: ✓ Check each box as you complete that item.

- ☐ Double-click on the *AutoCAD 2002* icon to open the program.
- ☐ When the *AutoCAD 2002 Today* dialog box appears, select the *Open a Drawing* tab, and use the *Browse* hyperlink to locate and open the drawing *M02A02-1.dwg* from the *Module02* subdirectory on the CD.
- ☐ After the drawing opens, click on the *Format* pull-down menu.
- ☐ Slide the mouse pointer down the list and click on *Units*. The *Drawing Units* dialog box will open. (See Figure 2-7.)
- ☐ For this activity, you will use the *Angle* section of this dialog box. As you read the description of each type of unit, use the drop-down lists to select units and precisions. The output is shown on the first line in the *Sample Output* area located near the bottom of the dialog box.

Decimal Degrees

A degree is obtained by dividing a full circle into 360 equal pieces with each piece equaling one degree. There are two different ways of describing the part of an angle that is less than one degree. The first method is by using decimals. 0.5° is equal to one half of a

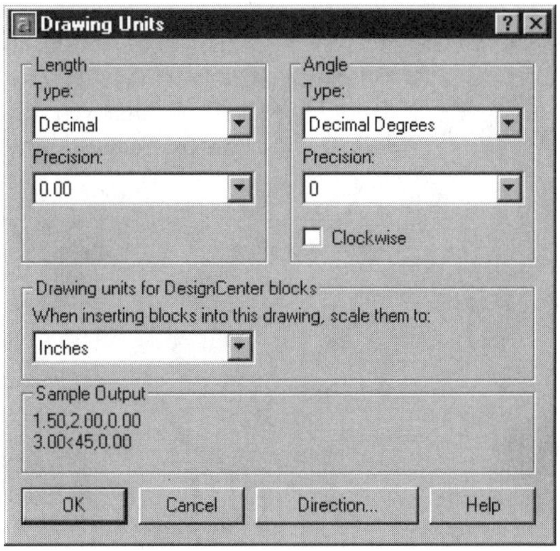

Figure 2-7
Drawing Units dialog box

Figure 2-8
Decimal degrees

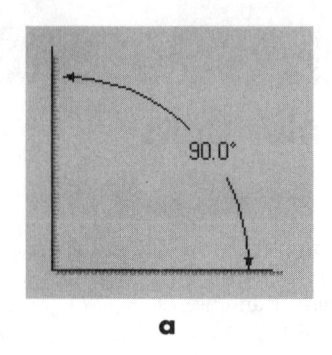

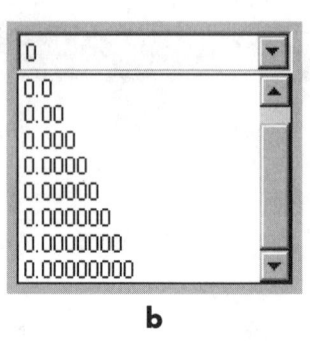

degree. 30.50°, 135.508°, and 90.00° are examples of decimal degrees. Figure 2-8a shows how a *Decimal Degree* would appear as a dimension on a drawing. Open the *Type* drop-down list and select *Decimal Degree* by clicking on it.

Like linear dimensions, precision also applies to angular units and indicates how exactly the angle is measured. Clicking on the *Precision* drop-down list (Figure 2-8b) shows that AutoCAD offers precisions for decimal degrees from 0 to 8 decimal places.

To enter decimal degrees for a drawing, type the number as it appears using the keyboard. You do not need to include the degree symbol (°) when you are working in these units. You also do not have to include the trailing zeros to the right of the decimal point because AutoCAD will always round everything to the precision you set. 30.50°, 135.508°, and 90.00°, for example, would be entered as 30.5, 135.508, and 90.

Degrees/Minutes/Seconds

Angles can be measured using degrees, minutes, and seconds. Minutes and seconds describe the part of an angle that is less than one degree.

A minute is obtained by dividing a degree into 60 parts. Therefore 1/2° equals 30 minutes. Minutes are noted by placing a single mark above and to the right of the number. 30 minutes is represented as 30′.

A second is obtained by dividing a minute into 60 parts. Therefore 1/2′ equals 30 seconds. Seconds are noted by placing two marks above and to the right of the number. 30 seconds is represented as 30″.

30°30′, 135°30′30″, and 90° are examples of *Deg/Min/Sec* units. Figure 2-9a shows how these units would appear as a dimension on a drawing. Open the *Type* drop-down list and select *Deg/Min/Sec* by clicking on it.

Precision for *Deg/Min/Sec* varies. Precision can be limited to whole degrees, whole minutes, or whole seconds, and greater precision can be entered as decimals of a second. Clicking on the *Precision* drop-down list (Figure 2-9b) shows that AutoCAD limits the precision to 4 decimal places on the seconds.

Entering *Deg/Min/Sec* from the keyboard requires that you provide the appropriate symbol for the value that you are entering. Degrees are followed by a "d" (indicating degrees), minutes are followed by an apostrophe ('), and seconds are followed with quota-

Figure 2-9
Degree/Minute/Second

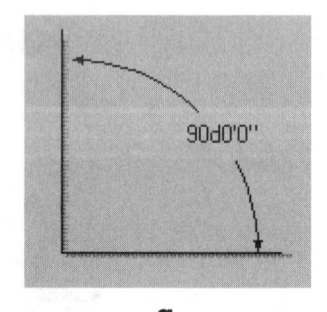

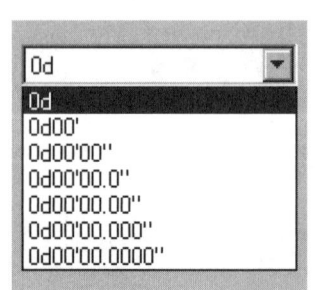

tion marks ("). If the angle you are entering does not have minutes and seconds, you do not have to enter the "d". 30°30′, 135°30′30″, and 90°, for example, are entered from the keyboard as 30d30′, 135d30′30″, and 90.

Gradients

Angles are sometimes measured in gradients. A gradient or grad is obtained by dividing 90° into 100 parts (or a full circle into 400 parts), each equaling one grad. 33.9g, 150.564g, and 100g are examples of grads. Figure 2-10a shows how these units would appear as a dimension on a drawing. Open the *Type* drop-down list and select *Grads* by clicking on it.

Clicking on the *Precision* drop-down list (Figure 2-10b) shows that AutoCAD offers precisions for gradients from 0 to 8 decimal places.

It is easy to enter grads from the keyboard. Simply enter them as they appear. The "g" symbol is not required because AutoCAD knows when you are entering an angle measure. 33.9g, 150.564g, and 100g, for example, are entered from the keyboard as 33.9, 150.564, and 100.

Radians

Radian measure is based on the relationship between the radius of a circle and the distance along the arc of the circle. There are 2π (6.283) radians in a full circle. One radian is approximately 57.3 degrees. 0.532r, 2.365r, and 1.571r are examples of radian measure. Figure 2-11a shows how these units would appear as a dimension on a drawing. Open the *Type* drop-down list and select *Radians* by clicking on it.

Clicking on the *Precision* drop-down list (Figure 2-11b) shows that AutoCAD offers precisions for radians from 0 to 8 decimal places.

It is easy to enter radians from the keyboard. Simply enter them as they appear. The "r" symbol is not required because AutoCAD knows when you are entering an angle measure. 0.532r, 2.365r, and 1.571r, for example, are entered from the keyboard as .532, 2.365, and 1.571.

Figure 2-10
Gradients

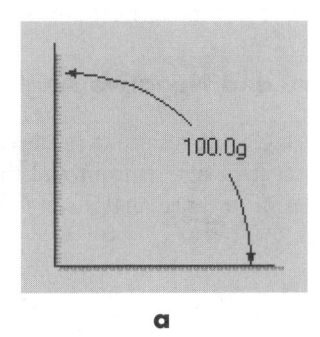

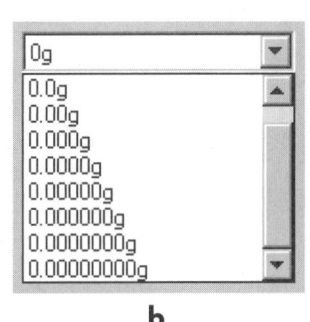

Figure 2-11
Radians

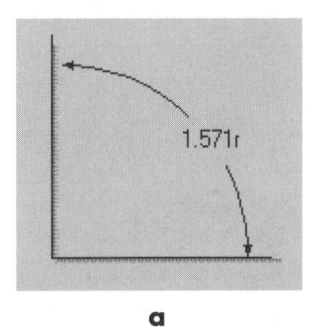

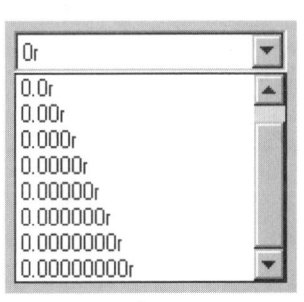

Figure 2-12
Surveyor's units

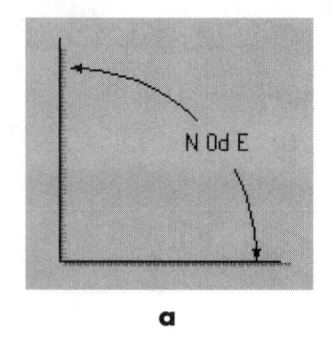

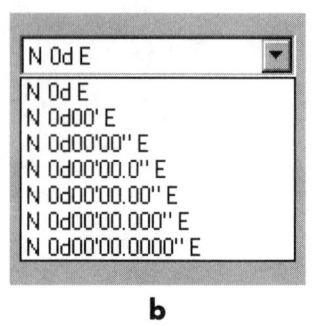

a

b

Surveyor's Units

Surveyor's units are based on the four compass points, North (N), South (S), East (E), and West (W). North is usually located at 90° and South at 270°. All angles start at either North or South with the given angle measured toward the East or the West of those locations. Surveyor's units use Deg/Min/Sec to measure the angles. N 30°30′ E, N 45°30′30″ W, and N are examples of surveyor's units. Figure 2-12a shows how these units would appear as a dimension on a drawing. Open the *Type* drop-down list and select *Surveyor's Units* by clicking on it.

Clicking on the *Precision* drop-down list (Figure 2-12b) shows that precisions for surveyor's units are the same as for Deg/Min/Sec.

Entering surveyor's units from the keyboard requires that you provide the starting location (N or S), the angle in Deg/Min/Sec, and the angle direction (E or W). If the angle is at 90° or 270°, then all you have to enter is N or S. N 30°30′ E, N 45°30′30″ W, and N, for example, are entered from the keyboard as N30d30'E, N45d30'30"W, and N.

Direction

Notice that the *Angle* section of the *Drawing Units* dialog box includes a *Clockwise* check box. Angles are usually measured counterclockwise. AutoCAD allows you to use either direction. If the *Clockwise* box is not checked, angles are measured in the standard counterclockwise direction. If the box is checked, angles will be measured clockwise.

Positive and Negative Angles

Positive angles are measured in the direction described above. You can also enter an angle with a negative sign in front and the angle will be measured in the opposite direction. Examples of negative angles are shown below. All are based on counterclockwise being positive.

$$270° = -90° \qquad 30° = -330° \qquad 225° = -135°$$

☐ This completes this activity. Exit the AutoCAD program using the *Close* button.

Activity 3

The Cartesian Coordinate System

Objectives: After completing this activity, you should be able to do the following:

- Describe the features of the coordinate system.
- Locate points on the "x" and "y" axis.
- Locate points using ordered (x, y) pairs.
- Sketch a simple figure using points described by ordered pairs.
- Locate the coordinate display on the *Status* bar.
- Set the Grid and Snap spacing and turn them on and off.
- Turn the *UCS* icon on and off.

You will make drawings in AutoCAD using the Cartesian coordinate system to locate points and to draw objects. The first part of this activity will introduce you to the coordinate system and how to locate points; and the second part will show you some of Auto-CAD's features based on this coordinate system.

The Number Line

The number line is used to describe the order and value of positive and negative numbers. A portion of the number line is shown in Figure 2-13.

The center mark (0) of the number line is called the *origin*. Numbers to the right of the origin are positive and numbers to the left are negative. Since a line is continuous, meaning that is has no breaks or spaces, the number line represents all possible numbers. Only whole numbers are shown in the figure, but you can easily imagine the location of 1 1/2 or –6 1/4. In fact, the distance between any two whole numbers can be divided into as many parts as you want. The distance between 1 and 2 could be divided into two parts (1/2 unit each), 100 parts (1/100 unit each), or one million parts (1/1000000 unit each); the possibilities are infinite.

The arrows at the ends of the number line indicate that it continues to infinity in both directions.

The number line not only describes the number system, it also describes distances. In Figure 2-14, the distance from the origin (0) to 4 is four units long and likewise, the distance from −5 to −1 is also four units long. When placed horizontally, the number line represents distances in one dimension and is often called the "x" axis.

Figure 2-13
The number line shows the order and value of positive and negative numbers.

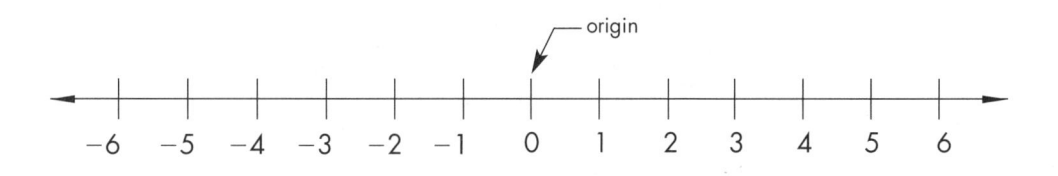

Figure 2-14
The number line describes distances.

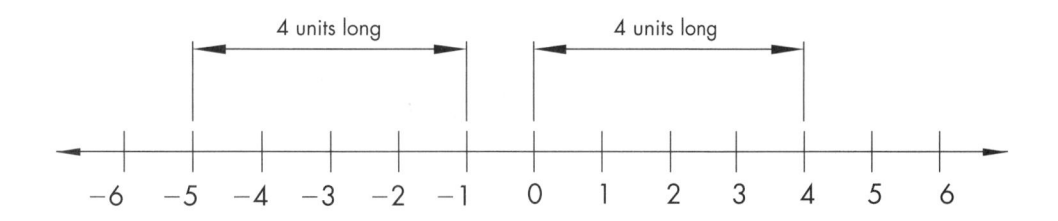

Figure 2-15

The Cartesian coordinate system

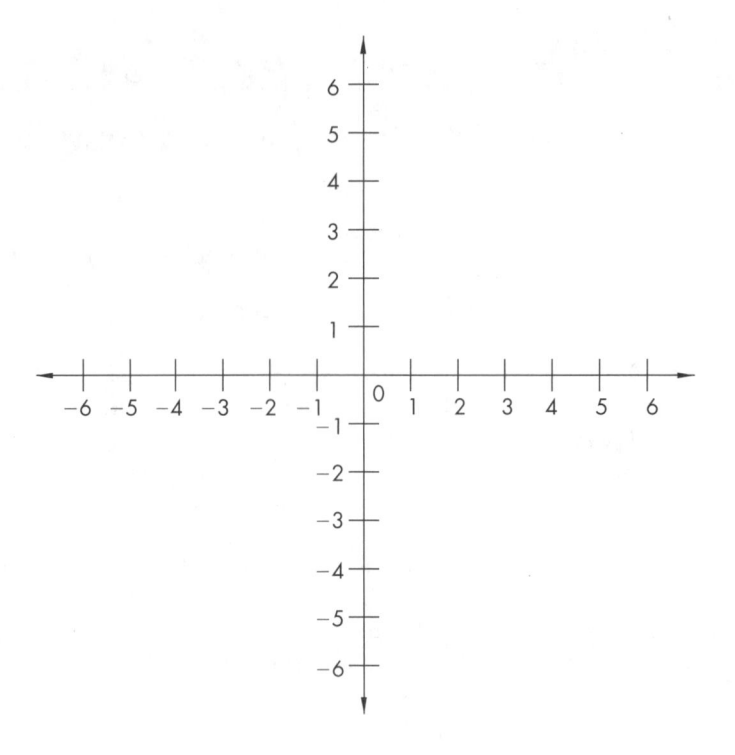

The Coordinate System

The number line described above works for one dimension. The majority of work you do in AutoCAD will be in two dimensions, so a second vertical number line, the "y" axis, is added. The combination of the two number lines is known as the 2D Cartesian coordinate system and it allows distance measurements to be made in two directions, vertical and horizontal. It is shown in Figure 2-15.

Ordered Pairs

Any location on the Cartesian coordinate system can be found by using an ordered pair. Ordered pairs specify the distance from the origin along each axis. An ordered pair has the format (x, y), where the "x" value specifies the location of an imaginary vertical line through that point on the x-axis and the "y" value specifies the location of an imaginary horizontal line through that point on the y-axis.

As shown in Figure 2-16, the ordered pair (4,5) is found by imagining a vertical line passing through 4 on the x-axis and a horizontal line passing through 5 on the y-axis. Where these two lines intersect is the point (4,5). It is very important that you specify the x-value first and the y-value second. There is a big difference between (4,5) and (5, 4).

Note that ordered pairs can also contain negative numbers. Points having negative x-values and positive y-values are left of the y-axis and above the x-axis. Likewise, points with both negative x- and y-values are to the left of the y-axis and below the x-axis.

In AutoCAD you will use ordered pairs to specify points for starting and ending lines, and to place objects like circles and rectangles. Mostly you will be working in the area of the coordinate system where both the x- and y-values are positive. You should imagine the edges of your AutoCAD drawing area as being in the area bounded by the y-axis on the left and the x-axis on the bottom.

In the following section you will see how the coordinate system is used with AutoCAD.

Figure 2-16
Location of point (4,5)

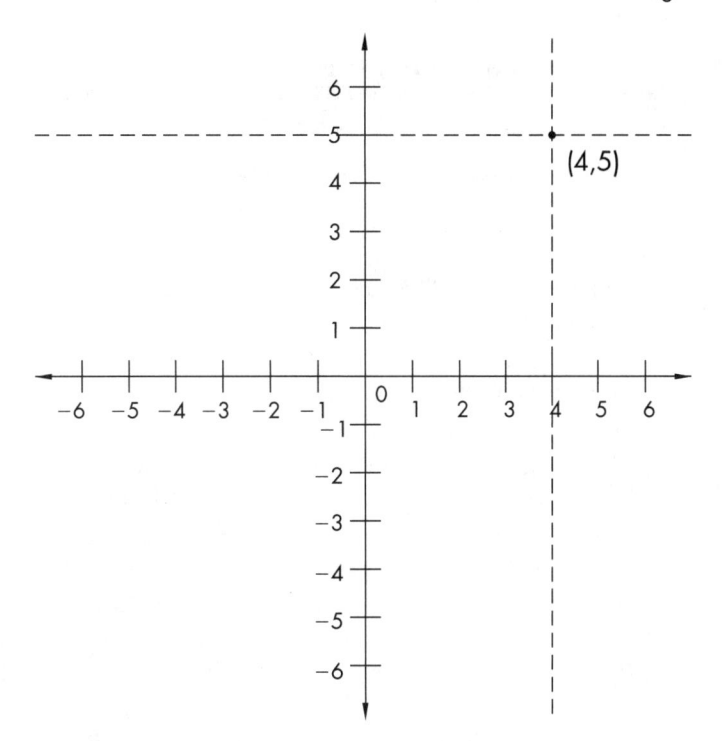

Procedure:

☑ Check each box as you complete that item.

☐ Double-click on the *AutoCAD 2002* icon to open the program.

☐ When the *AutoCAD 2002 Today* dialog box appears, select the *Open a Drawing* tab, and use the *Browse* hyperlink to locate and open the drawing *M02A03-1.dwg* from the *Module02* subdirectory on the CD.

☐ Make sure that all the *Drawing Features* buttons on the *Status* bar (SNAP, GRID ORTHO, POLAR, etc.), except for the MODEL button, are off, not depressed.

Snap, Grid, and Coordinates

☐ Use Figure 2-17 to help you locate the *Coordinates Display* on the *Status* bar. Move the graphics cursor around the screen and observe how the numbers change. The first number is the x-coordinate and changes as you move the mouse horizontally. The second number is the y-coordinate and changes as you move the mouse vertically. The third number is the z-coordinate. It remains at 0.000 because you are working in 2D space.

☐ Now click once on both the *Snap* and *Grid* buttons, also located on the *Status* bar, to turn them on. When a button is on, it will appear depressed. Your set of buttons

Figure 2-17
The *Coordinates Display* is located on the *Status* bar.

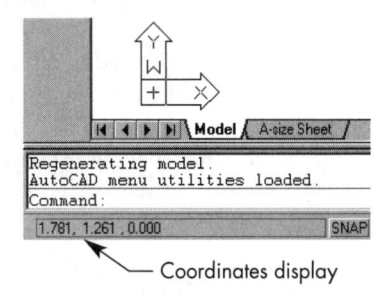

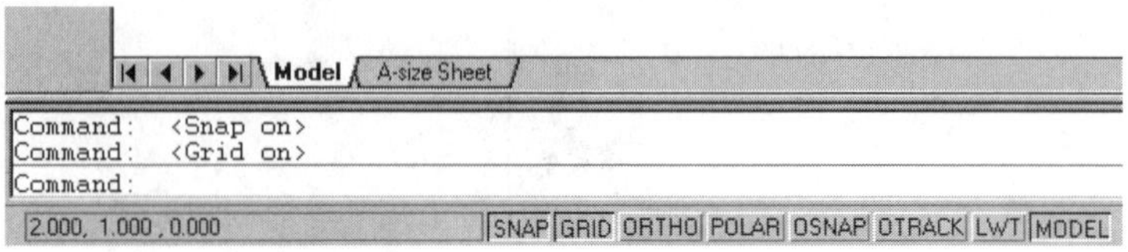

Figure 2-18
The *Snap*, *Grid*, and *Model* buttons should be selected and all others should be off.

should look exactly like those shown in Figure 2-18. If any of the other buttons are on and should be off, change them now.

☐ You should now see a series of dots on the screen. This is called the grid pattern. It was turned on when you clicked the *Grid* button. The dots are 1 unit apart in each direction.

☐ Move the graphics cursor around the screen. The cursor should jump to the nearest dot. This is called snap and it was turned on when you clicked the *Snap* button.

☐ Continue to move the graphics cursor around the screen and observe the coordinates display. Notice that it shows the x- and y-coordinates of each location you move to.

☐ Practice moving the cursor to the locations specified by the following ordered pairs.

(0,0)   (1,1)   (2,3)   (0,5)   (5,0)   (5,5)   (10,6)

☐ In locating the above coordinates, notice that the x-axis is located along the bottom of the screen and the y-axis is along the left side of the screen so you are always working with positive numbers.

☐ To understand the purpose of the *Snap* button, turn it off by clicking on it. Move the cursor around the drawing area. What happens? Click on the *Snap* button again to turn it back on.

☐ To understand the purpose of the *Grid* button, turn it off by clicking on it. What happened? Move the cursor around the drawing area. You will notice that the grid being off has no effect on the snap. Click on the *Grid* button again to turn it back on.

☐ You are not stuck with the settings of the grid and snap locations. As with most things in AutoCAD, they can be changed. Place the mouse pointer over the *Snap* button and click the *right* mouse button. A pop-up menu will appear as shown in Figure 2-19. Move the mouse pointer over the *Settings* selection on this menu to highlight it, and then click the left mouse button to select it.

☐ The *Drafting Settings* dialog box, shown in Figure 2-20, should appear. Since you clicked over either the *Snap* or the *Grid* button, the *Snap and Grid* tab will be active. The following gives a brief description of the features of this tab. The other tabs will be covered in detail in other activities.

■ **Snap On check box**—You can turn the snap on and off by checking or unchecking this box. The *F9* function key at the top of the keyboard can be used instead of clicking the *Snap* button on the *Status* bar.

Snap—This area is used to set the parameters of the invisible grid that controls the movement of the cursor on the screen.

■ **Snap X spacing**—The value that you place in the text box will set the distance between snap locations in the x-direction.

■ **Snap Y spacing**—The value that you place in the text box will set the distance between snap locations in the y-direction.

■ **Angle**—The value you place in the text box will rotate the snap and grid spacing to that angle. When set to zero, the spacing is horizontal and verti-

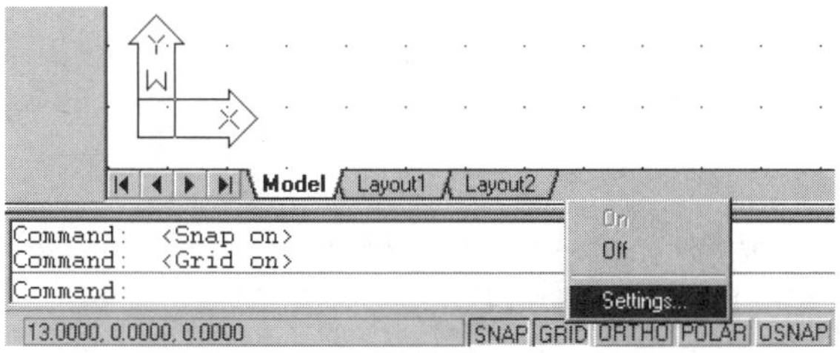

Putting Lines on a Drawing   49

Figure 2-19
Right-click over the *Snap* or *Grid* button to get the pop-up menu.

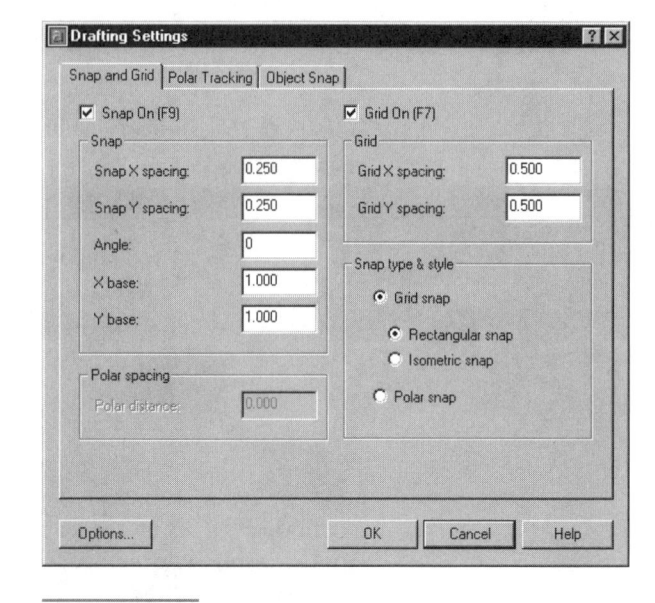

Figure 2-20
Set *Snap* and *Grid* spacing in the *Drafting Settings* dialog box.

cal. It is important to understand that you are only changing the orientation of the snap and grid and not the drawing's coordinate system. The drawing's x-axis and y-axis remain horizontal and vertical regardless of the value you enter here.

- **X base and Y base**—The value you place in these text boxes determines the origin of the snap and grid pattern. When set to zero, the origin of the drawing's coordinate system acts as the starting point of the snap and grid pattern. This option allows you to set new snap and grid locations based on an object or location on the drawing instead of being forced to always work from 0,0.

Polar spacing—This area is used to set the distance between snap points when the *Polar snap* option is selected.

- **Polar distance**—This type-in box allows you to enter the distance between points when you are using *Polar tracking*. If this value is set to zero, AutoCAD will use the *Grid X spacing* distance for the polar snap distance. *Polar tracking* will be covered in detail in a future activity

- **Grid On check box**—You can turn the snap on and off by checking or unchecking this box. The *F7* function key at the top of the keyboard can be used instead of clicking the *Grid* button on the *Status* bar.

Grid—This area is used to set the parameters of the series of dots that form a grid on the screen.

- **Grid X spacing**—The value that you place in the text box will set the distance between grid dots in the x-direction.

- **Grid Y spacing**—The value that you place in the text box will set the distance between grid dots in the y-direction.

Snap type & style—This area lets you choose the type of snap that will be active on the drawing.

- **Grid snap**—When this button is selected the snaps will be in the form of a grid pattern. The pattern can be either rectangular or isometric depending on the type of drawing you are making.

  - **Rectangular snap**—When selected, the grid will be a rectangular pattern.
  - **Isometric snap**—When selected, the grid will be an isometric pattern.
  - **Polar snap**—When this button is selected, the polar snap is activated. The *Polar spacing* area will become active and the *Snap* area will be grayed out.

☐ Change the *Snap X spacing* and the *Snap Y spacing* to .25. After you enter the x-value, hit the *Tab* key on the keyboard and the same value will be entered in the "Y" box. Using this same method, change the *Grid X spacing* and the *Grid Y spacing* to .50.

☐ Verify that the *Grid Snap* and *Rectangular Snap* buttons are selected in the *Snap type & style area*. If they are not, select them now by clicking on them.

☐ Click on the *OK* button to close the dialog box. The grid pattern should now look different. As you move the cursor around, you will notice that it not only snaps to the grid points, but also halfway between them.

The UCS Icon

The UCS icon is located in the lower left corner of the drawing area. UCS stands for User Coordinate System. In future activities you will learn how to move and rotate the coordinate system to make your drawing easier (thus it is called the *User* coordinate system). The original starting coordinate system of the drawing is called the World location. In the future when you start moving and rotating the coordinate system, it will be comforting to know you can restore things back to the original World position. Sometimes the UCS icon is in the way. In the following steps you will learn how to turn it on and off and how to change its appearance.

☐ Click on the *View* pull-down menu, and slide the mouse pointer down to the *Display* cascading menu and then to the right to open the *UCS Icon* cascading menu. Notice that the *ON* selection, as shown in Figure 2-21, has a check next to it. Place the mouse pointer over the *ON* and click the mouse button.

Figure 2-21
The *UCS Icon* can be turned on and off by clicking the *On* item.

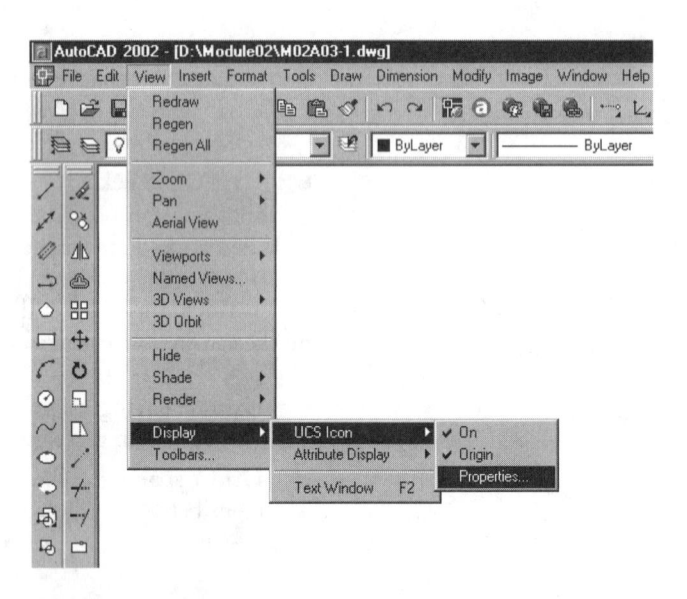

Figure 2-22
UCS Icon dialog box

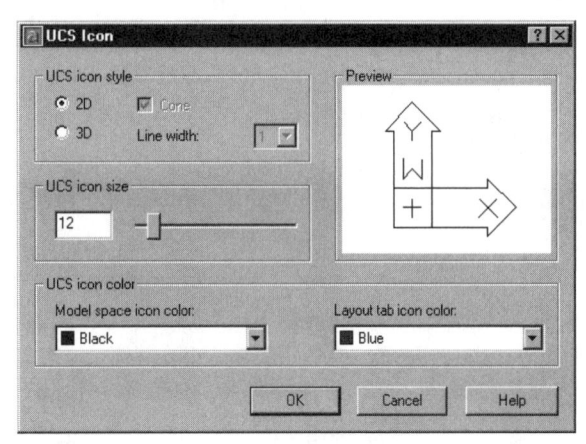

☐ The menus will close and you will return to the drawing. Notice that the UCS icon is gone. Repeat the above steps. You will notice this time the *ON* is not checked. Place the mouse pointer over it and click the button to turn it back on.

☐ Look at Figure 2-21. Notice that under the *ON*, there is another option called *Origin*. When this option is checked, the UCS icon will be displayed at the current origin (0,0,0). If you specify a new origin, the UCS icon will be displayed at that new point as long as it is located in the viewable drawing area. This will allow you to see the origin's location after moving it. If this option is not checked, or if the origin is off the screen (not in the viewable drawing area), the UCS icon will appear in the bottom left corner of the screen as long as the *On* item is checked.

☐ Click on the *View* pull-down menu, and slide the mouse pointer down to the *Display* cascading menu and then to the right to open the *UCS Icon* cascading menu. Slide the mouse pointer to highlight *Properties* and click the left mouse button. The *UCS Icon* dialog box, shown in Figure 2-22, will open. This dialog box gives you options for how the UCS icon will appear on the screen. In the style area you can set the icon for either 2D or 3D drawings. For the 3D arrangement, you have option of line weight and how the arrowheads will appear. In the size area, you can set the size of the icon, and in the color area, you can set the color of the icon for both Model and the *Layout* tab. Take a few minutes to explore the different options in this dialog box.

☐ You can set the values in the dialog box to any that you like. When you make changes here they are saved with the program, not with the drawing. If others are using your computer they may set the values differently, so you may not have the same setup when you next return to the computer. For the figures shown in these activities, the values in this dialog box will be set as shown below. You may want to use these as your standard values.

UCS Icon style: 2D
UCS Icon size: 12
UCS Icon color: Model = Black and Layout = Blue

☐ This completes this activity. Close the AutoCAD program without saving the drawing.

Assignment
for Module 2 – Activity 3

1. Locate the following points on the coordinate system in Figure 2-23. For each, put a point and label it with the ordered pair as shown in the example: (−3, 4).

A	(4,6)	F	(−5,6)	K	(−4,−4)	P	(10,−1)
B	(10,2)	G	(−10,8)	L	(−8,−10)	Q	(2,−7)
C	(6,12)	H	(−2,9)	M	(−1,−9)	R	(5,−11)
D	(9,10)	I	(−2,13)	N	(−5,−5)	S	(9,−9)
E	(7,7)	J	(−8,8)	O	(−12,−2)	T	(4,−6)

Figure 2-23

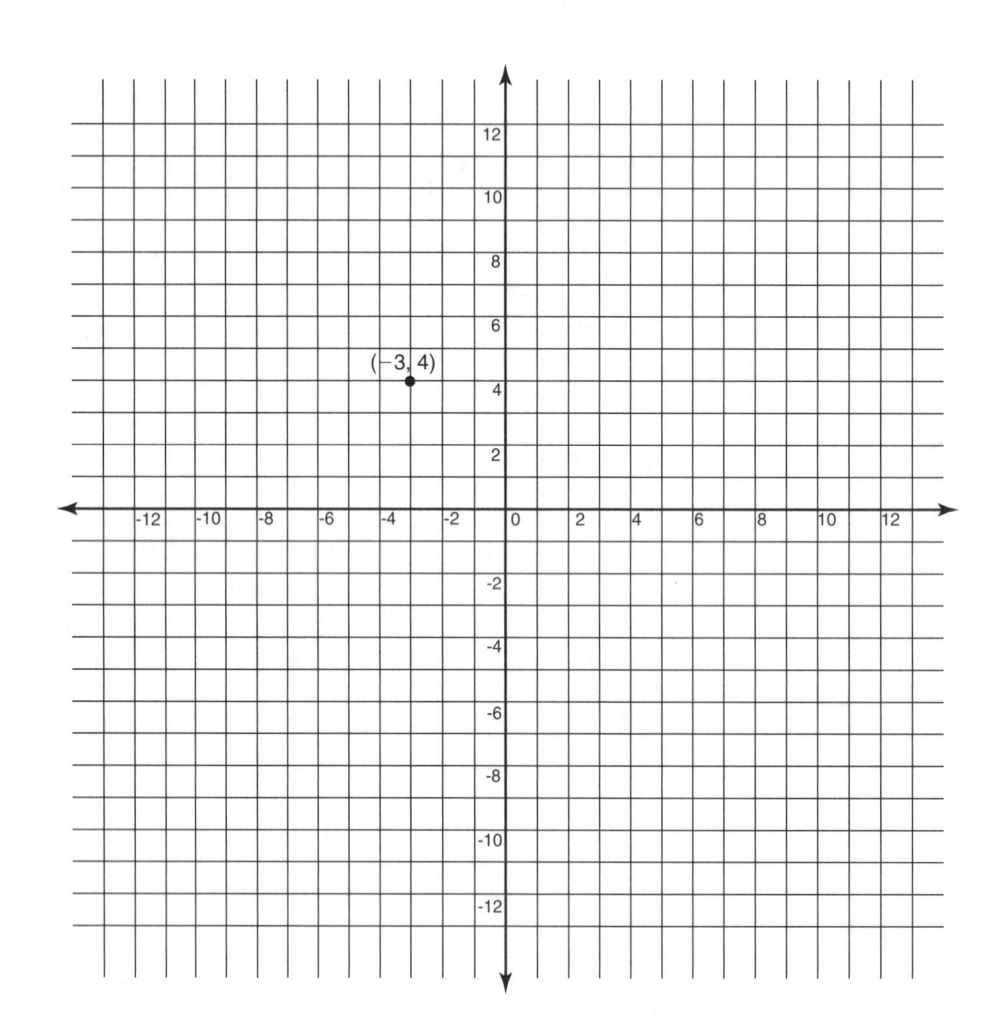

Putting Lines on a Drawing   53

2. Figure 2-24 is similar to the "Connect-the-dots" game that you may have played as a child. Locate points A and B and then draw a straight line between the two points. Next, locate point C and draw a straight line between points B and C. Continue connecting the points until you get to the last point. Finally connect the last point back to point A. Eventually you will make this same figure on AutoCAD using these same methods. Note that the squares are .5 units apart.

A	(1,1)	F	(1.5,6.5)	K	(6,3)	P	(7.5,3.5)
B	(1,2.5)	G	(3.5,6.5)	L	(6,6.5)	Q	(8.5,2.5)
C	(2,3.5)	H	(3.5,3)	M	(8,6.5)	R	(8.5,1)
D	(1,4.5)	I	(4,2.5)	N	(8.5,6)	S	(8,.5)
E	(1,6)	J	(5.5,2.5)	O	(8.5,4.5)	T	(1.5,.5)

Figure 2-24

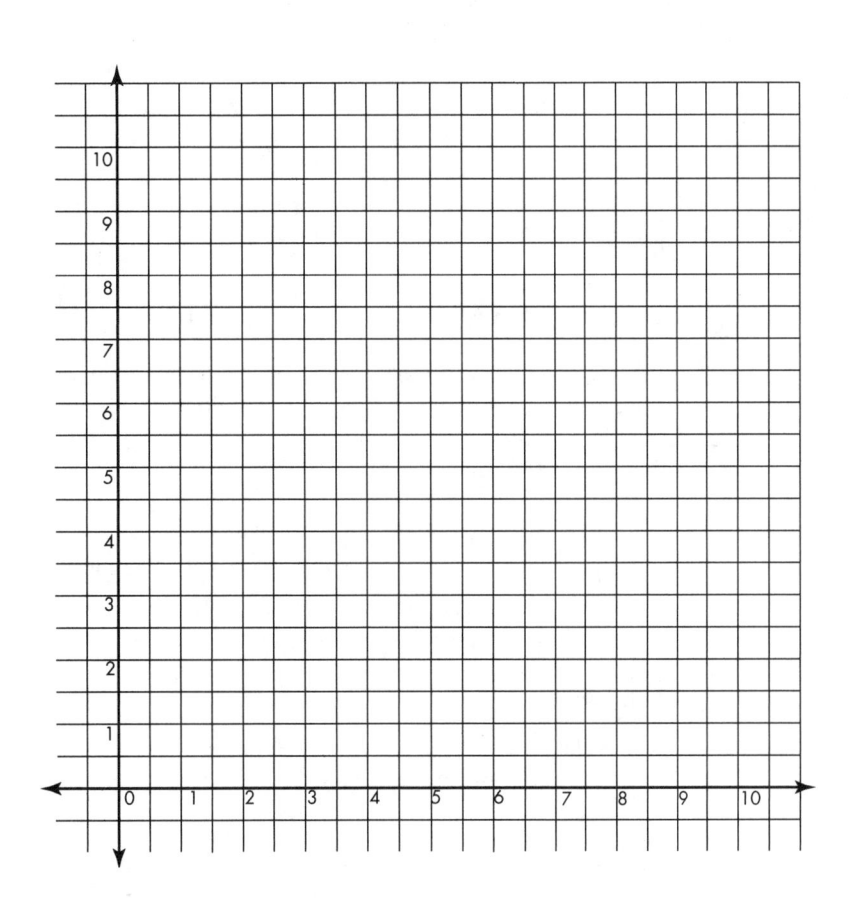

Activity 4

Drawing Lines Using Absolute Coordinates

Objectives: After completing this activity, you should be able to do the following:

- Locate and use the *Line* button on the *Draw* toolbar to draw a line.
- Start and end a line using absolute coordinates.
- Use the *Close* command to close a figure.
- Determine absolute coordinates for the endpoints of any straight line figure.
- Locate and use the *Endpoint* snap on the *Object Snap* toolbar to start a line from the end of another line.

Procedure: ☑ Check each box as you complete that item.

- ☐ Start *AutoCAD 2002*.
- ☐ When the *AutoCAD 2002 Today* dialog box appears, select the *Open a Drawing* tab, and use the *Browse* hyperlink to locate and open the drawing *M02A04-1.dwg* from the *Module02* subdirectory on the CD.
- ☐ Make sure that all the *Drawing Features* buttons on the *Status* bar (SNAP, GRID ORTHO, POLAR, etc.), except for the MODEL button, are off, not depressed.

Drawing a Line

In this section you will learn how to use the *Line* button on the *Draw* toolbar to draw a line. You will initially learn to draw lines without worrying about their length or direction. Later you will learn to draw lines by specifying their starting and ending locations using absolute coordinates.

- ☐ Use Figure 2-25 to help you locate the *Line* button on the *Draw* toolbar. It is the first button at the top of the toolbar since it is the most important drawing tool.
- ☐ Place the mouse pointer over the *Line* button and click the mouse button. The command line will appear as shown below.

Command:
Command:
Command: _line Specify first point:

Note: You must continuously check the command line. This is how AutoCAD communicates with you. The command line will let you know what information the program needs next or if there is a problem.

- ☐ Place the graphics cursor close to the lower left corner of the drawing area and click the mouse button. Check the command line; it is now asking for the next point.

Command:
Command: _line Specify first point:
Specify next point or [Undo]:

Putting Lines on a Drawing   55

Figure 2-25
The *Line* button is located at the top of the *Draw* toolbar.

Line button

☐ Move the graphics cursor around the drawing area and watch what happens. The line you are drawing appears from your original starting point to the location of your cursor. This is called the rubber-band effect. The line, like a rubber-band, stretches as you move the cursor. The purpose is to allow you to see what you are about to draw.

☐ Place the graphics cursor near the upper right corner of the drawing area and click the mouse button. Check the command line. Unlike some commands, the line command remains active even though you have finished drawing the first line. This allows you to continue drawing additional lines, each one starting at the point where the last ended.

Command: _line Specify first point:
Specify next point or [Undo]:
Specify next point or [Undo]:

☐ Hit the *Enter* key. The line command is now ended. You have just drawn your first line on AutoCAD.

☐ Click on the *Line* button again. This time draw a line from the upper left corner to the lower right corner. (Do not hit *Enter*.)

☐ Move the cursor to the middle top of the drawing area, and click the mouse button. Continue drawing lines by moving the cursor to a new location and clicking the mouse button to end the previous line and start the next. After you have placed several lines, hit the *Enter* key to end the line command.

In the next step you will learn to use the *Erase* command to remove all the lines you have placed on the drawing. This is only one of the many ways of erasing objects. Erasing will be covered in detail in Module 3.

☐ Use Figure 2-26 to help you locate and click on the *Erase* button on the *Modify* toolbar. Since it is the most commonly used modify button, it is located at the top.

Erase button

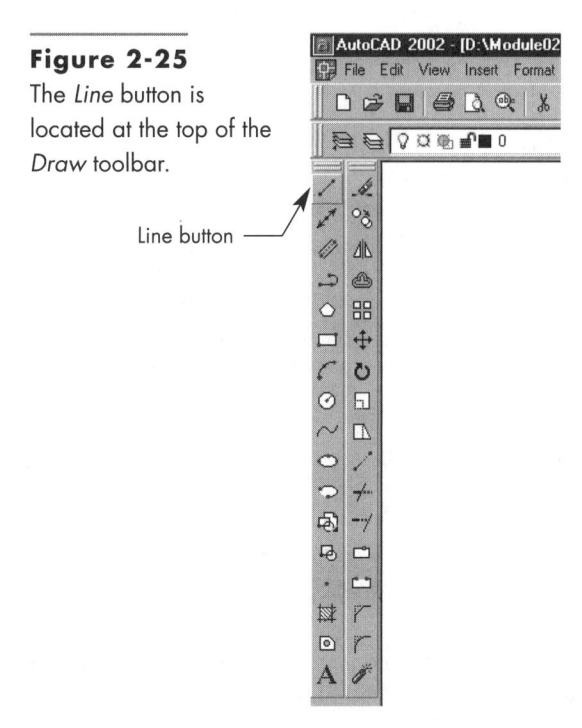

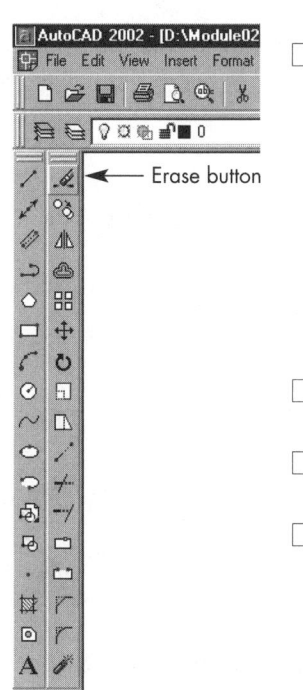

Figure 2-26
The *Erase* button is located on the *Modify* toolbar.

☐ Type **ALL** on the command line and hit *Enter* twice to erase all the lines you drew in the last section.

You should now have a basic understanding of how the *Line* command works. In the next section you will learn how to place lines in specific locations.

Draw a Line Using Absolute Coordinates

In this part of the activity you will place lines using absolute coordinates. The first figure you will draw is a 4 × 3 rectangle. The concepts of absolute coordinates were covered in the last activity. If you are unsure about absolute coordinates, you may want to do a quick review of that activity.

☐ Click on the *Line* button. Notice that AutoCAD is asking you for the first point.

Command:
Command:
Command: _line Specify first point:

☐ Type **2,2** on the command line and hit *Enter*. The line now starts at the point 2,2 and stretches to the location of the graphics cursor.

Command:
Command: _line Specify first point: 2,2
Specify next point or [Undo]:

☐ Type **6,2** on the command line and hit *Enter*.

Command: _line Specify first point: 2,2
Specify next point or [Undo]: 6,2
Specify next point or [Close/Undo]:

☐ Type **6,5** on the command line and hit *Enter*. You have now drawn two sides of the rectangle.

Specify next point or [Undo]: 6,2
Specify next point or [Close/Undo]: 6,5
Specify next point or [Close/Undo]:

☐ Type **2,5** on the command line and hit *Enter*.

Command: _line Specify first point: 6,5
Specify next point or [Undo]: 2,5
Specify next point or [Close/Undo]:

☐ You have now drawn three sides of the rectangle. You could now type in the final coordinates to finish the rectangle, but there is a better way. Notice that *Close* is one of the two available options inside the brackets on the command line. Using the *Close* option will close any figure that has at least two other sides. Type **C** on the command line and hit *Enter*.

Specify next point or [Close/Undo]: 2,5
Specify next point or [Close/Undo]: C
Command:

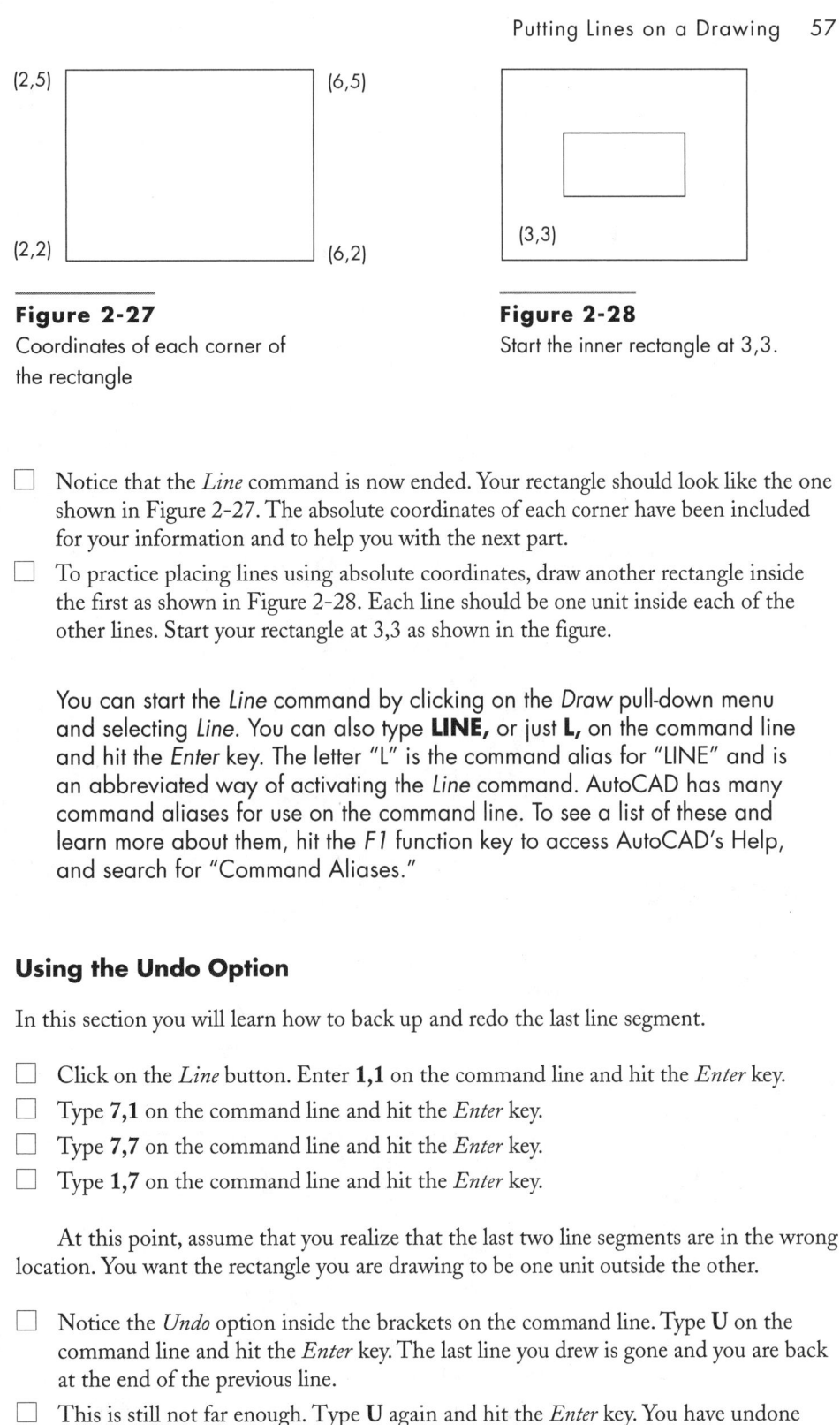

Putting Lines on a Drawing 57

Figure 2-27
Coordinates of each corner of the rectangle

Figure 2-28
Start the inner rectangle at 3,3.

- [ ] Notice that the *Line* command is now ended. Your rectangle should look like the one shown in Figure 2-27. The absolute coordinates of each corner have been included for your information and to help you with the next part.
- [ ] To practice placing lines using absolute coordinates, draw another rectangle inside the first as shown in Figure 2-28. Each line should be one unit inside each of the other lines. Start your rectangle at 3,3 as shown in the figure.

alternate method

You can start the *Line* command by clicking on the *Draw* pull-down menu and selecting *Line*. You can also type **LINE,** or just **L,** on the command line and hit the *Enter* key. The letter "L" is the command alias for "LINE" and is an abbreviated way of activating the *Line* command. AutoCAD has many command aliases for use on the command line. To see a list of these and learn more about them, hit the *F1* function key to access AutoCAD's Help, and search for "Command Aliases."

Using the Undo Option

In this section you will learn how to back up and redo the last line segment.

- [ ] Click on the *Line* button. Enter **1,1** on the command line and hit the *Enter* key.
- [ ] Type **7,1** on the command line and hit the *Enter* key.
- [ ] Type **7,7** on the command line and hit the *Enter* key.
- [ ] Type **1,7** on the command line and hit the *Enter* key.

At this point, assume that you realize that the last two line segments are in the wrong location. You want the rectangle you are drawing to be one unit outside the other.

- [ ] Notice the *Undo* option inside the brackets on the command line. Type **U** on the command line and hit the *Enter* key. The last line you drew is gone and you are back at the end of the previous line.
- [ ] This is still not far enough. Type **U** again and hit the *Enter* key. You have undone another line. Now you are ready to enter the correct coordinates and finish the figure.
- [ ] Type **7,6** on the command line and hit the *Enter* key.
- [ ] Type **1,6** on the command line and hit the *Enter* key.
- [ ] Type **C** and hit the *Enter* key to close the rectangle. You should now have three concentric rectangles as shown in Figure 2-29.

Figure 2-29
The three rectangles should look like this.

Figure 2-30
Erase the top line of the outer rectangle.

Using the Endpoint Object Snap

In this section you will learn how to snap to the end of a line to make it the starting point for another line.

☐ Click on the *Erase* button. (If you are unsure of its location refer to Figure 2-26.) The mouse cursor will change into a small square called a pickbox.

☐ Place the pickbox directly over the top line. Click the left mouse button to select the line and then hit the *Enter* key. The line, as shown in Figure 2-30, will be erased.

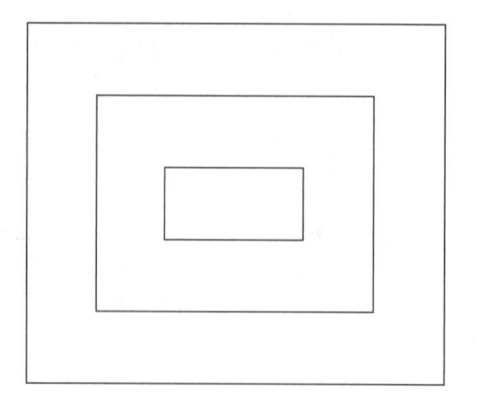

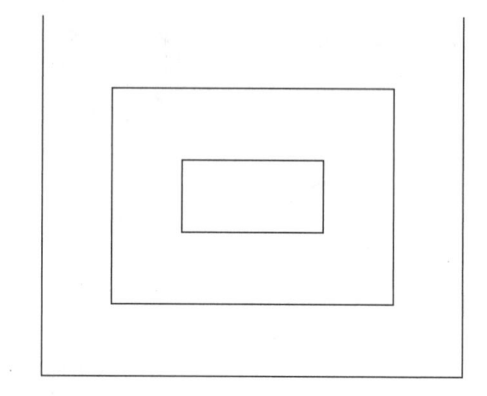

☐ You will now replace the line you erased with a new line. Assume that you do not remember the coordinates of both ends of the line. The *Endpoint* snap will help.

☐ Click on the *Line* button.

Command:
Command:
Command: _line Specify first point:

☐ Use Figure 2-31 to help you locate and click on the *Endpoint* button on the *Object Snap* toolbar. If this toolbar is not showing, you will have to turn it on as you learned in a previous activity. After clicking the *Endpoint* button, the command line should look as shown below.

Command:
Command:
Command: _line Specify first point: _endp of

☐ You have just activated the *Endpoint* snap command and AutoCAD is asking you to choose the endpoint of a line. Move the graphics cursor to the upper end of the right vertical line. A square box, called a marker, will appear at the end of that line.

☐ When the box is visible, click the left mouse button. The new line will now start exactly at the end of the vertical line. This process is called snapping to the endpoint of a line.

Command:
Command: _line Specify first point: _endp of
Specify next point or [Undo]:

Endpoint button

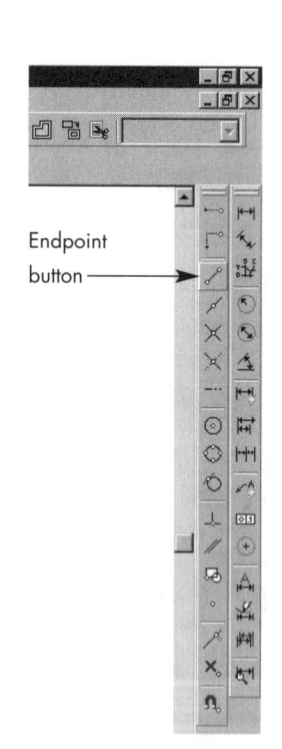

Figure 2-31
The *Endpoint* button is located on the *Object Snap* toolbar.

Figure 2-32
Draw diagonal lines between the corners.

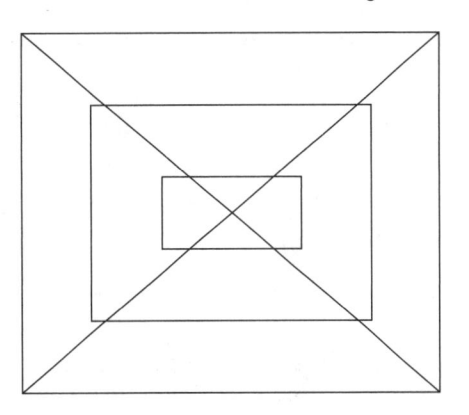

- [ ] You are now going to use the *Endpoint* snap to end the line at the other vertical line. The snap command is currently set up to end after each operation, so you will have to reactivate it to snap to the second line.
- [ ] Click on the *Endpoint* button. Don't worry; it is OK that the rubber-band line follows as you move the cursor to click on the button.

Command:
Command: _line Specify first point: _endp of
Specify next point or [Undo]: _endp of

- [ ] Move the graphics cursor to the upper end of the other vertical line. When the *Endpoint* snap marker appears, click the mouse button to complete the line between the two points.
- [ ] Hit the *Enter* key to complete the line command.
- [ ] For additional practice, use the line command and the *Endpoint* snap to draw diagonal lines between the corners as shown in Figure 2-32.
- [ ] This completes this activity. You may want to practice drawing using the absolute coordinates method. When you are done, close the AutoCAD program.

Assignment
for Module 2 – Activity 4

The purpose of this assignment is to give you practice making a drawing using absolute coordinates.

Procedure: ☑ Check each box as you complete that item.

- [ ] Start *AutoCAD 2002*.
- [ ] When the *AutoCAD 2002 Today* dialog box appears, select the *Open a Drawing* tab, and use the *Browse* hyperlink to locate and open the drawing *M02A04-2.dwg* from the *Module02* subdirectory on the CD.
- [ ] Use the absolute coordinates listed below to draw a closed figure. Start your first line at point A (1,1) and draw it to point B (1,2.5). Then continue drawing segments from B to C, then to D, etc. When you get to point T (1.5,.5), use the *Close* command to close the figure. (You may want to check your work against the sketch you made for Module 2, Activity 3. It should look the same.)

A	(1,1)	F	(1.5,6.5)	K	(6,3)	P	(7.5,3.5)
B	(1,2.5)	G	(3.5,6.5)	L	(6,6.5)	Q	(8.5,2.5)
C	(2,3.5)	H	(3.5,3)	M	(8,6.5)	R	(8.5,1)
D	(1,4.5)	I	(4,2.5)	N	(8.5,6)	S	(8,.5)
E	(1,6)	J	(5.5,2.5)	O	(8.5,4.5)	T	(1.5,.5)

- ☐ When you have completed the figure, click on the *A-size Sheet* tab. If you started your figure at 1,1, it will be centered on the paper.
- ☐ Save the drawing to your removable disk with the name M02A04-2.
- ☐ Print a copy of your drawing using the methods learned in Module 1, Activity 7.
- ☐ Neatly print your name and the date in the appropriate spaces in the title block.

Putting Lines on a Drawing 61

Activity 5

Drawing Lines Using Relative Coordinates

Objectives: After completing this activity, you should be able to do the following:

- Start a line using either an absolute coordinate or an endpoint, and end the line using a relative coordinate.
- Determine the relative coordinates required to draw a straight line figure.
- Start and/or end a line at the midpoint of another line using the *Midpoint* snap on the *Object Snap* toolbar.

Procedure: ☑ Check each box as you complete that item.

☐ Start *AutoCAD 2002*.

☐ When the *AutoCAD 2002 Today* dialog box appears, select the *Open a Drawing* tab, and use the *Browse* hyperlink to locate and open the drawing *M02A05-1.dwg* from the *Module02* subdirectory on the CD.

☐ Make sure that all the *Drawing Features* buttons on the *Status* bar (SNAP, GRID ORTHO, POLAR, etc.), except for the MODEL button, are off, not depressed.

Relative and Absolute Coordinates

Before you can draw lines using relative coordinates, you first need to know what they are and how they are calculated. It is very important to learn how to properly use relative coordinates because they can be used with many other AutoCAD commands like *Move*, *Copy*, and *Stretch*.

In the last activity you learned how to draw lines based on absolute coordinates. The line shown in Figure 2-33 starts at 2,2 and ends at 6,2. The coordinates 2,2 and 6,2 are absolute in that they describe an exact or absolute location of the endpoints of the line.

The same line can be drawn using another method. You will still start most lines by specifying either an exact location, like 2,2, or using the *Endpoint* snap to start at the end of another line. However, the second point can be located relative to the first. You can also get from 2,2 to point 6,2 by moving 4 units in the positive x-direction and 0 units in the y-direction. 4 and 0 are the relative coordinates of the second point. The format for relative coordinates is @4,0. The @ symbol, which is on the 2 key on the keyboard and requires using the *Shift* key, indicates that the coordinates are relative; the 4 indicates the number of units in the x-direction; and the 0 indicates the number of units in the y-direction. As with absolute coordinates, you have to be very careful to keep the x- and y-coordinates in their proper place. You must also remember to use the @ symbol or AutoCAD will use the coordinates you enter as absolute, which can produce some very strange results.

Now that you have an idea what relative coordinates are all about, you will draw the same rectangle you drew in Activity 4, except this time you will use relative instead of absolute coordinates.

(2,2)   (6,2)

Figure 2-33
The ends of the line are described by absolute coordinates.

☐ Click on the *Line* button on the *Draw* toolbar. Refer to Figure 2-25 if you are unsure of the button's location.

Command:
Command:
Command: _line Specify first point:

- ☐ Type **2,2** on the command line and hit *Enter*. The line now starts at the point 2,2 and stretches to the location of the graphics cursor.

  Command:
  Command: _line Specify first point: 2,2
  Specify next point or [Undo]:

- ☐ Type **@4,0** on the command line and hit *Enter*. The first side of the rectangle has been drawn. You are now at the absolute coordinate 6,2, but that is not important because with relative coordinates you don't have to keep track of absolute locations. This makes drawing much easier.

  Command: _line Specify first point: 2,2
  Specify next point or [Undo]: @4,0
  Specify next point or [Close/Undo]:

- ☐ Look at the absolute coordinates of the next line segment shown in Figure 2-34. Can you determine what the next relative coordinates will be?
- ☐ Type **@0,3** on the command line and hit *Enter*. The relative coordinates are 0,3 because you do not want to move in the x-direction, thus 0; but you do want to move 3 units in the positive y-direction.

  Specify next point or [Undo]: @4,0
  Specify next point or [Undo]: @0,3
  Specify next point or [Close/Undo]:

- ☐ Look at the absolute coordinates of the next line segment shown in Figure 2-35. Can you determine what the next relative coordinates will be?
- ☐ Type **@-4,0** on the command line and hit *Enter*. The relative coordinates are −4,0 because you want to go to the left, 4 units in the negative x-direction, but not move any units in the y-direction.

  Specify next point or [Undo]: @0,3
  Specify next point or [Undo]: @-4,0
  Specify next point or [Close/Undo]:

- ☐ Type **C** on the command line and hit *Enter* to close the figure. You could have typed the relative coordinates @0,−3 to get from 2,5 back to the starting point 2,2, but using the *Close* command is faster.

Figure 2-34
Determine the relative coordinates based on the absolute coordinates.

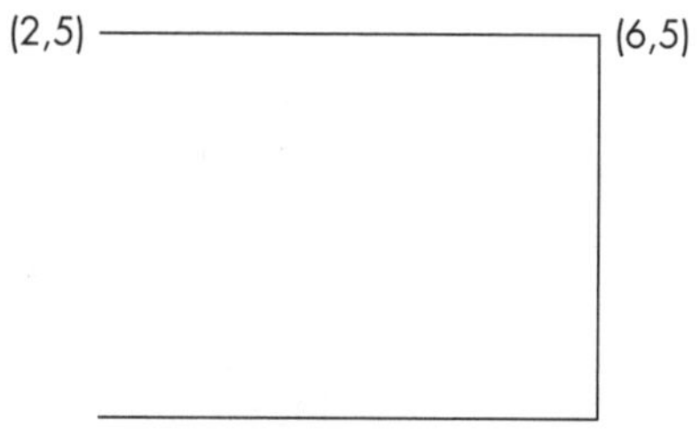

Figure 2-35
Determine the relative coordinates of the next line segment.

Putting Lines on a Drawing   63

Figure 2-36
Completed figure

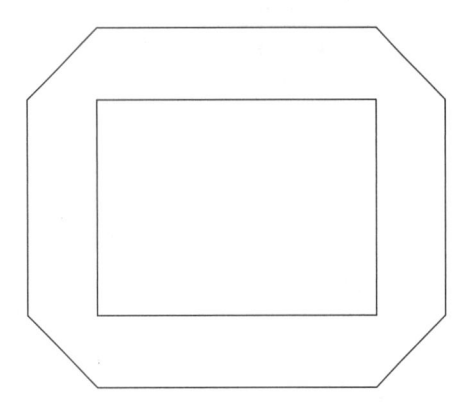

In the previous figure you moved in only one direction (x or y) during each command. In the next figure you will see that you can move in both directions at the same time. As you go through each step to draw the next figure, think about where the line is going to go before you hit the *Enter* key.

☐ Click on the *Line* button, type **2,1** on the command line, and hit *Enter*.

☐ Type **@4,0** on the command line and hit *Enter*.

☐ Type **@1,1** on the command line and hit *Enter*.

☐ Type **@0,3** on the command line and hit *Enter*.

☐ Type **@-1,1** on the command line and hit *Enter*.

☐ Type **@-4,0** on the command line and hit *Enter*.

☐ Type **@-1,-1** on the command line and hit *Enter*.

☐ Type **@0,-3** on the command line and hit *Enter*.

☐ Type **C** on the command line and hit *Enter* to close the figure. Your drawing should look like Figure 2-36.

Using the Midpoint Object Snap

In this section you will learn how to use another snap tool, the midpoint snap. This snap will allow you to locate and use the middle of a line as a starting or ending point. It is a convenient tool because sometimes it is not easy to determine the coordinates of a midpoint. With this tool, AutoCAD does the calculation for you, so all you have to do is pick the point.

☐ Click on the *Line* button on the *Draw* toolbar.

☐ Use Figure 2-37 to help you locate and click on the *Midpoint* button on the *Object Snap* toolbar.

☐ Move the mouse pointer around the screen and over the lines you have drawn. You will see a triangle appear when AutoCAD finds a line. The triangle appears at the midpoint of that line.

☐ Place the graphics cursor over the outside vertical line on the left and when the *Midpoint* marker appears, click the mouse button. The line now starts at the midpoint of the line and stretches to the location of the graphics cursor.

☐ Click on the *Midpoint* button and move the mouse pointer to the outside vertical line on the right. When the *Midpoint* marker appears, click the mouse button.

☐ Hit the *Enter* key to complete the line command. Your drawing should look like the one shown in Figure 2-38.

☐ Using the *Line* command and the *Midpoint* snap, draw a diagonal line from the midpoint of the opposite corners, as shown in Figure 2-39.

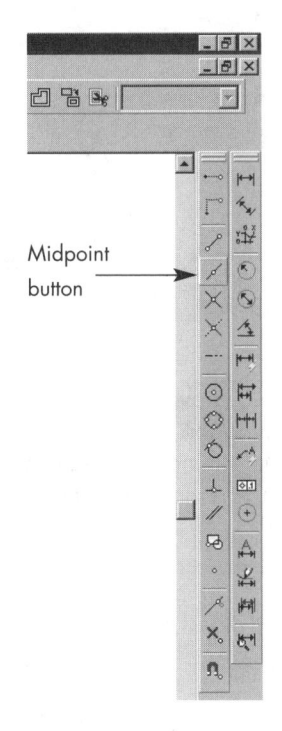

Figure 2-37
The *Midpoint* button is located on the *Object Snap* toolbar.

Figure 2-38
Completed figure

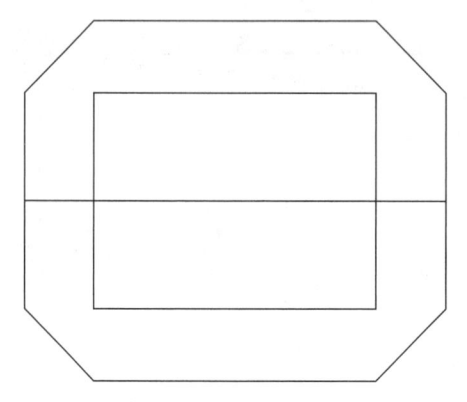

Figure 2-39
Completed figure

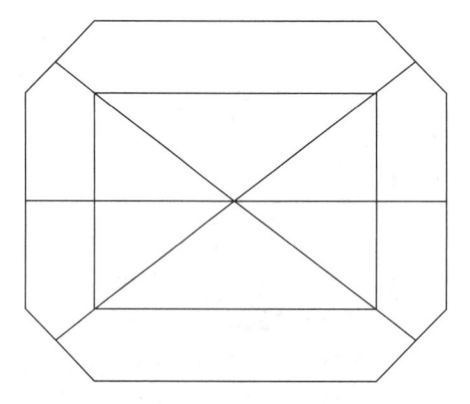

☐ This completes this activity. You should spend some time practicing drawing lines using absolute and relative coordinates. When you are done, close the AutoCAD program.

Assignment
for Module 2 – Activity 5

The purpose of this assignment is to give you practice making a drawing using relative coordinates. Before you start drawing, you must determine the relative coordinates for each step. Complete the following table by determining the relative coordinates needed to move from the first point to the second. The first set of coordinates has been completed for you as an example.

Line Segment	From Point	To Point	Relative Coordinates
1	(1,1)	(1,2.5)	@0,1.5
2	(1,2.5)	(2,3.5)	
3	(2,3.5)	(1,4.5)	
4	(1,4.5)	(1,6)	
5	(1,6)	(1.5,6.5)	
6	(1.5,6.5)	(3.5,6.5)	
7	(3.5,6.5)	(3.5,3)	
8	(3.5,3)	(4,2.5)	
9	(4,2.5)	(5.5,2.5)	
10	(5.5,2.5)	(6,3)	
11	(6,3)	(6,6.5)	
12	(6,6.5)	(8,6.5)	
13	(8,6.5)	(8.5,6)	
14	(8.5,6)	(8.5,4.5)	
15	(8.5,4.5)	(7.5,3.5)	
16	(7.5,3.5)	(8.5,2.5)	
17	(8.5,2.5)	(8.5,1)	
18	(8.5,1)	(8,.5)	
19	(8,.5)	(1.5,.5)	
20	(1.5,.5)	(1,1)	

Procedure: ☑ Check each box as you complete that item.

- ☐ Start *AutoCAD 2002*.
- ☐ When the *AutoCAD 2002 Today* dialog box appears, select the *Open a Drawing* tab, and use the *Browse* hyperlink to locate and open the drawing *M02A05-2.dwg* from the *Module02* subdirectory on the CD.
- ☐ Use the relative coordinates that you calculated above to draw a closed figure. Start your first line at point (1,1). (You may want to check your work against the drawing you made for Module 2, Activity 3. It should look the same.)
- ☐ When you have completed the figure, click on the *A-size Sheet* tab. If you started your figure at 1,1, it will be centered on the paper.
- ☐ Save the drawing to your removable disk with the name M02A05-2.
- ☐ Print a copy of your drawing using the methods learned in Module 1, Activity 7.
- ☐ Neatly print your name and the date in the appropriate spaces in the title block.

Activity 6

Drawing Lines Using Polar Coordinates

Objectives: After completing this activity, you should be able to do the following:

- Start a line using absolute coordinates, endpoint snap, or midpoint snap, and end the line using polar coordinates.
- Determine the polar coordinates required to draw any straight line figure.
- Start and/or end a line at the intersection of two or more lines using the *Intersection* snap on the *Object Snap* toolbar.

Procedure: ☑ Check each box as you complete that item.

☐ Start *AutoCAD 2002*.

☐ When the *AutoCAD 2002 Today* dialog box appears, select the *Open a Drawing* tab, and use the *Browse* hyperlink to locate and open the drawing *M02A06-1.dwg* from the *Module02* subdirectory on the CD.

☐ Make sure that all the *Drawing Features* buttons on the *Status* bar (SNAP, GRID ORTHO, POLAR, etc.), except for the MODEL button, are off, not depressed.

Polar Coordinates

In the last two activities, you learned how to draw lines using absolute and relative coordinates. In this activity you will learn to use polar coordinates to draw a line. Polar coordinates are also relative to the last point, but use distances and angles to define where the line should go. It is very important to learn how to properly use polar coordinates because they can be used with many other AutoCAD commands like *Move, Copy,* and *Stretch*.

In the first activity you drew the line shown in Figure 2-40 using the absolute coordinates 2,2 and 6,2.

(2,2) ———————— (6,2)

Figure 2-40
Absolute coordinates of first line

As stated in the last activity, most lines are still drawn by specifying an exact location, like 2,2, or by using snaps to determine their starting point. With polar coordinates, the second point of this line can be placed using a length of 4 units and a direction of 0°. The format is @4<0. The @ symbol indicates that it is relative; the 4 indicates the length of the line; the angle symbol (<), which is to the right of the M on the keyboard and requires using the *Shift* key, indicates that you are using polar coordinates. The 0 indicates the angle direction from the starting point.

Now that you have an idea how polar coordinates work, you will draw the same rectangle you drew in Activities 4 and 5, except this time you will use polar coordinates instead of absolute or relative coordinates.

☐ Click on the *Line* button on the *Draw* toolbar.

Command:
Command:
Command: _line Specify first point:

☐ Type **2,2** on the command line and hit *Enter*. The line now starts at the point 2,2 and stretches to the location of the graphics cursor.

Command:
Command: _line Specify first point: 2,2
Specify next point or [Undo]:

☐ Type **@4<0** on the command line and hit *Enter*. The first side of the rectangle is drawn and you are now at the absolute coordinates 6,2.

Command: _line Specify first point: 2,2
Specify next point or [Undo]: @4<0
Specify next point or [Close/Undo]:

☐ Look at the absolute coordinates of the second line segment shown in Figure 2-41. Can you determine what the next polar coordinates will be?

☐ Type **@3<90** on the command line and hit the *Enter* key. The polar coordinates are @3<90 because you want to move 3 units at an angle of 90° from the starting point.

Specify next point or [Undo]: @4<0
Specify next point or [Undo]: @3<90
Specify next point or [Close/Undo]:

☐ Look at the absolute coordinates of the next line segment shown in Figure 2-42. Can you determine what the next polar coordinates will be?

☐ Type **@4<180** on the command line and hit the *Enter* key. The polar coordinates are @4<180 because you want to go 4 units at an angle of 180 degrees from the starting point.

Specify next point or [Undo]: @3<90
Specify next point or [Undo]: @4<180
Specify next point or [Close/Undo]:

☐ Type **C** on the command line and hit *Enter* to close the figure. You could have typed the polar coordinates @3<270 to get from 2,5 back to the starting point 2,2, but using the *Close* command is faster.

In the last section you drew lines that were in the directions of 0°, 90°, 180°, and 270°. Polar coordinates can be used at any angle. In the next section you will learn how to use polar coordinates at any angle.

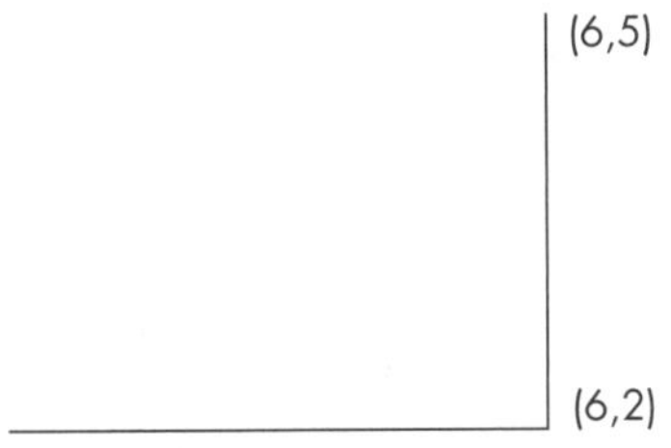

Figure 2-41
Determine the polar coordinates based on the absolute coordinates.

Figure 2-42
Determine the polar coordinates for the next line segment.

- ☐ Click on the *Line* button on the *Draw* toolbar.
- ☐ Click on the *Endpoint* snap button on the *Object Snap* toolbar.
- ☐ Move the graphics cursor to the upper right corner of the rectangle you just drew. When the endpoint marker appears, click the mouse button to start your line at that point.
- ☐ Type **@3<45** on the command line and hit the *Enter* key *twice*.

alternate method

You do not have to hit the *Enter* key twice to end the line command. After you place the last point, click the *right* mouse button and a pop-up menu will appear. The first item on this list will be *Enter*. Move the cursor to highlight it and then click the mouse button. The line command will end. To start the next line, hit the right mouse button again and the pop-up menu will appear with *Repeat Line* as the first item. Click on it and you are ready to start the next line. Using the right click pop-up menu keeps your eyes on the screen and increases your drawing speed. This method works for most commands that end by hitting the *Enter* key on the keyboard.

- ☐ Click on the *Line* button, and then click on the *Endpoint* object snap. Move the cursor back to the upper right corner of the rectangle and when the endpoint marker appears, click the mouse button to start the line.
- ☐ Type **@3<135** on the command line and hit the *Enter* key twice.
- ☐ Click on the *Line* button, and then click on the *Endpoint* object snap. Move the cursor back to the upper right corner of the rectangle and when the endpoint marker appears, click the mouse button to start the line.
- ☐ Type **@3<225** on the command line and hit the *Enter* key twice.
- ☐ Click on the *Line* button, and then click on the *Endpoint* object snap. Move the cursor back to the upper right corner of the rectangle and when the endpoint marker appears, click the mouse button to start the line.
- ☐ Type **@3<315** on the command line and hit the *Enter* key twice.
- ☐ You will now draw one additional line that will be used later in this activity.
- ☐ Click on the *Line* button, and then click on the *Endpoint* object snap. Move the cursor back to the *upper left* corner of the rectangle and when the endpoint mark appears, click the mouse button to start the line.
- ☐ Type **@3<315** on the command line and hit the *Enter* key twice.
- ☐ Your drawing should look like Figure 2-43.

Figure 2-43
Completed figure

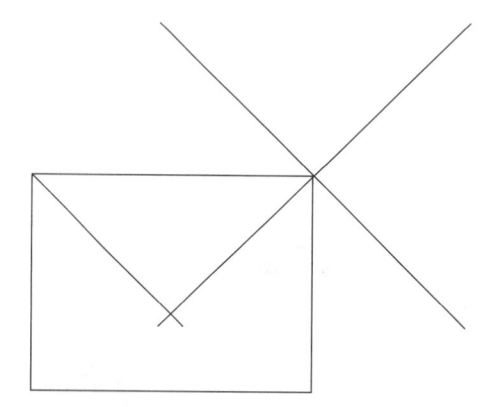

Relative vs. Polar Coordinates

It is very important that you understand that there is a big difference between the relative coordinates @2,2 and the polar coordinates @2<45. Both give you a line at a 45° angle, but there is a big difference in the lengths of these two lines. In the following steps you will draw both of these lines next to each other so you can see the difference.

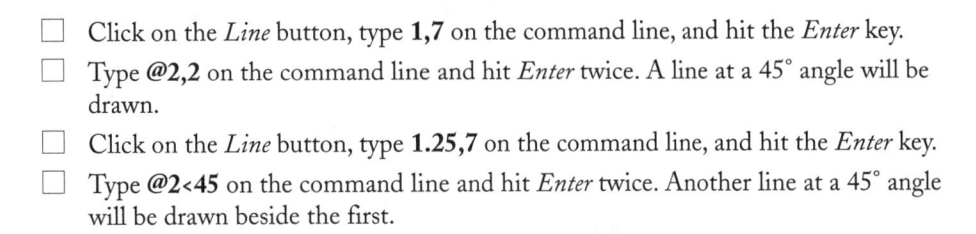

- ☐ Click on the *Line* button, type **1,7** on the command line, and hit the *Enter* key.
- ☐ Type **@2,2** on the command line and hit *Enter* twice. A line at a 45° angle will be drawn.
- ☐ Click on the *Line* button, type **1.25,7** on the command line, and hit the *Enter* key.
- ☐ Type **@2<45** on the command line and hit *Enter* twice. Another line at a 45° angle will be drawn beside the first.

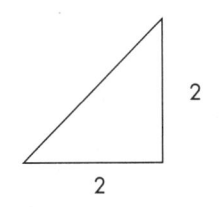

Notice the difference in length of the two lines. When you use relative coordinates, you specify how far the endpoint will be in both the x- and y-directions from the starting point. If you have ever taken geometry you may remember that the first line you drew was the hypotenuse of a triangle with a base length of 2 and a height of 2. This triangle is shown in Figure 2-44. The hypotenuse is always longer than either of the two sides.

For this triangle, the length of the hypotenuse and the length of the line formed by using @2,2 will be:

$$\sqrt{2^2 + 2^2} = \sqrt{4 + 4} = \sqrt{8} \cong 2.8284$$

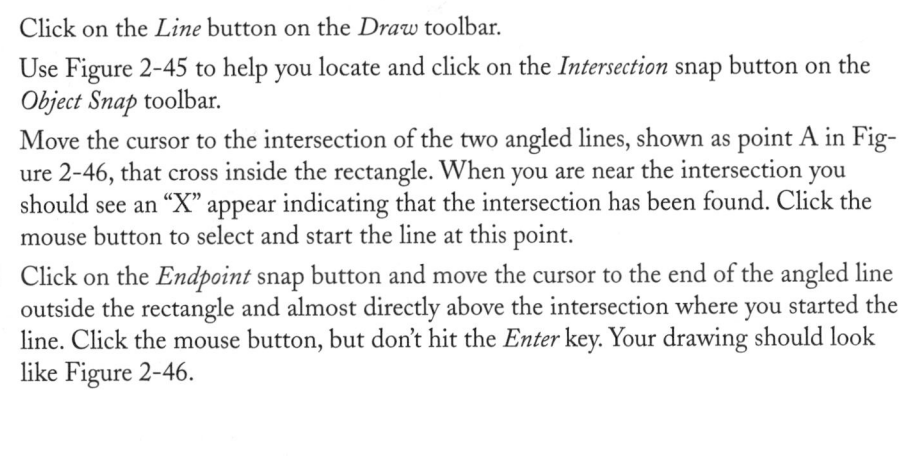

Figure 2-44
Right angle triangle with base and height of 2

For the line you drew using the polar coordinates @2<45, the length was 2. So @2,2 and @2<45 do not produce the same results.

You should also notice the ≅ symbol in the calculation. This symbol means approximately equal to. You should not use your calculator to make a calculation like the one above, and then use that value to draw the line using polar coordinates. The lengths of @2,2 and @2.8284<45 will still be different because 2,2 gives exact starting and ending points whereas 2.8284 is approximately the length of the line between these two points.

So, what should you do when you want to draw a line? Until now, you have learned three methods for drawing lines. No one method works best in all situations. Most of the time you will mix and match the methods so you can complete your drawing in the fastest, most precise way. The most important thing is that you know how to use the three methods and that you know their limitations.

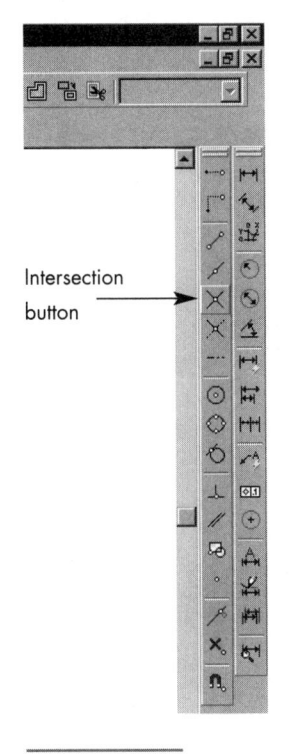

Using the Intersection Object Snap

In this section you will learn another method of locating the starting or ending point for a line. This new snap allows you to start or end at the intersection of two or more lines.

- ☐ Click on the *Line* button on the *Draw* toolbar.
- ☐ Use Figure 2-45 to help you locate and click on the *Intersection* snap button on the *Object Snap* toolbar.
- ☐ Move the cursor to the intersection of the two angled lines, shown as point A in Figure 2-46, that cross inside the rectangle. When you are near the intersection you should see an "X" appear indicating that the intersection has been found. Click the mouse button to select and start the line at this point.
- ☐ Click on the *Endpoint* snap button and move the cursor to the end of the angled line outside the rectangle and almost directly above the intersection where you started the line. Click the mouse button, but don't hit the *Enter* key. Your drawing should look like Figure 2-46.

Figure 2-45
The *Intersection* button is located on the *Object Snap* toolbar.

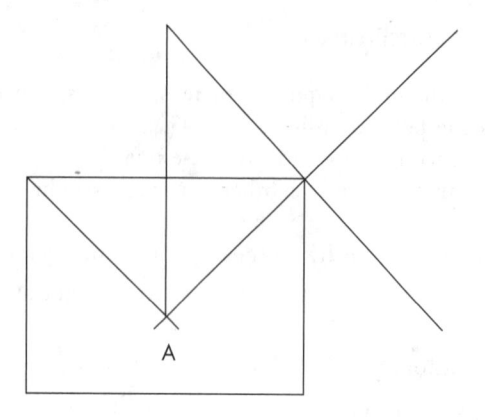

Figure 2-46
Use the *Intersection* snap to start the line at point A.

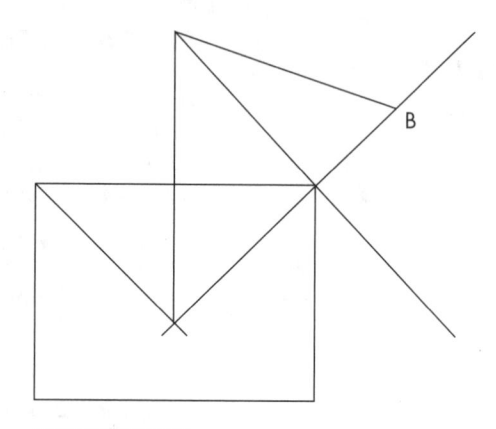

Figure 2-47
Use the *Midpoint* snap to end the second line segment at B.

Figure 2-48
Use the *Intersection* snap to end the line segment at C.

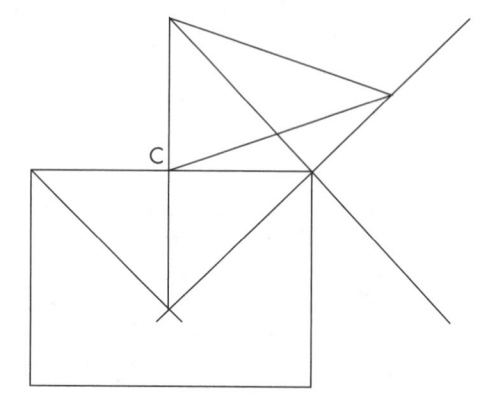

- ☐ Click on the *Midpoint* snap button, and move the cursor near the midpoint of the angled line to the right. When the midpoint marker appears, click the mouse button to select this point. Your drawing should look like Figure 2-47.
- ☐ Click on the *Intersection* snap button, move the cursor near to the point where your first line crossed the rectangle, and click the mouse button when you see the "X" marker. Your drawing should look like Figure 2-48.
- ☐ Hit the *Enter* key to end the line command.
- ☐ You now know three ways of snapping to exact locations for starting and ending lines. You now have several lines intersecting on your drawing. You may want to spend some time practicing using all three snaps.
- ☐ This completes this activity. Close the AutoCAD program when you are done.

Assignment
for Module 2 – Activity 6

The purpose of this assignment is to give you practice in making a drawing using polar coordinates. Before you start drawing, you must determine the polar coordinates for each step. Complete the following table by determining the polar coordinates needed to move from the first point to the second. The first set of coordinates has been completed for you as an example. All the lines in this object are either horizontal or vertical. You can determine the direction of the line (0°, 90°, 180°,

Putting Lines on a Drawing   71

or 270°) by determining whether it is the x-coordinate and/or the y-coordinate that is changing and which way.

Line Segment	From Point	To Point	Relative Coordinates
1	(1,1)	(3.75,1)	@2.75<0
2	(3.75,1)	(3.75,1.75)	_____
3	(3.75,1.75)	(1.75,1.75)	_____
4	(1.75,1.75)	(1.75,3.25)	_____
5	(1.75,3.25)	(2.5,3.25)	_____
6	(2.5,3.25)	(2.5,2.5)	_____
7	(2.5,2.5)	(6.5,2.5)	_____
8	(6.5,2.5)	(6.5,3.25)	_____
9	(6.5,3.25)	(7.25,3.25)	_____
10	(7.25,3.25)	(7.25,1.75)	_____
11	(7.25,1.75)	(5.25,1.75)	_____
12	(5.25,1.75)	(5.25,1)	_____
13	(5.25,1)	(8,1)	_____
14	(8,1)	(8,6.5)	_____
15	(8,6.5)	(7.25,6.5)	_____
16	(7.25,6.5)	(7.25,5.75)	_____
17	(7.25,5.75)	(5.75,5.75)	_____
18	(5.75,5.75)	(5.75,3.75)	_____
19	(5.75,3.75)	(3.25,3.75)	_____
20	(3.25,3.75)	(3.25,5.75)	_____
21	(3.25,5.75)	(1.75,5.75)	_____
22	(1.75,5.75)	(1.75,6.5)	_____
23	(1.75,6.5)	(1,6.5)	_____
24	(1,6.5)	(1,1)	CLOSE

Procedure: ✓ Check each box as you complete that item.

- ☐ Start *AutoCAD 2002*.
- ☐ When the *AutoCAD 2002 Today* dialog box appears, select the *Open a Drawing* tab, and use the *Browse* hyperlink to locate and open the drawing M02A06-2.dwg from the *Module02* subdirectory on the CD.
- ☐ Use the polar coordinates you calculated above to draw a closed figure. Start your first line at point (1,1).
- ☐ When you have completed the figure, click on the *A-size Sheet* tab. If you started your figure at 1,1, it will be centered on the paper.
- ☐ Save the drawing to your removable disk with the name M02A06-2.
- ☐ Print a copy of your drawing using the methods learned in Module 1, Activity 7.
- ☐ Neatly print your name and the date in the appropriate spaces in the title block.

Applying the Concepts

Your company manufactures a repair kit for their model L-2002 stamping machine. The kit includes both large parts and numerous smaller parts, which are shipped together in a wooden crate. Lately customers have complained that some of the smallest parts are missing when they receive their repair kits. They wonder if these may be falling through the cracks in the crate. Your company decides to ship the smaller parts in a cardboard box inside the crate. Your boss designs a box he feels will hold the parts perfectly, but since your company intends to order hundreds of these custom boxes, he wants to make sure his design works before placing the order.

Your boss knows that you have learned how to draw lines on AutoCAD. He wants you to make a drawing of his box pattern so that he can cut it out, fold it up, and verify that it will work. It is very important that you make a drawing to the exact dimensions shown on your boss's sketch (Figure 2-49). A three-dimensional view of the box has been provided to help you visualize how the finished box will look.

- ☐ Start *AutoCAD 2002*.
- ☐ When the *AutoCAD 2002 Today* dialog box appears, open the drawing *M02APP.dwg* located in the *Module02* subdirectory on the CD.
- ☐ Using absolute, relative, and/or polar coordinates, draw the layout of the box pattern. Start your drawing at point 2.5, .750, as shown in the figure.

Figure 2-49
Box pattern

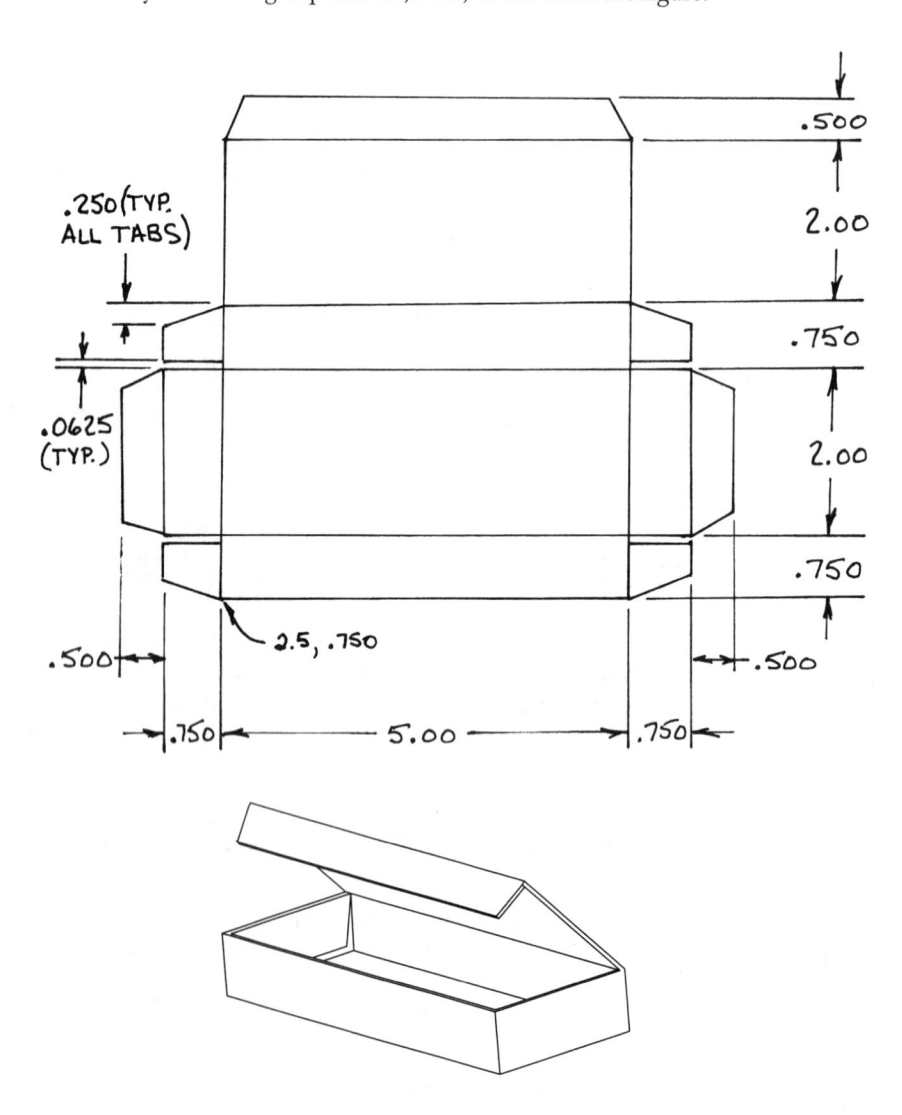

- [ ] When you have completed the drawing, click on the *A-size Sheet* tab. If you started your drawing at the correct point, it will be centered on the drawing.
- [ ] Save the drawing to your removable disk with the name M02APP.
- [ ] Print a copy of your drawing.
- [ ] Neatly print your name and the date in the appropriate spaces in the title block.
- [ ] If you would like to see what your finished box looks like, print an additional copy of the layout, cut it out, and fold it into a box, as shown in the 3D figure.

Module 2 Review Questions

These questions are provided to help you review the topics and concepts covered in this module.

True or False

Determine whether the statement is true or false. Place your answer, either T or F, in the blank.

____ 1. The *Precision* setting allows you to draw lines more accurately.

____ 2. AutoCAD requires you to specify when you are working in metric units instead of inches.

____ 3. Decimal units are commonly used for metric units.

____ 4. Architectural units are only used for drawing buildings and structures.

____ 5. The snap points can be set so they are not at the same locations as the grid points.

____ 6. You can set the x- and y-values of the grid settings to different values.

____ 7. The USC icon will always be located in the lower left corner of the screen.

____ 8. @12<45 produces the same length line as @6,6.

____ 9. A line from point 5,5 to point 5,10 can be drawn starting at 5,5 and using the relative polar coordinates @5<90.

____ 10. A line starting at 2,2 and ending at 6,8 can be drawn starting at 2,2 and using the relative coordinates @6,4.

____ 11. A line between the points 10,10 and 5,4 can be drawn starting at 5,4 and using the relative coordinates @5,6.

____ 12. **C** is the keyboard shortcut for *Cut*.

____ 13. Although you can draw a line using absolute, relative, or polar coordinates, the absolute method is the fastest and easiest in all cases.

Multiple-choice

Place the letter of the best answer in the blank.

1. 2'- 8.5" is an example of ____ linear units.
   a. Decimal
   b. Fractional
   c. Engineering
   d. Architectural

2. 37d15'36" is an example of ____ angular units.
   a. Decimal
   b. Deg/Min/Sec
   c. Radians
   d. Surveyor's

3. .877r is an example of ____ angular units.
   a. Decimal
   b. Deg/Min/Sec
   c. Radians
   d. Surveyor's

4. 24.325 is an example of ____ linear units.
   a. Decimal
   b. Fractional
   c. Engineering
   d. Architectural

5. 45 is an example of ____ angular units.
   a. Decimal
   b. Deg/Min/Sec
   c. Gradients
   d. Surveyor's

6. 12'- 2 15/16 is an example of ____ linear units.
   a. Decimal
   b. Fractional
   c. Engineering
   d. Architectural

7. 2 5/8 is an example of ____ linear units.
   a. Decimal
   b. Fractional
   c. Engineering
   d. Architectural

8. S 15d30" W is an example of ____ angular units.
   a. Decimal
   b. Deg/Min/Sec
   c. Gradients
   d. Surveyor's

9. 17g is an example of ____ angular units.
   a. Decimal
   b. Deg/Min/Sec
   c. Gradients
   d. Surveyor's

10. ____ is the only true example of surveyor's units listed below.
    a. N16d05"E
    b. W14d15'17"S
    c. N30d15'S
    d. E22s14'N

11. @12<45 is an example of ____ coordinates.
    a. absolute
    b. relative
    c. polar
    d. exact

12. 15,12 is an example of ____ coordinates.
    a. absolute
    b. relative
    c. polar
    d. exact

13. @15,12 is an example of ____ coordinates.
    a. absolute
    b. relative
    c. polar
    d. exact

14. The endpoint of a line starting at point 2,2 drawn with the relative coordinates @5,7 is ____.
    a. 9,7
    b. 5,7
    c. 7,9
    d. 7,5

76　Module 2

15. This button is used to activate the ____ command.
    a. Intersection snap
    b. Center snap
    c. Endpoint snap
    d. Line

16. This button is used to activate the ____ command.
    a. Line
    b. Endpoint snap
    c. Intersection snap
    d. Move

17. This button is used to activate the ____ command.
    a. Line
    b. Endpoint snap
    c. Intersection snap
    d. Copy

18. This button is used to activate the ____ command.
    a. Center snap
    b. Intersection snap
    c. Midpoint snap
    d. Endpoint snap

Module 3

Modifying Objects on a Drawing

Activity 1

Erasing

Objectives: After completing this activity, you should be able to do the following:

- Erase individual lines or objects from a drawing.
- Select and erase several lines or objects from a drawing.
- Use the *Erase All* command to erase everything from a drawing.
- Locate and use the *Undo* button on the *Standard* toolbar to undo one or more previous commands.
- Use the *Erase Window* command to erase objects contained within a rectangular area.
- Use the *Erase Crossing Box* command to erase objects inside and crossing a rectangular area.
- Remove and add objects to a selection set of objects to be erased.
- Erase individual objects that are stacked.
- Use the erase *Window Polygon, Crossing Polygon,* and *Fence* commands to erase objects.

Procedure: ☑ Check each box as you complete that item.

- ☐ Start *AutoCAD 2002*.
- ☐ When the *AutoCAD 2002 Today* dialog box appears, open the drawing *M03A01-1.dwg* located in the *Module03* subdirectory on the CD.
- ☐ After the program has completely loaded, verify that the *Model* button is the only button on the *Status* bar that is selected. You will have difficulty completing this activity if any of the other buttons appear depressed, meaning they are selected.

Erasing a Single Line or Object

In this section you will learn how to erase individual objects from a drawing.

77

Figure 3-1
The *Erase* button is located on the *Modify* toolbar.

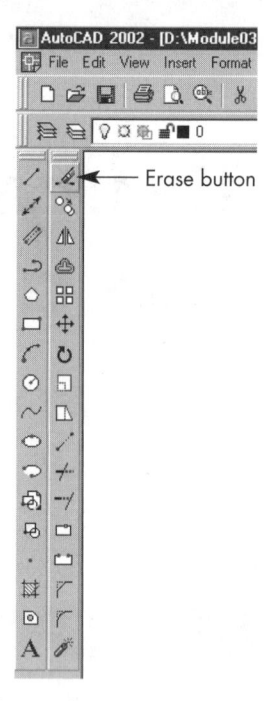

- Use Figure 3-1 to help you locate the *Erase* button located at the top of the *Modify* toolbar.

Note: If you cannot find the *Erase* button, it may be that the *Modify* toolbar is not turned on. Use the methods learned in previous activities to turn it on.

- Click on the *Erase* button and then move the mouse pointer back to the drawing area. Notice that the graphics cursor has now turned into a square called a *pickbox*. The *pickbox* is used to pick the objects you want to erase.
- Place the *pickbox* over the left vertical line of the rectangle in View A. Click the left mouse button. The line will turn into a dashed line indicating that it has been selected (picked).
- Hit the *Enter* key on the keyboard and the line will be erased.

alternate method: You can start the *Erase* command by clicking on the *Modify* pull-down menu and selecting *Erase*. You can also type **ERASE,** or just **E,** on the command line and hit the *Enter* key.

Erasing Several Lines of Objects

In this section you will learn to erase several objects at the same time.

- Click on the *Erase* button.
- Place the *pickbox* over one of the other lines of the rectangle in View A and click the left mouse button. The line will turn dashed.
- Move the pickbox over one of the other lines and click the mouse button again. That line will also become dashed. (Do not hit the *Enter* key yet.)
- Repeat the procedure for the other line and the circle. As you select each, it will become dashed indicating that it has been selected.
- Hit the *Enter* key on the keyboard and all the selected objects will be erased.

Modifying Objects on a Drawing 79

Instead of hitting Enter on the keyboard you can click the right mouse button to end the Select objects command. You may want to try this method as it is faster than returning to the keyboard.

Erasing Everything

In this section you will learn to use the *Erase All* command to remove all lines and objects from a drawing.

- ☐ Click on the *Erase* button.
- ☐ Type **ALL** from the keyboard. Notice that ALL appears next to *Select objects:* on the command line, as shown in Figure 3-2.
- ☐ Hit the *Enter* key. Notice that all the lines, text, and objects on the drawing appear dashed. This means they all are selected and will be erased.
- ☐ Hit the *Enter* key again. Everything is gone.

Using the *Undo* button

In this section you will learn to undo the last completed command.

- ☐ Use Figure 3-3 to help you locate the *Undo* button on the *Standard* toolbar. When this button is clicked, the last operation will be undone.
- ☐ Click the *Undo* button once. All the objects you erased in the last section have now returned.
- ☐ Click the *Undo* button again. The circle and three lines of the rectangle have returned.
- ☐ Click the *Undo* button a third time. You are now back at the original drawing.

You must be careful using Erase All. In a future activity you will learn how to add drawing layers and turn these layers on and off so that objects on those layers are visible or invisible on the computer screen. Erase All will erase objects on all layers even if some of those objects are invisible on layers that are turned off. You will learn how to Freeze and/or Lock layers to prevent this from happening.

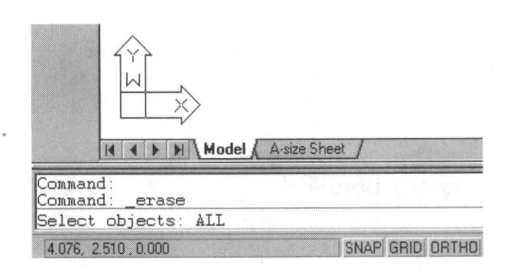

Figure 3-2
Type **ALL** from the keyboard to select and erase all the objects.

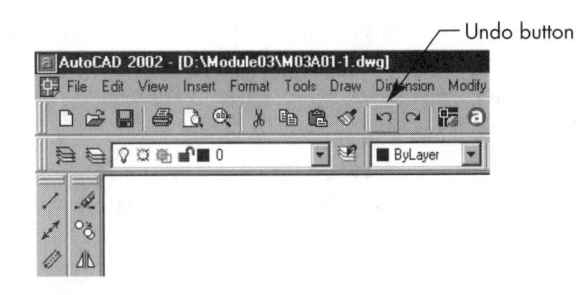

Figure 3-3
The *Undo* button is located on the *Standard* toolbar.

80   Module 3

Figure 3-4
Draw an *Erase Window* around the objects to be erased.

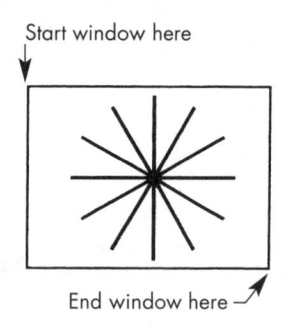

Using the *Erase Window* Command

Erasing objects one at a time can be time consuming when you have lots of objects to erase. In this section you will learn to erase several objects at once using the *Erase Window* command.

☐ Click on the *Erase* button.

☐ Place the *pickbox* above and to the left of the pinwheel of lines (View B), as shown in Figure 3-4.

☐ Click the left mouse button and drag toward the lower right of the pinwheel. As you drag, a rectangular shaped box will appear. This is the *Erase Window*.

Note: If you find you started the window at the wrong location, hit the *Esc* key and try again.

☐ When the window completely surrounds the pinwheel, click the left mouse button again. All the lines of the pinwheel will appear dashed and the window will disappear. The window was used to select the lines to be erased.

☐ Hit *Enter*, or hit the right mouse button, and the pinwheel will be erased.

☐ Click on the *Undo* button on the *Standard* toolbar to restore the pinwheel.

☐ Click on the *Erase* button.

☐ Place the *pickbox* above and to the left of the pinwheel of lines, as shown in Figure 3-5.

☐ Click the mouse button and drag toward the right and just past the horizontal center of the pinwheel, as shown in the figure. Click the mouse button again.

☐ When your window is similar to the one in the figure, click the left mouse button. What lines have become dashed? What is the relationship between the window and the dashed lines?

☐ Hit the *Enter* key. The dashed lines are erased. Using an *Erase Window* will only erase the lines and objects that are contained completely inside the window. Any line or object that is outside and/or crossing the window's boundary will not be erased.

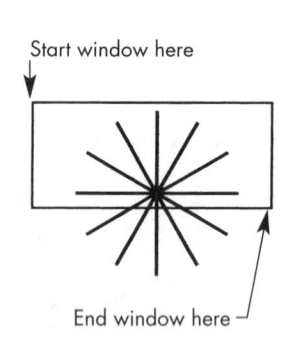

Figure 3-5
Only the objects *completely* inside the *Erase Window* will be selected to be erased.

Note: When you use the window method of selection, you will select only the objects that are completely inside the window's borders.

☐ Click on the *Undo* button on the *Standard* toolbar to restore the pinwheel.

☐ Take some time to practice using the *Erase Window* command on other parts of the drawing. Remember to use the *Undo* command each time you erase something so that you will have all the objects to continue this activity.

Modifying Objects on a Drawing   81

Using the *Erase Crossing Box*

In this section you will learn to erase objects using the *Crossing Box*. Unlike the *Erase Window*, the *Crossing Box* not only erases objects inside it, but also any object that crosses its boundary.

- ☐ Click on the *Erase* button.
- ☐ Place the *pickbox* to the *right* and just below the horizontal center of the pinwheel, as shown in Figure 3-6.
- ☐ Click the mouse button and drag the mouse up and to the left, as shown in the figure, to create a *Crossing Box*. Notice that the lines of the *Crossing Box* are dashed while the lines of an *Erase Window* are solid.
- ☐ When your *Crossing Box* is similar to the one in the figure, click the mouse button again.
- ☐ Notice that all the lines inside the box and all the lines crossing the boundary of the box were selected.
- ☐ Hit the *Enter* key and the pinwheel will be erased.
- ☐ Click on the *Undo* button on the *Standard* toolbar to restore the pinwheel.
- ☐ Take some time practicing using the *Crossing Box* command on other parts of the drawing. Remember to use the *Undo* command each time you erase something so that you will have all the sketches to continue this activity.

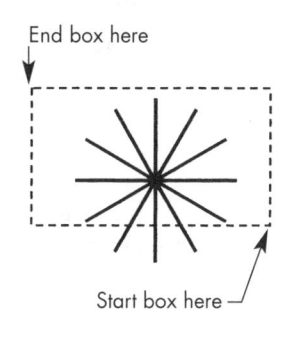

Figure 3-6
To draw an *Erase Crossing Box*, you start on the right and move left.

Note: When you use the crossing box method of selection, you will select the objects that are completely inside the box's borders *and* all objects that cross the box's borders.

Adding and Removing Objects to the Set of Objects to be Erased

This section will show you how to add or remove objects from the group of objects you have selected to be erased.

- ☐ Click on the *Erase* button. Notice that the command line reads *Select objects*.
- ☐ Place the *pickbox* over any one of the lines in View C and click the left mouse button. That line will become dashed, indicating that it was selected. Also notice that the command line is still reading *Select objects*, which indicates that you can select another object to be erased.
- ☐ Place the *pickbox* over another line in View C and click the mouse button to select that line. Now two lines are dashed.
- ☐ Select a third line using the same procedure.
- ☐ Hit *Enter* and all three lines will be erased.
- ☐ Click on the *Undo* button on the *Standard* toolbar to restore the lines.

This method of adding lines to be erased works for all methods of selection. In the following section you will use all three methods, *pickbox*, *Window*, and *Crossing Box*, to select a group of lines to be erased.

- ☐ Click on the *Erase* button.
- ☐ Use the *pickbox* to select any line or object in any figure on the drawing.
- ☐ Use the *Erase Window* method to select any group of lines or objects on the drawing. Notice that the original object you selected and the objects you included in the window are all dashed.

- ☐ Use the *Crossing Box* method to select another group of lines of objects on the drawing. These will be added to your selection group.
- ☐ Hit the *Enter* key and all the objects you selected will be erased. It is usually easier to select all or most of the objects and erase them at one time than to erase each individually.
- ☐ Click on the *Undo* button on the *Standard* toolbar to restore everything you erased.

Sometimes you may include too many lines or objects in your selection set and may need to remove one or more of them. The next section will show you how to do this.

- ☐ Click on the *Erase* button and use the *Erase Window* command to select all the lines in View D.

If you hit *Enter* now everything would be erased; but you realize that you want to leave the four lines that make up the middle rectangle.

- ☐ Press and hold the *Shift* key on the keyboard. Now place the *pickbox* over one of the lines of the middle rectangle and click the mouse button. That line now turns from dashed to solid, indicating that it is no longer selected.
- ☐ Continue to hold the *Shift* key and select each of the other three lines using the same method. When you finish, the outer two rectangles should be dashed and the inner one should be solid.
- ☐ Hit the *Enter* key. Only one rectangle remains.
- ☐ Click on the *Undo* button on the *Standard* toolbar to restore everything you erased.
- ☐ Spend some time practicing adding and removing objects from the selected items to be erased. Remember to use the *Undo* command each time you erase something so that you will have all the objects to continue this activity.

Erase Objects That Are Stacked

Sometimes you have two or more objects stacked together and you need to select one for erasing and leave the other(s). Look at View D on the screen. On the left vertical line on the upper rectangle there are actually two lines, one on top of the other. (The line is noted in Figure 3-7.) One line goes from the bottom to the top of the rectangle, and the other line only goes halfway from the bottom toward the top. You will learn how to delete the second line in the following section.

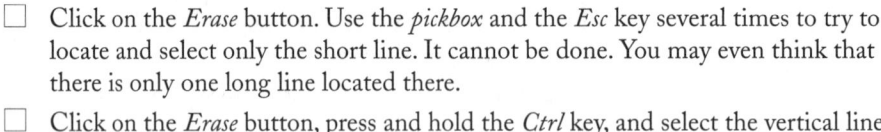

- ☐ Click on the *Erase* button. Use the *pickbox* and the *Esc* key several times to try to locate and select only the short line. It cannot be done. You may even think that there is only one long line located there.
- ☐ Click on the *Erase* button, press and hold the *Ctrl* key, and select the vertical line near the bottom again. Notice that <Cycle on> appears on the command line. Release the *Ctrl* key.

Figure 3-7
There are two lines, one short and one long, along the edge of the rectangle.

There are two lines located along this edge.

Modifying Objects on a Drawing

Figure 3-8
The short line is selected to be erased.

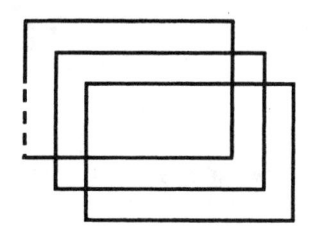

- [ ] Click the left mouse button. Only half of the line appears dashed. You have selected the shorter line. Click the left mouse button several more times and notice that you cycle back and forth between the two lines. If there were lots of lines all stacked together, you would be cycling among all of them one at a time.
- [ ] Click the left mouse button until you have selected the short line, as shown in Figure 3-8.
- [ ] Hit the *Enter* key twice, once to exit cycle and the second time to erase the line.
- [ ] Click on the *Undo* button on the *Standard* toolbar to restore the line you erased.
- [ ] Now use this method to erase the long line and leave the short line. Remember to replace all objects that you erase using the *Undo* command.

Erasing Using the *Window Polygon* Command

Although the following erase commands are used less often than those you learned above, they will be useful when you are trying to erase objects that are surrounded by, or near other objects you do not want to erase. The *Window Polygon* command allows you to create a closed figure with multiple sides and erase what is contained in the figure.

- [ ] Click on the *Erase* button.
- [ ] Type **WP** (for *Window Polygon*) on the command line and hit the *Enter* key.
- [ ] Place the crosshairs between the two lines as shown above in Figure 3-9a. Click the left mouse button to start the polygon at this point.
- [ ] Move the crosshairs to point 2, as shown in Figure 3-9b, and click the mouse button. This will make the second vertex of the polygon.
- [ ] Move the pointer to point 3, click; then point 4, click; etc. all the way around to form the polygon shown in the figure. Notice that the sides of the polygon go through the vertical and horizontal lines and go outside the angled lines.
- [ ] When you get to the last point, hit the *Enter* key. Your drawing should look like Figure 3-8c, with only the angled lines selected. Hit *Enter* again and they will be erased.
- [ ] Click on the *Undo* button on the *Standard* toolbar to restore the lines you erased.

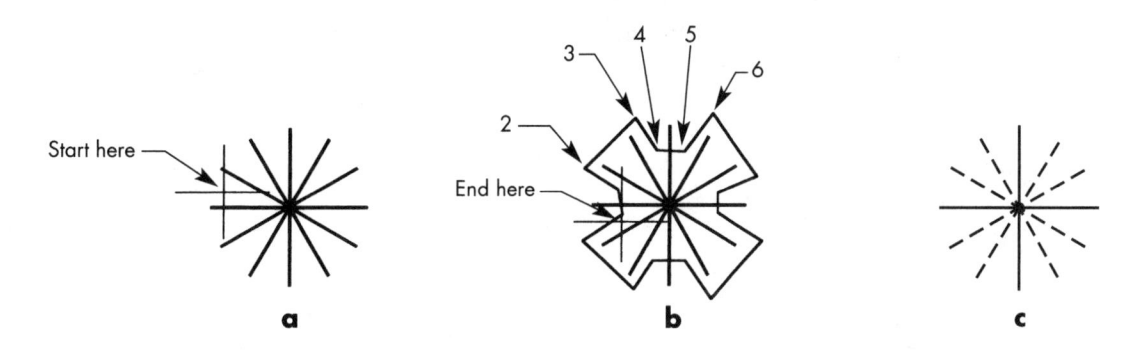

Figure 3-9
Draw a *Window Polygon* to erase selected objects.

Note: When you use the window polygon method of selection, you will select only the objects that are completely inside the polygon's borders.

Erasing Using the *Crossing Polygon* Command

The *Crossing Polygon* works exactly the same as a *Crossing Box*. All objects completely inside the polygon or crossing any boundary of the polygon will be erased. Try erasing the four angled line segments on the left side of View B using a *Crossing Polygon*. Type *CP* instead of *WP* to start a *Crossing Polygon* and then choose a starting point. Remember that you need to draw a figure that has the four lines you want to erase passing through its boundary but none of the other lines.

Note: When you use the crossing polygon method of selection, you will select the objects that are completely inside the polygon's borders *and* all objects that cross the polygon's borders.

Erasing Using the *Fence* Command

The *Fence* command is also a crossing figure. Instead of being a closed figure like a box or polygon, the fence is just a line with one or more vertexes.

- ☐ Click on the *Erase* button, type **F** for *Fence*, and hit the *Enter* key. *First fence point:* will appear on the command line.
- ☐ Place the crosshairs at the first point, shown in Figure 3-10, and click the mouse button. Move to the second point, click, and then to the last point, and click.
- ☐ Hit the *Enter* key. All the lines that the *Fence* passed through will be selected. Hit the *Enter* key again and they will be erased.
- ☐ Click on the *Undo* button on the *Standard* toolbar to restore the lines you erased.

Practice erasing lines using all the methods you learned in this activity.

- ☐ When you are done, close the AutoCAD program. When AutoCAD asks if you want to save, select *No*.

Figure 3-10
A *Crossing Fence* is used to erase only the lines that pass through it.

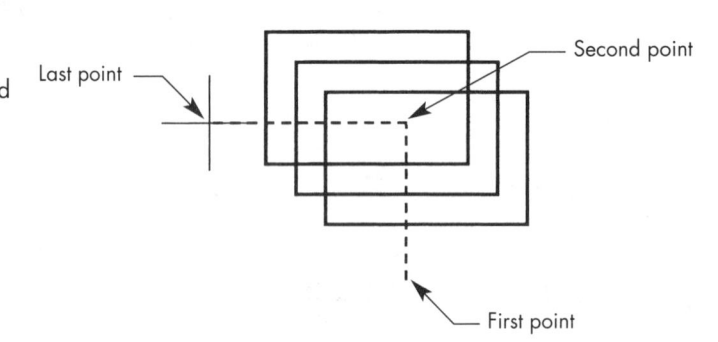

Activity 2

Trim, Extend, Move, and Copy

Objectives: After completing this activity, you should be able to do the following:

- Locate and use the *Trim* button on the *Modify* toolbar to trim a line to another line.
- Locate and use the *Extend* button on the *Modify* toolbar to extend a line to another line.
- Locate and use the *Move* button on the *Modify* toolbar to move an object to a specific location on a drawing.
- Locate and use the *Copy* button on the *Modify* toolbar to copy an object to a specific location on a drawing.

Procedure: ☑ Check each box as you complete that item.

- ☐ Start *AutoCAD 2002*.
- ☐ When the *AutoCAD 2002 Today* dialog box appears, open the drawing *M03A02-1.dwg* located in the *Module03* subdirectory on the CD.
- ☐ Make sure that all the *Drawing Features* buttons on the *Status* bar, except for the *Model* button, are off.

Using the *Trim* Command

The *Trim* command allows you to trim one line to another line. This can be handy when you want a line to stop exactly at another line, but you do not know the coordinates of the point where the line must end. To help you choose the correct lines in this exercise, a figure has been included with each set of instructions.

Setting the Trim Variable

In the following section you will set one of the variables associated with trimming. This variable allows you to trim to a line even if the two lines do not intersect. You will do this later in the activity, but for now you must make sure the variable is set correctly.

- ☐ Type **EDGEMODE** on the command line and hit the *Enter* key. Your command line should look like the one shown below. You may have 0 instead of 1 in the brackets. When this variable is set to 0, it is off; and when it is set to 1, it is on. You want it on.

    AutoCAD menu utilities loaded
    Command: EDGEMODE
    Enter new value for EDGEMODE <1>:

- ☐ If 1 appears in the brackets, hit the *Enter* key. If 0 appears in the brackets, type **1** on the command line and hit the *Enter* key.
- ☐ You have now turned the EDGEMODE variable on.

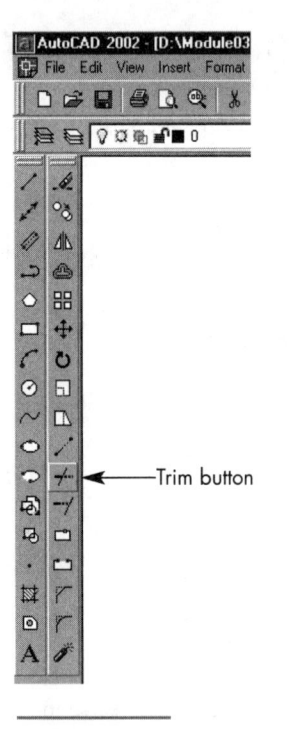

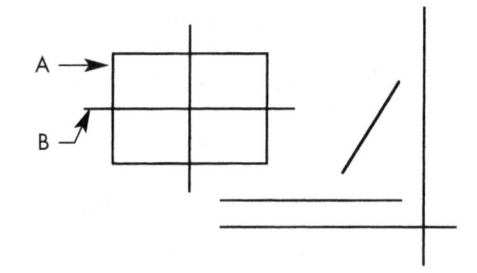

Figure 3-11
The *Trim* button is located on the *Modify* toolbar.

Figure 3-12
Trim line B to line A.

Trimming a Single Line

☐ Use Figure 3-11 to help you locate and click on the *Trim* button on the *Modify* toolbar.

Current settings: Projection=UCS Edge=Extend
Select cutting edges...
Select objects:

☐ A check of the command line shows that AutoCAD is asking you to select cutting edges (the line you want to trim to). Select the left vertical line of the rectangle (shown as A in Figure 3-12) by placing the square pickbox over the line and clicking the mouse button. The line will become dashed to indicate that it has been selected.

☐ Hit the *Enter* key to go from selecting the cutting edge to selecting the line or object to trim.

Select objects: 1 found
Select objects:
Select object to trim or shift-select to extend or [Project/Edge/Undo]:

☐ When selecting the line to trim, it is very important where you click on that line. The segment of the line you click on is the segment that will be trimmed away. Place the square pickbox over the left end of the horizontal line passing through the rectangle, shown as B in Figure 3-12, and click the mouse button. The segment will disappear.

☐ Hit the *Enter* key to end the *Trim* command.

Modifying Objects on a Drawing 87

*You can start the Trim command by clicking on the Modify pull-down menu and selecting Trim. You can also type **TRIM,** or just **TR,** on the command line and hit the Enter key.*

Trimming Between Two Lines

Sometimes you want to trim a line, removing the portion that is between two lines, as shown in Figure 3-13.

- ☐ Click the *Trim* button on the *Modify* toolbar.
- ☐ Select the top (C) and the bottom (D) lines of the rectangle as the cutting edges by placing the pickbox over each and clicking the mouse button. The lines will become dashed when selected.
- ☐ Hit the *Enter* key, or click the *right* mouse button, to end selecting cutting edges.
- ☐ Place the *pickbox* over the vertical line (E) passing through the rectangle. Make sure that you are between the two cutting edges when you select this line. As soon as you pick the line, that segment will disappear.
- ☐ Hit the *Enter* key to end the *Trim* command.
- ☐ For additional practice, trim off the line segment (F) that is projecting from the right side of the rectangle, as shown in Figure 3-14.

Trimming the Cutting Edge

In this section you will select two lines as cutting edges and then trim both of them to the other.

- ☐ Click the *Trim* button on the *Modify* toolbar.
- ☐ Use the pickbox to select lines G and H, shown in Figure 3-15, as cutting edges. Hit the *Enter* key to end selecting cutting edges.
- ☐ Place the pickbox over line segment I and click the mouse button. That part of the line will disappear. Repeat, clicking on segment J.
- ☐ Hit the *Enter* key to end the *Trim* command.

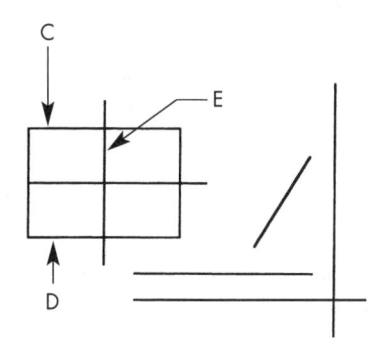

Figure 3-13
Trim off line E between lines C and D.

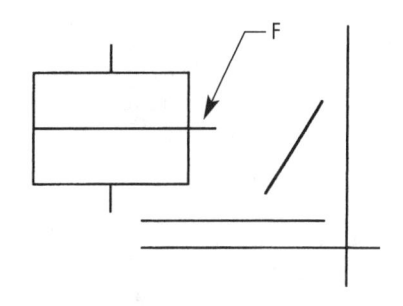

Figure 3-14
Trim off line segment F.

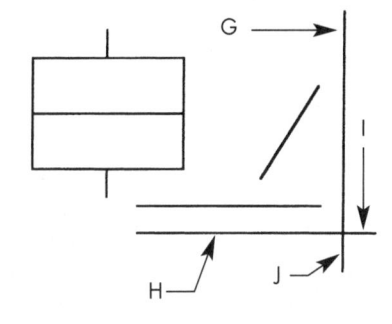

Figure 3-15
Trim off line segments I and J.

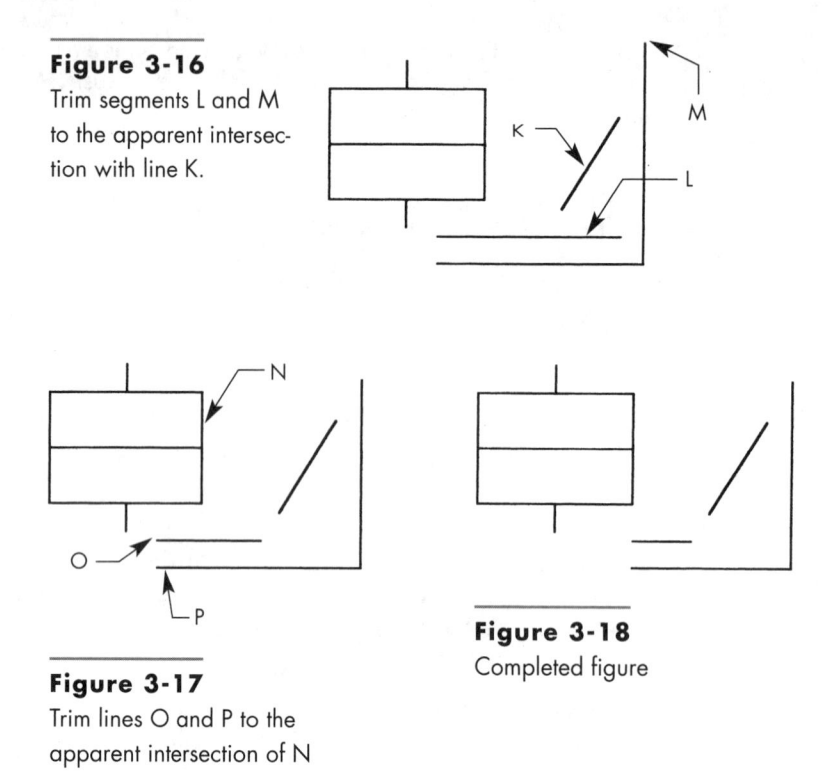

Figure 3-16
Trim segments L and M to the apparent intersection with line K.

Figure 3-17
Trim lines O and P to the apparent intersection of N

Figure 3-18
Completed figure

Trimming to an Apparent Intersection

In this section you will find that you can trim one line to another even if they do not intersect, as shown in Figure 3-16. It was for this operation that you turned the EDGEMODE variable on.

☐ Click the *Trim* button on the *Modify* toolbar.
☐ Use the pickbox to select the angled line K as the cutting edge. Hit the *Enter* key to end selecting cutting edges.
☐ Place the pickbox over the right end of line L and click the mouse button. The right end of the line will be trimmed to the apparent intersection of lines K and L.
☐ Place the pickbox over the upper end of line M and click the mouse button. This end of the line will be trimmed to the apparent intersection of lines K and M.
☐ Hit the *Enter* key to end the *Trim* command.
☐ For additional practice, use the right side of the rectangle (N) as the cutting edge and trim the left end of lines O and P to their apparent intersection with N (see Figure 3-17). When you are done your drawing should look like that shown in Figure 3-18.

Using the *Extend* Command

The *Extend* command enables you to extend one line to another line or object. This can be handy when you want a line to stop exactly at another line, but you do not know the coordinates of the point where the line must end. As with the *Trim* command, the lines do not have to actually meet.

Modifying Objects on a Drawing 89

Extend a Single Line

☐ Use Figure 3-19 to locate and click on the *Extend* button on the *Modify* toolbar.

Current settings: Projection=UCS Edge=Extend
Select boundary edges...
Select objects:

☐ A check of the command line shows that AutoCAD is asking you to select the boundary edges (the lines you want to extend to). Select the angled line, shown as Q in Figure 3-20, by placing the square pickbox over the line and clicking the mouse button. The line will become dashed to indicate that it has been selected.

☐ Hit the *Enter* key to go from selecting the boundary edge to selecting the object to extend.

Select objects: 1 found
Select objects:
Select object to extend or shift-select to trim or [Project/Edge/Undo]:

☐ When selecting the line to extend, it is very important where you click on that line. You must click on the end of the line that will be extended, i.e., some place past the center of the line that is toward the boundary edge. Place the square pickbox over the right end of the horizontal line, shown as R in Figure 3-20, and click the mouse button. The line will be extended to the angled line.

☐ Hit the *Enter* key to end the *Extend* command.

alternate method

You can start the *Extend* command by clicking on the *Modify* pull-down menu and selecting *Extend*. You can also type **EXTEND,** or just **EX,** on the command line and hit the *Enter* key.

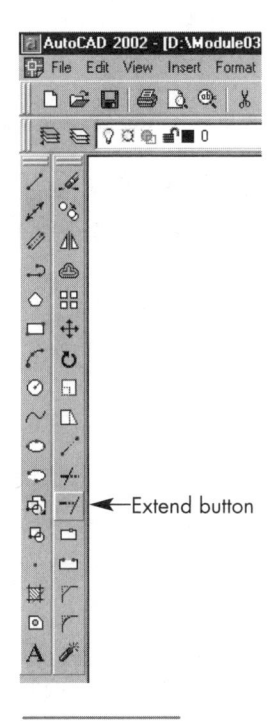

Figure 3-19
The *Extend* button is located on the *Modify* toolbar.

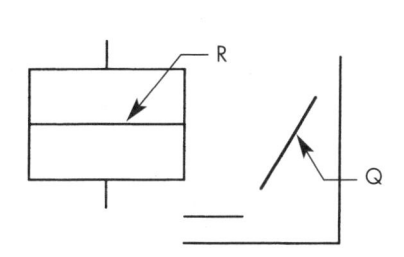

Figure 3-20
Extend line R to line Q.

Figure 3-21
Extend line U to both lines S and T.

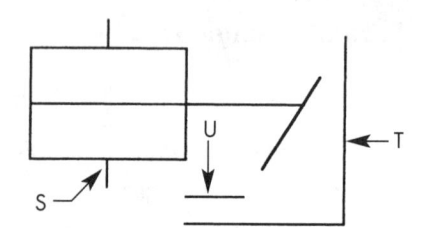

Selecting Two Lines to Extend to

- ☐ Click on the *Extend* button.
- ☐ Use the pickbox to select line S and line T, shown in Figure 3-21, as the boundary edges. Hit the *Enter* key to end selecting boundaries.
- ☐ Use the pickbox to click on the right end and then the left end of line U. As you click each end, the line will be extended to the boundary line near that end.
- ☐ Hit the *Enter* key to end the *Extend* command.

Extending to the Apparent Intersection

- ☐ Click on the *Extend* button.
- ☐ Use the pickbox to select the top of the rectangle, line V (shown in Figure 3-22), as the boundary. Hit the *Enter* key.
- ☐ Use the pickbox to select the top end of the angled line W. It will be extended to the apparent intersection with line V.
- ☐ Hit the *Enter* key to end the *Extend* command.

Extending the Boundary Lines

Extend can also be used to make two lines meet to form a corner.

- ☐ Click on the *Extend* button.
- ☐ Use the pickbox to select lines X and Y, shown in Figure 3-23, as the boundaries. Hit the *Enter* key.
- ☐ Now use the pickbox to select the lower end of line X and the left end of line Y. Both lines will be extended to meet at the same point forming a corner.
- ☐ Hit the *Enter* key to end the *Extend* command.

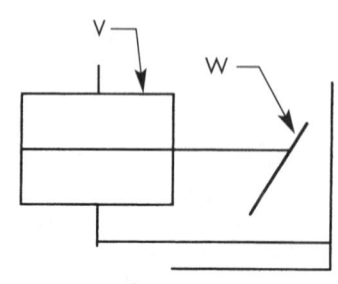

Figure 3-22
Extend line W to the apparent intersection with line V.

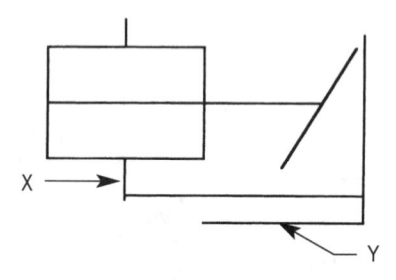

Figure 3-23
Extend lines X and Y so they join to form a corner.

Using the *Move* Command

The *Move* command allows you to move existing objects to a new location on a drawing. Moving is a three-step process. First, choose the object or objects you want to move. Next, select a starting point, known as the base point, for the move. Finally, choose the ending point for the move.

Moving a Single Object

In this part you will move a line to a new location without worrying about the exact final location. This procedure is sometimes used when you want to move an object out of the way, but not erase it. You can later go back and restore it to its original position or move it to a new location.

☐ Click on the *Ortho* button on the *Status* bar to activate it. It should appear depressed like the *Model* button, but all other buttons should be off. *Ortho* allows you to move only in the x- or y-direction.

☐ Use Figure 3-24 to locate and click on the *Move* button on the *Modify* toolbar.

Command:
Command: _move
Select objects:

☐ Place the pickbox over line Z, shown in Figure 3-25, and click the mouse button to select it. Hit the *Enter* key to end select objects.

Select objects: 1 found
Select objects:
Specify base point or displacement:

☐ A check of the command line shows that AutoCAD is asking you to locate the starting or base point for the move. For now you are not going to worry about a specific starting point, only an approximate one. Place the graphics cursor, now appearing as a cross, somewhere over line Z and click the mouse button.

Select objects: 1 found
Select objects:
Specify base point or displacement: Specify second point of displacement or <use first...

☐ Move your mouse around the drawing area and observe what happens. Although you can move the cursor to any location, the line you are moving will only move right and left or up and down. This is the result of having the *Ortho* button on.

Figure 3-24
The *Move* button is located on the *Modify* toolbar.

Figure 3-25
Move line Z to a new location at AA.

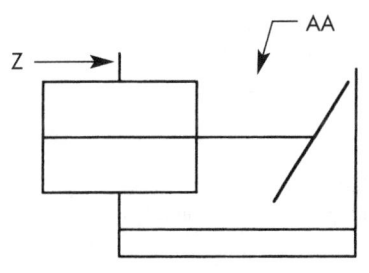

92   Module 3

☐ Move the graphics cursor to the right of line Z to a location somewhere between the end of the rectangle and the angled line. The position should be somewhere around point AA, as shown in Figure 3-25. Click the mouse button to select the new location and end the *Move* command. The line is now at its new location.

☐ Click on the *Ortho* button to turn it off.

alternate method

You can start the *Move* command by clicking on the *Modify* pull-down menu and selecting *Move*. You can also type **MOVE,** or just **M,** on the command line and hit the *Enter* key.

In the next part you will move the same line to another location, but this time you will specify the starting and ending points of the move.

☐ Click on the *Move* button on the *Modify* toolbar.

☐ Place the pickbox over line AB, shown in Figure 3-26, and click the mouse button to select it. Hit the *Enter* key to end select objects.

☐ Click on the *Endpoint* button on the *Object Snap* toolbar. Move the cursor to the bottom end of line AB. When the endpoint marker appears, click the mouse button to select the bottom end of the line as the base point.

☐ Click on the *Endpoint* button on the *Object Snap* toolbar. Move the cursor to the corner of the rectangle, shown as point AC in the figure. When the endpoint marker appears, click the mouse button to select it as the second point. The line has now moved and extends upward from the corner.

In this part you will see that the distance of the move can be based on two points not related to the object you are moving.

☐ Click on the *Move* button on the *Modify* toolbar.

☐ Place the pickbox over line AD, shown in Figure 3-27, and click the mouse button to select it. Hit the *Enter* key to end select objects.

☐ Click on the *Endpoint* button on the *Object Snap* toolbar. Move the cursor to the bottom left corner of the rectangle, shown as point AE in the figure. When the endpoint marker appears, click the mouse button to select it as the base point.

☐ Click on the *Endpoint* button on the *Object Snap* toolbar. Move the cursor to the upper left corner of the rectangle, shown as point AF in the figure. When the endpoint marker appears, click the mouse button to select it as the second point. The line has now moved upward a distance equal to the distance between points AE and AF.

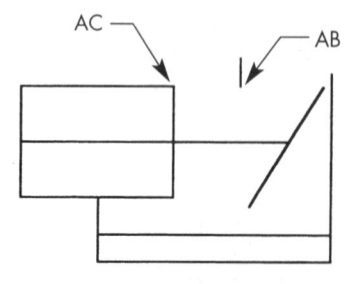

Figure 3-26
Move line AB to point AC.

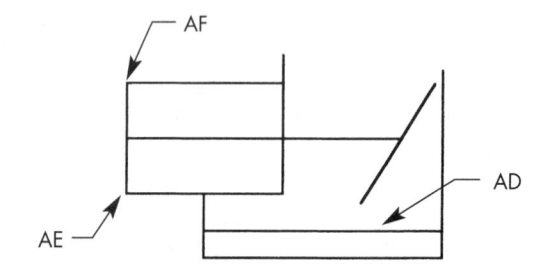

Figure 3-27
Move line AD upward a distance equal to the distance between points AE and AF.

Moving an Object Using Relative or Polar Coordinates

In this section you will use relative or polar coordinates to move an object instead of locating starting and ending points based on specific locations of objects on the drawing.

Moving Using Relative Coordinates

☐ Click on the *Move* button on the *Modify* toolbar.

☐ Place the pickbox over line AG, shown in Figure 3-28, and click the mouse button to select it. Hit the *Enter* key to end select objects.

☐ For relative coordinates, it does not matter what location you use for the base point. Place the crosshairs anywhere in the drawing area and click the left mouse button to set a base point.

☐ Type **@2,0** on the command line and hit the *Enter* key. The line will move two units to the right.

Moving Using Polar Coordinates

☐ Click on the *Move* button on the *Modify* toolbar.

☐ Place the pickbox over the same line you moved above and click the mouse button to select it. Hit the *Enter* key to end select objects.

☐ Place the crosshairs anywhere in the drawing area and click the left mouse button to select a base point.

☐ Type **@2<180** on the command line and hit the *Enter* key. The line will move two units to the left, back to its original position.

Moving Several Objects at the Same Time

☐ Click on the *Move* button on the *Modify* toolbar.

☐ Use the pickbox to select the four lines AH, AI, AJ, and AK, shown in Figure 3-29, to move. Hit the *Enter* button to end select objects.

☐ Click on the *Endpoint* button on the *Object Snap* toolbar. Move the cursor to the top of line AH. When the endpoint marker appears, click the mouse button to select it as the base point.

☐ Click on the *Endpoint* button on the *Object Snap* toolbar. Move the cursor to the lower left corner of the rectangle, shown as point AL in the figure. When the endpoint marker appears, click the mouse button to select it as the second point. Your drawing will look like Figure 3-30.

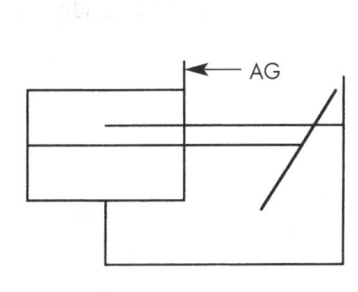

Figure 3-28
Move line AG using relative and polar coordinates.

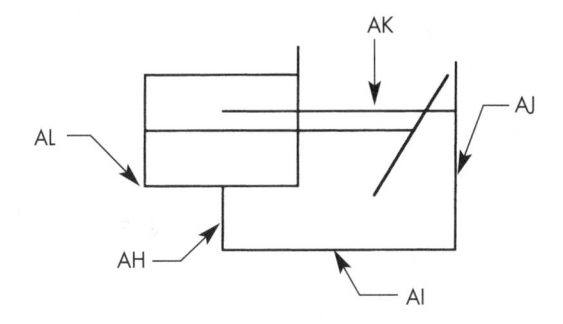

Figure 3-29
Move four lines at the same time.

Figure 3-30
Completed figure

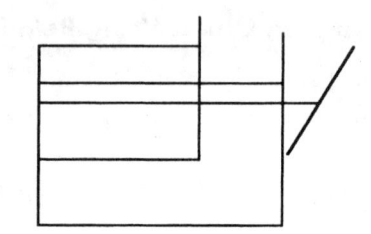

Using the *Copy* Command

The *Copy* command enables you to make a copy of an existing object and place it at a new location on a drawing. Like moving, copying is a three-step process. First, choose the object or objects you want to copy. Next, select a starting point, known as the base point, for the move. Finally, choose the ending point that will define the displacement for the copied object.

Copy a Single Object

☐ Use Figure 3-31 to locate and click on the *Copy* button on the *Modify* toolbar.

Command:
Command: _copy
Select objects:

☐ Place the pickbox over line AM, shown in Figure 3-32, and click the mouse button to select it. Hit the *Enter* key to end select objects.

Select objects: 1 found
Select objects:
Specify base point or displacement or [Multiple]:

☐ A check of the command line shows that AutoCAD is asking you to locate the starting or base point for the copy. Click on the *Endpoint* button on the *Object Snap* toolbar. Move the cursor to the bottom end of line AM, shown as point AN in the figure. When the endpoint marker appears, click the mouse button to select it as the base point.

Select objects: 1 found
Select objects:
Specify base point or displacement or [Multiple]: _endp of Specify second point of displacement...

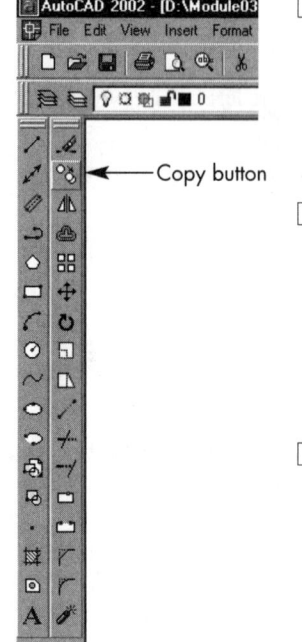

Figure 3-31
The *Copy* button is located on the *Modify* toolbar.

Figure 3-32
Make a copy of line AM that starts at point AO.

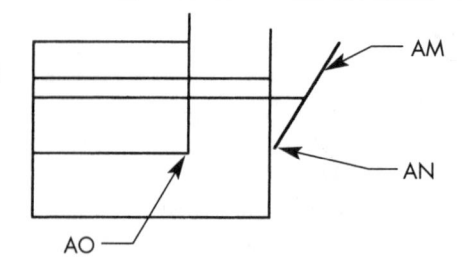

☐ Click on the *Endpoint* button on the *Object Snap* toolbar. Move the cursor to the lower right corner of the rectangle, shown as point AO in the figure. When the endpoint marker appears, click the mouse button to select it as the second point. A copy of the original angled line now appears at the new location.

alternate method

You can start the Copy command by clicking on the Modify pull-down menu and selecting Copy. You can also type **COPY,** or just **CO,** on the command line and hit the Enter key.

Multiple Copies of an Object

☐ Locate and click on the *Copy* button on the *Modify* toolbar.
☐ Place the pickbox over line AP, shown in Figure 3-33, and click the mouse button to select it. Hit the *Enter* key to end select objects.
☐ Type **M** on the command line to make multiple copies of line AP. Hit the *Enter* key.
☐ Click on the *Endpoint* button on the *Object Snap* toolbar. Move the cursor to the bottom end of line AP, shown as point AQ in the figure. When the endpoint marker appears, click the mouse button to select it as the base point.
☐ Click on the *Midpoint* button on the *Object Snap* toolbar. Move the cursor to the bottom line of the rectangle, shown as point AR in the figure. When the midpoint marker appears, click the mouse button to select it as the second point. A copy of the original angled line now appears at that location. Notice that the *Copy* command is still active and a copy of the original line is still attached to the cursor.
☐ Click on the *Endpoint* button on the *Object Snap* toolbar. Move the cursor to the lower left corner of the rectangle, shown as point AS in the figure. When the endpoint marker appears, click the mouse button to select it as the second point.
☐ Click on the *Endpoint* button on the *Object Snap* toolbar. Move the cursor to point AT, as shown in the figure. When the endpoint marker appears, click the mouse button to select it as the second point.
☐ Hit the *Enter* key to end the copy multiple command. Your drawing should look like Figure 3-34.
☐ To make the next section easier to understand, click on the *Erase* button and erase the five angled lines from the drawing.

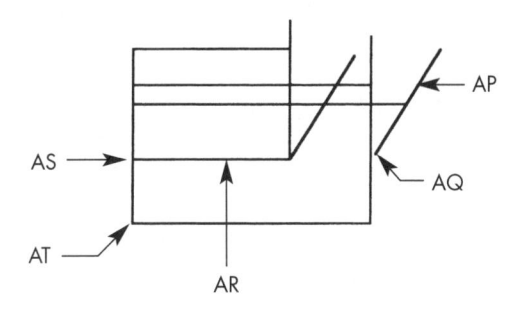

Figure 3-33
Make multiple copies of line AP.

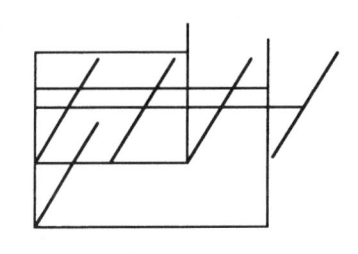

Figure 3-34
Completed figure

Copying an Object Using Relative or Polar Coordinates

In this section you will use relative or polar coordinates to copy an object to a new location.

Copy Using Relative Coordinates

- [ ] Click on the *Copy* button on the *Modify* toolbar.
- [ ] Use the pickbox to select line AU, shown in Figure 3-35. Hit the *Enter* key to end select objects.
- [ ] As with the move command for relative coordinates, it does not matter what location you use for the base point. Place the crosshairs anywhere in the drawing area and click the left mouse button to set a base point.
- [ ] Type **@-2,-2** on the command line and hit the *Enter* key. The new line will appear inside the smaller rectangle.

Copy Using Polar Coordinates

- [ ] Click on the *Copy* button on the *Modify* toolbar.
- [ ] Use the pickbox to select the line you just made, line AV in Figure 3-36. Hit the *Enter* key to end select objects.
- [ ] Place the crosshairs anywhere in the drawing area and click the mouse button to set a base point.
- [ ] Type **@4<315** on the command line and hit the *Enter* key. The new line will appear crossing the bottom line.
- [ ] This completes this activity. You should spend some additional time practicing the things you learned in this activity. When you are done, close the AutoCAD program.

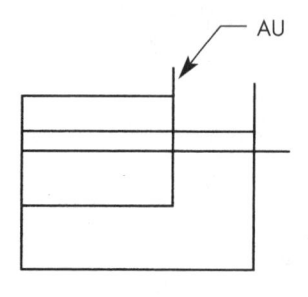

Figure 3-35
Copy line AU using relative coordinates.

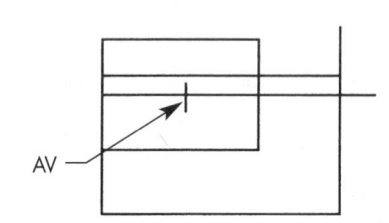

Figure 3-36
Move line AV using polar coordinates.

Modifying Objects on a Drawing 97

Applying the Concepts

Your boss is aware that you are relatively new to using AutoCAD, but he has a project he is sure you can complete because you know how to draw lines and use the *Erase, Trim, Extend, Copy,* and *Move* commands. The project involves making changes to an existing electrical schematic drawing. The layout for the final schematic is shown in Figure 3-37. You must copy or erase some of the electrical components, and move others. Lines must be added, deleted, shortened, or extended to connect the components. Each component is made up of multiple lines and text that are grouped together into a single object. When you try to move or erase a component, all the parts of that component act as if they are one object. Although the component's parts are joined together, you can still use the object snaps, like *Endpoint* or *Midpoint*, to snap to any of the individual lines making up that component. Note that each component is identified by a letter and a number code. These too are grouped with the component and move with it. When modifying the schematic, you must make sure that the correct components, including the codes, are in the proper location.

This project is your opportunity to show your boss what you have learned. Make sure that you make the schematic exactly as it appears in Figure 3-37. Your company plans to produce 10,000 circuit boards with this circuit on it. It would be very costly to the company if you made a mistake; it could also be very costly to you if you lose your job.

Procedure: ✓ Check each box as you complete that item.

- ☐ Start *AutoCAD 2002*.
- ☐ When the *AutoCAD 2002 Today* dialog box appears, open the drawing *M03APP.dwg* located in the *Module03* subdirectory on the CD.
- ☐ The drawing will open to the existing schematic. Make all the necessary changes to make it look like Figure 3-37.
- ☐ When you have completed the work, click on the *A-size Sheet* tab.
- ☐ Save the drawing to your removable disk with the name M03APP.
- ☐ Print a copy of your drawing.
- ☐ Neatly print your name and the date in the appropriate spaces in the title block.

Figure 3-37
Final schematic*

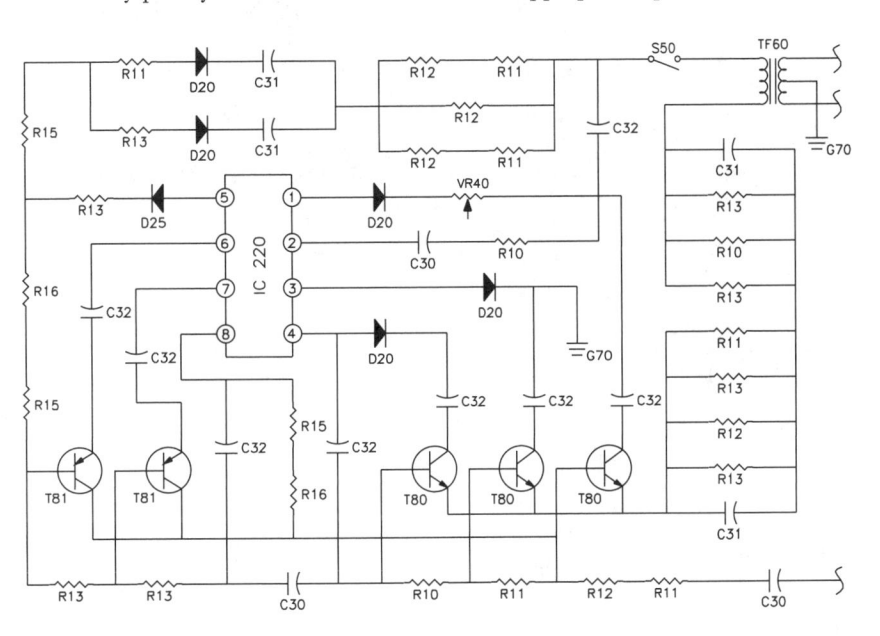

*This is not an actual working electrical circuit. Its sole intent is to provide practice using AutoCAD.

Module 3 Review Questions

These questions are provided to help you review the topics and concepts covered in this module.

True or False

Determine whether the statement is true or false. Place your answer, either T or F, in the blank.

____ 1. The edges of the *Erase Window* are dashed lines.

____ 2. The *Crossing Fence* will erase only the objects that it crosses.

____ 3. An *Erase Window* is drawn moving left to right, and an *Erase Crossing Box* is drawn right to left.

____ 4. *Crossing Fence, Crossing Box,* and *Crossing Polygons* will only erase lines and objects that their edges cross.

____ 5. The edges of the *Erase Crossing Box* are dashed lines.

____ 6. Holding the *Shift* key while selecting an object to erase allows you to cycle between objects that are stacked together.

____ 7. The *Window Polygon* enables you to draw an irregular shaped object around only the objects you want to select to erase.

____ 8. Once you select objects using a *Crossing Box*, you cannot add or delete objects from that group.

____ 9. *Erase All* removes all objects from a drawing, even those that are on a layer that is invisible, unless that layer is locked or frozen.

____ 10. The *Undo* button allows you to back up only once to the previous command.

____ 11. You cannot use relative coordinates with the *Copy* and *Move* commands.

____ 12. You can use a *Crossing Box* as a method for selecting objects to be copied or moved.

____ 13. You can move or copy only one object at a time.

____ 14. You cannot use the *Extend* command to join two parallel lines.

____ 15. You can only trim a line to another line if both lines actually cross each other, thus producing a 90° corner.

____ 16. *Ortho* allows you to draw straight horizontal or vertical lines.

Multiple-choice

Place the letter of the best answer in the blank.

1. This button is used to activate the ____ command.
   a. Erase
   b. Extend
   c. Trim
   d. Copy

2. This button is used to activate the ____ command.
   a. Move
   b. Extend
   c. Erase
   d. Copy

3. This button is used to activate the ____ command.
   a. Move
   b. Extend
   c. Trim
   d. Erase

4. This button is used to activate the ____ command.
    a. Move
    b. Erase
    c. Trim
    d. Copy

5. This button is used to activate the ____ command.
    a. Move
    b. Erase
    c. Trim
    d. Copy

Module 4

Drawing Regular-Shaped Objects

Activity 1

Drawing Rectangles

Objectives: After completing this activity, you should be able to do the following:

- Locate and use the *Rectangle* button on the *Draw* toolbar.
- Draw a rectangle with specified length and height using absolute, relative, and polar coordinates.
- Draw a square with specified dimensions.
- Use the chamfer, fillet, and width variables with the rectangle command.
- Locate and use the *Explode* button on the *Modify* toolbar.

Procedure: ☑ Check each box as you complete that item.

- ☐ Start *AutoCAD 2002*.
- ☐ When the *AutoCAD 2002 Today* dialog box appears, open the drawing *M04A01-1.dwg* located in the *Module04* subdirectory on the CD.
- ☐ Make sure that all the *Drawing Features* buttons, except for the *Model* button, on the *Status* bar are off.

Drawing Rectangles

Until now you have created rectangles by drawing the four sides one side at a time. There is an easier way. AutoCAD provides a command for drawing rectangles that only requires specifying the locations of two diagonally opposite corners. In this section you will learn how to draw rectangles using absolute, relative, and polar coordinates.

- ☐ Use Figure 4-1 to locate and click on the *Rectangle* button located on the *Draw* toolbar.

Figure 4-1
The *Rectangle* button is located on the *Draw* toolbar.

Rectangle button →

```
Command:
Command: _rectang
Specify first corner point or [Chamfer/Elevation/Fillet/Thickness/Width]:
```

☐ A check of the command line shows that AutoCAD is asking you to specify the first corner of the rectangle.

☐ Type **0,5.5** on the command line and hit the *Enter* key.

```
Command: _rectang
Specify first corner point or [Chamfer/Elevation/Fillet/Thickness/Width]: 0,5.5
Specify other corner point:
```

☐ AutoCAD now asks that you provide the location of the other corner. This corner is *always* the one that is diagonally opposite the first corner, i.e., if you start with the lower left corner, you must specify the upper right corner, or if you start with the upper left corner, you then specify the lower right corner. You can also start a rectangle at one of the right side corners and end on the diagonally opposite left side corner. The location of the second corner can be specified in absolute, relative, or polar coordinates. For this rectangle you will use absolute coordinates.

☐ Type **2,7** on the command line and hit the *Enter* key. A rectangle having a length of 2″ and a height of 1.5″ is drawn and the rectangle command ends.

```
Specify first corner point or [Chamfer/Elevation/Fillet/Thickness/Width]: 0,5.5
Specify other corner point: 2,7
Command:
```

alternate method

You can start the *Rectangle* command by clicking on the *Draw* pull-down menu and selecting *Rectangle*. You can also type **RECTANGLE,** or just **RECTAN,** on the command line and hit the *Enter* key.

Drawing Regular-Shaped Objects   103

In the following steps you will draw a rectangle starting at the upper right corner and then use relative coordinates to specify the lower left corner.

☐ Click on the *Rectangle* button.

Command:
Command: _rectang
Specify first corner point or [Chamfer/Elevation/Fillet/Thickness/Width]:

☐ Type **2,3** on the command line and hit the *Enter* key.

Command: _rectang
Specify first corner point or [Chamfer/Elevation/Fillet/Thickness/Width]: 2,3
Specify other corner point:

☐ Type **@-2,-1.5** (don't forget to include the minus signs) on the command line and hit the *Enter* key. A rectangle having a length of 2″ and a height of 1.5″ is drawn. Using relative coordinates is a good way to draw rectangles because you specify the rectangle's actual length and height.

Specify first corner point or [Chamfer/Elevation/Fillet/Thickness/Width]: 2,3
Specify other corner point: @-2,-1.5
Command:

In the following steps you will draw a rectangle using polar coordinates.

☐ Click on the *Rectangle* button.

Command:
Command: _rectang
Specify first corner point or [Chamfer/Elevation/Fillet/Thickness/Width]:

☐ Type **0,3.5** on the command line and hit the *Enter* key.

Command: _rectang
Specify first corner point or [Chamfer/Elevation/Fillet/Thickness/Width]: 0,3.5
Specify other corner point:

☐ Type **@2.5<36.87** on the command line and hit the *Enter* key. A rectangle having an approximate length of 2″ and an approximate height of 1.5″ is drawn. This is not the best way to draw rectangles and should only be used when the rectangle is based on a diagonal distance between two points, not a length and a height. Note that the diagonal of the rectangle forms the hypotenuse of a triangle. If you try to determine the length of this line and its angle by using trigonometry, your calculation will result in approximate numbers, which are not acceptable when making CAD drawings. The rectangle you drew is based on a 3, 4, 5 triangle, where a 2.5″ hypotenuse produces a base of 2″ and a height of 1.5″. Although this rectangle appears to be exactly the same size as the one above it, the approximate angle of 36.87° produces sides that are not truly 2″ and 1.5″.

Specify first corner point or [Chamfer/Elevation/Fillet/Thickness/Width]: 0,3.5
Specify other corner point: @2.5<36.87
Command:

In the following steps you will use the rectangle command to draw a square.

- ☐ Click on the *Rectangle* button.
- ☐ Type **3.5,5.5** on the command line and hit the *Enter* key.
- ☐ Type **@1.5,1.5** on the command line and hit the *Enter* key.

Drawing Rectangles with Wider Lines

It is possible to draw rectangles that have wide lines. These are sometimes used as borders for drawings or views on a drawing.

- ☐ Click on the *Rectangle* button.

  Command:
  Command: _rectang
  Specify first corner point or [Chamfer/Elevation/Fillet/Thickness/Width]:

- ☐ Type **W** on the command line to activate the *Width* option, and hit the *Enter* key.

  Command: _rectang
  Specify first corner point or [Chamfer/Elevation/Fillet/Thickness/Width]: W
  Specify line width for rectangles <0.0000>:

- ☐ Type **.05** on the command line and hit the *Enter* key. The lines of the rectangle will now be drawn .05″ wide.

  Specify first corner point or [Chamfer/Elevation/Fillet/Thickness/Width]: W
  Specify line width for rectangles <0.0000>: .05
  Specify first corner point or [Chamfer/Elevation/Fillet/Thickness/Width]:

- ☐ Type **3.5,3.5** on the command line and hit the *Enter* key.

  Specify line width for rectangles <0.0000>: .05
  Specify first corner point or [Chamfer/Elevation/Fillet/Thickness/Width]: 3.5,3.5
  Specify other corner point:

- ☐ Type **@2,1.5** on the command line and hit the *Enter* key. Compare the width of the lines of the rectangle just drawn to the others.

  Specify first corner point or [Chamfer/Elevation/Fillet/Thickness/Width]: 3.5,3.5
  Specify other corner point: @2,1.5
  Command:

Note: Do not confuse the *Width* option with the *Thickness* option. *Width* sets the width of the line. *Thickness* is only used in three-dimensional (3D) drawings and sets the thickness of the rectangle in the z-direction. The *Elevation* option is also used only in 3D and will not be covered here.

- ☐ For additional practice, place a 2″ long × 1.5″ wide rectangle at point 3.5,1.5 that has a line width of .125″.

Drawing Regular-Shaped Objects 105

Note: When you set the width, it stays at that value until you change it. You will reset the value to zero in this section.

☐ Click on the *Rectangle* button.

Command:
Command: _rectang
Specify first corner point or [Chamfer/Elevation/Fillet/Thickness/Width]:

☐ Type **W** on the command line and hit the *Enter* key.

Command: _rectang
Specify first corner point or [Chamfer/Elevation/Fillet/Thickness/Width]: W
Specify line width for rectangles <0.1250>:

☐ Type **0** on the command line and hit the *Enter* key. This resets the width to the original default value.

Specify first corner point or [Chamfer/Elevation/Fillet/Thickness/Width]: W
Specify line width for rectangles <0.1250>: 0
Specify first corner point or [Chamfer/Elevation/Fillet/Thickness/Width]:

☐ You do not have to continue drawing the rectangle. The width has been set and will stay the same until you change it. Hit the *Esc* key to cancel the *Rectangle* command. You will find as you continue with this activity that the line width is now set to the default.

Specify line width for rectangles <0.1250>: 0
Specify first corner point or [Chamfer/Elevation/Fillet/Thickness/Width]: *Cancel*
Command:

Drawing Rectangles with Fillets

Fillets are rounded corners on objects. Fillets (or rounds) are often used on outer edges of objects to eliminate a sharp corner that could hurt someone. Therefore, many objects you draw will contain fillets. The *Rectangle* command offers fillets as an option. When using this option, all four corners are filleted (rounded) at the same time and all have the same radius. You will want to use this option only if all the corners are the same. In a later module you will learn a command that enables you to fillet individual corners of objects.

☐ Click on the *Rectangle* button.

Command:
Command: _rectang
Specify first corner point or [Chamfer/Elevation/Fillet/Thickness/Width]:

☐ Type **F** on the command line to activate the *Fillet* command, and hit the *Enter* key.

Command: _rectang
Specify first corner point or [Chamfer/Elevation/Fillet/Thickness/Width]: F
Specify line width for rectangles <0.0000>:

☐ Type **.25** on the command line and hit the *Enter* key. The fillets on the corners of the rectangle will now be drawn with a .25" radius.

Specify first corner point or [Chamfer/Elevation/Fillet/Thickness/Width]: F
Specify fillet radius for rectangles <0.0000>: .25
Specify first corner point or [Chamfer/Elevation/Fillet/Thickness/Width]:

☐ Type **7,5.5** on the command line and hit the *Enter* key.

Specify fillet radius for rectangles <0.0000>: .25
Specify first corner point or [Chamfer/Elevation/Fillet/Thickness/Width]: 7,5.5
Specify other corner point:

☐ Type **@2,1.5** on the command line and hit the *Enter* key. Compare the fillets on this rectangle to those on the previous rectangle.

Specify first corner point or [Chamfer/Elevation/Fillet/Thickness/Width]: 7,5.5
Specify other corner point: @2,1.5
Command:

Note: Just like the *Width* option, the *Fillet* option stays on until you reset it to zero. In the following steps you will reset the value to zero.

☐ Click on the *Rectangle* button.

Command:
Command: _rectang
Specify first corner point or [Chamfer/Elevation/Fillet/Thickness/Width]:

☐ Type **F** on the command line and hit the *Enter* key.

Command: _rectang
Specify first corner point or [Chamfer/Elevation/Fillet/Thickness/Width]: F
Specify fillet radius for rectangles <0.2500>:

☐ Type **0** on the command line and hit the *Enter* key. This resets the fillet to the default value.

Specify first corner point or [Chamfer/Elevation/Fillet/Thickness/Width]: F
Specify fillet radius for rectangles <0.2500>: 0
Specify first corner point or [Chamfer/Elevation/Fillet/Thickness/Width]:

☐ You do not have to continue drawing the rectangle. Hit the *Esc* key to end the *Rectangle* command.

Specify fillet radius for rectangles <0.2500>: 0
Specify first corner point or [Chamfer/Elevation/Fillet/Thickness/Width]: *Cancel*
Command:

Drawing a Rectangle with Chamfers

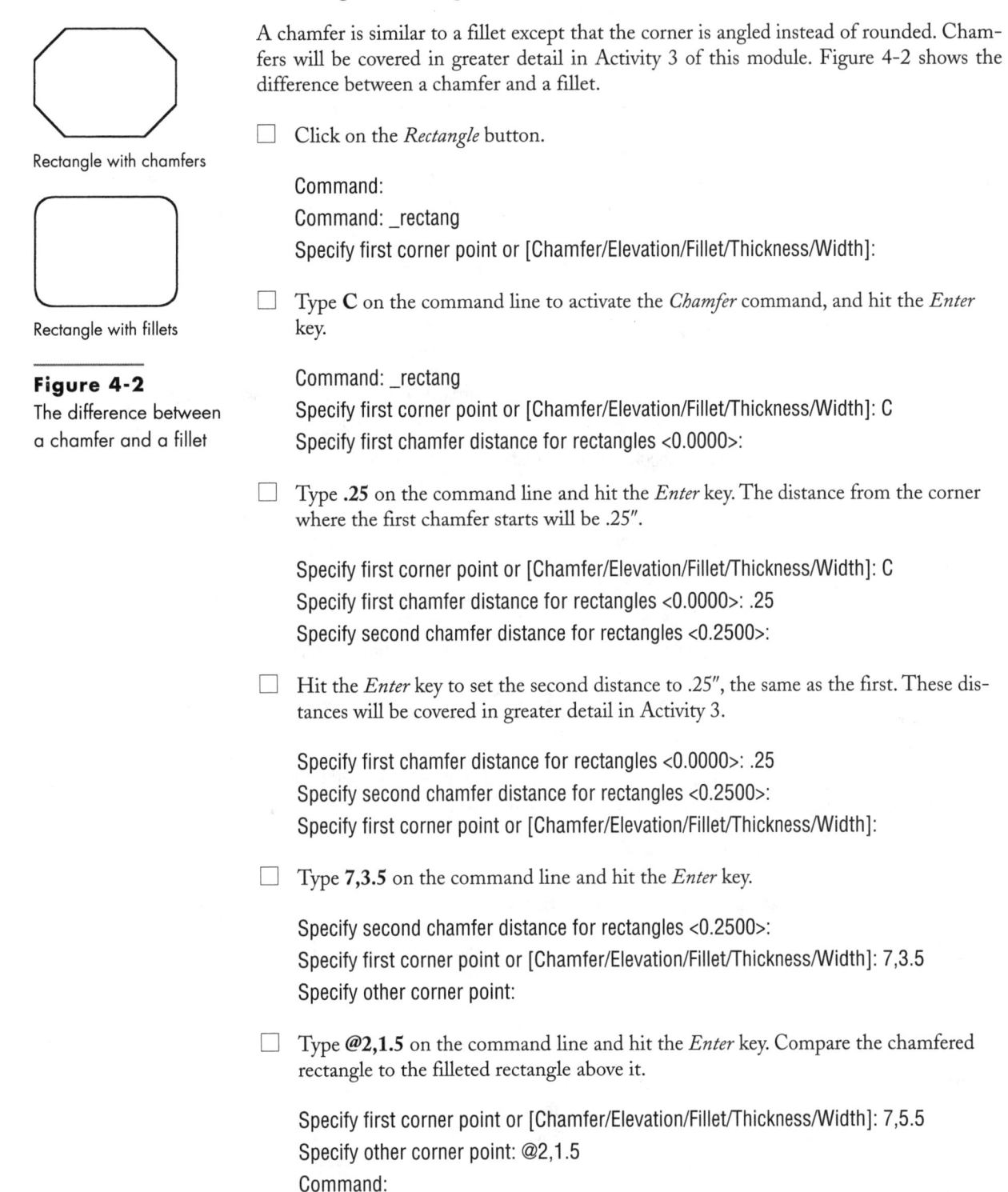

A chamfer is similar to a fillet except that the corner is angled instead of rounded. Chamfers will be covered in greater detail in Activity 3 of this module. Figure 4-2 shows the difference between a chamfer and a fillet.

Rectangle with chamfers

Rectangle with fillets

Figure 4-2
The difference between a chamfer and a fillet

☐ Click on the *Rectangle* button.

```
Command:
Command: _rectang
Specify first corner point or [Chamfer/Elevation/Fillet/Thickness/Width]:
```

☐ Type **C** on the command line to activate the *Chamfer* command, and hit the *Enter* key.

```
Command: _rectang
Specify first corner point or [Chamfer/Elevation/Fillet/Thickness/Width]: C
Specify first chamfer distance for rectangles <0.0000>:
```

☐ Type **.25** on the command line and hit the *Enter* key. The distance from the corner where the first chamfer starts will be .25".

```
Specify first corner point or [Chamfer/Elevation/Fillet/Thickness/Width]: C
Specify first chamfer distance for rectangles <0.0000>: .25
Specify second chamfer distance for rectangles <0.2500>:
```

☐ Hit the *Enter* key to set the second distance to .25", the same as the first. These distances will be covered in greater detail in Activity 3.

```
Specify first chamfer distance for rectangles <0.0000>: .25
Specify second chamfer distance for rectangles <0.2500>:
Specify first corner point or [Chamfer/Elevation/Fillet/Thickness/Width]:
```

☐ Type **7,3.5** on the command line and hit the *Enter* key.

```
Specify second chamfer distance for rectangles <0.2500>:
Specify first corner point or [Chamfer/Elevation/Fillet/Thickness/Width]: 7,3.5
Specify other corner point:
```

☐ Type **@2,1.5** on the command line and hit the *Enter* key. Compare the chamfered rectangle to the filleted rectangle above it.

```
Specify first corner point or [Chamfer/Elevation/Fillet/Thickness/Width]: 7,5.5
Specify other corner point: @2,1.5
Command:
```

Note: Just like the *Width* and *Fillet* options, the *Chamfer* option stays on until you reset it to zero. In the following steps you will reset the value to zero.

108   Module 4

☐ Click on the *Rectangle* button.

Command:
Command: _rectang
Specify first corner point or [Chamfer/Elevation/Fillet/Thickness/Width]:

☐ Type **C** on the command line and hit the *Enter* key.

Command: _rectang
Specify first corner point or [Chamfer/Elevation/Fillet/Thickness/Width]: C
Specify first chamfer distance for rectangles <0.2500>:

☐ Type **0** on the command line and hit the *Enter* key. This resets the first distance to the default value.

Specify first corner point or [Chamfer/Elevation/Fillet/Thickness/Width]: C
Specify first chamfer distance for rectangles <0.2500>: 0
Specify second chamfer distance for rectangles <0.2500>:

☐ Type **0** on the command line and hit the *Enter* key. This resets the second distance to the default value.

Specify first chamfer distance for rectangles <0.2500>: 0
Specify second chamfer distance for rectangles <0.2500>: 0
Specify first corner point or [Chamfer/Elevation/Fillet/Thickness/Width]:

☐ You do not have to continue drawing the rectangle. Hit the *Esc* key to end the *Rectangle* command.

Specify second chamfer distance for rectangles <0.2500>: 0
Specify first corner point or [Chamfer/Elevation/Fillet/Thickness/Width]: *Cancel*
Command:

Using the *Explode* Button

The *Explode* button allows you to break a single object, like a rectangle, into its individual parts.

☐ When you use the *Rectangle* command to draw a rectangle, it is not made of four individual lines; it is a single object. To prove this, click on the *Erase* button located on the *Modify* toolbar.

☐ Select the first rectangle you drew, the one in the upper left corner of the drawing, by clicking on it. Notice that the entire rectangle becomes dashed.

☐ Hit the *Enter* key to erase the rectangle and end the *Erase* command.

☐ Use Figure 4-3 to locate and click on the *Explode* button on the *Modify* toolbar.

☐ Select the second rectangle you drew by clicking on it. The entire rectangle will become dashed as it did when you used the *Erase* command.

☐ Hit the *Enter* key to explode the rectangle and end the *Explode* command. It appears that nothing has happened.

☐ Click on the *Erase* button and select the left vertical line and the right vertical line of the rectangle you just exploded. Note that only these two lines become dashed.

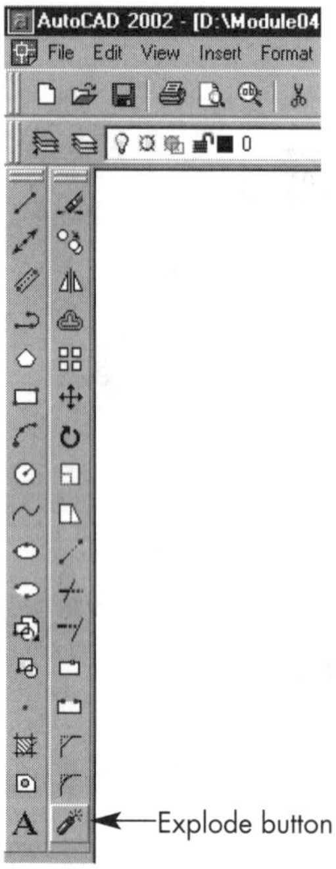

Figure 4-3
The *Explode* button is located on the *Modify* toolbar.

Drawing Regular-Shaped Objects 109

☐ Hit the *Enter* key and the two lines are erased leaving the other two. The *Explode* command changed the rectangle into four individual lines.

☐ Click on the *Explode* button. Select the rectangle with the wide lines in the middle of the middle row by clicking on it.

☐ Hit the *Enter* key to explode the rectangle and end the command. Note that because the rectangle is now four individual lines the line width went back to the default.

☐ Click on the *Explode* button. Select the two rectangles, the one with the fillets and the one with the chamfers, by clicking on them.

☐ Hit the *Enter* key to explode the rectangle and end the command. Use the *Erase* command to erase various parts of these two rectangles, especially a chamfer and a fillet. When using the *Explode* command, each feature becomes an individual object.

alternate method

You can also access the *Explode* command by clicking on the *Modify* pull-down menu and selecting *Explode*, or you can type **EXPLODE,** or just **X,** on the command line and hit the *Enter* key.

☐ This completes this activity. You should spend some time practicing what you learned in this activity. When you are done, close the AutoCAD program.

Assignment
for Module 4 – Activity 1

Procedure: ☑ Check each box as you complete that item.

☐ Start *AutoCAD 2002*.

☐ When the *AutoCAD 2002 Today* dialog box appears, open the drawing M04A01-2.dwg located in the *Module04* subdirectory on the CD.

☐ For this assignment you will draw six rectangles. Use the information in the following table to place and size each rectangle.

	Coordinates of Lower Left Corner	Size l × w	Line Width (Default = 0)	Chamfer Size	Fillet Size
1.	.5,.5	9.0 × 6.5	.05	None	None
2.	1.25,1.25	2.25 × 2.75	Default	None	None
3.	1.25,4.75	2.25 × 1.5	Default	None	None
4.	4.25,1.25	1.5 × 5.0	Default	.375 × .375	None
5.	6.5,4.0	2.25 × 2.25	Default	None	.50R
6.	6.5,1.25	2.25 × 2.0	Default	None	None

☐ Erase the bottom line of rectangle number 6.

☐ When you have completed the figure, click on the *A-size Sheet* tab. If you placed each rectangle at the specified starting point, they will be centered on the paper.

- ☐ Save the drawing to your removable disk with the name M04A01-2.
- ☐ Print a copy of your drawing.
- ☐ Neatly print your name and the date in the appropriate spaces in the title block.

Activity 2

Drawing Polygons

Objectives: After completing this activity, you should be able to do the following:

- Locate and use the *Polygon* button on the *Draw* toolbar.
- Draw a polygon with a specified number of sides.
- Describe the difference between inscribed and circumscribed polygons.
- Draw both an inscribed and a circumscribed polygon.
- Draw a polygon with a specified number of sides based on the length of an edge.

Procedure: ☑ Check each box as you complete that item.

- ☐ Start *AutoCAD 2002*.
- ☐ When the *AutoCAD 2002 Today* dialog box appears, open the drawing *M04A02-1.dwg* located in the *Module04* subdirectory on the CD.
- ☐ Make sure that all the *Drawing Features* buttons, except for the *Model* button, on the *Status* bar are off.

Drawing Polygons

A polygon is a multisided figure with three or more equal sides and equal angles. In AutoCAD you can draw polygons having anywhere from 3 to 1024 sides. Polygons are drawn based on the radius of a circle. A polygon can be drawn either inside a circle, called inscribed, or outside a circle, called circumscribed. Examples of inscribed and circumscribed polygons are shown in Figure 4-4. You should note that when you draw an inscribed polygon you are specifying the distance across the corners, and when you draw a circumscribed polygon you are specifying the distance across the flats. The *Polygon* command draws *only* the polygon. The circle is shown only to help your understanding of the difference.

- ☐ Use Figure 4-5 to locate and click on the *Polygon* button on the *Draw* toolbar.

  Command:
  Command:
  Command: _polygon Enter number of sides <4>:

Figure 4-4
The difference between an inscribed and a circumscribed polygon

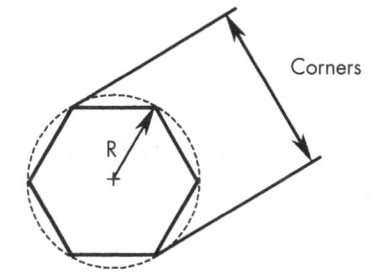

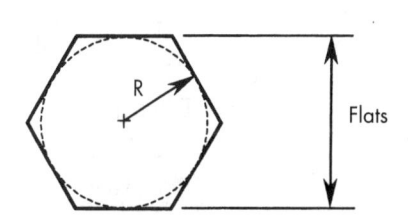

Inscribed polygon

Circumscribed polygon

Figure 4-5
The *Polygon* button is located on the *Draw* toolbar.

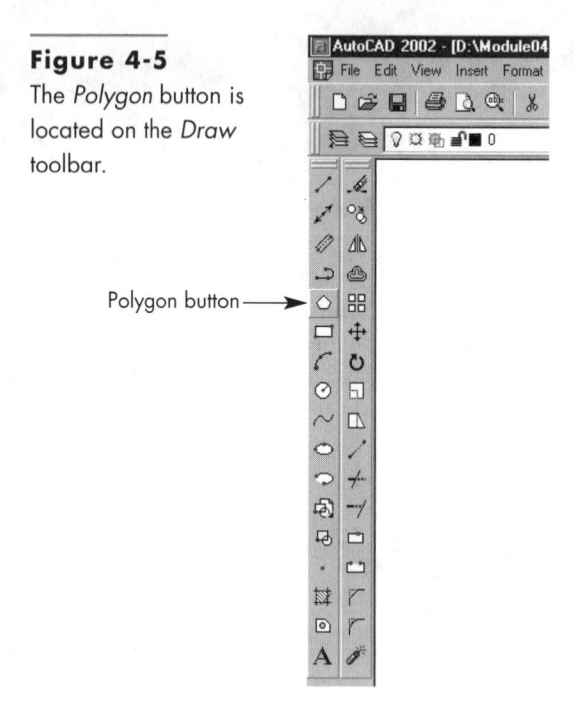

Polygon button

☐ AutoCAD asks that you provide the number of sides for the polygon. Type **8** on the command line and hit the *Enter* key.

Command:
Command: _polygon Enter number of sides <4>: 8
Specify center of polygon or [Edge]:

☐ Type **2,6** on the command line to specify the center of the polygon and hit the *Enter* key.

Command: _polygon Enter number of sides <4>: 8
Specify center of polygon or [Edge]: 2,6
Enter an option [Inscribed in circle/Circumscribed about circle] <I>:

☐ You now have to specify whether you want an inscribed or a circumscribed polygon. An "I" for inscribed appears inside the angled brackets as the default. Hit the *Enter* key to accept the default.

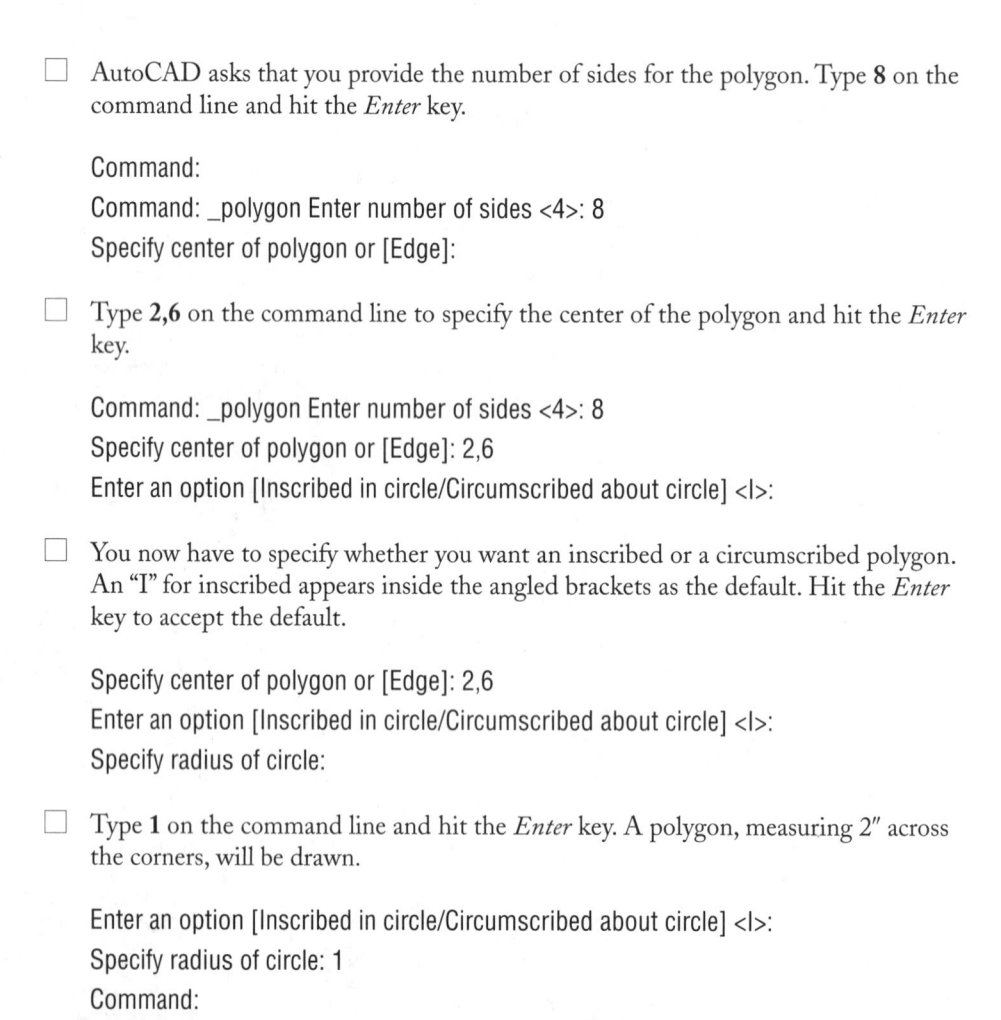

Specify center of polygon or [Edge]: 2,6
Enter an option [Inscribed in circle/Circumscribed about circle] <I>:
Specify radius of circle:

☐ Type **1** on the command line and hit the *Enter* key. A polygon, measuring 2″ across the corners, will be drawn.

Enter an option [Inscribed in circle/Circumscribed about circle] <I>:
Specify radius of circle: 1
Command:

Drawing Regular-Shaped Objects   113

- ☐ Click on the *Polygon* button.

    Command:
    Command:
    Command: _polygon Enter number of sides <8>:

- ☐ Hit the *Enter* key to accept 8 as the number of sides for the polygon. AutoCAD remembers the number of sides of the last polygon you drew and makes that the default.

    Command:
    Command: _polygon Enter number of sides <8>:
    Specify center of polygon or [Edge]:

- ☐ Type **2,3** on the command line to specify the center of the polygon and hit the *Enter* key.

    Command: _polygon Enter number of sides <8>:
    Specify center of polygon or [Edge]: 2,3
    Enter an option [Inscribed in circle/Circumscribed about circle] <I>:

- ☐ Type **C** on the command line to draw a circumscribed polygon and hit the *Enter* key.

    Specify center of polygon or [Edge]: 2,3
    Enter an option [Inscribed in circle/Circumscribed about circle] <I>: C
    Specify radius of circle:

- ☐ Type **1** on the command line and hit the *Enter* key. A polygon, measuring 2″ across the flats, will be drawn. You should notice that AutoCAD does *not* remember the last radius drawn.

    Enter an option [Inscribed in circle/Circumscribed about circle] <I>: C
    Specify radius of circle: 1
    Command:

    It may be a little hard to see, but you should note that the second polygon is larger than the first. This is because both are based on the same size circle, but the first was inscribed (drawn inside the circle) and the second was circumscribed (drawn outside the circle).

- ☐ For additional practice, draw a triangle (3-sided polygon), inscribed in a 1″ radius circle, at 5,6.
- ☐ Draw a pentagon (5-sided polygon), inscribed in a 1″ radius circle, at 5,3.

alternate method
You can also draw a polygon by clicking on the *Draw* pull-down menu and selecting *Polygon*, or you can type **POLYGON,** or just **POL,** on the command line and hit the *Enter* key.

Now that you have drawn four polygons you should note that the flat side is always drawn on the bottom. This is the standard position. In a future activity you will learn how to rotate these and other objects to any angle.

- [ ] For this section you must draw two construction lines to use as snap points. Draw a line from 8,5 to 8,4.5 and one from 8.5,6.5 to 10,6.5.
- [ ] Click on the *Polygon* button.

Command:
Command:
Command: _polygon Enter number of sides <5>:

- [ ] Type **3** on the command line and hit the *Enter* key.

Command:
Command: _polygon Enter number of sides <5>: 3
Specify center of polygon or [Edge]:

- [ ] Type **E** on the command line to activate the *Edge* option and hit the *Enter* key.

Command: _polygon Enter number of sides <5>: 3
Specify center of polygon or [Edge]: E
Specify first endpoint of edge:

- [ ] Click on the *Endpoint* button on the *Object Snap* toolbar. Select the top endpoint of the vertical line by clicking on it.

Command: _polygon Enter number of sides <5>: 3
Specify center of polygon or [Edge]: E
Specify first endpoint of edge:

- [ ] Click on the *Endpoint* button on the *Object Snap* toolbar. Select the left endpoint of the horizontal line by clicking on it. A triangle having sides equal to the distance between the two points will be drawn.

Specify first endpoint of edge: _endp of
Specify second endpoint of edge: _endp of
Command:

If you erase a polygon, you will find that it is a single object just like the rectangles you drew in Activity 1. As with rectangles, polygons can be exploded and individual sides erased or modified.

- [ ] This completes this activity. You should spend some time practicing what you learned in this activity. When you are done, close the AutoCAD program.

Assignment
for Module 4 – Activity 2

Procedure: ☑ Check each box as you complete that item.

☐ Start *AutoCAD 2002*.

☐ When the *AutoCAD 2002 Today* dialog box appears, open the drawing *M04A02-2.dwg* located in the *Module04* subdirectory on the CD.

☐ For this assignment you will draw nine polygons. Use the information in the following table to place and size each rectangle.

	Number of Sides	Coordinates of Center	Inscribed or Circumscribed	Radius
1.	5	1.5,6.5	C	.75
2.	6	1.5,4.5	C	.75
3.	7	1.5,2.5	C	.75
4.	8	5.25,4.5	I	1.0
5.	9	5.25,4.5	I	1.5
6.	10	5.25,4.5	I	2.0
7.	11	9,6.5	C	.75
8.	12	9,4.5	C	.75
9.	13	9,2.5	C	.75

☐ When you have completed the figure, click on the *A-size Sheet* tab. If you placed the polygons at their specified center points, they will be centered on the paper.

☐ Save the drawing to your removable disk with the name M04A02-2.

☐ Print a copy of your drawing.

☐ Neatly print your name and the date in the appropriate spaces in the title block.

116   Module 4

Activity 3

Drawing Chamfers

Objectives: After completing this activity, you should be able to do the following:

- Locate and use the *Chamfer* button on the *Modify* toolbar to place angled lines between two lines or objects.
- Set the chamfer for equal or unequal distances.
- Draw chamfers based on a distance and an angle.

Chamfers

Chamfers are small angled corners on objects. Chamfers are often used on outer edges of objects to eliminate sharp corners that could hurt someone; and they are sometimes used on inner corners to maintain the strength of a part. In this activity you will learn how to draw chamfers with both equal and unequal distances. Figure 4-6 shows the difference between equal and unequal chamfer distances.

Procedure: ☑ Check each box as you complete that item.

☐ Start *AutoCAD 2002*.

☐ When the *AutoCAD 2002 Today* dialog box appears, open the drawing *M04A03-1.dwg* located in the *Module04* subdirectory on the CD.

☐ Make sure that all the *Drawing Features* buttons on the *Status* bar, except for the *Model* button, are off.

☐ To prepare for this activity, you need to draw a few lines to act as chamfer points. Using the *Line* command and absolute coordinates listed in the table draw the following lines. When you are done, your screen should look like Figure 4-7, but without the letters. Some of the lines are lettered so that you can identify the correct line to be used in making the chamfers. You should refer to this figure as you go through this activity.

	From	To		From	To
a)	0,5	0,7	k)	3,4	6,4
b)	0,7	2,7	l)	6,4	4,2
c)	2,7	2,5	m)	4,2	3,4
d)	2,5	0,5	n)	8,5	8,7
e)	0,2.5	0,3.5	o)	8,7	10,7
f)	.5,4	1.5,4	p)	10,7	10,5
g)	2,3.5	2, 2.5	q)	10,5	8,5
h)	1.5,2	.5,2	r)	8,4	9.5,4
i)	3,7	6,7	s)	10,3.5	10,2
j)	5.5,7.5	5.5,5	t)	8,4	9,2.5

Drawing Regular-Shaped Objects   117

No chamfer   Equal chamfer distance   Unequal chamfer distance

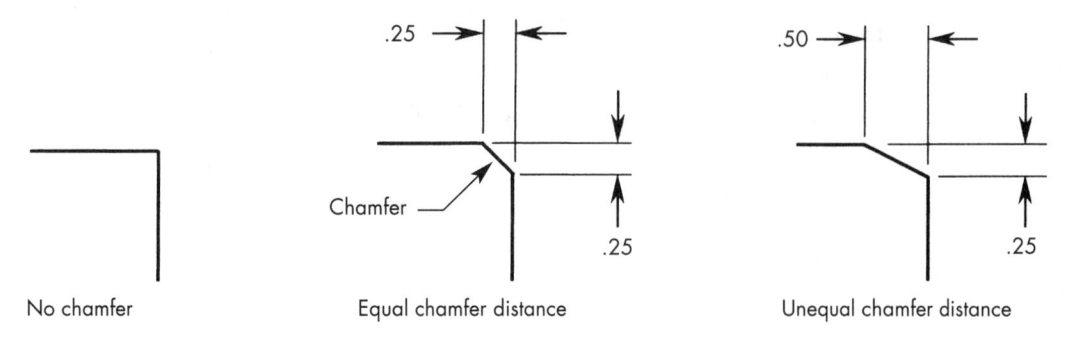

Figure 4-6
Equal and unequal chamfers

Figure 4-7
When finished, your screen should look like this.

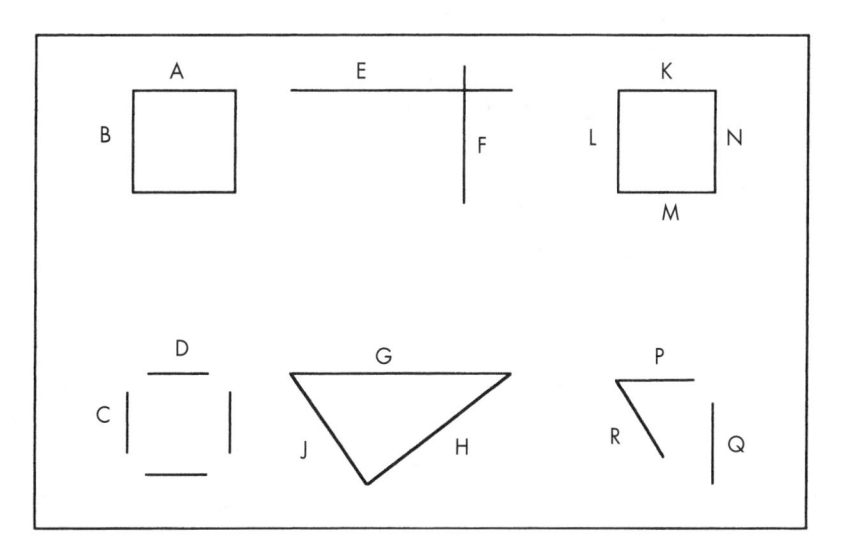

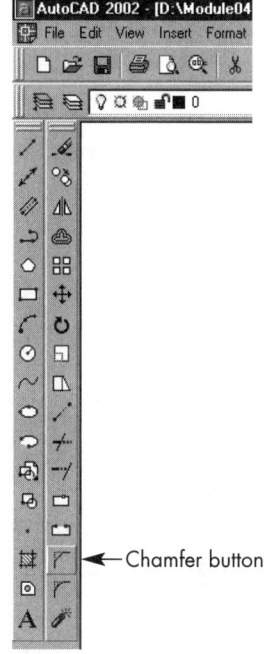

Figure 4-8
The *Chamfer* button is located on the *Modify* toolbar.

← Chamfer button

Setting the Trim and Distance Options

☐ Use Figure 4-8 to locate and click on the *Chamfer* button on the *Modify* toolbar. Note that the *Chamfer* button looks similar to the *Fillet* button, which is directly below it. Make sure you click on the right one.

Command: _chamfer
(TRIM mode) Current chamfer Dist1 = 0.5000, Dist2 = 0.5000
Select first line or [Polyline/Distance/Angle/Trim/Method]:

☐ For this section you will work with the *Trim* mode turned on. The following steps will ensure that your computer is set correctly.

☐ Type **T** on the command line to select the *Trim* option and hit the *Enter* key.

(TRIM mode) Current chamfer Dist1 = 0.5000, Dist2 = 0.5000
Select first line or [Polyline/Distance/Angle/Trim/Method]: T
Enter Trim mode option [Trim/No trim] <Trim>:

☐ If *Trim* appears inside the angled brackets, hit the *Enter* key. If *No trim* appears, then type **T** on the command line and hit the *Enter* key.

Select first line or [Polyline/Distance/Angle/Trim/Method]: T
Enter Trim mode option [Trim/No trim] <Trim>:
Select first line or [Polyline/Distance/Angle/Trim/Method]:

☐ Hit the *Enter* key to end the *Chamfer* command.

Drawing a Chamfer

☐ Click on the *Chamfer* button.

Command: _chamfer
(TRIM mode) Current chamfer Dist1 = 0.5000, Dist2 = 0.5000
Select first line or [Polyline/Distance/Angle/Trim/Method]:

☐ The cursor has turned into a square pickbox. Move the pickbox to line A, shown in Figure 4-7. When the cursor is over the line, click the mouse button. Line A will become dashed.

(TRIM mode) Current chamfer Dist1 = 0.5000, Dist2 = 0.5000
Select first line or [Polyline/Distance/Angle/Trim/Method]:
Select second line:

☐ Using the same method, select line B. A .5" × .5" chamfer will appear at the corner between the two lines and the *Chamfer* command will end. It is not important where you click on the two lines because AutoCAD determines where the lines intersect and places the chamfer there.

Select first line or [Polyline/Distance/Angle/Trim/Method]:
Select second line:
Command:

☐ For practice, chamfer the other three corners of the square.
☐ Lines do not have to intersect for a chamfer to be drawn. Click on the *Chamfer* button.

Command: _chamfer
(TRIM mode) Current chamfer Dist1 = 0.5000, Dist2 = 0.5000
Select first line or [Polyline/Distance/Angle/Trim/Method]:

☐ Use the pickbox to select line C.

(TRIM mode) Current chamfer Dist1 = 0.5000, Dist2 = 0.5000
Select first line or [Polyline/Distance/Angle/Trim/Method]:
Select second line:

☐ Use the pickbox to select line D. The two lines will be joined with a chamfer and the *Chamfer* command will end.

Select first line or [Polyline/Distance/Angle/Trim/Method]:
Select second line:
Command:

Drawing Regular-Shaped Objects 119

☐ For additional practice, chamfer the three other open corners of the square.

☐ If the lines intersect and go past the intersection, a chamfer can still be drawn between them. Click on the *Chamfer* button.

☐ Select line E by clicking on it. Make sure you select the line *left* of the intersection on the longest part of the line.

☐ Select line F by clicking on it. Make sure you select the line *below* the intersection on the longest part of the line. The lines will be trimmed and a chamfer will be placed between them.

alternate method

You can also access the Chamfer command by clicking on the Modify pull-down menu and selecting Chamfer, or you can type **CHAMFER,** or just **CHA,** on the command line and hit the Enter key.

Note

When lines extend past an intersection point, it is very important where you select the line. AutoCAD will retain the part of the line you select and trim off the part of the line that extends past the intersection. If you had selected one short segment and one long segment, the chamfer would have been different. You may want to use the Undo button on the Standard toolbar to undo the last Chamfer command. You can then practice clicking different line segments to see what chamfers are drawn. When you are done, put the original chamfer back.

☐ Lines do not have to meet at a right angle to be chamfered. Click on the *Chamfer* button.

☐ Select line G by clicking on it.

☐ Select line H by clicking on it. A chamfer with distances of .5″ will be placed between the two lines. Notice that AutoCAD calculates the correct location and angle for the chamfer.

☐ For additional practice, chamfer the other two corners of the triangle formed by lines G, H, and J.

Placing Unequal Distance Chamfers

In this section you will place chamfers that have a different distance from the corner for the two sides. For unequal distance chamfers it is very important which side you pick first. The first line you choose will be given the first distance and the second line you choose will be given the second distance. Figure 4-9 shows how the picking order changes the chamfer. In this example, distance 1 is .5 and distance 2 is .25.

Figure 4-9
The orientation of the chamfer depends on which line you click first.

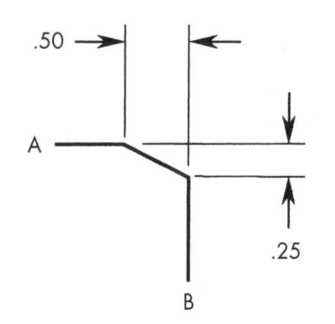

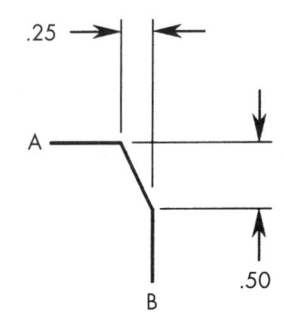

Setting the Distances

☐ Click on the *Chamfer* button.

Command: _chamfer
(TRIM mode) Current chamfer Dist1 = 0.5000, Dist2 = 0.5000
Select first line or [Polyline/Distance/Angle/Trim/Method]:

☐ Type **D** on the command line to select the *Distance* option and hit the *Enter* key.

Enter Trim mode option [Trim/No trim] <Trim>:
Select first line or [Polyline/Distance/Angle/Trim/Method]: D
Specify first chamfer distance <0.5000>:

☐ Hit the *Enter* key to accept the current default and set the first chamfer distance to .5".

Select first line or [Polyline/Distance/Angle/Trim/Method]: D
Specify first chamfer distance <0.5000>:
Specify second chamfer distance <0.5000>:

☐ Type **.25** on the command line and hit the *Enter* key to set the second distance to .25".

Specify first chamfer distance <0.5000>:
Specify second chamfer distance <0.5000>: .25
Select first line or [Polyline/Distance/Angle/Trim/Method]:

☐ Select line L by clicking on it.
☐ Select line K by clicking on it. The chamfer will be drawn and the command will end. Note that the first line you choose has the longest chamfer distance.
☐ Click on the *Chamfer* button.
☐ Select line K by clicking on it.
☐ Select line N by clicking on it. Compare this chamfer to the previous one. Make sure that you understand how the order of selecting the first and second lines can change the chamfer.

Placing Chamfers Based on an Angle

It is also possible to draw chamfers based on the distance of the first side and an angle. Figure 4-10 shows how this chamfer is defined.

Figure 4-10
Chamfer size can be set using a distance and an angle.

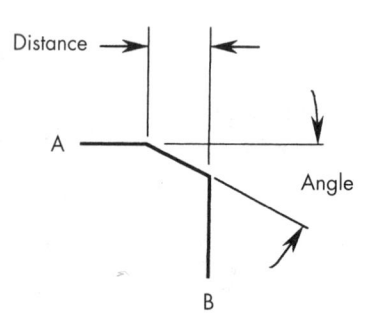

Drawing Regular-Shaped Objects   121

☐ Click on the *Chamfer* button.

Command: _chamfer
(TRIM mode) Current chamfer Dist1 = 0.5000, Dist2 = 0.2500
Select first line or [Polyline/Distance/Angle/Trim/Method]:

☐ Type **A** on the command line to select the *Angle* option and hit the *Enter* key.

(TRIM mode) Current chamfer Dist1 = 0.5000, Dist2 = 0.2500
Select first line or [Polyline/Distance/Angle/Trim/Method]: A
Specify chamfer length on the first line <0.1000>:

☐ Type **.375** on the command line and hit the *Enter* key to set the first line chamfer distance.

Select first line or [Polyline/Distance/Angle/Trim/Method]: A
Specify chamfer length on the first line <0.1000>: .375
Specify chamfer angle from the first line <0>:

☐ Type **60** on the command line and hit the *Enter* key to set the angle to 60°.

Specify chamfer length on the first line <0.1000>: .375
Specify chamfer angle from the first line <0>: 60
Select first line or [Polyline/Distance/Angle/Trim/Method]:

☐ Select line N by clicking on it.
☐ Select line M by clicking on it. A chamfer having a distance of .375″ on the first line and an angle of 60° from the first line will be drawn.
☐ Click on the *Chamfer* button.
☐ Select line M by clicking on it.
☐ Select line L by clicking on it. Compare this chamfer to the previous one. Make sure that you understand how the line selection and the angle are related.

A Special Use of the *Chamfer* Command

☐ Click on the *Chamfer* button.

Command: _chamfer
(TRIM mode) Current chamfer Length = 0.3750, Angle = 60
Select first line or [Polyline/Distance/Angle/Trim/Method]:

☐ Type **D** on the command line to select the *Distance* option and hit the *Enter* key.

(TRIM mode) Current chamfer Length = 0.3750, Angle = 60
Select first line or [Polyline/Distance/Angle/Trim/Method]: D
Specify first chamfer distance <0.5000>:

☐ Type **0** on the command line and hit the *Enter* key.

Select first line or [Polyline/Distance/Angle/Trim/Method]: D
Specify first chamfer distance <0.5000>: 0
Specify second chamfer distance <0.0000>:

☐ Hit the *Enter* key to accept 0 as the second distance.

Specify first chamfer distance <0.5000>: 0
Specify second chamfer distance <0.0000>:
Select first line or [Polyline/Distance/Angle/Trim/Method]:

☐ Select line P by clicking on it.
☐ Select line Q by clicking on it. The corner will be completed with no chamfer.
☐ Click on the *Chamfer* button.
☐ Complete the triangle by clicking on lines Q and R.
☐ This completes this activity. You should spend some time practicing what you learned in this activity. When you are done, close the AutoCAD program.

Assignment
for Module 4 – Activity 3

Procedure: ☑ Check each box as you complete that item.

☐ Start *AutoCAD 2002*.
☐ When the *AutoCAD 2002 Today* dialog box appears, open the drawing *M04A03-2.dwg* located in the *Module04* subdirectory on the CD.
☐ For this assignment you will draw the object shown in Figure 4-11 using the methods learned in this and previous activities.
☐ Start the object at point 2.5,.500 as indicated on the drawing. Follow the dimensions shown for the object. Do not include any of the dimensions, dimension lines, or letters on your drawing, only the lines and chamfers.

Figure 4-11

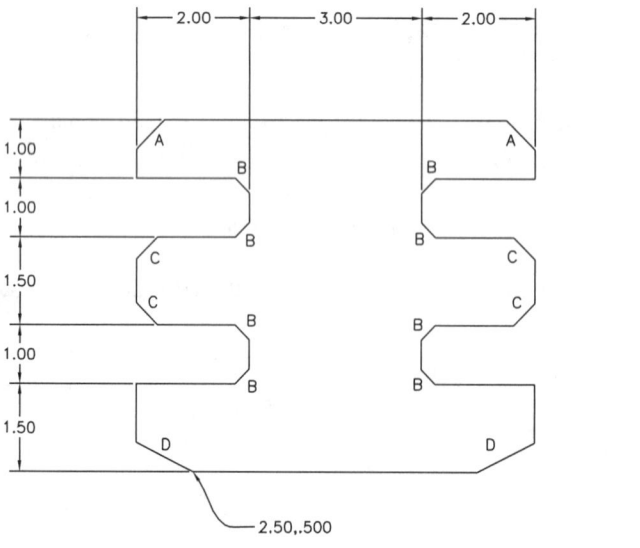

A = .5 X .5
B = .25 X .25
C = .375 X .375
D = 1.0 X .5

- [ ] The letter at each chamfer indicates its size. The first number is the first dimension and the second number is the second dimension. Refer to the key at the right of the object.
- [ ] When you have completed the figure, click on the *A-size Sheet* tab. If you started the object at the specified point, it will be centered on the paper.
- [ ] Save the drawing to your removable disk with the name M04A03-2.
- [ ] Print a copy of your drawing.
- [ ] Neatly print your name and the date in the appropriate spaces in the title block.

Applying the Concepts

Your company uses small steel shafts of various sizes and shapes in manufacturing their products. The receiving department is responsible for hand sorting the shaft sizes they receive and then placing them in various bins based on their size and shape. When a specific size shaft is required, the bin containing it is taken to the assembly line. Lately bins containing a mixture of different sized shafts have been delivered to the assembly line. This stops the production line as the bin must be returned to receiving, the shafts rechecked, and the correct size shafts returned to the production line. This is too much down time, which in turn affects production and profits.

Your boss has decided to remedy the situation by creating a gauge that receiving can use to verify a shaft's size so that it is placed in the proper bin. He has asked you to do a layout drawing of the gauge for checking both square and hexagon shafts. (The sizes of the shafts to be checked are listed below.) The gauge will be made from a 7.5" × 4.5" thin steel plate. It is your job to determine the best layout of the sizing holes so that all needed sizes fit on the one plate. The holes should be laid out in some reasonable pattern, i.e., the centers or edges of the holes aligned and located with increasing or decreasing shaft size. There also needs to be at least 1/4" of material between any two holes to ensure that the gauge will not break with use.

To ensure that the gauge slips easily over each shaft, you need to add fifteen-thousandths of an inch (0.015") across the flats of each size hole. For example, to check a 5/8" hex shaft you need to provide a hex hole that is 0.640" across the flats (0.625 + 0.015 = 0.640). Make sure that you provide this additional clearance on all the holes in your gauge. You do not want your boss to get a call from the receiving department telling him that your gauge does not work.

To demonstrate what he wants, your boss shows you a similar gauge for checking round shafts. This gauge, slipped on a shaft, is shown in Figure 4-12.

Square shaft sizes to be checked: 1/2", 5/8", 3/4", 7/8", 1", 1 1/8", 1 1/4", 1 1/2"
Hex shaft sizes to be checked: 1/2", 5/8", 3/4", 7/8", 1", 1 1/8", 1 1/4", 1 1/2"

Procedure: ☑ Check each box as you complete that item.

☐ Start *AutoCAD 2002*.

☐ When the *AutoCAD 2002 Today* dialog box appears, open the drawing *M04APP.dwg* located in the *Module04* subdirectory on the CD.

☐ Draw a 7.5" × 4.5" rectangle to represent the plate the gauge will be made from. To ensure that your drawing will be centered, start the bottom corner of the rectangle at

Figure 4-12
Gauge for checking round shafts

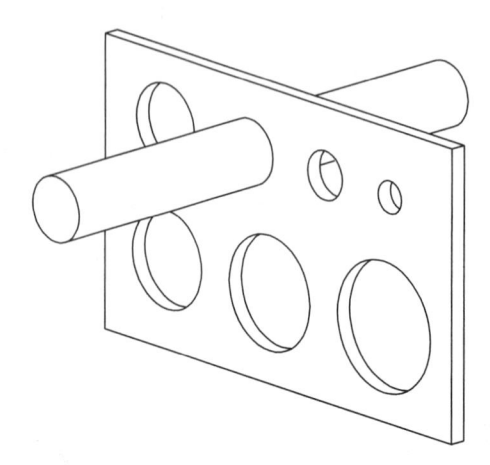

point 1.5,1.5. You may want to put a small chamfer on the plate's four corners so that anyone using the gauge will not be injured.

- [ ] Lay out the gauge with all the size and shape holes listed above. Don't forget to add the additional size for clearance.
- [ ] When you have completed the drawing, click on the *A-size Sheet* tab. If you started your drawing at the correct point, it will be centered on the drawing.
- [ ] Save the drawing to your removable disk with the name M04APP.
- [ ] Print a copy of your drawing.
- [ ] Neatly print your name and the date in the appropriate spaces in the title block.

Module 4 Review Questions

These questions are provided to help you review the topics and concepts covered in this module.

True or False

Determine whether the statement is true or false. Place your answer, either T or F, in the blank.

_____ 1. You can draw a rectangle using absolute, relative, or polar coordinates to specify the second corner.

_____ 2. An *Inscribed* polygon will be larger than a *Circumscribed* polygon if both are based on the same size circle.

_____ 3. You cannot use the *Chamfer* command to make a 90° corner.

_____ 4. A triangle is not a polygon, but a square is a polygon.

_____ 5. A square can only be made using relative coordinates to specify the second corner.

_____ 6. When drawing an unequal chamfer, it is not important what line of the corner you choose first because chamfers are always based on positive angles.

_____ 7. The *Chamfer* and *Fillet* commands that are part of the *Rectangle* command can be used on different corners of the same rectangle.

_____ 8. To draw a 3/8" hex bolt head, you would use a 6-sided *Inscribed* polygon.

_____ 9. You cannot erase an individual side of an object made with the *Rectangle* command without exploding the figure first.

_____ 10. Any two non-parallel lines can be joined to form a 90° corner by using the *Chamfer* command and setting the chamfer distance to 0.

Multiple-choice

Place the letter of the best answer in the blank.

1. A rectangle with opposite corners at 2,2 and 8,10 can be drawn using the *Rectangle* command, placing the first corner at 2,2, and using the relative coordinates _____.
    a. @8,6
    b. @8,10
    c. @6,8
    d. @10,8

2. This button is used to start the _____ command.
    a. Rectangle
    b. Explode
    c. Polygon
    d. Chamfer

3. This button is used to start the _____ command.
    a. Rectangle
    b. Explode
    c. Polygon
    d. Chamfer

4. This button is used to start the ____ command.
   a. Rectangle
   b. Explode
   c. Polygon
   d. Chamfer

5. This button is used to start the ____ command.
   a. Rectangle
   b. Explode
   c. Polygon
   d. Chamfer

Module 5

Getting in Close and Moving Around a Drawing

Activity 1

Zooming In and Out

Objectives: After completing this activity, you should be able to do the following:

- Zoom using a window.
- Zoom to the previous view.
- Zoom using the *All* and *Extents* toolbar buttons.
- Zoom *Realtime*.
- Cancel a command using the *Esc* key.

Procedure: ☑ Check each box as you complete that item.

AutoCAD drawings can be very complicated and contain thousands of lines. While you may be working on a drawing that will eventually be printed on a 34″ × 44″ piece of paper, AutoCAD's drawing area on your computer monitor is approximately 12″ wide by 9″ high or about ¼ the size of the finished drawing. Imagine squeezing a large drawing with thousands of lines down to that small area on your screen and trying to work on it. It is almost impossible. In this activity you will learn how to zoom in and out on the drawing so you can get in close to make changes and then move back out to view the overall drawing.

- ☐ Double-click on the *AutoCAD 2002* icon to open the program.
- ☐ When the *AutoCAD 2002 Today* dialog box appears, open the drawing *Wilhome.dwg*. It is located in the *Sample* subdirectory in the *AutoCAD2002* directory on your computer's C: drive.
- ☐ Verify that the MODEL tab is selected at the bottom of the drawing area. If not, select it now.

Zoom a Drawing Using a Window and Previous Commands

In this activity you will learn how to zoom in on a region of a drawing and then zoom back out to a previous view. As you look at the drawing, you will see why it is important to learn to zoom in on a drawing; you cannot read any of the text or dimensions on the drawing.

☐ The drawing navigation options, including *Zoom*, are located on the *Standard* toolbar. Use Figure 5-1 to locate them now.

☐ Toolbar buttons that have a small arrowhead in the lower right corner have a feature called a flyout. Flyouts are similar to cascading menus in that they provide additional options. The *Zoom* flyout has eight zoom option buttons, as seen in Figure 5-2. To open a flyout, place the mouse pointer over the flyout button, press and hold the left mouse button, and then slide the pointer down the list to the option you want. When you release the mouse button, that option will be selected and the flyout will close. The button you selected will replace the previous flyout button. This saves time if you use that same option over and over again. The next time you return to the flyout, that option is on top and is available by clicking (not holding the mouse button) on the flyout button. You do not have to reopen the flyout until you want a different option.

☐ Place your mouse pointer over the flyout button, and press and hold the left mouse button. The flyout will open. Release the left mouse button and the flyout will retract to its original position. Hit the *Esc* key to cancel the zoom command you just activated.

☐ Press and hold the left mouse button again, and this time slide the mouse pointer up and down the set of buttons on the flyout and observe how each is highlighted as you pass over it. While over any one of the buttons, release the left mouse button. The flyout will close and the flyout button will now be the same as the operation you selected. Hit the *Esc* key to cancel the zoom command you just activated.

☐ Activate the flyout again and locate the *Zoom Window* button. Move the mouse pointer down until you highlight this button and then release the left mouse button. The *Zoom Window* is now selected.

Figure 5-1
The drawing *Navigation Tools* are located on the *Standard* toolbar.

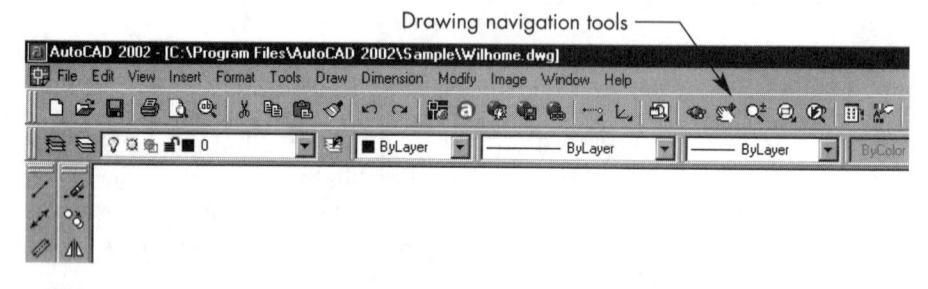

Figure 5-2
Press and hold the mouse button to see additional options on a flyout button.

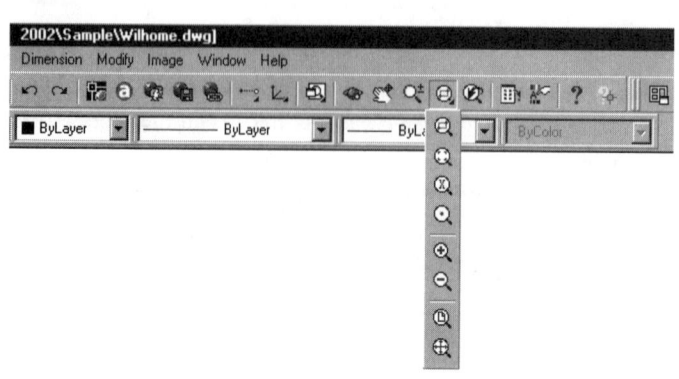

- ☐ The *Zoom Window* allows you to draw a box (window) around the area of the drawing you want to zoom in on. Making a window is done by placing the mouse pointer in the *upper left* corner where you want the box to start, clicking the left mouse button at that location, and then dragging the mouse pointer diagonally down to the *lower right* corner where you want the box to end. As you do this operation, you should see the box being drawn around the area you selected.

  If you start drawing a window and find that you started the box in the wrong location, you can cancel the operation by hitting the *Esc* key on your keyboard. If you use *Esc*, you will have to select the *Zoom Window* command again. The *Esc* key can be used to cancel almost every operation you start in AutoCAD, so if you make a mistake or choose the wrong command, use this method to start over again.

- ☐ On the drawing you will see what appears to be a large layout on the right half of the drawing and about a dozen green-colored detail views on the left. You are now going to zoom in on the detail view at the lower left corner of the drawing. Make sure the *Zoom Window* command is activated. You will see *Specify first corner:* on the command line. If not, select *Zoom Window* again.

- ☐ Place the mouse pointer, now appearing as a cross, above and to the left of the view you are going to zoom in on. Click the left mouse button and drag the window to the lower right corner of the view. The size of the window is not important; just make sure the window is around the entire view. If you did not get the starting point in a good location, hit *Esc,* reselect *Zoom Window,* and try again. When you are happy with the window and its location, click the left mouse button again and you will zoom in on the detail view.

- ☐ The *Zoom Previous* button is located to the right of the flyout and is used to take you back to the last view before you zoomed. Locate and click the *Zoom Previous* button now. You will again see the overall view of the drawing.

- ☐ Click on the *Zoom Window* button, which is now located as the flyout button. (You do not have to activate the flyout when the operation you need is showing as the flyout button. Click on the button once and you have activated that command.) Again zoom in on the detail view in the lower left corner of the drawing.

- ☐ Locate the arrow from the *OVEN/MICRO COMBO* note. Click on the *Zoom Window* button; draw the window, starting with the upper left corner, around the control panel that the arrow points to; and click the left mouse button. You are now zoomed in close on that panel.

- ☐ Click the *Zoom Window* button again and zoom in on the four circular controls in the middle of the panel. *Zoom Window* again and zoom in on one of the circular controls. *Zoom Window* allows you to zoom in closer and closer. You may notice that the controls do not look round, but appear as polygons. This is caused by multiple zooming of the original screen. Type **REGEN** on the command line and hit the *Enter* key. This will regenerate the drawing and make the controls circular again.

- ☐ Click on the *Zoom Previous* button four times to get back to the original full drawing.

- ☐ You now know how to use *Zoom Window*. You may want to practice zooming in on different parts of the drawing until you feel comfortable with the operation. Make sure to *Zoom Previous* back to the original drawing each time you are done zooming in.

Using *Zoom All* and *Zoom Extents*

Zoom All and *Zoom Extents* sometimes produce the same or similar results and therefore can be confusing. The way they zoom is dependent on what and where things are drawn. The *Extents* of your drawing are the furthest outside edges of all the objects you have drawn. Both are very useful because they enable you to get an overall view of everything that has been drawn. Either button is useful for finding lost objects. Sometimes you use the *Move* or *Copy* command and an object seems to disappear. In reality it may have been copied to a distant location, hundreds of feet away, and therefore does not appear on the screen. Using *Zoom All* or *Zoom Extents* helps you locate these lost items.

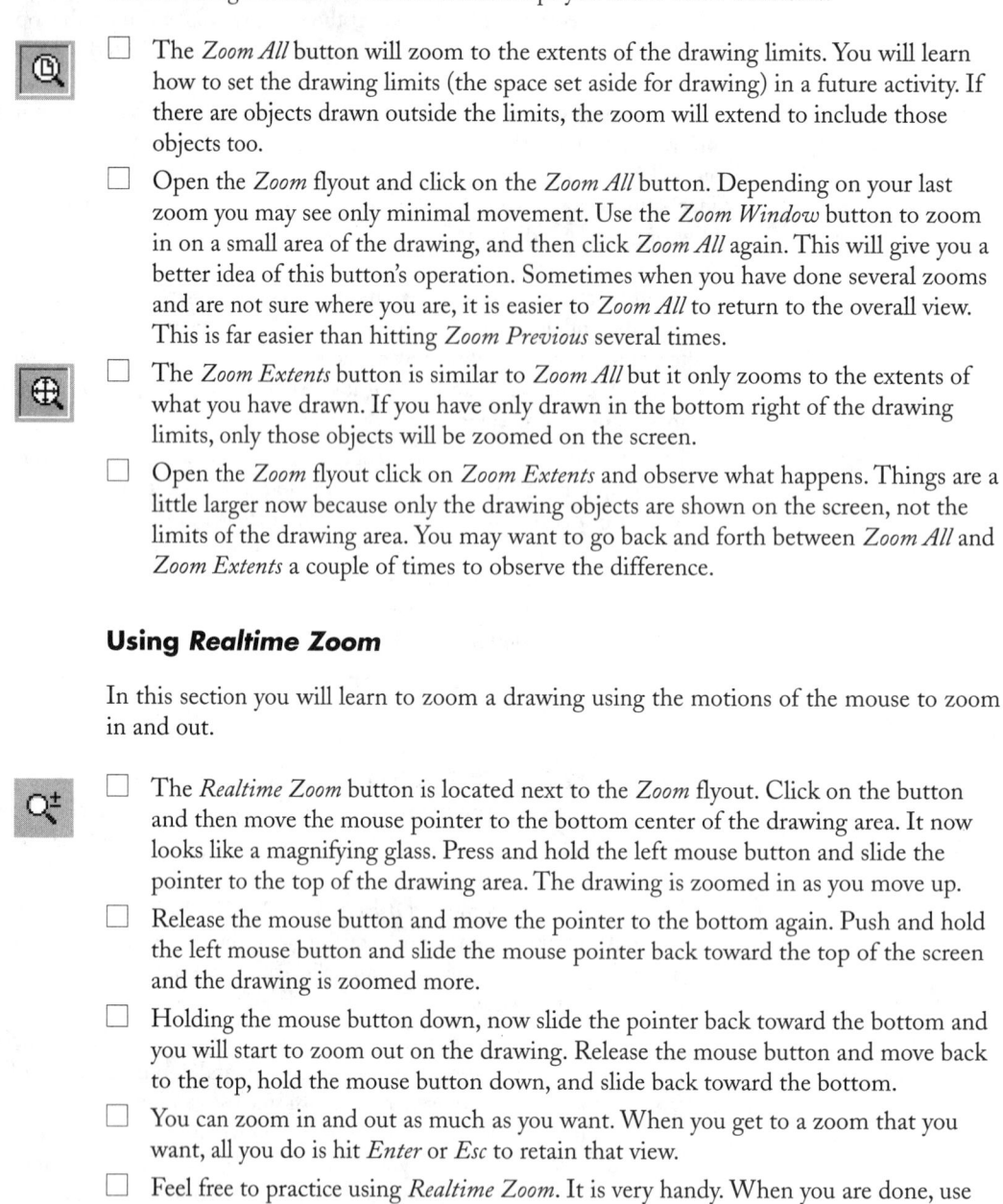

- ☐ The *Zoom All* button will zoom to the extents of the drawing limits. You will learn how to set the drawing limits (the space set aside for drawing) in a future activity. If there are objects drawn outside the limits, the zoom will extend to include those objects too.

- ☐ Open the *Zoom* flyout and click on the *Zoom All* button. Depending on your last zoom you may see only minimal movement. Use the *Zoom Window* button to zoom in on a small area of the drawing, and then click *Zoom All* again. This will give you a better idea of this button's operation. Sometimes when you have done several zooms and are not sure where you are, it is easier to *Zoom All* to return to the overall view. This is far easier than hitting *Zoom Previous* several times.

- ☐ The *Zoom Extents* button is similar to *Zoom All* but it only zooms to the extents of what you have drawn. If you have only drawn in the bottom right of the drawing limits, only those objects will be zoomed on the screen.

- ☐ Open the *Zoom* flyout click on *Zoom Extents* and observe what happens. Things are a little larger now because only the drawing objects are shown on the screen, not the limits of the drawing area. You may want to go back and forth between *Zoom All* and *Zoom Extents* a couple of times to observe the difference.

Using *Realtime Zoom*

In this section you will learn to zoom a drawing using the motions of the mouse to zoom in and out.

- ☐ The *Realtime Zoom* button is located next to the *Zoom* flyout. Click on the button and then move the mouse pointer to the bottom center of the drawing area. It now looks like a magnifying glass. Press and hold the left mouse button and slide the pointer to the top of the drawing area. The drawing is zoomed in as you move up.

- ☐ Release the mouse button and move the pointer to the bottom again. Push and hold the left mouse button and slide the mouse pointer back toward the top of the screen and the drawing is zoomed more.

- ☐ Holding the mouse button down, now slide the pointer back toward the bottom and you will start to zoom out on the drawing. Release the mouse button and move back to the top, hold the mouse button down, and slide back toward the bottom.

- ☐ You can zoom in and out as much as you want. When you get to a zoom that you want, all you do is hit *Enter* or *Esc* to retain that view.

- ☐ Feel free to practice using *Realtime Zoom*. It is very handy. When you are done, use *Zoom Extents* to get back to the full drawing.

The Other Zoom Commands

Zoom Window and *Zoom Previous* are the two most often used zoom commands. You will use them quite often. The next section will give you an overview of the other zoom commands. It is not intended to make you an expert at using them, only to make you aware that they exist and how they work.

- ☐ *Zoom Dynamic* is similar to zoom window in that it allows you to specify a rectangular-shaped area on the drawing for zooming. The difference is that *Zoom Dynamic* allows you to adjust the size and position of the rectangle several times before making the actual zoom. The length and width of the rectangle are also automatically sized to be the same proportions as the drawing area on your monitor, so you know exactly everything that will be seen after you zoom.

- [ ] Click on the *Zoom Dynamic* button on the *Zoom* flyout. You will notice three rectangular-shaped colored boxes. The blue dotted box shows the *extents* of the drawing that contains drawn objects, the green dotted box shows the boundary of the *current view* before you started the zoom, and the white solid box with an "X" in the center is the *panning view* box that shows the area that will be zoomed.

- [ ] Move the mouse around and observe how the panning view moves. Place the box's "X" approximately in the middle of the drawing and click the left mouse button. The "X" disappears and an arrow appears, pointing toward the right edge of the box. This is called the *zooming view* box. Move the mouse around and observe how this box reacts.

- [ ] Size the box so that its width is about as wide as the detail views (about 1/3 the total drawing width) along the left of the drawing. Click the left mouse button again and the box will change back to a *panning view* box. Move the box to the lower left corner of the drawing to the same view you zoomed on in the last section. Click the left mouse button to change back to a *zooming view* box, and resize it again to bring it closer to the size of the detail view. Continue going back and forth between the two boxes until you feel you have the detail contained inside and then hit the *Enter* key. You are now zoomed in on the area inside the last box that was on the screen.

- [ ] Click the *Zoom Dynamic* button again and you will see the overall drawing. The current view box shows the part of the drawing where you are currently zoomed, and the panning box will still be the same size as it was last set. Move the panning box to surround the detail view to the right of the previous view (you can resize the box if you like), and hit *Enter*.

- [ ] Hit the *Zoom Previous* button twice and it will take you back to the original overall view of the drawing.

Feel free to practice using *Zoom Dynamic;* however, you must return to the overall view before continuing this exercise.

- [ ] *Zoom Scale* zooms in and out based on the number you enter from the keyboard, e.g., entering 2 will make the view twice its current size and entering .5 will make the view half its current size. The zooming occurs about the center of the screen. In the next activity, you will learn how to move the drawing around to place things in the center of the screen.

- [ ] Click on the *Zoom Scale* button, type **2X** on the command line, and hit the *Enter* key. The drawing is now twice as big. Click on the *Zoom Scale* button again, type **.25X** on the command line, and hit the *Enter* key. The drawing is now half its original size (one-fourth the size of the previous view).

Note

Including the "X" in the *Zoom Scale* command zooms the objects based on what you currently see on the screen. If you do not include the "X", the zoom is based on the overall drawing. For example, "2X" makes the objects you see on the screen twice as large. Using "2" returns you to the original overall drawing and zooms it twice as large.

- [ ] Hit the *Zoom Previous* button twice to return to the original overall view of the drawing.
- [ ] *Zoom Center* allows you to specify the center that you are going to zoom about before specifying the zoom scale.

- ☐ Click on the *Zoom Center* button, move the mouse's crosshairs to the center of the detail view in the lower left corner of the drawing, and click the mouse button. Type **5X** on the command line, and hit *Enter*. You are now zoomed in on that view. When entering the scale factor, you must include the "X". The command line gives you an option of entering either a magnification or a height, and if you do not include the "X", AutoCAD assumes you are entering a height. This will make the screen 5" high, not scale it the 5 times you need to see the entire view.

- ☐ Click on the *Zoom Center* button, hit enter to accept the last selected zoom point, type **1/5X** on the command line, and hit *Enter*. You are now zoomed back to the original size of the drawing but you are centered on the detail view.

- ☐ Hit the *Zoom Previous* button twice and it will take you back to the original overall view of the drawing.

- ☐ *Zoom In* button makes a 2X zoom about the center of the screen.

- ☐ Click on the *Zoom In* button and observe what happens. You will zoom back out in the next step.

- ☐ *Zoom Out* button makes a .5X zoom about the center of the screen.

- ☐ Click on the *Zoom In* button and observe what happens. You should be back to the original full view.

alternate method

There are two additional ways of activating the zoom commands. You can click on the *View* pull-down menu, slide the mouse pointer to the *Zoom* option, and select any of the zoom options from the cascading menu. Or you can type **ZOOM** (or the letter **Z**) next to *Command:* in the *Command* window and hit the *Enter* key. You can then select one of the zoom options from the command line list. Using command line options will be covered in a later activity.

If you have a mouse with a roller wheel button, you can use the wheel to zoom in and out. Roll the wheel up to zoom out and down to zoom in. You can also zoom to the extents of the drawing by double-clicking the wheel.

- ☐ This completes this activity; close the AutoCAD program without saving the drawing.

Activity 2

Panning

Objectives: After completing this activity, you should be able to move around the drawing using the following:

- Scroll bars
- Point Pan
- Realtime Pan

Panning is used to move horizontally and vertically around a drawing so you can place the area you want to work on in the center of the computer screen. In this activity you will learn three methods of panning: *scrolling, Point Pan,* and *Realtime Pan.*

Procedure: ☑ Check each box as you complete that item.

- ☐ Double-click on the *AutoCAD 2002* icon to open the program.
- ☐ When the *AutoCAD 2002 Today* dialog box appears, open the drawing *Wilhome.dwg.* It is located in the *Sample* subdirectory in the *AutoCAD2002* directory on your computer's C: drive.
- ☐ Verfiy that the MODEL tab is selected at the bottom of the drawing area. If not, select it now.

Using the *Scroll Bars* to Pan

Scroll bars is a Windows feature that enables you to move around in a document that is larger than the computer screen. This method works very well for small drawings or where you only have to move a short distance. Figure 5-3 shows the scroll bars that are located along the right side and bottom of the work area.

- ☐ Using the *Zoom Window* command that you learned in the last activity, zoom in on the kitchen detail located at the bottom and to the right of the column of green detail views.
- ☐ Place your mouse pointer on the dark gray square in the horizontal bottom scroll bar. Press and hold the left mouse button, slowly moving the mouse right and left, dragging the square with it. As you move the mouse, you should see the drawing move back and forth too.
- ☐ Now, using the same method, try moving the vertical scroll bar and observe the drawing's motion.

Figure 5-3
Scroll bars are used to move around in the drawing on the screen.

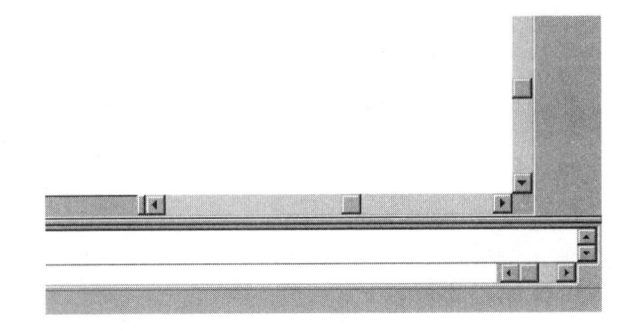

- ☐ Drag both squares back to their original position so the kitchen view is again in the center of the computer screen.
- ☐ Another method for moving the scroll bar is to use the arrow buttons located at each end of the bar. Place the mouse pointer over the left arrow button on the bottom scroll bar and click the left mouse button several times. Observe how the drawing moves.
- ☐ Practice using all the arrow buttons on both the horizontal and vertical scroll bars.
- ☐ When you are done practicing, move back to the original position with the kitchen view in the center of the screen, using either method described above.

Note

After doing several pans, you will not be able to use the *Zoom Previous* button to take you back to the original view. If you get lost, use the *Zoom All* or *Zoom Extents* button to get an overview of the drawing and then you can use the *Zoom Window* to get back to the kitchen view.

Using *Point Pan*

Point Pan is used to move a specific point to a new location on the computer screen. This is very convenient when you want to center a different part of the drawing view on the screen. The *Point Pan* command is located in the *Pan* cascading menu under the *View* pull-down menu, as seen in Figure 5-4.

- ☐ Click on the *View* pull-down menu, slide the mouse pointer down the list to *Pan*, slide the pointer to the right and down to highlight *Point*, and then click the left mouse button.
- ☐ The graphics cursor now appears as a set of crosshairs. Place the crosshairs over the small blue circle in the upper left corner of the kitchen view. (This is part of the kitchen lighting.) Click the left mouse button to select this location.
- ☐ Drag the cursor to the middle of the computer screen. You will see a line extending from the circle to the location of the crosshairs. This line indicates the pan distance. The circle will move from its original location, along the line, to where the crosshairs are located. Click the left mouse button and the drawing view will move placing the circle in the middle of the screen (if that is where you had the crosshairs).
- ☐ Practice using this method of panning. First move the blue circle to the lower left corner of the screen, then to the upper left corner, the upper right corner, the lower right corner, and finally back to the center.

Figure 5-4
Select the *Point* option from the *Pan* cascading menu.

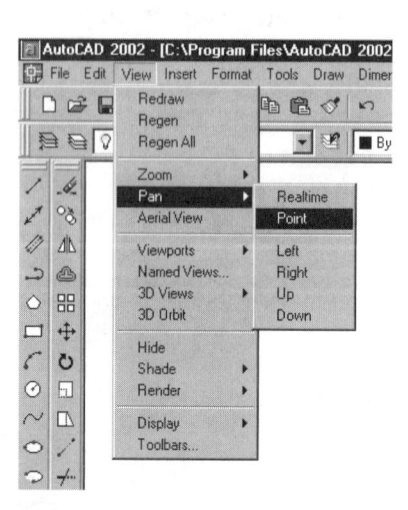

Getting in Close and Moving Around a Drawing   137

> If you do not want to keep returning to the *View* pull-down menu to get the *Point Pan* command, you can hit the right mouse button, while the mouse pointer is in the drawing area of the screen, and a pop-up menu will appear. The first item on this menu will be *Repeat Point*. Move the mouse pointer to highlight *Repeat Point* and click the mouse button. This will select the command. This method can be used to repeat almost any command.

- [ ] Reposition the kitchen view in the center of the screen using any of the panning methods you have learned.

Using *Realtime Pan*

Realtime Pan is probably the most useful *Pan* command. It is so useful that the *Realtime Pan* button is included on the *Standard* toolbar. *Realtime Pan* allows you to easily move around the drawing.

- [ ] Locate the *Realtime Pan* button on the *Standard* toolbar. Place the mouse pointer over the button and click the left mouse button.
- [ ] When you move the pointer back to the drawing area, you will see that it has turned into a hand. This hand is used to "grab" the drawing and pull it to a new location.
- [ ] Place the hand in the middle of the screen, press and hold down the left mouse button, and drag the hand to the right side of the screen. The drawing will move with the mouse.
- [ ] Release the left mouse button. Note that the hand is still visible. *Realtime Pan* stays active until you hit the *Enter* or *Esc* key on the keyboard.
- [ ] Press and hold the left mouse button again and practice dragging the drawing around the screen. When you are done, move the kitchen view back to the middle of the screen.
- [ ] *Realtime Pan* can also be used to move over long distances on the drawing. Place the hand at the top center of the drawing area. Press and hold the left mouse button and move the hand straight down to the bottom of the screen. Release the mouse button.
- [ ] Again, move the hand to the top center of the drawing area, press and hold the left mouse button, and move the hand straight down to the bottom of the drawing area.
- [ ] Repeat this method two more times. You should be somewhere close to the top of the drawing.
- [ ] Reverse the above method starting with the hand at the bottom of the screen and moving up until you get back to the kitchen view.
- [ ] Use *Realtime Pan* to place the kitchen view in the middle of the screen. Hit the *Enter* key on the keyboard to stop the *Realtime Pan* function.

alternate method

If you have a mouse with a roller wheel button, you can use the wheel to do a realtime pan. Press and hold the wheel and the pointer will turn into a hand that enables you to pan around the drawing.

Note

Zooming and panning usually go together. Often you will zoom to a portion of a drawing and then pan to place the exact location you want in the center of the screen. This is sometimes followed by another zoom to get things a little larger. If you do not have a roller wheel mouse, or you are more comfortable using *Realtime* zooms, you can easily move between these two commands by clicking the *right* mouse button. This brings up a menu that contains both *Realtime Zoom* and *Pan*. This is a convenient way to quickly switch from one command to the other.

- [ ] This completes this activity. You may want to spend some time *Panning* and *Zooming* around the drawing so that you are familiar with both operations. When you are done close the AutoCAD program.

Module 5 Review Questions

These questions are provided to help you review the topics and concepts covered in this module.

True or False

Determine whether the statement is true or false. Place your answer, either T or F, in the blank.

_____ 1. When using *Point Pan* you can only move the drawing left and right.
_____ 2. *Realtime Zoom* and *Pan* are usually used together.
_____ 3. The mouse roller wheel button can be used to zoom and pan the drawing.
_____ 4. *Zoom Previous* can only be used to back up once.
_____ 5. *Zoom Extents* is a good way to locate objects that were incorrectly drawn or moved far from the drawing limits.
_____ 6. The best way to move around a drawing is to use the *scroll bars*.
_____ 7. Double-clicking the mouse roller wheel button will *Zoom Extents*.
_____ 8. *Zoom Extents* will always take you to the extents of the drawing limits.
_____ 9. Sometimes *Pan Point* must be used several times to get to the part of the drawing where you want to work.
_____ 10. *Zoom All* will always take you to the extents of the drawing limits.

Multiple-choice

Place the letter of the best answer in the blank.

1. This button is used to start the ____ command.
   a. Realtime Pan
   b. Realtime Zoom
   c. Zoom In
   d. Zoom Out

2. This button is used to start the ____ command.
   a. Zoom Extents
   b. Zoom All
   c. Zoom Dynamic
   d. Zoom Window

3. This button is used to start the ____ command.
   a. Zoom Previous
   b. Realtime Zoom
   c. Realtime Pan
   d. Zoom Scale

4. This button is used to start the ____ command.
   a. Realtime Zoom
   b. Realtime Pan
   c. Zoom In
   d. Zoom Out

5. This button is used to start the ____ command.
   a. Zoom In
   b. Zoom Dynamic
   c. Zoom Center
   d. Zoom Out

6. This button is used to start the ____ command.
   a. Zoom All
   b. Zoom Window
   c. Zoom Extents
   d. Zoom Previous

7. This button is used to start the ____ command.
   a. Zoom Window
   b. Zoom Extents
   c. Zoom All
   d. Zoom Center

8. This button is used to start the ____ command.
   a. Zoom Out
   b. Zoom In
   c. Zoom All
   d. Zoom Center

9. This button is used to start the ____ command.
   a. Zoom Extents
   b. Zoom Window
   c. Zoom All
   d. Zoom Scale

10. This button is used to start the ____ command.
    a. Zoom In
    b. Zoom Out
    c. Zoom Scale
    d. Zoom Center

11. This button is used to start the ____ command.
    a. Zoom Center
    b. Zoom Scale
    c. Zoom Extents
    d. Zoom In

Module 6

Drawing Curved Shapes

Activity 1

Drawing Circles

Objectives: After completing this activity, you should be able to do the following:

- Locate and use the *Circle* button on the *Draw* toolbar.
- Draw a circle having a specific radius at a given location on a drawing.
- Draw a circle having a specific diameter at a given location on a drawing.
- Draw a circle tangent to a line or another circle.
- Draw a circle based on two or three points.
- Draw a line tangent to a circle using the *Tangent* snap from the *Object Snap* toolbar.
- Locate and use the *Center* button on the *Object Snap* toolbar.
- Locate and use the *Quadrant* button on the *Object Snap* toolbar

Procedure: ☑ Check each box as you complete that item.

- ☐ Start *AutoCAD 2002*.
- ☐ When the *AutoCAD 2002 Today* dialog box appears, open the drawing *M06A01-1.dwg* located in the *Module06* subdirectory on the CD.
- ☐ Make sure that all the *Drawing Features* buttons, except for the *Model* button, on the *Status* bar are all off.

Drawing a Circle

In this part you will learn how to draw and place a circle, having a specific diameter or radius, in a defined location on a drawing. Circles are commonly found on drawings where they usually represent cylindrically shaped objects or holes. Figure 6-1 shows the difference between a circle's radius and diameter.

141

142   Module 6

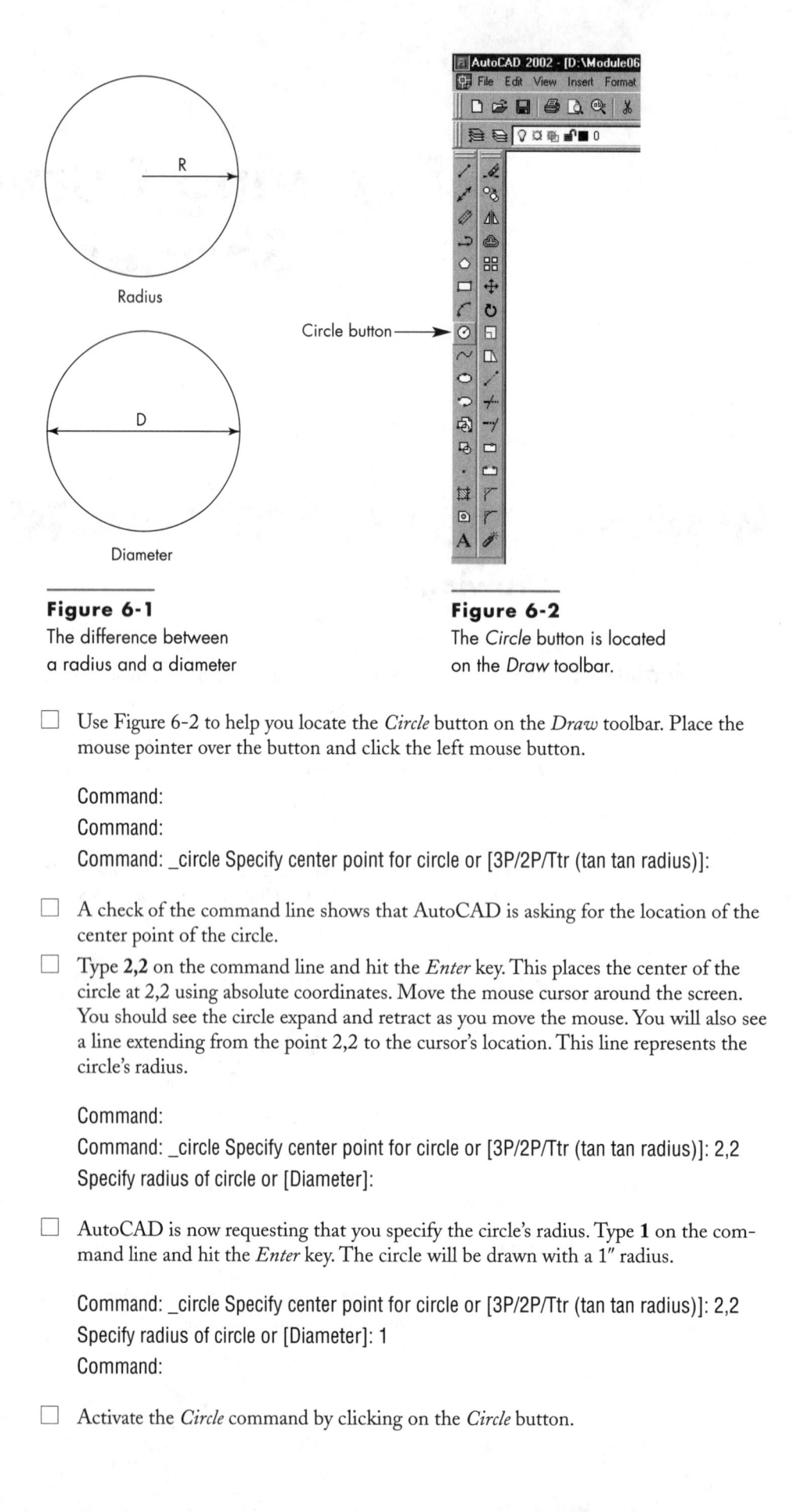

Figure 6-1
The difference between
a radius and a diameter

Figure 6-2
The *Circle* button is located
on the *Draw* toolbar.

☐ Use Figure 6-2 to help you locate the *Circle* button on the *Draw* toolbar. Place the mouse pointer over the button and click the left mouse button.

Command:
Command:
Command: _circle Specify center point for circle or [3P/2P/Ttr (tan tan radius)]:

☐ A check of the command line shows that AutoCAD is asking for the location of the center point of the circle.

☐ Type **2,2** on the command line and hit the *Enter* key. This places the center of the circle at 2,2 using absolute coordinates. Move the mouse cursor around the screen. You should see the circle expand and retract as you move the mouse. You will also see a line extending from the point 2,2 to the cursor's location. This line represents the circle's radius.

Command:
Command: _circle Specify center point for circle or [3P/2P/Ttr (tan tan radius)]: 2,2
Specify radius of circle or [Diameter]:

☐ AutoCAD is now requesting that you specify the circle's radius. Type **1** on the command line and hit the *Enter* key. The circle will be drawn with a 1″ radius.

Command: _circle Specify center point for circle or [3P/2P/Ttr (tan tan radius)]: 2,2
Specify radius of circle or [Diameter]: 1
Command:

☐ Activate the *Circle* command by clicking on the *Circle* button.

Command:
Command:
Command: _circle Specify center point for circle or [3P/2P/Ttr (tan tan radius)]:

☐ Type **2,5** on the command line and hit the *Enter* key.

Command:
Command: _circle Specify center point for circle or [3P/2P/Ttr (tan tan radius)]: 2,5
Specify radius of circle or [Diameter]<1.0000>:

☐ The command line asks you to specify the radius of the circle. AutoCAD also offers another option indicated by *or [Diameter]*. Items appearing in square brackets are options. (Do not confuse this feature with the value option in the angled brackets that provides the last value entered.) To activate a bracketed option, you must type the option on the command line. Since typing is time consuming, AutoCAD offers a shortcut. You only need to type what is capitalized. To specify the diameter, for example, you only have to type "D".

☐ Type a **D** on the command line and hit the *Enter* key.

Command: _circle Specify center point for circle or [3P/2P/Ttr (tan tan radius)]: 2,5
Specify radius of circle or [Diameter]<1.0000>: D
Specify diameter of circle <2.0000>:

☐ Notice that the value option in the angled brackets has changed from 1.0000 to 2.0000. Remember that the diameter is twice the radius. Hit the *Enter* key to accept the default value. The second circle is drawn above the first. Both circles are the same size.

alternate method   You can also access the *Circle* command by clicking on the *Draw* pull-down menu and selecting either *Center, Radius* or *Center, Diameter* from the *Circle* cascading menu. You can also type **CIRCLE,** or just **C,** on the command line to start the *Circle* command.

Drawing a Circle Tangent to a Line or a Circle

Sometimes it is necessary to place a circle based on the location of another object. In this part you will place three circles: one tangent to two circles, one tangent to a circle and a line, and one tangent to two lines. Tangency is defined as a line or object meeting a curved line at only one point and not intersecting the curved line. Figure 6-3 shows examples of circles and lines that are tangent. In each example the points of tangency are indicated by an arrow.

Figure 6-3
Tangencies

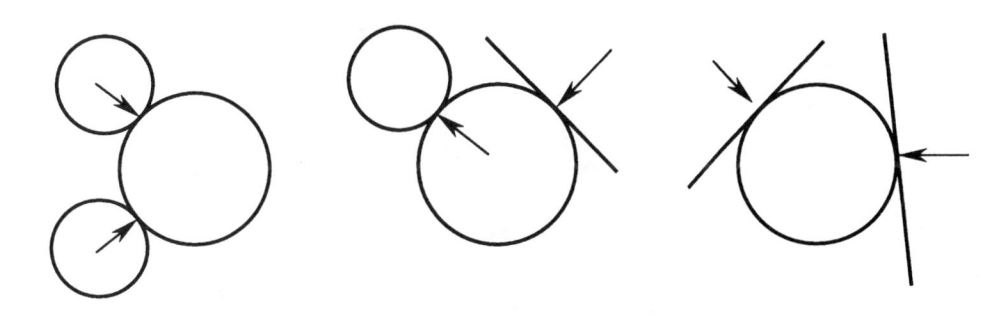

- [ ] Activate the *Circle* command by clicking on the *Circle* button.

  Command:
  Command:
  Command: _circle Specify center point for circle or [3P/2P/Ttr (tan tan radius)]:

- [ ] Type **T** on the command line to accept the tan, tan, radius option, and hit the *Enter* key. As stated previously, to select the Ttr option you only have to type the capitalized portion of the option.

  Command:
  Command: _circle Specify center point for circle or [3P/2P/Ttr (tan tan radius)]: T
  Specify point on object for first tangency of circle:

Note: It is very important where you click on the circle as that indicates the point of tangency. Follow the directions carefully.

- [ ] Move the mouse pointer to the upper right part (somewhere between 0° and 90°) on the first circle you drew. The *Tangent* snap marker that looks like a circle and a line will appear. When the marker is on, click the mouse button.

  Command: _circle Specify center point for circle or [3P/2P/Ttr (tan tan radius)]: T
  Specify point on object for first tangency of circle:
  Specify point on object for second tangency of circle:

- [ ] Move the mouse pointer to the lower right part (somewhere between 270° and 360°) on the second circle you drew. When the *Tangent* snap marker appears, click the mouse button to select the second point of tangency.

  Specify point on object for first tangency of circle:
  Specify point on object for second tangency of circle:
  Specify radius of circle <1.0000>:

- [ ] Type **1.5** on the command line and hit the *Enter* key. A circle having a radius of 1.5 will be drawn that is tangent to both of the circles.
- [ ] You are now going to add a couple of lines so you can practice drawing a circle tangent to a line. Click on the *Line* button on the *Draw* toolbar.
- [ ] Type **4,6** on the command line and hit the *Enter* key.
- [ ] Type **10,6** on the command line and hit the *Enter* key.
- [ ] Type **6,1** on the command line and hit the *Enter* key twice to end the *Line* command.
- [ ] Activate the *Circle* command by clicking on the *Circle* button.

  Command:
  Command:
  Command: _circle Specify center point for circle or [3P/2P/Ttr (tan tan radius)]:

- [ ] Type **T** on the command line to accept the tan, tan, radius option, and hit the *Enter* key.

Command:

Command: _circle Specify center point for circle or [3P/2P/Ttr (tan tan radius)]: T
Specify point on object for first tangency of circle:

☐ Move the mouse pointer to the upper right part (somewhere between 0° and 90°) on the large circle you drew. When the *Tangent* snap marker appears, click the mouse button.

Command: _circle Specify center point for circle or [3P/2P/Ttr (tan tan radius)]: T
Specify point on object for first tangency of circle:
Specify point on object for second tangency of circle:

☐ Move the mouse pointer to the horizontal line over the large circle. When the *Tangent* snap marker appears, click the mouse button to select the second point of tangency.

Specify point on object for first tangency of circle:
Specify point on object for second tangency of circle:
Specify radius of circle <1.0000>:

☐ Type **.75** on the command and hit the *Enter* key. The new circle will be drawn tangent to both the circle and the line.

☐ Activate the *Circle* command by clicking on the *Circle* button.

Command:
Command:
Command: _circle Specify center point for circle or [3P/2P/Ttr (tan tan radius)]:

☐ Type **T** on the command line to accept the tan, tan, radius option, and hit the *Enter* key.

Command:
Command: _circle Specify center point for circle or [3P/2P/Ttr (tan tan radius)]: T
Specify point on object for first tangency of circle:

☐ Move the mouse pointer to the horizontal line. When the *Tangent* snap marker appears, click the mouse button.

Command: _circle Specify center point for circle or [3P/2P/Ttr (tan tan radius)]: T
Specify point on object for first tangency of circle:
Specify point on object for second tangency of circle:

☐ Move the mouse pointer to the angled line. When the *Tangent* snap marker appears, click the mouse button to select the second point of tangency.

Specify point on object for first tangency of circle:
Specify point on object for second tangency of circle:
Specify radius of circle <1.0000>:

☐ Type **1** on the command and hit the *Enter* key. The new circle will be drawn tangent to both lines.

Figure 6-4
Tangencies

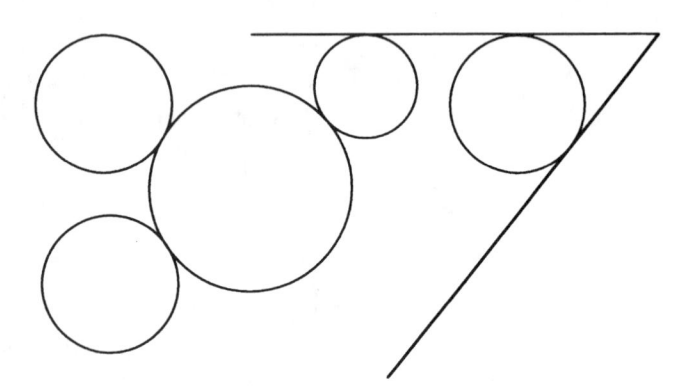

- [ ] Take a little time to look at the objects on the screen to make sure you understand the different operations that have been covered to this point.
- [ ] Compare your screen with Figure 6-4. If they are not the same, you need to go back and repeat this section until you can do it right.
- [ ] Things are getting a little cluttered. Click on the *Erase* button, type **ALL** on the command line, and hit the *Enter* key twice. This will erase all objects on the screen.

The next section will show you the importance of where you select the tangency points.

- [ ] Using the procedures you learned above, place two 1" radius circles, one centered at 5.5,2 and the other centered at 5.5,5.
- [ ] Activate the *Circle* command by clicking on the *Circle* button.
- [ ] Type **T** on the command line to accept the tan, tan, radius option, and hit the *Enter* key.
- [ ] Move the mouse pointer to the upper right part (somewhere between 0° and 90°) on the bottom circle you drew. When the *Tangent* snap marker appears, click the mouse button.
- [ ] Move the mouse pointer to the lower right part (somewhere between 270° and 360°) on the top circle you drew. When the *Tangent* snap marker appears, click the mouse button to select the second point of tangency.
- [ ] Type **3** on the command line and hit the *Enter* key. A circle having a radius of 3" will be drawn to the right of and tangent to both circles.
- [ ] Activate the *Circle* command by clicking on the *Circle* button.
- [ ] Type **T** on the command line to accept the tan, tan, radius option, and hit the *Enter* key.
- [ ] Move the mouse pointer to the lower left part (somewhere between 180° and 270°) on the bottom small circle you drew. When the *Tangent* snap marker appears, click the mouse button.
- [ ] Move the mouse pointer to the upper left part (somewhere between 90° and 180°) on the top small circle you drew. When the *Tangent* snap marker appears, click the mouse button to select the second point of tangency.
- [ ] Type **3** on the command line (or accept the default value from the last circle you drew) and hit the *Enter* key. A circle having a radius of 3" will be drawn tangent to both circles. Notice that this circle contains the original two circles.
- [ ] Activate the *Circle* command by clicking on the *Circle* button.
- [ ] Type **T** on the command line to accept the tan, tan, radius option, and hit the *Enter* key.

Figure 6-5
Tangencies

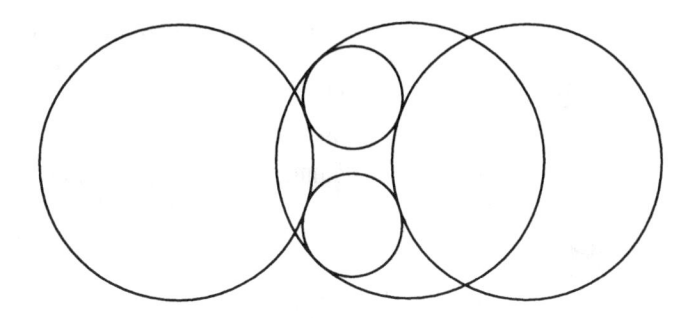

☐ Move the mouse pointer to the upper left part (somewhere between 90° and 180°) on the bottom small circle you drew. When the *Tangent* snap marker appears, click the mouse button.

☐ Move the mouse pointer to the lower left part (somewhere between 180° and 270°) on the top small circle you drew. When the *Tangent* snap marker appears, click the mouse button to select the second point of tangency.

☐ Type **3** on the command line (or accept the default value from the last circle you drew) and hit the *Enter* key. A circle having a radius of 3″ will be drawn tangent to both circles, but this time the circle opens to the left with the smaller circles outside.

☐ Compare your screen with Figure 6-5. If they are not the same, you need to go back and repeat this section until you can do it right.

Drawing Two- and Three-Point Circles

Sometimes the location of the center of a circle and its diameter are not important. It may be necessary to draw a circle based on the location of other objects.

☐ Again things are getting cluttered. Use *Erase ALL* to clear the screen.

☐ For this section you will draw four lines. Using the *Line* command and absolute coordinates draw the following individual lines. (They will not be connected.) When you are done your screen should look like Figure 6-6.

  a) From 3,4 to 4,4
  b) From 5,4 to 6,4
  c) From 8,3 to 9,2
  d) From 8,6 to 9,7

In this first part you will use the two-point option to draw a circle between the two horizontal lines you drew above.

Figure 6-6
Lines used for drawing two- and three-point circles

☐ Activate the *Circle* command by clicking on the *Circle* button.

Command:
Command:
Command: _circle Specify center point for circle or [3P/2P/Ttr (tan tan radius)]:

☐ Type **2P** on the command line to accept the two-point option, and hit the *Enter* key.

Command:
Command: _circle Specify center point for circle or [3P/2P/Ttr (tan tan radius)]: 2P
Specify first endpoint of circle's diameter:

☐ Click on the *Endpoint* snap button. Select the right end of the left horizontal line and click the mouse button to select the point.

Command: _circle Specify center point for circle or [3P/2P/Ttr (tan tan radius)]: T
Specify first endpoint of circle's diameter: _endp of
Specify second endpoint of circle's diameter:

☐ Click the *Endpoint* snap again, select the left end of the right horizontal line, and click the mouse button. The circle will be drawn with its diameter between the two lines and the *Circle* command will end.

In this section, you will draw a circle based on the endpoints of three lines.

☐ Activate the *Circle* command by clicking on the *Circle* button.
☐ Type **3P** on the command line to accept the three-point option, and hit the *Enter* key.
☐ Click on the *Endpoint* snap button. Select the right end of the right horizontal line and click the mouse button to select the point.
☐ Click the *Endpoint* snap again, select the lower end of the top angled line, and click the mouse button.
☐ Click the *Endpoint* snap a third time, select the upper end of the bottom angled line, and click the mouse button. The circle will be drawn so that its edge touches each of the three lines.
☐ Compare your screen with Figure 6-7. If they are not the same, you need to go back and repeat this section until you can do it right.

Figure 6-7
Completed figure

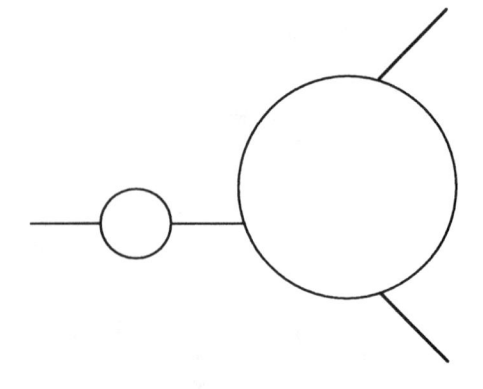

Drawing Curved Shapes 149

Drawing a Line Tangent to a Circle

Sometimes you need to draw a line that is tangent to a circle. In the next part, you will draw two lines that are tangent to both circles.

- ☐ Click on the *Line* button on the *Draw* toolbar to activate the *Line* command.
- ☐ Use Figure 6-8 to help you locate and click on the *Tangent* snap button located on the *Object Snap* toolbar.
- ☐ Move the mouse pointer to the upper left part (somewhere between 90° and 180°) on the larger circle. When the *Tangent* snap marker appears, click the mouse button. You will not see the line appear at this time because AutoCAD does not yet know exactly where the line will start.
- ☐ Click on the *Tangent* snap button again.
- ☐ Move the mouse pointer to the upper left part (somewhere between 90° and 180°) on the smaller circle. When the *Tangent* snap marker appears, click the mouse button. The line will be drawn tangent to both circles.
- ☐ Hit the *Enter* key to end the *Line* command.
- ☐ Click on the *Line* button on the *Draw* toolbar to activate the *Line* command.
- ☐ Click on the *Tangent* snap button located on the *Object Snap* toolbar.
- ☐ Move the mouse pointer to the lower left part (somewhere between 180° and 270°) on the smaller circle. When the *Tangent* snap marker appears, click the mouse button.
- ☐ Click on the *Tangent* snap button.
- ☐ Move the mouse pointer to the lower left part (somewhere between 180° and 270°) on the larger circle. When the *Tangent* snap marker appears, click the mouse button. The line will be drawn tangent to both circles.
- ☐ Hit the *Enter* key to end the *Line* command.
- ☐ Compare your screen with Figure 6-9. If they are not the same, you need to go back and repeat this section until you can do it right.

Using the *Center* Snap

Another snap tool that is useful is the *Center* snap. This snap allows you to snap to the center of a circle or arc. This section will show you how to use this snap.

- ☐ Click on the *Line* button.
- ☐ Use Figure 6-10 to locate and click on the *Center* snap button located on the *Object Snap* toolbar.

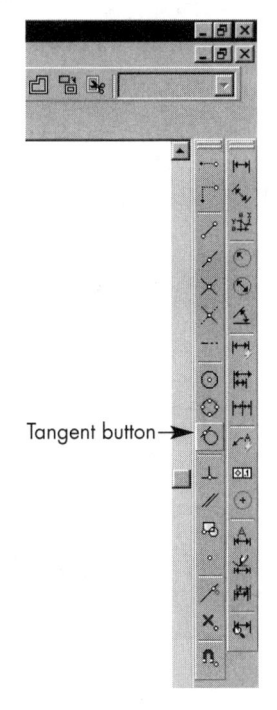

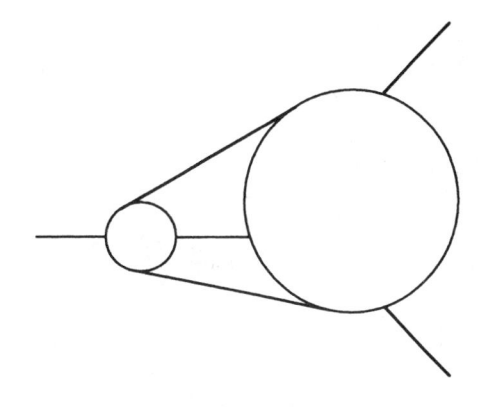

Figure 6-8
The *Tangent* button is located on the *Object Snap* toolbar.

Figure 6-9
Completed figure

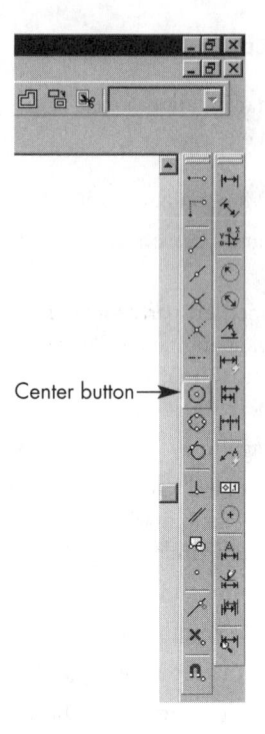

Figure 6-10
The *Center* button is located on the *Object Snap* toolbar.

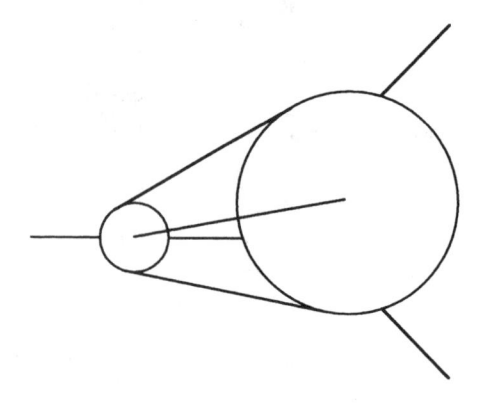

Figure 6-11
Completed figure

☐ Move the mouse pointer around the screen to get an idea of how the *Center* snap marker is activated. You will see that being near the circle or being near the center of the circle activates the marker.

☐ Move the mouse to the center of the larger circle. When the *Center* snap marker appears, click the mouse button.

☐ Click on the *Center* snap button again and move the mouse to the center of the smaller circle. When the *Center* snap marker appears, click the mouse button. A line will be drawn between the two centers.

☐ Hit the *Enter* key to end the *Line* command. Your drawing should look like Figure 6-11.

Using the *Quadrant* Snap

The *Quadrant* snap allows you to snap to each of the four quadrants of a circle. Quadrants are defined as the 0°, 90°, 180°, and 270° points on a circle, as based on the current user coordinate system (UCS). In this part you will draw lines between each of the four quadrants of the larger circle.

☐ Click on the *Line* button.

☐ Use Figure 6-12 to locate and click on the *Quadrant* snap button on the *Object Snap* toolbar.

☐ Move the mouse cursor to the right side of the large circle at the 0° location. A diamond that represents the *Quadrant* snap will appear. When the marker appears, click the mouse button to start the line.

☐ Click on the *Quadrant* snap button.

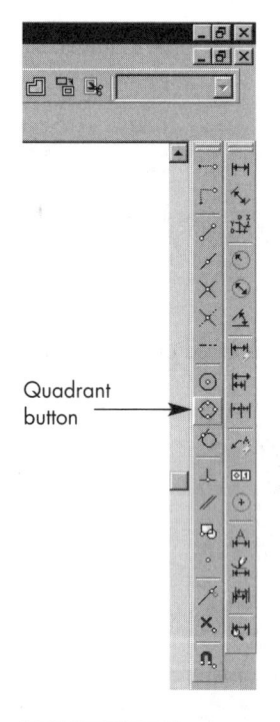

Figure 6-12
The *Quadrant* button is located on the *Object Snap* toolbar.

Figure 6-13
Completed figure

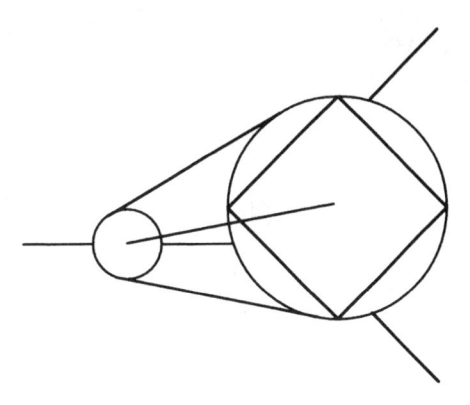

- [ ] Move the mouse cursor to the top of the large circle at 90°. When the *Quadrant* marker appears, click the mouse button.
- [ ] Click on the *Quadrant* snap button.
- [ ] Move the mouse cursor to the left side of the large circle at 180°. When the *Quadrant* marker appears, click the mouse button.
- [ ] Click on the *Quadrant* snap button.
- [ ] Move the mouse cursor to the bottom of the large circle at 270°. When the *Quadrant* marker appears, click the mouse button.
- [ ] Type **C** on the command and hit the *Enter* key to close the figure. Your drawing should look like Figure 6-13.
- [ ] This completes this activity. You should spend some time practicing what you learned in this activity. When you are done, close the AutoCAD program.

Assignment
for Module 6 – Activity 1

Procedure: ☑ Check each box as you complete that item.

- [ ] Start *AutoCAD 2002*.
- [ ] When the *AutoCAD 2002 Today* dialog box appears, open the drawing *M06A01-2.dwg* located in the *Module06* subdirectory on the CD.
- [ ] For this assignment you will draw the four groups of objects shown in Figure 6-14 using the methods learned in this and previous activities. Start each group at the points shown in the figure.
- [ ] The larger circles are 2" in diameter and the smaller circles are 1" in diameter. You must place the objects relative to each other based on the dimensions shown on the drawing. Do not include any of the dimensions or dimension lines on your drawing, only the lines and circles.
- [ ] The lengths of the two lines that form a 45° angle are not important as long as they extend past their tangency points with the circle.

In Module 5 you learned how to use the *Pan* command. In the following steps you will use this command to center the objects you drew on the drawing paper. It is important that you follow the steps carefully. DO NOT use the *Zoom* command during these steps or the finished drawing will not be to scale, and that is unacceptable for engineering drawings.

Figure 6-14

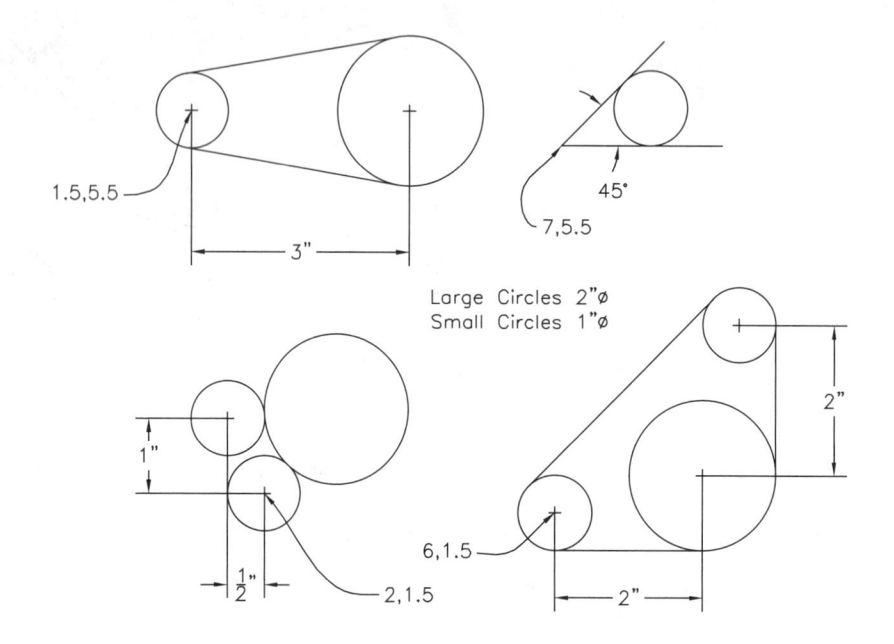

- ☐ When you have drawn the figure, click on the *A-size Sheet* tab to go to paper space. You will see the objects you drew inside the blue rectangle on the paper, but they are probably not centered inside the rectangle.
- ☐ Look at the *Drawing Features* buttons on the *Status* bar. The last button says *Paper* for paper space. Click on this button. It will change to read *Model* and the blue rectangle on the paper will thicken. You are now in model space working through a "hole" in the paper. The blue rectangle represents the hole.
- ☐ Click on the *Pan* button, and move the cursor to the center of the drawing area. The cursor will now appear as a hand. Press and hold the left mouse button and move the figure around the area. You will notice that when parts of the figure get past the edges of the blue rectangle they can no longer be seen.
- ☐ Move the figure you drew so that it is centered in the blue rectangle. It will also be centered on the paper. Hit the *Enter* key to end the *Pan* command. Be careful not to use the *Zoom* command during this operation.
- ☐ **Don't miss this step!** Click on the *Model* button on the *Status* bar to change back to paper space. The blue line will get thinner. You are now back working on the piece of paper and are ready to print the drawing.
- ☐ Save the drawing to your removable disk with the name M06A01-2.
- ☐ Print a copy of your drawing.
- ☐ Neatly print your name and the date in the appropriate spaces in the title block.

Activity 2

Drawing Arcs

Objectives: After completing this activity, you should be able to do the following:

- Locate and use the *Arc* button on the *Draw* toolbar.
- Draw an arc through three points.
- Draw an arc based on a start point, a center point, and an endpoint.
- Draw an arc based on a start point, a center point, and an angle.
- Draw an arc based on a start point, a center point, and a chord length.
- Draw an arc based on a start point, an endpoint, and a radius.
- Continue an arc from a previously drawn arc or line.

Procedure: ☑ Check each box as you complete that item.

☐ Start *AutoCAD 2002*.

☐ When the *AutoCAD 2002 Today* dialog box appears, open the drawing *M06A02-1.dwg* located in the *Module06* subdirectory on the CD.

☐ Make sure that all the *Drawing Features* buttons, except for the *Model* button, on the *Status* bar are off.

Drawing an Arc

In this section you will learn how to draw an arc based on different variables such as endpoints, center point, and radius. Arcs are commonly found on drawings where they usually represent curved surfaces. Figure 6-15 shows some of the terms you need to know that are used with arcs.

☐ To prepare for this activity, you need to draw a few lines to act as snap points. Using the *Line* command and absolute coordinates, draw the following individual lines. (They will not be connected.) When you are done, your screen should look like Figure 6-16 without the letters. The letters represent locations to be used as snap points for constructing arcs. You should refer to this figure as you work through this activity.

	From	To		From	To
a)	0,5	1,5	i)	6,3	6,5
b)	2,6	2,7	j)	6,2	6,1
c)	3,5	4,5	k)	9,7	9,6
d)	.5,1.5	1,2	l)	9,5	9,4
e)	2,2	2,3	m)	9,3	9,2
f)	3,2	3.5,1.5	n)	10.25,7	10.25,6
g)	5.25,6	5.25,7	o)	10.25,6.5	11,6.5
h)	6.75,6	6.75,7	p)	10.25,5	10.25,4

Figure 6-15
Terms associated with arcs

Figure 6-16
Your screen should look like this, without the letters, when you are done.

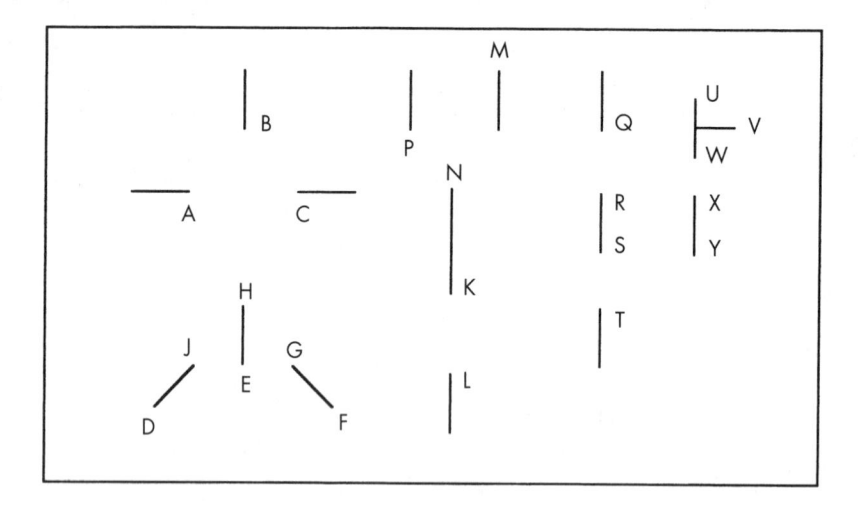

Drawing a Three-Point Arc

Three-point arcs are drawn using a starting point, second point, and endpoint, as shown in Figure 6-17.

☐ Use Figure 6-18 to help you locate and click on the *Arc* button on the *Draw* toolbar.

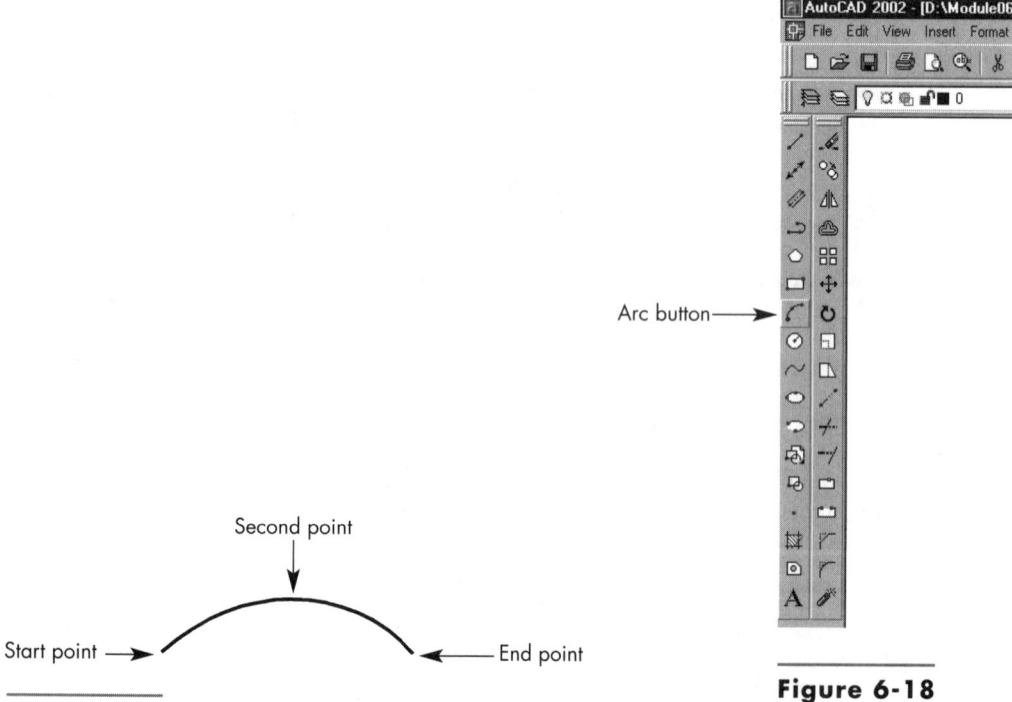

Figure 6-17
Draw an arc using three points.

Figure 6-18
The Arc button is located on the *Draw* toolbar.

Command:

Command:

Command: _arc Specify start point of arc or [Center]:

☐ Click on the *Endpoint* button on the *Object Snap* toolbar. Move the cursor to point A, shown in Figure 6-16. When the *Endpoint* snap marker appears, click the mouse button.

Command:

Command: _arc Specify start point of arc or [Center]:_endp of

Specify second point of arc or [Center/End]:

☐ Click on the *Endpoint* button on the *Object Snap* toolbar. Move the cursor to point B. When the *Endpoint* snap marker appears, click the mouse button.

Command: _arc Specify start point of arc or [Center]:_endp of

Specify second point of arc or [Center/End]: _endp of

Specify end point of arc:

☐ You have now drawn two of the three points. The arc now appears on the screen attached to the mouse cursor. Before placing the next point, move the cursor around the screen to see how the arc reacts. Make sure you check all directions; above, below, to the left, and to the right of the second point.

☐ Click on the *Endpoint* button on the *Object Snap* toolbar. Move the cursor to point C. When the *Endpoint* snap marker appears, click the mouse button. The arc is now complete and the *Arc* command ends.

☐ For additional practice, place a second three-point arc using the other end of each of the three lines as the snap points.

Drawing an Arc Using Start, Center, and End Points

The three points for this arc are shown in Figure 6-19.

☐ Click on the *Arc* button.

Command:

Command:

Command: _arc Specify start point of arc or [Center]:

☐ Click on the *Endpoint* button. Move the cursor to point D. When the *Endpoint* snap marker appears, click the mouse button.

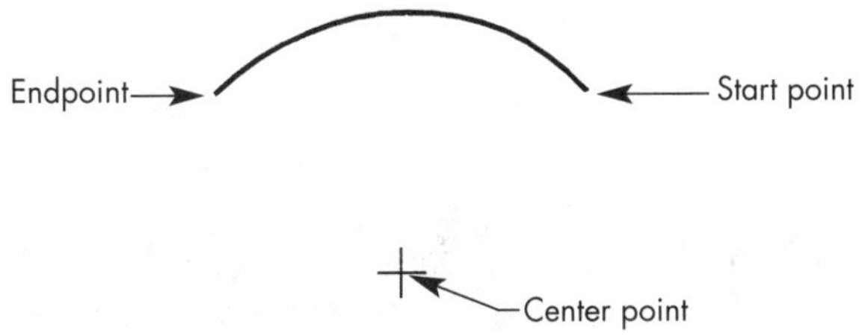

Figure 6-19
Draw an arc using endpoints and a center point.

Command:
Command: _arc Specify start point of arc or [Center]:_endp of
Specify second point of arc or [Center/End]:

☐ A look at the command line shows that you have three options at this point. Type **C** on the command line to activate the *Center* option and hit the *Enter* key.

Command: _arc Specify start point of arc or [Center]:_endp of
Specify second point of arc or [Center/End]: CE
Specify center point of arc:

☐ Click on the *Endpoint* button. Move the cursor to point E. When the *Endpoint* snap marker appears, click the mouse button.

Specify second point of arc or [Center/End]: CE
Specify center point of arc or: _end of
Specify end point of arc or [Angle/chord Length]:

☐ Click on the *Endpoint* button. Move the cursor to point F. When the *Endpoint* snap marker appears, click the mouse button. The arc will be drawn between points D and F, with its center at E.

Note that the arc is drawn counterclockwise between the two points. Since this type of arc is always drawn counterclockwise, it is very important that you choose your starting and ending points correctly. Reversing the two points will give you a completely different arc. In the next part you will draw another arc starting with a point on the right and ending with a point on the left.

☐ Click on the *Arc* button.

Command:
Command:
Command: _arc Specify start point of arc or [Center]:

☐ Click on the *Endpoint* button. Move the cursor to point G. When the *Endpoint* snap marker appears, click the mouse button.

Command:
Command: _arc Specify start point of arc or [Center]:_endp of
Specify second point of arc or [Center/End]:

☐ Type **C** on the command line to activate the *Center* option and hit the *Enter* key.

Command: _arc Specify start point of arc or [Center]:_endp of
Specify second point of arc or [Center/End]: CE
Specify center point of arc:

☐ Click on the *Endpoint* button. Move the cursor to point H. When the *Endpoint* snap marker appears, click the mouse button.

Specify second point of arc or [Center/End]: C
Specify center point of arc or: _end of
Specify end point of arc or [Angle/chord Length]:

Drawing Curved Shapes 157

☐ Click on the *Endpoint* button. Move the cursor to point J. When the *Endpoint* snap marker appears, click the mouse button. The arc will be drawn between points G and J, with its center at H.

For additional practice, and to prove that an arc is drawn counterclockwise, draw an arc starting at J, ending at G, and having a center at H. When you are satisfied with the results, erase this arc.

Drawing an Arc Using Start, Center, and Angle

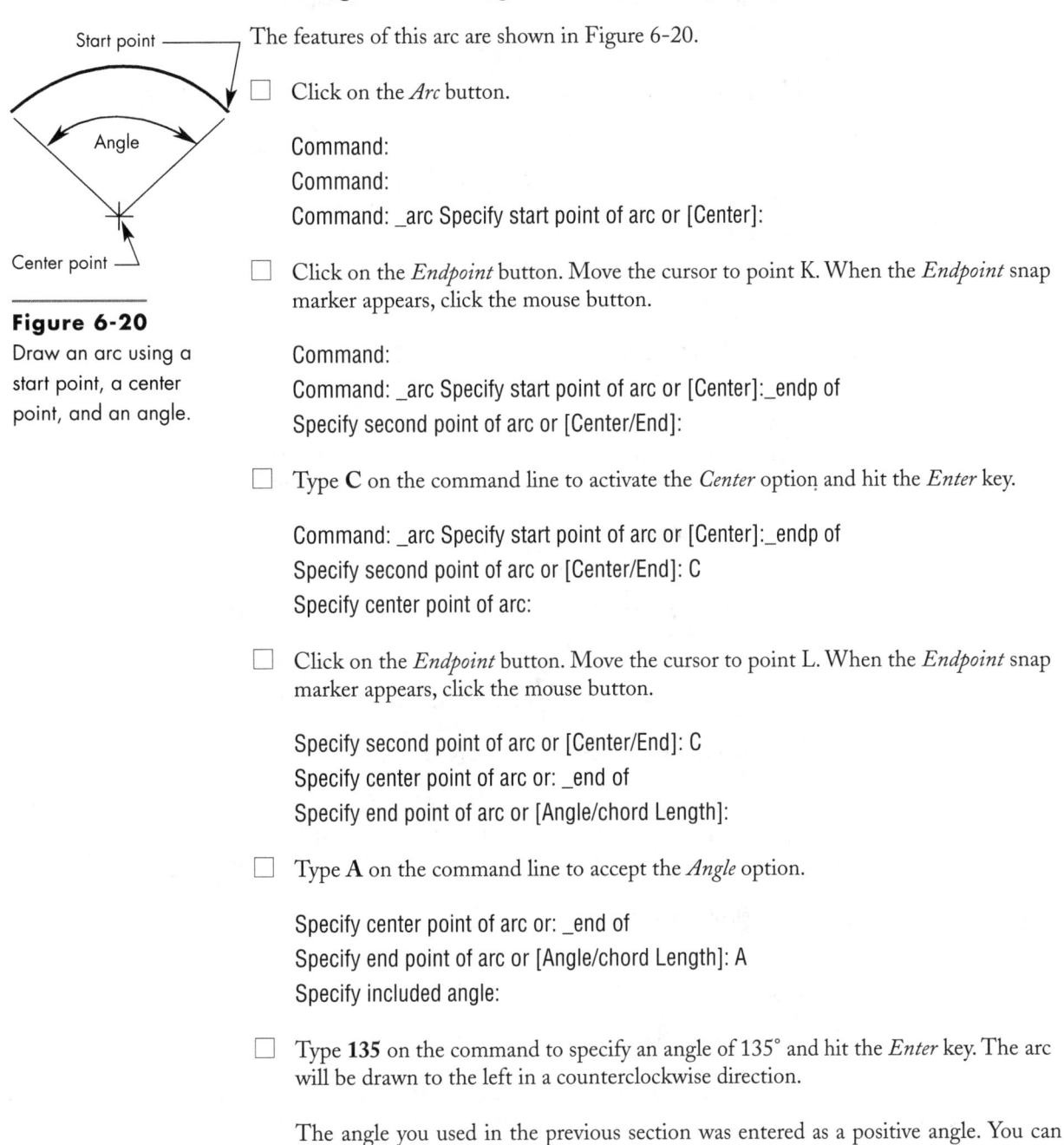

The features of this arc are shown in Figure 6-20.

☐ Click on the *Arc* button.

Command:
Command:
Command: _arc Specify start point of arc or [Center]:

☐ Click on the *Endpoint* button. Move the cursor to point K. When the *Endpoint* snap marker appears, click the mouse button.

Command:
Command: _arc Specify start point of arc or [Center]:_endp of
Specify second point of arc or [Center/End]:

☐ Type **C** on the command line to activate the *Center* option and hit the *Enter* key.

Command: _arc Specify start point of arc or [Center]:_endp of
Specify second point of arc or [Center/End]: C
Specify center point of arc:

☐ Click on the *Endpoint* button. Move the cursor to point L. When the *Endpoint* snap marker appears, click the mouse button.

Specify second point of arc or [Center/End]: C
Specify center point of arc or: _end of
Specify end point of arc or [Angle/chord Length]:

☐ Type **A** on the command line to accept the *Angle* option.

Specify center point of arc or: _end of
Specify end point of arc or [Angle/chord Length]: A
Specify included angle:

☐ Type **135** on the command to specify an angle of 135° and hit the *Enter* key. The arc will be drawn to the left in a counterclockwise direction.

The angle you used in the previous section was entered as a positive angle. You can also specify a negative angle to draw an arc in a clockwise direction. This is explained in the next section.

☐ Click on the *Arc* button.

Figure 6-20
Draw an arc using a start point, a center point, and an angle.

Command:
Command:
Command: _arc Specify start point of arc or [Center]:

☐ Click on the *Endpoint* button. Move the cursor to point K. When the *Endpoint* snap marker appears, click the mouse button.

Command:
Command: _arc Specify start point of arc or [Center]:_endp of
Specify second point of arc or [Center/End]:

☐ Type **C** on the command line to activate the *Center* option and hit the *Enter* key.

Command: _arc Specify start point of arc or [Center]:_endp of
Specify second point of arc or [Center/End]: C
Specify center point of arc:

☐ Click on the *Endpoint* button. Move the cursor to point L. When the *Endpoint* snap marker appears, click the mouse button.

Specify second point of arc or [Center/End]: C
Specify center point of arc or: _end of
Specify end point of arc or [Angle/chord Length]:

☐ Type **A** on the command line to accept the *Angle* option.

Specify center point of arc or: _end of
Specify end point of arc or [Angle/chord Length]: A
Specify included angle:

☐ Type **-135** on the command line to specify an angle of 135° in a clockwise direction and hit the *Enter* key. The arc will be drawn to the right of the starting point.

Drawing an Arc Using Start, Center, and Chord Length

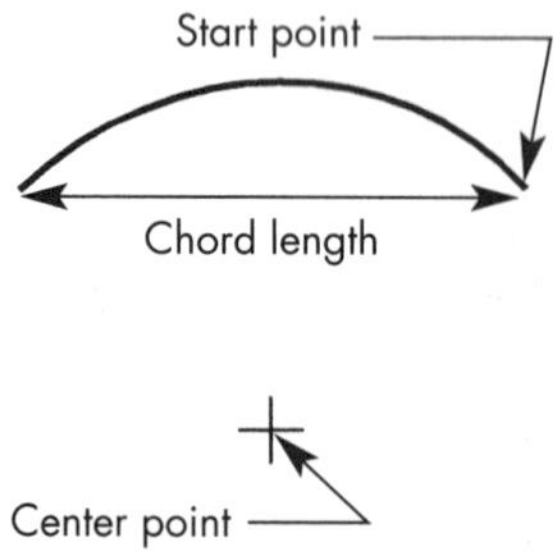

The features of this arc are shown in Figure 6-21. Notice that if you drew a line at right angles to the chord, through the center point, the chord would be bisected, with half the chord length on each side of the line.

☐ Click on the *Arc* button.

Command:
Command:
Command: _arc Specify start point of arc or [Center]:

☐ Click on the *Endpoint* button. Move the cursor to point M. When the *Endpoint* snap marker appears, click the mouse button.

Command:
Command: _arc Specify start point of arc or [Center]:_endp of
Specify second point of arc or [Center/End]:

Figure 6-21
Draw an arc using a start point, a center point, and a chord length.

Drawing Curved Shapes 159

☐ Type **C** on the command line to activate the *Center* option and hit the *Enter* key.

Command: _arc Specify start point of arc or [Center]:_endp of
Specify second point of arc or [Center/End]: C
Specify center point of arc:

☐ Click on the *Endpoint* button. Move the cursor to point N. When the *Endpoint* snap marker appears, click the mouse button.

Specify second point of arc or [Center/End]: C
Specify center point of arc or: _end of
Specify end point of arc or [Angle/chord Length]:

☐ Type **L** on the command line to accept the *Chord Length* option.

Specify center point of arc or: _end of
Specify end point of arc or [Angle/chord Length]: L
Specify length of chord:

☐ Type **1.5** on the command to specify a chord length of 1.5" toward the left and hit the *Enter* key. The arc will be drawn to the left of the starting point in a counter-clockwise direction. The 1.5" length was chosen so that the arc spans the two lines you drew earlier.

As with the other *Arc* commands, the angle is drawn in a positive direction. In the following section you will see the effect of entering a negative chord length.

☐ Click on the *Arc* button.

Command:
Command:
Command: _arc Specify start point of arc or [Center]:

☐ Click on the *Endpoint* button. Move the cursor to point P. When the *Endpoint* snap marker appears, click the mouse button.

Command:
Command: _arc Specify start point of arc or [Center]:_endp of
Specify second point of arc or [Center/End]:

☐ Type **C** on the command line to activate the *Center* option and hit the *Enter* key.

Command: _arc Specify start point of arc or [Center]:_endp of
Specify second point of arc or [Center/End]: C
Specify center point of arc:

☐ Click on the *Endpoint* button. Move the cursor to point N. When the *Endpoint* snap marker appears, click the mouse button.

Specify second point of arc or [Center/End]: C
Specify center point of arc or: _end of
Specify end point of arc or [Angle/chord Length]:

160 Module 6

☐ Type **L** on the command line to accept the *Chord Length* option.

Specify center point of arc or: _end of
Specify end point of arc or [Angle/chord Length]: L
Specify length of chord:

☐ Type **-1.5** on the command to specify a chord length of 1.5″ toward the right and hit the *Enter* key. The arc will be drawn to the right of the starting point. The 1.5″ length was chosen so that the arc spans the two lines you drew earlier.

Drawing an Arc Using Start, End, and Radius

The features of this arc are shown in Figure 6-22. This type of arc can be drawn without knowing the location of the center point. Like the other arcs, the sign (±) of the radius produces a different arc. However, with this option the positive radius gives the smallest possible arc and the negative radius gives the largest arc. The two arcs will be demonstrated in the following steps. As with all arcs, they will always be drawn counterclockwise, so the starting and ending points are very important.

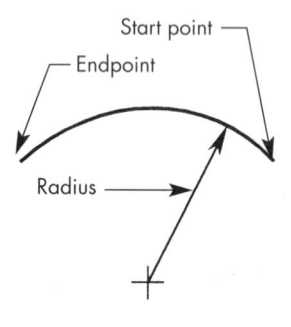

Figure 6-22
Draw an arc using a start point, an endpoint, and a radius.

☐ Click on the *Arc* button.

Command:
Command:
Command: _arc Specify start point of arc or [Center]:

☐ Click on the *Endpoint* button. Move the cursor to point Q. When the *Endpoint* snap marker appears, click the mouse button.

Command:
Command: _arc Specify start point of arc or [Center]:_endp of
Specify second point of arc or [Center/End]:

☐ Type **E** on the command line to activate the *Endpoint* option and hit the *Enter* key.

Command: _arc Specify start point of arc or [Center]:_endp of
Specify second point of arc or [Center/End]: E
Specify end point of arc:

☐ Click on the *Endpoint* button. Move the cursor to point R. When the *Endpoint* snap marker appears, click the mouse button.

Specify second point of arc or [Center/End]: E
Specify end point of arc or: _end of
Specify center point of arc or [Angle/Direction/Radius]:

☐ Type **R** on the command line to accept the *Radius* option.

Specify end point of arc or: _end of
Specify center point of arc or [Angle/Direction/Radius]: R
Specify radius of arc:

☐ Type **.75** on the command line to specify a radius of .75″ and hit the *Enter* key. The arc will be drawn to the left of the starting point.

The next section will show the results of using a negative radius. When you are finished with this section, compare the two arcs.

☐ Click on the *Arc* button.

Command:
Command:
Command: _arc Specify start point of arc or [Center]:

☐ Click on the *Endpoint* button. Move the cursor to point S. When the *Endpoint* snap marker appears, click the mouse button.

Command:
Command: _arc Specify start point of arc or [Center]:_endp of
Specify second point of arc or [Center/End]:

☐ Type **E** on the command line to activate the *Endpoint* option and hit the *Enter* key.

Command: _arc Specify start point of arc or [Center]:_endp of
Specify second point of arc or [Center/End]: E
Specify end point of arc:

☐ Click on the *Endpoint* button. Move the cursor to point T. When the *Endpoint* snap marker appears, click the mouse button.

Specify second point of arc or [Center/End]: E
Specify end point of arc or: _end of
Specify center point of arc or [Angle/Direction/Radius]:

☐ Type **R** on the command line to accept the *Radius* option.

Specify end point of arc or: _end of
Specify center point of arc or [Angle/Direction/Radius]: R
Specify radius of arc:

☐ Type **-.75** on the command to specify a radius of .75″ and hit the *Enter* key. The arc will be drawn to the left of the starting point but is a larger arc than the one drawn above.

Continuing an Arc from a Previous Arc

It is possible to draw one arc and then continue with a second arc that starts at the end of the first. When continuing an arc, the transition between the two arcs will always be smooth and tangent. The features of the *Continue* operation are shown in Figure 6-23. When doing this section, notice the smooth transitions between the arcs.

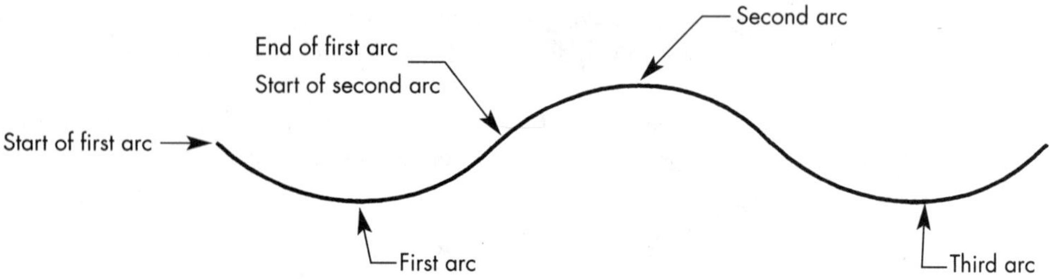

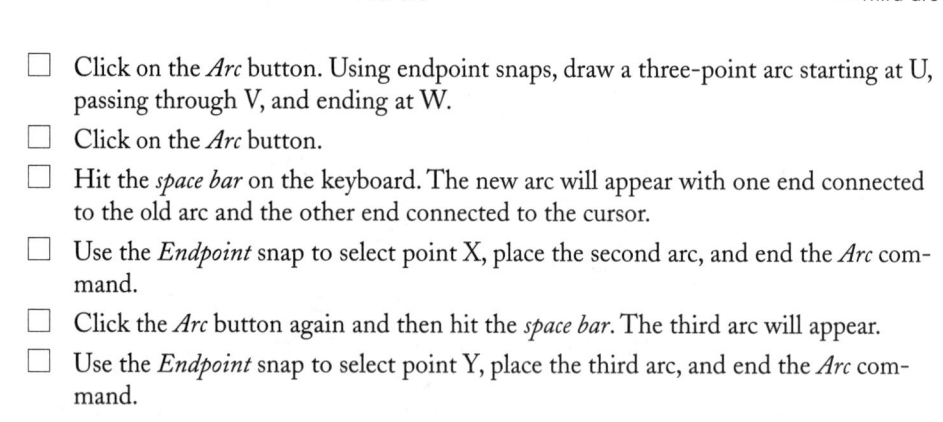

Figure 6-23
Continuing an arc from a previous arc

- ☐ Click on the *Arc* button. Using endpoint snaps, draw a three-point arc starting at U, passing through V, and ending at W.
- ☐ Click on the *Arc* button.
- ☐ Hit the *space bar* on the keyboard. The new arc will appear with one end connected to the old arc and the other end connected to the cursor.
- ☐ Use the *Endpoint* snap to select point X, place the second arc, and end the *Arc* command.
- ☐ Click the *Arc* button again and then hit the *space bar*. The third arc will appear.
- ☐ Use the *Endpoint* snap to select point Y, place the third arc, and end the *Arc* command.

Continuing an Arc from a Previous Line

It is possible to draw an arc starting at the end of a line as shown in Figure 6-24.

- ☐ Click on the *Line* button and draw a line from point (9.75,2.75) to (9.75,1.25). When done, hit the *Enter* key to complete the *Line* command.
- ☐ Click on the *Arc* button and then hit the *space bar*. The arc will appear with one end attached to the end of the line and the other end attached to the cursor.
- ☐ Type **@1<0** on the command line and hit the *Enter* key. The arc will be placed on the drawing and the *Arc* command will end.

The *Continue* function also works with lines.

- ☐ Click on the *Line* button and hit the *space bar*. A line appears attached to the end of the arc you just drew.
- ☐ Type **@1.5<90** on the command line and hit the *Enter* key twice. The line will be placed on the drawing and the *Line* command will end.
- ☐ Click on the *Arc* button and then hit the *space bar*. Another arc will appear with one end attached to the end of the second line.
- ☐ Type **9.75,2.75** on the command line and hit the *Enter* key. The arc will be placed on the drawing. This will complete the figure. You should have a "racetrack"-shaped oval.

Note that in the previous instructions, absolute, relative, and polar coordinates were used to place the lines and arcs. You will find that each of these methods of specifying

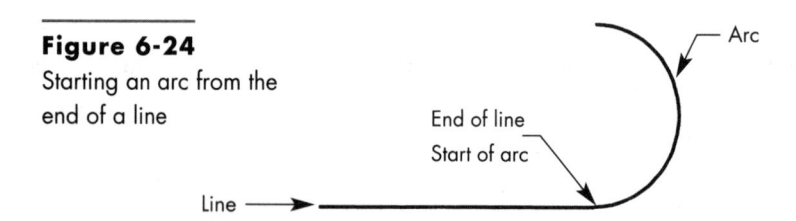

Figure 6-24
Starting an arc from the end of a line

Drawing Curved Shapes 163

points and directions is used often. It is very important that you practice using them so that you can become efficient as an AutoCAD operator.

alternate method

You can start the *Arc* command by clicking on the *Draw* pull-down menu and selecting one of the methods for drawing an arc from the *Arc* cascading menu. You can also type **ARC,** or just **A,** on the command line and hit the *Enter* key.

☐ This completes this activity. You should spend some time practicing what you learned in this activity. When you are done, close the AutoCAD program.

Assignment
for Module 6 − Activity 2

Procedure: ☑ Check each box as you complete that item.

☐ Start *AutoCAD 2002*.

☐ When the *AutoCAD 2002 Today* dialog box appears, open the drawing *M06A02-2.dwg* located in the *Module06* subdirectory on the CD.

☐ For this assignment you will draw the two objects shown in Figure 6-25 using the methods learned in this and previous activities. Position the two objects based on the coordinates of the points shown in the figure.

☐ Follow the dimensions shown for each object. Do not include any of the dimensions or dimension lines on your drawing, only the lines, arcs, and circles.

☐ *Typical*, which is abbreviated (TYP.) on the drawing, indicates that all similar items on that object are the same. For example, if a circle is marked 2"Ø (TYP.), then all circles on that part are 2" in diameter unless noted otherwise.

☐ When you have completed the figure, click on the *A-size Sheet* tab. You will see the objects you drew inside the blue rectangle on the paper, but they are probably not centered inside the rectangle.

☐ As you did in the previous activities, center the objects on the paper by changing to model space, using the *Pan* command, and then changing back to

Figure 6-25

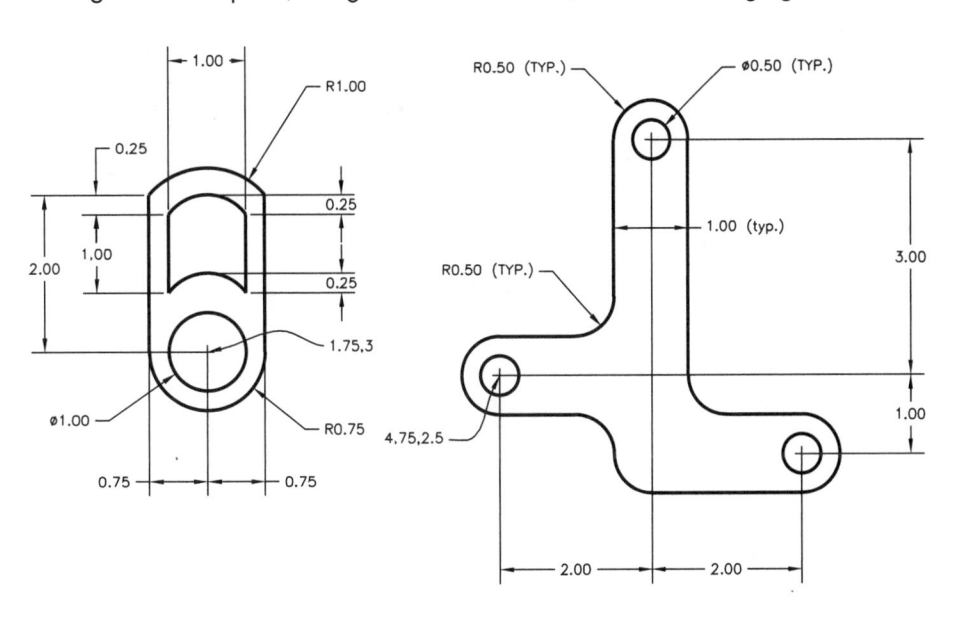

paper space. Be careful not to use the *Zoom* command during this operation. If you are unsure of how to do this, refer to the Assignment for Module 6 – Activity 1.
- ☐ Save the drawing to your removable disk with the name M06A02-2.
- ☐ Print a copy of your drawing.
- ☐ Neatly print your name and the date in the appropriate spaces in the title block.

Activity 3

Drawing Ellipses

Objectives: After completing this activity, you should be able to do the following:

- Locate and use the *Ellipse* button on the *Draw* toolbar.
- Draw an ellipse based on a center point and the major or minor axis.
- Draw an ellipse based on a center point and a rotation angle.
- Draw an elliptical arc.

When you look at a circle at an angle, you see an ellipse. Ellipses are often drawn in engineering drawings because holes or other round objects that are circles may lay on an angled surface and therefore would not appear on the drawing as circles. In this activity you will learn how to draw ellipses and elliptical arcs.

The features of an ellipse are shown in Figure 6-26. The major axis will always be the longest axis and the minor axis will always be the shortest.

Procedure: ☑ Check each box as you complete that item.

- ☐ Start *AutoCAD 2002*.
- ☐ When the *AutoCAD 2002 Today* dialog box appears, open the drawing *M06A03-1.dwg* located in the *Module06* subdirectory on the CD.
- ☐ Make sure that all the *Drawing Features* buttons on the *Status* bar, except for the *Model* button, are off.
- ☐ To prepare for this activity, you need to draw a few lines to act as snap points. Using the *Line* command and absolute coordinates, draw the following individual lines. (They will not be connected.) When you are done, your screen should look like Figure 6-27 without the letters. The letters represent locations that will be used as snap points for constructing ellipses. You should refer to this figure as you go through this activity.

	From	To		From	To
a)	0,6	3,6	e)	7,6	10,6
b)	1.5,7	1.5,5	f)	8.5,7	8.5,5
c)	0,2.5	3,2.5	g)	7,2.5	10,2.5
d)	1.5,3.5	1.5,1.5	h)	8.5,3.5	8.5,1.5

Figure 6-26
The major axis and minor axis of an ellipse

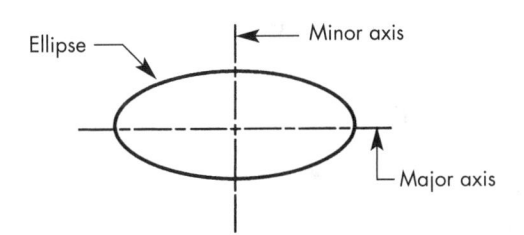

166 Module 6

Figure 6-27

Your screen should look like this, without the letters, when you are done.

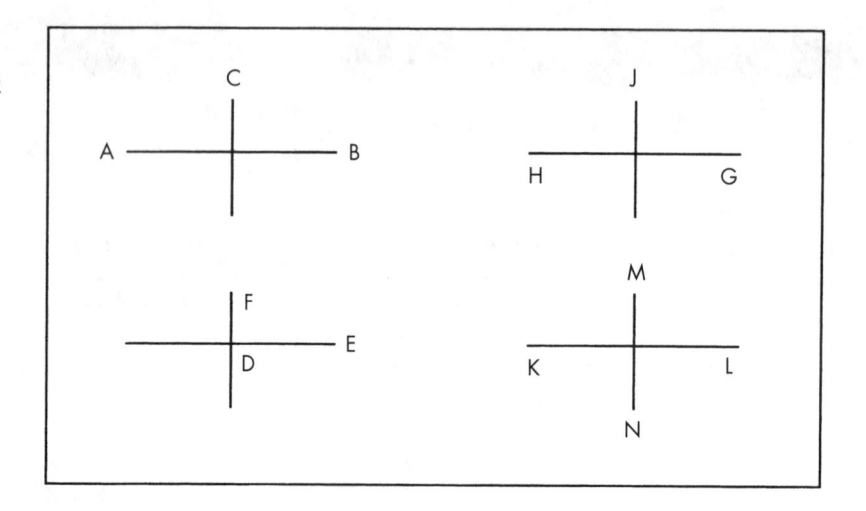

Drawing an Ellipse Using Three Axis Endpoints

In this section you will learn how to draw an ellipse based on the two endpoints along one axis and one endpoint along the other axis. These points are shown in Figure 6-28.

☐ Use Figure 6-29 to locate and click on the *Ellipse* button on the *Draw* toolbar.

Command:
Command: _ellipse
Specify axis endpoint of ellipse or [Arc/Center]:

☐ Click the *Endpoint* button located on the *Object Snap* toolbar. Move the cursor to point A (refer to Figure 6-27). When the *Endpoint* snap marker appears, click the mouse button. This selects the endpoint of the first axis.

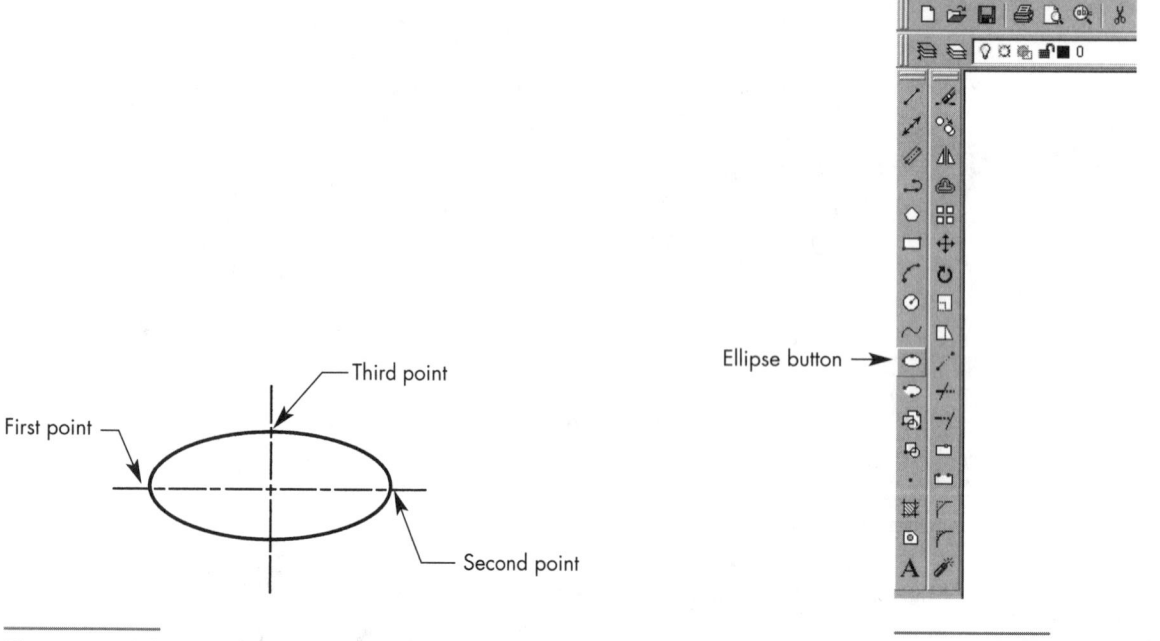

Figure 6-28

Ellipse drawn using three endpoints

Figure 6-29

The *Ellipse* button is located on the *Draw* toolbar.

Command: _ellipse
Specify axis endpoint of ellipse or [Arc/Center]: _endp of
Specify other endpoint of axis:

☐ A check of the command line shows that you must now specify the other end of the axis. Click on the *Endpoint* button. Move the cursor to point B. When the *Endpoint* snap marker appears, click the mouse button. This selects the second endpoint of the first axis.

Specify axis endpoint of ellipse or [Arc/Center]: _endp of
Specify other endpoint of axis: _endp of
Specify distance to other axis or [Rotation]:

☐ AutoCAD is now asking for the endpoint of the other axis. Click on the *Endpoint* button. Move the cursor to point C. When the *Endpoint* snap marker appears, click the mouse button. This selects the endpoint of the second axis and the ellipse is drawn.

It is always possible to place objects and specify distances on the drawing using coordinates instead of endpoints. In the next section, you will draw an ellipse using absolute and polar coordinates to locate the endpoints.

☐ Click on the *Ellipse* button.

Command:
Command: _ellipse
Specify axis endpoint of ellipse or [Arc/Center]:

☐ Type **3.5,7** on the command line and hit the *Enter* key. These absolute coordinates locate the first axis endpoint.

Command: _ellipse
Specify axis endpoint of ellipse or [Arc/Center]: 3.5,7
Specify other endpoint of axis:

☐ Type **6.5,7** on the command line and hit the *Enter* key. These absolute coordinates locate the second axis endpoint.

Specify axis endpoint of ellipse or [Arc/Center]: 3.5,7
Specify other endpoint of axis: 6.5,7
Specify distance to other axis or [Rotation]:

☐ Type **@.5<90** on the command line and hit the *Enter* key. These relative coordinates locate the endpoint of the second axis completing the ellipse.

Drawing an Ellipse Using the Center Point and the Axes Endpoints

In this section you will learn to draw an ellipse based on its center point and an endpoint of each axis. These points are shown in Figure 6-30.

☐ Click on the *Ellipse* button on the *Draw* toolbar.

Figure 6-30

Ellipse drawn using center and two endpoints

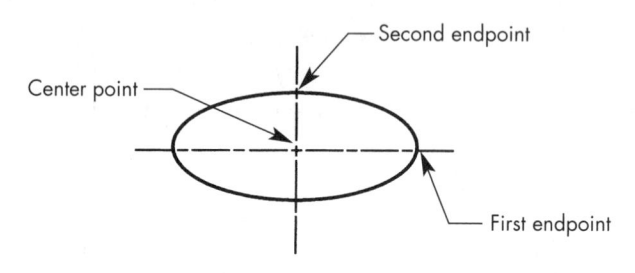

```
Command:
Command: _ellipse
Specify axis endpoint of ellipse or [Arc/Center]:
```

☐ Type **C** on the command line and hit the *Enter* key to accept the *Center* option.

```
Command: _ellipse
Specify axis endpoint of ellipse or [Arc/Center]: C
Specify center of ellipse:
```

☐ Locate and click the *Intersection* button on the *Object Snap* toolbar. Move the cursor to the intersection of the two axes. (See Figure 6-27.) When the *Intersection* snap marker appears, click the mouse button. This specifies the ellipse's center point.

```
Specify axis endpoint of ellipse or [Arc/Center]: C
Specify center of ellipse: _int of
Specify endpoint of axis:
```

☐ Click on the *Endpoint* button located on the *Object Snap* toolbar. Move the cursor to point E. When the *Endpoint* snap marker appears, click the mouse button.

```
Specify center of ellipse: _int of
Specify endpoint of axis: _endp of
Specify distance to other axis or [Rotation]:
```

☐ Click on the *Endpoint* button. Move the cursor to point F. When the *Endpoint* snap marker appears, click the mouse button and the ellipse will be drawn.

alternate method

You can also start the *Ellipse* command by clicking on the *Draw* pull-down menu, sliding the cursor to the *Ellipse* item, and selecting either *Center* or *Axis, End* from the cascading menu. You can also start the command by typing **ELLIPSE** on the command line and hitting the *Enter* key.

Drawing an Ellipse Based on Endpoints and Rotation

It is also possible to draw an ellipse based on the major axis and the angle the circle is rotated. This method is often used when the angle of rotation is known. Figure 6-31 shows the front and side views of a round object tilted at a 45° angle. To draw the ellipse based on endpoints, you need to know the length of the minor axis and the distance from the major axis to the endpoint of the minor axis. (The major axis is the circle's diameter.) This distance is not a difficult calculation if you know trigonometry, but the results of the calculation are approximate, not exact. To draw the ellipse using the rotation method, you just enter the major axis endpoints and the 45° angle.

Drawing Curved Shapes 169

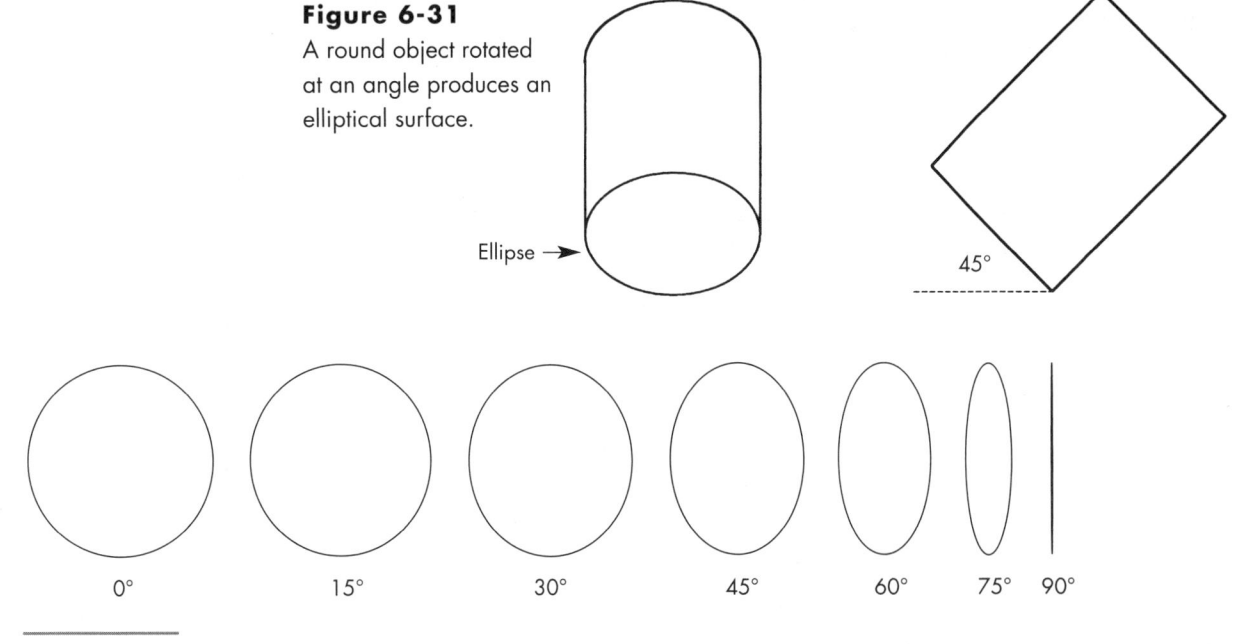

Figure 6-31
A round object rotated at an angle produces an elliptical surface.

0°   15°   30°   45°   60°   75°   90°

Figure 6-32
A circle rotated along an axis produces an ellipse.

Figure 6-32 gives you an indication of how an ellipse looks at different angles. (At 90° it is no longer an ellipse but a line.) In this section you will draw three ellipses having a major axis length of 2″ and rotated at 30°, 45°, and 60°.

☐ Click the *Ellipse* button.

Command:
Command: _ellipse
Specify axis endpoint of ellipse or [Arc/Center]:

☐ Type **4,5** on the command line and hit the *Enter* key to select the first endpoint of the major axis.

Command: _ellipse
Specify axis endpoint of ellipse or [Arc/Center]: 4,5
Specify other endpoint of axis:

☐ Type **6,5** on the command line and hit the *Enter* key to select the other endpoint of the major axis.

Specify axis endpoint of ellipse or [Arc/Center]: 4,5
Specify other endpoint of axis: 6,5
Specify distance to other axis or [Rotation]:

☐ Type **R** on the command line to select the *Rotation* option and hit the *Enter* key.

Specify other endpoint of axis: 6,5
Specify distance to other axis or [Rotation]: R
Specify rotation around major axis:

- ☐ Type **30** on the command line to specify a rotation angle of 30° and hit the *Enter* key. The ellipse will be drawn.
- ☐ Click on the *Ellipse* button.

    Command:
    Command: _ellipse
    Specify axis endpoint of ellipse or [Arc/Center]:

- ☐ Type **4,3** on the command line and hit the *Enter* key to select the first endpoint of the major axis.

    Command: _ellipse
    Specify axis endpoint of ellipse or [Arc/Center]: 4,3
    Specify other endpoint of axis:

- ☐ Type **6,3** on the command line and hit the *Enter* key to select the other endpoint of major axis.

    Specify axis endpoint of ellipse or [Arc/Center]: 4,3
    Specify other endpoint of axis: 6,3
    Specify distance to other axis or [Rotation]:

- ☐ Type **R** on the command line to select the *Rotation* option and hit the *Enter* key.

    Specify other endpoint of axis: 6,3
    Specify distance to other axis or [Rotation]: R
    Specify rotation around major axis:

- ☐ Type **45** on the command line to specify a rotation angle of 45° and hit the *Enter* key. The ellipse will be drawn.
- ☐ Click on the *Ellipse* button.

    Command:
    Command: _ellipse
    Specify axis endpoint of ellipse or [Arc/Center]:

- ☐ Type **4,1** on the command line and hit the *Enter* key to select the first endpoint of the major axis.

    Command: _ellipse
    Specify axis endpoint of ellipse or [Arc/Center]: 4,1
    Specify other endpoint of axis:

- ☐ Type **6,1** on the command line and hit the *Enter* key to select the other endpoint of the major axis.

    Specify axis endpoint of ellipse or [Arc/Center]: 4,1
    Specify other endpoint of axis: 6,1
    Specify distance to other axis or [Rotation]:

- ☐ Type **R** on the command line to select the *Rotation* option and hit the *Enter* key.

Specify other endpoint of axis: 6,1
Specify distance to other axis or [Rotation]: R
Specify rotation around major axis:

☐ Type **60** on the command line to specify a rotation angle of 60° and hit the *Enter* key. The ellipse will be drawn.

Drawing Elliptical Arcs

Often when you are drawing ellipses, you will also need to draw elliptical arcs. Figure 6-33 shows the elliptical arc formed by the rotation a cylindrical object.

Elliptical arcs are based on ellipses, so you must first specify the shape and the size of the ellipse, as you did previously, and then specify the part of the ellipse that will become the arc. When drawing elliptical arcs, you must consider where to start the major axis because all arcs are drawn counterclockwise and angles will be important. Although the ellipse drawn in this section will use three endpoints, you can make the ellipse using all the methods you learned in this activity.

☐ Use Figure 6-34 to locate and click on the *Ellipse Arc* button. The *Ellipse Arc* button was added in AutoCAD 2002. If you are using an earlier version of AutoCAD, you can still draw an elliptical arc by clicking the *Ellipse* button and then typing **A** on the command line to select the *Arc* option. If you look at the second command line in AutoCAD 2002, the *Arc* option is already there.

Command: _ellipse
Specify axis endpoint of ellipse or [Arc/Center]: _a
Specify axis endpoint of elliptical arc or [Center]:

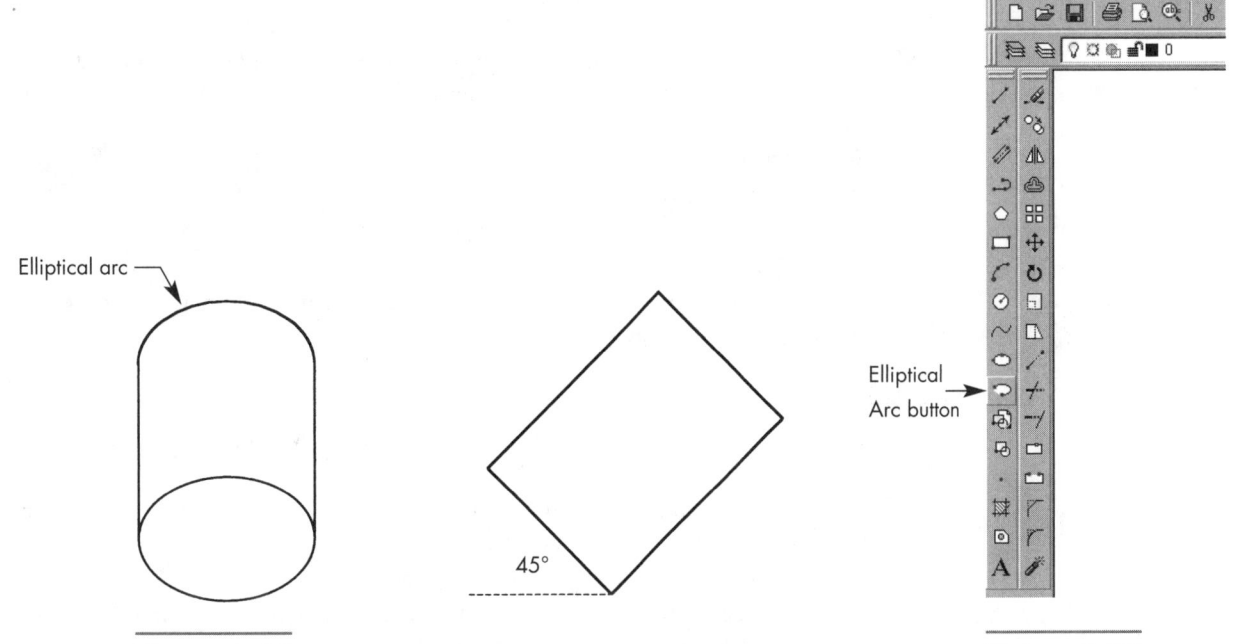

Figure 6-33
An elliptical arc is formed by rotating a cylindrical object.

Figure 6-34
The *Ellipse Arc* button is located on the *Draw* toolbar.

☐ Click the *Endpoint* button. Move the cursor to point G (refer to Figure 6-27). When the *Endpoint* snap marker appears, click the mouse button.

Specify axis endpoint of ellipse or [Arc/Center]: _a
Specify axis endpoint of ellipse or [Center]: _endp of
Specify other endpoint of axis:

☐ Click on the *Endpoint* button. Move the cursor to point H. When the *Endpoint* snap marker appears, click the mouse button.

Specify axis endpoint of elliptical arc or [Center]: _endp of
Specify other endpoint of axis: _endp of
Specify distance to other axis or [Rotation]:

☐ Click on the *Endpoint* button. Move the cursor to point J. When the *Endpoint* snap marker appears, click the mouse button. The ellipse is now complete and it is time to specify the starting and ending points of the arc.

Specify other endpoint of axis: _endp of
Specify distance to other axis or [Rotation]: _endp of
Specify start angle or [Parameter]:

☐ A check of the command line shows that AutoCAD is requesting the starting angle of the arc. The angle will be measured counterclockwise from the first point you choose. In this example, point G is 0°, point J is 90°, and point H is 180°.

☐ Type **45** on the command line to specify a starting angle of 45° and hit the *Enter* key.

Specify distance to other axis or [Rotation]: _endp of
Specify start angle or [Parameter]: 45
Specify end angle or [Parameter/Included angle]:

☐ Type **135** on the command line to specify an ending angle of 135° and hit the *Enter* key. The elliptical arc will be drawn starting at 45° and ending at 135°.

Specify distance to other axis or [Rotation]: _endp of
Specify start angle or [Parameter]: 45
Specify end angle or [Parameter/Included angle]: 135

For additional practice you will now draw a second arc having different starting and ending points on this same figure.

☐ Click on the *Ellipse Arc* button.
☐ Click the *Endpoint* button. Move the cursor to point G. When the *Endpoint* snap marker appears, click the mouse button.
☐ Click on the *Endpoint* button. Move the cursor to point H. When the *Endpoint* snap marker appears, click the mouse button.
☐ Click on the *Endpoint* button. Move the cursor to point J. When the *Endpoint* snap marker appears, click the mouse button. The ellipse is now complete and it is time to specify the starting and ending points of the arc.
☐ Type **180** on the command line to specify a starting angle of 180° and hit the *Enter* key.

Drawing Curved Shapes 173

☐ Type **360** on the command line to specify an ending angle of 360° and hit the *Enter* key. The elliptical arc will be drawn starting at 180° and ending at 360°.

The following section will show how the starting point affects the angle of the elliptical arc.

☐ Click on the *Ellipse Arc* button.

Command: _ellipse
Specify axis endpoint of ellipse or [Arc/Center]: _a
Specify axis endpoint of elliptical arc or [Center]:

☐ Click the *Endpoint* button. Move the cursor to point K. When the *Endpoint* snap marker appears, click the mouse button.

Specify axis endpoint of ellipse or [Arc/Center]: _a
Specify axis endpoint of ellipse or [Center]: _endp of
Specify other endpoint of axis:

☐ Click on the *Endpoint* button. Move the cursor to point L. When the *Endpoint* snap marker appears, click the mouse button.

Specify axis endpoint of elliptical arc or [Center]: _endp of
Specify other endpoint of axis: _endp of
Specify distance to other axis or [Rotation]:

☐ Click on the *Endpoint* button. Move the cursor to point M. When the *Endpoint* snap marker appears, click the mouse button.

Specify other endpoint of axis: _endp of
Specify distance to other axis or [Rotation]: _endp of
Specify start angle or [Parameter]:

☐ Remember that angles are measured counterclockwise from the first point you choose. In this example, point K is 0°, point N is 90°, and point L is 180°.

☐ Type **0** on the command line to specify a starting angle of 0° and hit the *Enter* key.

Specify distance to other axis or [Rotation]: _endp of
Specify start angle or [Parameter]: 0
Specify end angle or [Parameter/Included angle]:

☐ Type **270** on the command line to specify an ending angle of 270° and hit the *Enter* key. The elliptical arc will be drawn starting at 0° and ending at 270°.

Specify distance to other axis or [Rotation]: _endp of
Specify start angle or [Parameter]: 0
Specify end angle or [Parameter/Included angle]: 270

alternate method

You can also start the *Ellipse Arc* command by clicking on the *Draw* pull-down menu, sliding the cursor to the *Ellipse* item, and selecting *Arc* from the cascading menu. You can also start the command by typing **ELLIPSE** on the command line, hitting the *Enter* key, and then typing **A** to select the *Arc* option.

174 Module 6

☐ This completes this activity. You should spend some time practicing what you learned in this activity. When you are done, close the AutoCAD program.

Assignment
for Module 6 – Activity 3

Procedure: ☑ Check each box as you complete that item.

☐ Start *AutoCAD 2002*.

☐ When the *AutoCAD 2002 Today* dialog box appears, open the drawing *M06A03-2.dwg* located in the *Module06* subdirectory on the CD.

☐ For this assignment you will draw the objects shown in Figure 6-35 using the methods learned in this and previous activities. Place the objects based on the coordinates of the points shown in the figure. For the objects on the right, place the center of each arc 1" below the previous arc.

☐ Follow the dimensions shown for each object. Do not include any of the dimensions or dimension lines on your drawing, only the lines, arcs, and circles.

☐ When you have completed the figure, click on the *A-size Sheet* tab. You will see the objects you drew inside the blue rectangle on the paper, but they are probably not centered inside the rectangle.

☐ As you did in the previous activities, center the objects on the paper by changing to model space, using the *Pan* command, and then changing back to paper space. Be careful not to use the *Zoom* command during this operation. If you are unsure of how to do this, refer to the Assignment for Module 6 – Activity 1.

☐ Save the drawing to your removable disk with the name M06A03-2.

☐ Print a copy of your drawing.

☐ Neatly print your name and the date in the appropriate spaces in the title block.

Figure 6-35

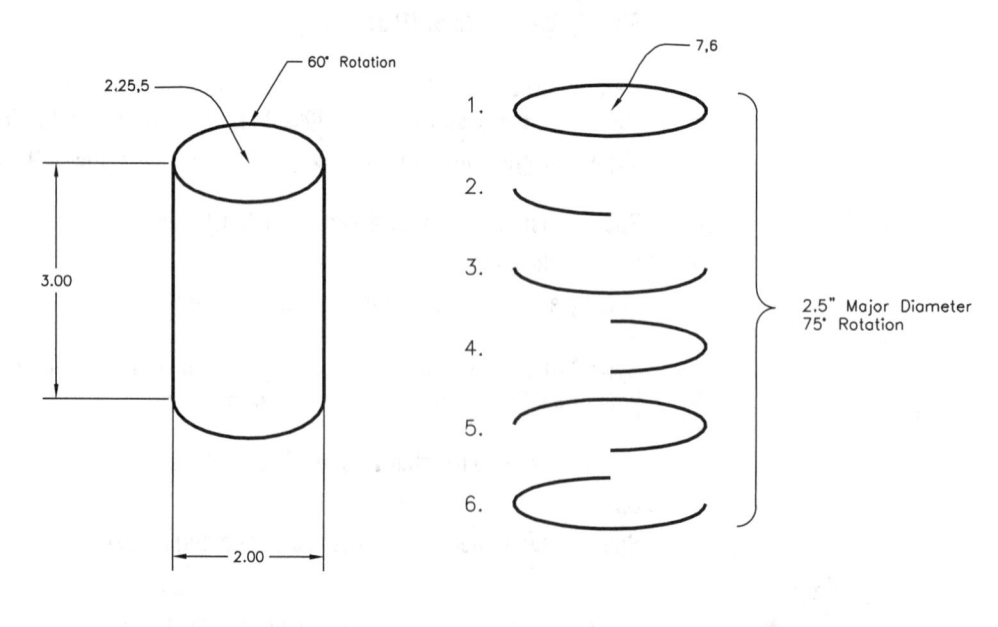

Activity 4

Drawing Donuts and Solid Circles

Objectives: After completing this activity, you should be able to do the following:

- Draw donuts of a specified inside and outside radius or diameter.
- Draw solid circles.
- Use the FILL variable to produce solid or segmented donuts and solid circles.

Procedure: ☑ Check each box as you complete that item.

☐ Start *AutoCAD 2002*.

☐ When the *AutoCAD 2002 Today* dialog box appears, open the drawing *M06A04-1.dwg* located in the *Module06* subdirectory on the CD.

☐ Make sure that all the *Drawing Features* buttons, except for the *Model* button, on the *Status* bar are off.

Drawing Donuts

Donuts come in two flavors, one with a hole and one without. In reality, a donut is a closed figure made up of a very thick line, called a polyline. (You will study polylines in detail in a future activity.) When you make the line's width less than the circle's radius, the donut has a hole; and when you make it equal to the circle's radius, you have a donut without a hole.

☐ To start this activity you will draw solid filled donuts. To ensure that the AutoCAD variable is set correctly, you will set it now. Type **FILL** on the command line and hit the *Enter* key.

Command:
Command: FILL
Enter mode [ON/OFF] <ON>: ON

☐ You have two options for this variable, on and off. If Fill is currently on, you will see ON inside the angle brackets. All you need to do is hit the *Enter* key to leave it on. If it is off, you must type ON on the command line and hit the *Enter* key to turn it on. Remember, you must type all the capitalized letters to select a particular option. For this option, you should type either ON or OFF to set the fill. Do whichever is appropriate now.

Command: FILL
Enter mode [ON/OFF] <ON>: ON
Command:

☐ *Donut* is located in the *Draw* pull-down menu, as shown in Figure 6-36. Click on the *Draw* pull-down menu to open it, slide the cursor down the menu to highlight the *Donut* command, and click the mouse button.

Figure 6-36
The *Donut* command is located on the *Draw* pull-down menu.

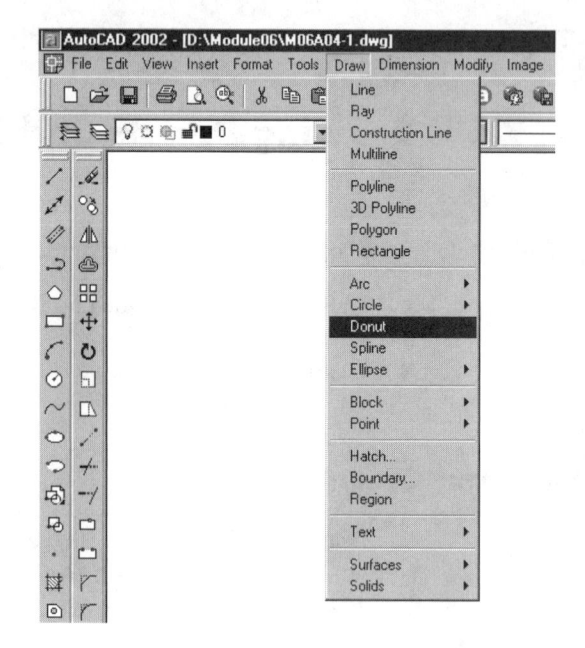

Command:
Command: _donut
Command: Specify inside diameter of donut <0.5000>:

☐ A check of the command line shows that AutoCAD is requesting the inside diameter of the donut. Note that this is asking for a *diameter* and *not a radius* like most other curved objects such as circles and arcs.

Command:
Command: _donut
Specify inside diameter of donut <0.5000>:

☐ Type **.375** on the command line and hit the *Enter* key.

Command: _donut
Specify inside diameter of donut <0.5000>: .375
Specify outside diameter of donut <1.0000>:

☐ Type **.75** on the command line and hit the *Enter* key. The donut will appear on the screen attached to the cursor.

Specify inside diameter of donut <0.5000>: .375
Specify outside diameter of donut <1.0000>: .75
Specify center of donut or <exit>:

☐ Type **1,6** on the command line and hit the *Enter* key to place the donut.

Specify outside diameter of donut <1.0000>: .75
Specify center of donut or <exit>: 1,6
Specify center of donut or <exit>:

☐ Note that there is still a donut attached to your cursor. The donut command is set to place multiple copies of a donut. Type **1,4** on the command line and hit the *Enter* key *twice* to place another donut and to end the donut command.

Specify center of donut or <exit>: 1,6
Specify center of donut or <exit>: 1,4
Command:

In this section you will draw a different size donut with a smaller difference between inside and outside diameters.

☐ Click on the *Draw* pull-down menu to open it, slide the cursor down the menu to highlight the *Donut* command, and click the mouse button.

Command:
Command: _donut
Command: Specify inside diameter of donut <0.3750>:

☐ Type **1.5** on the command line and hit the *Enter* key.

Command: _donut
Specify inside diameter of donut <0.3750>: 1.5
Specify outside diameter of donut <0.7500>:

☐ Type **1.75** on the command line and hit the *Enter* key. The donut will appear attached to the cursor on the screen.

Specify inside diameter of donut <0.3750>: 1.5
Specify outside diameter of donut <0.7500>: 1.75
Specify center of donut or <exit>:

☐ Type **3,5** on the command line and hit the *Enter* key twice to place the donut and end the donut command.

Specify center of donut or <exit>: 3.5
Specify center of donut or <exit>:
Command:

☐ With a little imagination you should be able to see that the donut is actually made from a thick continuous line. The width of the line is determined by taking half the difference between the inside and outside diameters. The width of the last line you drew is calculated below.

$$\text{Line thickness} = \frac{OD - ID}{2} = \frac{1.75 - 1.5}{2} = \frac{.25}{2} = .125$$

alternate method

You can start the *Donut* command by typing **DONUT,** or just **DO,** on the command line and hitting the *Enter* key.

Drawing a Solid Circle

A solid circle is a donut that has a zero inside diameter.

- ☐ Click on the *Draw* pull-down menu to open it, slide the cursor down the menu to highlight the *Donut* command, and click the mouse button.

  Command:
  Command: _donut
  Command: Specify inside diameter of donut <1.5000>:

- ☐ Type **0** on the command line and hit the *Enter* key.

  Command: _donut
  Specify inside diameter of donut <1.5000>: 0
  Specify outside diameter of donut <1.7500>:

- ☐ Type **.75** on the command line and hit the *Enter* key. The donut will appear attached to the cursor on the screen.

  Specify inside diameter of donut <0.5000>: 0
  Specify outside diameter of donut <1.750>: .75
  Specify center of donut or <exit>:

- ☐ Type **1,5** on the command line and hit the *Enter* key to place the solid circle.

  Specify outside diameter of donut <1.750>: .75
  Specify center of donut or <exit>: 1,5
  Specify center of donut or <exit>:

- ☐ Type **1,3** on the command line and hit the *Enter* key *twice* to place the second solid circle and to end the donut command.

  Specify center of donut or <exit>: 1,5
  Specify center of donut or <exit>: 1,3
  Command:

Drawing Donuts with the Fill Off

When the *Fill* is off, the donuts appear with a series of lines that indicate the solid part of the donut.

- ☐ Type **FILL** on the command line and hit the *Enter* key. Type **OFF** and hit the *Enter* key to turn *Fill* off.
- ☐ Place a donut having a 1″ ID and a 1.5″ OD at point 6,6. Note the look of the donut now that *Fill* is off.
- ☐ Place a solid circle having a 1.5″ OD at point 6,3.

It appears that the original donuts you drew are still filled and the new ones are not. In reality AutoCAD only allows *Fill* to be on or off for all the objects on the entire drawing. The only reason the original donuts are still solid is that the screen has not been regenerated (redrawn) since you drew them. The following steps will show you that none of the donuts are filled.

- ☐ Type **REGEN** on the command line and hit the *Enter* key. All the donuts are not filled.

- ☐ Type **FILL** on the command line and hit the *Enter* key. Type **ON** and hit the *Enter* key to turn *Fill* on.
- ☐ Type **REGEN** again on the command line and hit the *Enter* key. All the donuts are now filled.
- ☐ This completes this activity. You can close the AutoCAD program now or you can practice placing more donuts.

Activity 5

Drawing Fillets

Objectives: After completing this activity, you should be able to do the following:

- Locate and use the *Fillet* button on the *Modify* toolbar.
- Draw a fillet between two lines or objects.
- Set the radius of a fillet to a specified value.
- Turn the *Fillet Trim* mode on and off and describe its effects.

Fillets are rounded corners on objects. Fillets (or rounds) are often used on outer edges of objects to eliminate sharp corners that could hurt someone, and they are used on inner corners to maintain the strength of the part. Therefore, a lot of objects you draw will contain fillets. In this activity you will learn how to specify the radius of a fillet and how to place fillets between different shapes. Figure 6-37 shows inside and outside fillets.

Procedure: ☑ Check each box as you complete that item.

- ☐ Start *AutoCAD 2002*.
- ☐ When the *AutoCAD 2002 Today* dialog box appears, open the drawing *M06A05-1.dwg* located in the *Module06* subdirectory on the CD.
- ☐ Make sure that all the *Drawing Features* buttons on the *Status* bar, except for the *Model* button, are off.
- ☐ To prepare for this activity, you must draw a few lines to act as fillet points. Using the *Line* command and absolute coordinates, draw the following lines. When you are done, your screen will look like Figure 6-38 without the letters. Some of the lines are lettered so you can identify the correct line to be used in making the fillets. You should refer to this sketch as you go through this activity.

	From	To		From	To
a)	0,5	0,7	k)	3,4	6,4
b)	0,7	2,7	l)	6,4	4,2
c)	2,7	2,5	m)	4,2	3,4
d)	2,5	0,5	n)	8,5	8,7
e)	0,2.5	0,3.5	o)	8,7	10,7
f)	.5,4	1.5,4	p)	10,7	10,5
g)	2,3.5	2,2.5	q)	10,5	8,5
h)	1.5,2	.5,2	r)	8,4	9.5,4
i)	3,7	6,7	s)	10,3.5	10,2
j)	5.5,7.5	5.5,5	t)	8,4	9,2.5

Setting the Trim and Radius Options

- ☐ Use Figure 6-39 to help you locate and click on the *Fillet* button on the *Modify* toolbar.

Drawing Curved Shapes   181

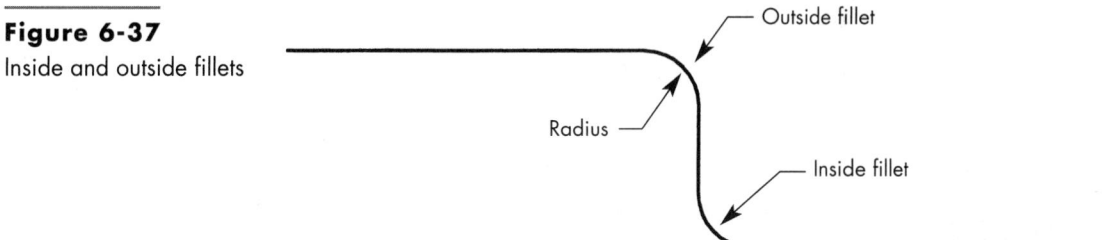

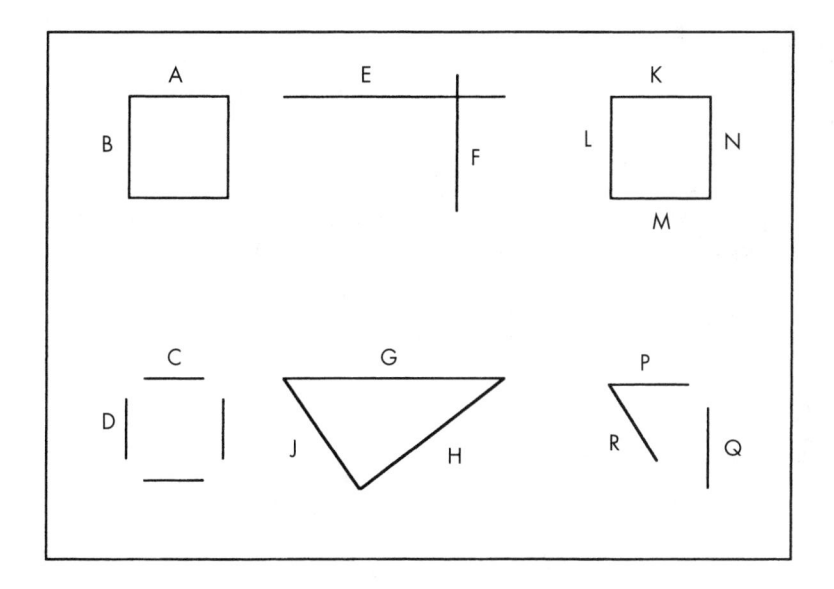

Figure 6-37
Inside and outside fillets

Figure 6-38
Your screen should look like this, except for the letters, when you are done.

Figure 6-39
The *Fillet* button is located on the *Modify* toolbar.

Command: _fillet
Current settings: Mode = TRIM, Radius = 0.5000
Select first object or [Polyline/Radius/Trim]:

☐ For this section you will work with the *Trim* mode turned on. The following steps will ensure that your computer is set correctly.

☐ Type **T** on the command line to select the *Trim* option and hit the *Enter* key.

Current settings: Mode = TRIM, Radius = 0.5000
Select first object or [Polyline/Radius/Trim]: T
Enter Trim mode option [Trim/No trim] <Trim>:

☐ If *Trim* appears inside the angled brackets, hit the *Enter* key. If *No trim* appears, type **T** on the command line and hit the *Enter* key twice.

Select first object or [Polyline/Radius/Trim]: T
Enter Trim mode option [Trim/No trim] <Trim>:
Select first object or [Polyline/Radius/Trim]:
Command:

Drawing a Fillet

☐ Click on the *Fillet* button.

Command: _fillet
Current settings: Mode = TRIM, Radius = 0.5000
Select first object or [Polyline/Radius/Trim]:

☐ The cursor has turned into a square pickbox. Move the pickbox to line A. (See Figure 6-38.) When the cursor is over the line, click the mouse button. Line A will become dashed.

Current settings: Mode = TRIM, Radius = 0.5000
Select first object or [Polyline/Radius/Trim]:
Select second object:

☐ Using the same method, select line B. A .5″ fillet will appear at the corner between the two lines and the *Fillet* command will end. It is not important where you click on the two lines because AutoCAD determines where the lines intersect and places the fillet there.

Select first object or [Polyline/Radius/Trim]: R
Select second object:
Command:

☐ For practice, fillet the other three corners of the square.

Note
If you do not want to keep returning to the *Modify* toolbar to select the *Fillet* button, you can repeat the *Fillet* command by clicking the *right* mouse button and selecting *Repeat Fillet* from the pop-up menu that appears. (You can use this method to immediately repeat any command. When you hit the *right* mouse button, the pop-up menu will open and *Repeat <your last command>* will appear as a selection at the top of the menu.)

alternate method
You can start the *Fillet* command by clicking on the *Modify* pull-down menu and selecting *Fillet*. You can also type **FILLET,** or just **F,** on the command line and hit the *Enter* key.

☐ Lines do not have to intersect for a fillet to be drawn. Click on the *Fillet* button.

Command: _fillet
Current settings: Mode = TRIM, Radius = 0.5000
Select first object or [Polyline/Radius/Trim]:

☐ Use the pickbox to select line C. (See Figure 6-38.)

Current settings: Mode = TRIM, Radius = 0.5000
Select first object or [Polyline/Radius/Trim]:
Select second object:

☐ Use the pickbox to select line D. The two lines will be joined with a fillet and the *Fillet* command will end.

Select first object or [Polyline/Radius/Trim]: R
Select second object:
Command:

- [ ] For additional practice, fillet the three other open corners of the square.
- [ ] If the lines intersect and go past the intersection, a fillet can still be drawn between them. Click on the *Fillet* button.
- [ ] Select line E by clicking on it. Make sure you select the line *left* of the intersection on the longest part of the line.
- [ ] Select line F by clicking on it. Make sure you select the line *below* the intersection on the longest part of the line. The lines will be trimmed and a fillet will be placed between them.

Note: When lines extend past an intersection point, it is very important where you select the line. AutoCAD will retain the part of the line you select and trim off the part of the line that extends past the intersection. If you had selected one short segment and one long segment, the fillet would have been different. You may want to use the *Undo* button on the *Standard* toolbar to undo the last *Fillet* command. You can then practice clicking on different line segments to see what fillets are drawn. When you are done, put the original fillet back.

- [ ] Lines do not have to meet at a right angle to be filleted. Click on the *Fillet* button.
- [ ] Select line G (see Figure 6-38) by clicking on it.
- [ ] Select line H by clicking on it. A fillet with radius .5 will be placed between the two lines. Notice that AutoCAD calculates the correct location and angle for the fillet so that it meets both lines tangent.
- [ ] For additional practice, fillet the other two corners of the triangle formed by lines G, H, and J.

Changing the Radius for the Fillet

Until now you have been placing all fillets with a .5″ radius. In this section you will place fillets with different radii.

- [ ] Click on the *Fillet* button.
- [ ] Type **R** on the command line to select the radius mode and hit the *Enter* key.

Enter Trim mode option [Trim/No trim] <Trim>:
Select first object or [Polyline/Radius/Trim]: R
Specify fillet radius <0.5000>:

- [ ] Type **.25** on the command line and hit the *Enter* key.

Select first object or [Polyline/Radius/Trim]: R
Specify fillet radius <0.5000>: .25
Select first object or [Polyline/Radius/Trim]:

- [ ] Place a .25″ radius fillet between lines K and L.
- [ ] Click on the *Fillet* button.
- [ ] Type **R** on the command line to select the *Radius* option and hit the *Enter* key.

Enter Trim mode option [Trim/No trim] <Trim>:
Select first object or [Polyline/Radius/Trim]: R
Specify fillet radius <0.2500>:

☐ Type **.75** on the command line and hit the *Enter* key.

Select first object or [Polyline/Radius/Trim]: R
Specify fillet radius <0.2500>: .75
Select first object or [Polyline/Radius/Trim]:

☐ Place a .75" radius fillet between lines L and M.
☐ Click on the *Fillet* button.
☐ Type **R** on the command line to select the *Radius* option and hit the *Enter* key.

Enter Trim mode option [Trim/No trim] <Trim>:
Select first object or [Polyline/Radius/Trim]: R
Specify fillet radius <0.7500>:

☐ Type **1** on the command line and hit the *Enter* key.

Select first object or [Polyline/Radius/Trim]: R
Specify fillet radius <0.7500>: 1
Select first object or [Polyline/Radius/Trim]:

☐ Place a 1.0" radius fillet between lines M and N.
☐ Click on the *Fillet* button.
☐ Type **R** on the command line to select the *Radius* option and hit the *Enter* key.

Enter Trim mode option [Trim/No trim] <Trim>:
Select first object or [Polyline/Radius/Trim]: R
Specify fillet radius <1.000>:

☐ Type **1.5** on the command line and hit the *Enter* key.

Select first object or [Polyline/Radius/Trim]: R
Specify fillet radius <1.0000>: 1.5
Select first object or [Polyline/Radius/Trim]:

☐ Try to place a 1.5" radius fillet between lines N and K. You will get an error message indicating that the radius is too large. AutoCAD does not allow you to place a fillet that does not fit. Hit the *Esc* key and then click on the *Fillet* button, change the radius to .5, and fillet the corner between lines N and K.

A Special Use of the *Fillet* Command

☐ Click on the *Fillet* button.
☐ Type **R** on the command line to select the *Radius* option and hit the *Enter* key.

Enter Trim mode option [Trim/No trim] <Trim>:
Select first object or [Polyline/Radius/Trim]: R
Specify fillet radius <0.5000>:

Drawing Curved Shapes 185

☐ Type **0** on the command line and hit the *Enter* key.

Select first object or [Polyline/Radius/Trim]: R
Specify fillet radius <0.5000>: 0
Select first object or [Polyline/Radius/Trim]:

☐ Select line P by clicking on it.

Current settings: Mode = TRIM, Radius = 0.0000
Select first object or [Polyline/Radius/Trim]:
Select second object:

☐ Select line Q by clicking on it. The two lines will be extended to form a square corner. Setting the radius to zero allows you to extend and trim at the same time to form a perfect corner.
☐ Click on the *Fillet* button and select lines Q and R to finish the triangle.
☐ This completes this activity. You should spend some time practicing what you learned in this activity. When you are done, close the AutoCAD program.

Assignment
for Module 6 – Activity 5

Procedure: ☑ Check each box as you complete that item.

☐ Start *AutoCAD 2002*.
☐ When the *AutoCAD 2002 Today* dialog box appears, open the drawing M06A05-2.dwg located in the *Module06* subdirectory on the CD.
☐ For this assignment you will draw the object shown in Figure 6-40 using the methods learned in this and previous activities. Place the object based on the coordinates of the points shown in the figure.

Figure 6-40

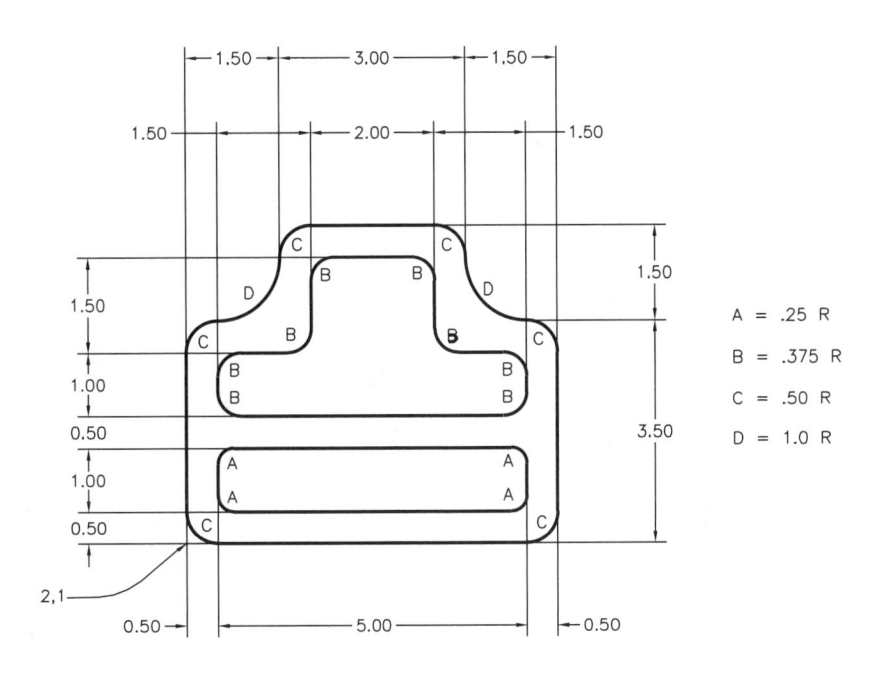

A = .25 R
B = .375 R
C = .50 R
D = 1.0 R

- ☐ Follow the dimensions shown for the object. Do not include any of the dimensions, dimension lines, or letters on your drawing, only the lines and fillets.
- ☐ The letter at each fillet indicates the size of the radius for that fillet. Refer to the radius key at the right of the object.
- ☐ When you have completed the figure, click on the *A-size Sheet* tab. You will see the object you drew inside the blue rectangle on the paper, but it is probably not centered inside the rectangle.
- ☐ As you did in the previous activities, center the object on the paper by changing to model space, using the *Pan* command, and then changing back to paper space. Be careful not to use the *Zoom* command during this operation. If you are unsure of how to do this, refer to the Assignment for Module 6 – Activity 1.
- ☐ Save the drawing to your removable disk with the name M06A05-2.
- ☐ Print a copy of your drawing.
- ☐ Neatly print your name and the date in the appropriate spaces in the title block.

Applying the Concepts

Your company has a burning machine that can burn through 3"-thick steel plate. Intricate shapes can be produced by using the machine's follower attachment. This attachment uses a laser light to follow lines on a drawing so that the burn head cuts out the exact shape shown on the drawing.

Your boss has made a sketch of a spacer, shown in Figure 6-41, that must be burned from 2 1/2" steel plate. He wants you to make a drawing of the part that he can give to the machine shop to be used with the burner's follower attachment. You must make the drawing exactly as shown in his sketch because the cost of 2 1/2" steel plate and the burning time is very expensive. A three-dimensional picture of the part is included in the figure to help you visualize what it will look like.

Procedure: ☑ Check each box as you complete that item.

☐ Start *AutoCAD 2002*.

☐ When the *AutoCAD 2002 Today* dialog box appears, open the drawing *M06APP.dwg* located in the *Module06* subdirectory on the CD.

Figure 6-41
Steel spacer

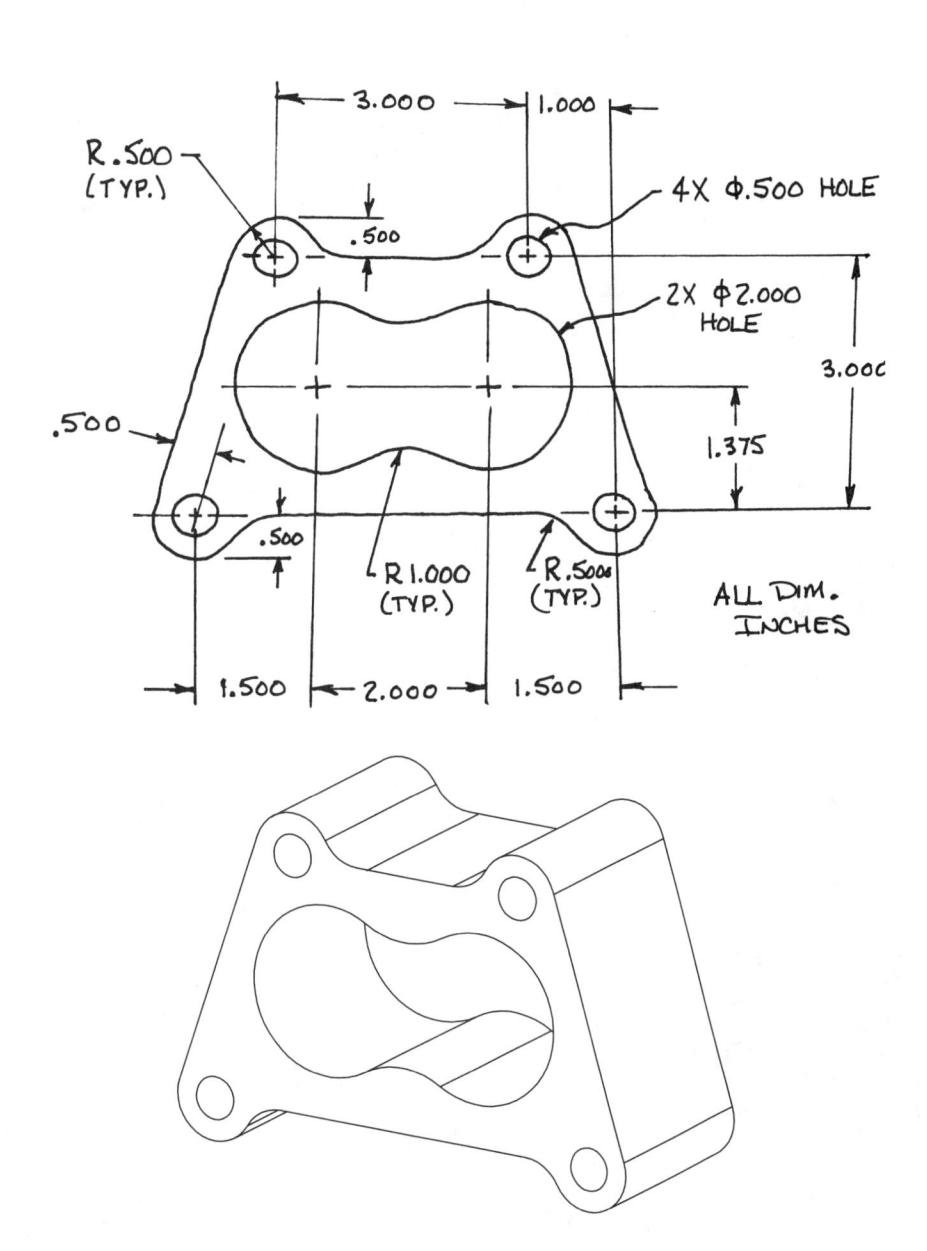

- ☐ Lay out the spacer as shown in the figure.
- ☐ When you are done, click on the *A-size Sheet* tab. As you did in the previous activities, center the object on the paper.
- ☐ Save the drawing to your removable disk with the name **M06APP**.
- ☐ Print a copy of your drawing.
- ☐ Neatly print your name and the date in the appropriate spaces in the title block.

Module 6 Review Questions

These questions are provided to help you review the topics and concepts covered in this module.

True or False

Determine whether the statement is true or false. Place your answer, either T or F, in the blank.

_____ 1. You can draw a circle based on its center location and diameter.

_____ 2. An ellipse can represent a circle viewed from an angle.

_____ 3. Donuts can have a zero inside diameter.

_____ 4. A line can be tangent to a circle, but cannot be tangent to another line.

_____ 5. Fillets are used to break sharp corners.

_____ 6. A circle's radius is twice its diameter.

_____ 7. The chord distance of an arc is the distance along the arc's curved surface.

_____ 8. The *Quadrant snap* button allows you to snap to every 45° segment of a circle or arc.

_____ 9. An ellipse based on a 15° rotation has a longer minor axis than one based on a 75° rotation.

_____ 10. When using the *Tangent* option to draw circles, the location on the circle where you snap to is not important as long as you pick a point on the edge of the circle and not its center.

_____ 11. The *Center* snap can be used to snap to the center of a circle, but cannot be used to snap to the center of an arc.

_____ 12. An ellipse can be drawn by specifying the endpoints of its minor axis and one endpoint of its major axis.

_____ 13. An ellipse's major axis is always horizontal and its minor axis is always vertical.

_____ 14. The radius of a fillet is set by default by AutoCAD and cannot be changed.

_____ 15. An arc is just a segment of a circle. It can be drawn using a center point, radius, and angle.

Multiple-choice

Place the letter of the best answer in the blank.

1. This button is used to start the _____ command.
   a. Circle
   b. Arc
   c. Ellipse Arc
   d. Ellipse

2. This button is used to start the _____ command.
   a. Tangent snap
   b. Center snap
   c. Circle snap
   d. Quadrant snap

3. This button is used to start the _____ command.
   a. Circle
   b. Arc
   c. Ellipse Arc
   d. Ellipse

4. This button is used to start the _____ command.
   a. Circle
   b. Arc
   c. Ellipse Arc
   d. Ellipse

5. This button is used to start the _____ command.
   a. Tangent snap
   b. Center snap
   c. Circle snap
   d. Quadrant snap

6. This button is used to start the _____ command.
   a. Circle
   b. Arc
   c. Ellipse Arc
   d. Ellipse

7. This button is used to start the _____ command.
   a. Tangent snap
   b. Center snap
   c. Circle snap
   d. Quadrant snap

Module 7

Putting Text on a Drawing

Activity 1

Dynamic Text

Objectives: After completing this activity, you should be able to do the following:

- Place dynamic text on a drawing using the *DTEXT* command.
- Set the position, height, justification, and rotation of the dynamic text.
- Insert special symbols using dynamic text.
- Underscore and overscore dynamic text.
- Create and use a new text style using the *Text Style* dialog box and dynamic text.

In AutoCAD, words on a drawing are referred to as text. Every drawing has text. Text is used for notes and to identify views. On the drawing paper, it is used to identify the drawing number, the drawing title, the name of who made the drawing, and the date it was made. In this activity you will learn how to place *Dynamic Text* on a drawing. *Dynamic Text* is single-line text. Although you can type several lines of text while using this command, each text line is separate from the others so it can be changed, moved, and erased without affecting the other lines of text.

Most companies have standards that specify the size and type of text to be used on their drawings. Usually 1/8" (0.125") is the minimum text size for a drawing because it allows good readable reproduction. In this activity we will set the standards for text on all future drawings in this course.

Procedure: ☑ Check each box as you complete that item.

- ☐ Start *AutoCAD 2002*.
- ☐ When the *AutoCAD 2002 Today* dialog box appears, open the drawing *M07A01-1.dwg* located in the *Module07* subdirectory on the CD.
- ☐ When the program has loaded, you will notice that the drawing has opened in *Paper Space*. You can tell this because the *A-size Sheet* tab at the bottom of the drawing area is selected and the *Paper* button on the *Status* bar is depressed. You are going to place text on the paper shown on your screen and then print it. *Paper Space* is being used

because it is always printed 1:1 (or full size); therefore, when text is 1/8″ high in *Paper Space*, it will print 1/8″ high.

☐ Verify that all the other buttons on the *Status* bar, except for *Paper*, are not selected.

Using the *DTEXT* Command

In this section you will learn how to activate the *Dynamic Text* command, specify a starting location, height, and rotation angle for the text, and then enter the text from the keyboard. When entering text, you must refer to the bottom command line often because this is where the AutoCAD program requests different information at different times. Three lines of the command window are included with many of the following steps so that you know what to look for. (These are indented and in a smaller font size beneath each step.) Make sure that you have a minimum of three (3) lines of text in your command window visible so that you can compare them to the examples.

☐ Type **DT** (for *Dynamic Text*) on the keyboard.

AutoCAD menu utilities loaded.
Command:
Command: DT

☐ Hit the *Enter* key.

DTEXT
Current text style: "Standard" Text height: 0.2000
Specify start point of text or [Justify/Style]:

☐ Place the crosshairs somewhere inside the drawing border, near the left edge of the paper, and click the left mouse button. Do not worry if the location you choose leads to some of the text being off the drawing; you will eventually erase it anyway.

Current text style: "Standard" Text height: 0.2000
Specify start point of text or [Justify/Style]:
Specify height <0.2000>:

☐ Type **.25** on the keyboard.

Current text style: "Standard" Text height: 0.2000
Specify start point of text or [Justify/Style]:
Specify height <0.2000>: .25

☐ Hit the *Enter* key.

Specify start point of text or [Justify/Style]:
Specify height <0.2000>: .25
Specify rotation angle of text <0>:

☐ Hit *Enter* to select the default rotation angle of 0.

Specify height <0.2000>: .25
Specify rotation angle of text <0>:
Enter text:

- Notice that an *I-bar* that looks like a capital I now appears on the drawing where the text will go. Type (in capital letters) **THIS IS MY FIRST LINE OF TEXT** on the keyboard. Observe that the text appears on the drawing as you type.

  Specify height <0.2000>: .25
  Specify rotation angle of text <0>:
  Enter text: THIS IS MY FIRST LINE OF TEXT

Note: For clarity, capital letters are *always* used for text on engineering drawings. Hit the *Caps Lock* key to activate it so you don't have to worry about hitting the shift key for every letter you type. The commands you type on the keyboard are not case sensitive, so having the *Caps Lock* on will not cause any problems. For the rest of these activities you should work with the *Caps Lock* on so that the commands you enter will appear as capital letters.

- Hit the *Enter* key. Notice that the I-bar moves down and to the left to start the next line of text.

  Specify rotation angle of text <0>:
  Enter text: THIS IS MY FIRST LINE OF TEXT
  Enter text:

- Type **THIS IS MY SECOND LINE OF TEXT** and hit the *Enter* key.

  Enter text: THIS IS MY FIRST LINE OF TEXT
  Enter text: THIS IS MY SECOND LINE OF TEXT
  Enter text:

- Hit *Enter* again to exit the dynamic text command.

  Enter text: THIS IS MY SECOND LINE OF TEXT
  Enter text:
  Command:

- To prove that you are typing single-line text, click on the *Erase* button, use the *pickbox* to select the second line of text, and hit the *Enter* key. Only the first line remains.

  Congratulations, you have successfully entered text on a drawing. In the next section you will learn some of the options you have when entering text.

alternate method: You can also start the *Dynamic Text* command by clicking on the *Draw* pull-down menu, sliding the pointer to the *Text* menu item, and selecting *Single Line Text* from the cascading menu that appears.

Rotation Angle

- Type **DT** and hit the *Enter* key.

  DTEXT
  Current text style: "Standard" Text height: 0.2500
  Specify start point of text or [Justify/Style]:

- ☐ Place the crosshairs somewhere near the bottom, center, and inside the border. Click the left mouse button. Don't worry about the exact starting location.

  Current text style: "Standard" Text height: 0.2500
  Specify start point of text or [Justify/Style]:
  Specify height <0.2500>:

- ☐ Notice that the default is now 0.2500, the last value you used. Hit *Enter* to accept the default.

  Specify start point of text or [Justify/Style]:
  Specify height <0.2500>:
  Specify rotation angle of text <0>:

- ☐ Type **90** on the keyboard to rotate the text so that it is placed on the drawing at an angle of 90°. Hit the *Enter* key. Notice that the I-bar is now sideways, ready to type upward.

  Specify height <0.2500>:
  Specify rotation angle of text <0>: 90
  Enter text:

- ☐ Type **THIS IS AT 90 DEGREES** on the keyboard and hit *Enter* twice.

  Enter text: THIS IS AT 90 DEGREES
  Enter text:
  Command:

- ☐ Practice placing more text on the drawing using angles of 135°, 180°, 270°, and 315°.
- ☐ When you are done practicing, use the *Erase* command to erase all the text you have put on the screen including your first line of text.

Justification

Justification refers to the position of the text based on the starting point you choose. The default is at the bottom left corner of the first character you type. This means that the starting point you select with the crosshairs will be the bottom left corner of the line of text. There are 14 justification options for dynamic text. Only one, *Center*, will be covered in detail here. A brief description of the others will be given at the end of this section.

- ☐ Type **DT** and hit the *Enter* key.

  DTEXT
  Current text style: "Standard" Text height: 0.2500
  Specify start point of text or [Justify/Style]:

- ☐ The usual operation at this point would be to select a starting point for the text. You have two additional options: *Justify* and *Style*.
- ☐ Type **J** and hit the *Enter* key.

  Current text style: "Standard" Text height: 0.2500
  Specify start point of text or [Justify/Style]:
  Enter an option [Align/Fit/Center/Middle/Right/TL/TC/TR/ML/MC/MR/BL/BC/BR]:

- Look at all the options you have. The first five (Align/Fit/Center/Middle/Right) have single-letter shortcuts, A,F,C,M, and R, and the rest have two-letter shortcuts.
- Type **C** (for Center) and hit the *Enter* key.

Specify start point of text or [Justify/Style]:
Enter an option [Align/Fit/Center/Middle/Right/TL/TC/TR/ML/MC/MR/BL/BC/BR]: C
Specify center point of text:

- Place the crosshairs somewhere in the center of the paper and click the mouse button.

Enter an option [Align/Fit/Center/Middle/Right/TL/TC/TR/ML/MC/MR/BL/BC/BR]: C
Specify center point of text:
Specify height <0.2500>:

- Hit *Enter* to select the .2500 text height, type **0**, and then hit *Enter* to set the rotation angle at 0°.

Specify height <0.2500>:
Specify rotation angle of text <315>: 0
Enter text:

- Type **THIS IS CENTERED TEXT**. Notice that the text is to the right of the starting location. Don't worry; AutoCAD will correct the problem when you are done entering all your text.

Specify rotation angle of text <315>: 0
Enter text: THIS IS CENTERED TEXT
Enter text:

- Hit *Enter* twice to complete the dynamic text command. What happened to the text when you hit the second *Enter*?

Enter text: THIS IS CENTERED TEXT
Enter text:
Command:

- Use the *Erase* command to erase all text from the screen.

The following gives a brief description of the other justification options. When you have time you should practice placing text using each of these options. Although they are not used extensively, every one is useful; and if you continue to use AutoCAD, you will eventually find the need to use these options on a drawing.

Align—This option requires you to pick two points. AutoCAD then fits the text along an imaginary line, called a baseline, between these two points. To make the text fit, AutoCAD adjusts the text height, keeping each letter's height and width proportional to the original font. If you have a lot of text to fit between two close points, the text will become very small. If you have a small amount of text to fit between two distant points, the text will be large. With *Align*, the baseline can be horizontal or at any angle, so you can align it with an object on the drawing. Be careful how you use this option. It is not recommended for multiple lines of text because the change in size can cause one line to overlap the next. With single lines, the text can become so small it is unreadable or below company size standards.

Fit—This option is very similar to *Align*. Again you select two points to form a baseline and AutoCAD fits the text along the baseline between the two points. The difference is that you are asked to specify the text height. AutoCAD holds that height constant and changes the width of the characters so they will fit between the two points. Again use this option sparingly because it can produce strange-looking text.

Middle—This option aligns the text so it will be centered horizontally and vertically on the point you choose. It is similar to *Center* except that *Center* uses the bottom of the text line and *Middle* uses the middle of the text line.

Right—This option aligns the bottom right edge of the text with the point you select.

TL (Top Left)—This option aligns the top left edge of the text with the point you select.

TC (Top Center)—This option aligns the top center edge of the text with the point you select.

TR (Top Right)—This option aligns the top right edge of the text with the point you select.

ML (Middle Left)—This option aligns the middle left edge of the text with the point you select.

MC (Middle Center)—This option aligns the middle center edge of the text with the point you select. This option is the same as selecting *Middle*.

MR (Middle Right)—This option aligns the middle right edge of the text with the point you select.

BL (Bottom Left)—This option aligns the bottom left edge of the text with the point you select. This is the same as the default *Left* justification.

BC (Bottom Center)—This option aligns the bottom center edge of the text with the point you select. This is the same as using the *Center* option.

BR (Bottom Right)—This option aligns the bottom right edge of the text with the point you select. This is the same as using the *Right* option.

Inserting Special Characters

Three special characters are frequently used in drawings that do not appear on the keyboard: the degree symbol (°), the plus/minus sign (±), and the diameter symbol (∅). In the next section, you will learn how to include these in your dynamic text.

- [ ] Type **DT** and hit the *Enter* key.
- [ ] Place the crosshairs somewhere near the left side, toward the top, and inside the border. Click the mouse button.
- [ ] Hit *Enter* twice to accept the defaults 0.25 and 0.
- [ ] Type the following exactly as is appears. **STEEL SHAFT 4.5"%%C**
- [ ] Hit the *Enter* key. What happened? Hit the *Enter* key again to end the dynamic text command. What happened? %%C is the code for the diameter symbol (∅) special character.

You need to know, and memorize, the following codes for these three special characters.

%%D	Degrees symbol (°)
%%P	Plus/minus sign (±)
%%C	Diameter symbol (∅)

Putting Text on a Drawing 197

☐ Practice typing some lines of text that contain each of these special characters.

Underscoring and Overscoring Text

Sometimes you need to use text that has a line under or over it, or both. %%U turns on the underscoring and %%O turns on the overscoring. To end either, place the same code (%%U or %%O) at the location in the line where you want it to end. If you do not type in an end code, the underscoring or overscoring will continue to the end of the line you are working on. You must memorize both of these codes.

☐ Activate dynamic text and type the following line:

%%UUNDERSCORED%%U AND %%OOVERSCORED

☐ Hit the *Enter* key to go to another line. Type the following on the second line:

%%U%%OTHIS IS BOTH

☐ Hit the *Enter* key twice and look at the results.
☐ Take some time and practice placing dynamic text with both the special characters and the score codes learned above.
☐ When you are finished, erase all the text on the drawing.

Setting up a New *Text Style*

You may have noticed that a second option, *Style*, was available when you were using dynamic text. In this section, you will learn how to set up a new text style called *Mechanical* that you will use in most future drawings.

☐ Click on the *Format* pull-down menu, slide the mouse pointer down to the menu *Text Style*, and click the mouse button. (See Figure 7-1.)
☐ The *Text Style* dialog box, seen in Figure 7-2, will appear. The following gives a brief description of the features in this dialog box.

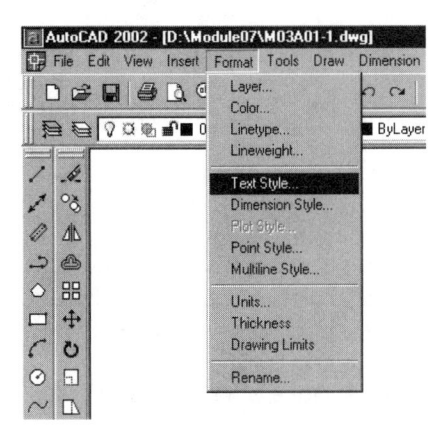

Figure 7-1
Select *Text Style* from the *Format* pull-down menu.

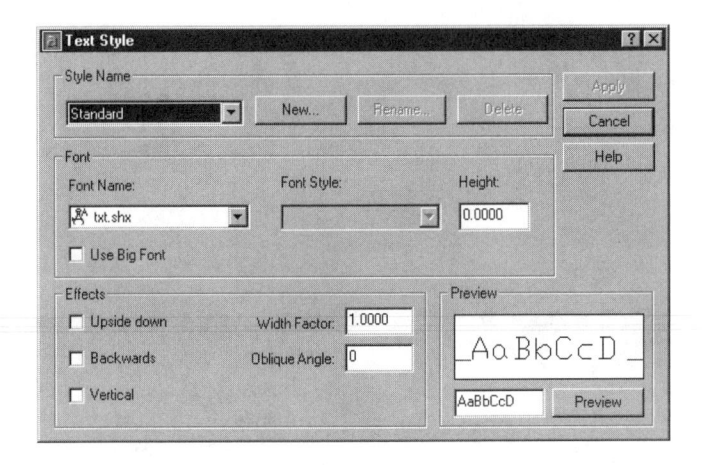

Figure 7-2
The *Text Style* dialog box allows you to customize different styles of text.

Style Name—This area provides a drop-down list where you can activate a style. Buttons are provided in this area to *Add*, *Rename*, and *Delete* styles. The default style in AutoCAD is *Standard* and it cannot be renamed or deleted.

Font—This area allows you to specify the font characteristics used with a text style.

- **Font Name**—This drop-down list provides the names of all the fonts available on your computer. Clicking on the name of a font will activate it and close the drop-down list. The txt.sht font is the default for the *Standard* text style, but you can change it to any available font.
- **Font Style**—This area provides options like Bold or Italics if those are available with the chosen font. If they are not, this area is grayed out.
- **Height**—This text box allows you to specify the height for the text. If this value is set to anything other than zero, you will not have the option of specifying the height while placing text on the drawing. This value should always be set to zero so you have the options of using different text heights on the drawing.

Effects—This area provides a way to make additional changes to the text style. As you read each description, you may want to make the change and see how it affects the text in the preview window. If you do, remember to reset each one to its original condition or value.

- **Upside down**—When checked, this box will make the text appear upside down.
- **Backwards**—When checked, this box will make the text appear backwards.
- **Vertical**—When checked, this box this will make the text vertical. This option is not available for all fonts.
- **Width Factor**—This text box allows you to set a value that will expand or compress the font. Entering 2 makes the text twice as wide and entering .5 makes it half as wide.
- **Oblique Angle**—This text box allows you to specify the amount of slant on the text. (This is not the same as setting the rotation angle.) A positive value will slant the text to the right, a negative value will slant the text to the left, and zero makes the text upright. You can enter any value from −85 to +85.

Apply Button—This button allows you to apply any changes you make to the drawing. If you do not click *Apply*, any changes you make will not take affect.

Close/Cancel Button—This button appears as either a *Close* button or a *Cancel* button and allows you to exit the dialog box without applying the changes that you made.

Help Button—This button provides you with additional information about the options in this dialog box.

> **Note:** Any changes you make to an existing text style will affect the text *already placed on the drawing* that used that style. If you placed text on the drawing using the *Standard* text style, then opened the dialog box, checked the *Backwards* box, and hit the *Apply* button, all the *Standard* text already on the drawing would appear backwards. Before you can enter text of a different style, you must do two things. First, you must make a new text style; and second, you must make it active.

- [ ] For your new *Mechanical* text style, you will use *romans*. Open the *Font Name* drop-down list, use the scroll bar to locate the *romans* font, and select it by clicking on it. Be careful as there are several roman fonts; make sure you select *romans*.
- [ ] Locate the *Height* box at the right of the *Font Name* box and make sure the value is zero.

> **Note:** NEVER, never set this value to anything but "0" for activities in this book. If this is set to a value other than zero, any text or dimension you place on the drawing will be that size regardless of any other settings you have made in the drawing. Setting this to a value other than zero also removes the "select height" option when placing dynamic text, which prevents you from specifying a different height. It is recommended that you leave this value at zero to eliminate possible problems in this and future activities. Sometimes it is useful to set the text height to a value other than zero. If your company has a standard that requires specific text to be a certain height, then you may want to create a text style for use in only those situations. It is not recommended that you use this special text style for dimensioning where the text height needs to be changed within the same drawing.

- [ ] Click on the *New* button that is located next to the *Style Name* box. The *New Text Style* dialog box will open, as shown in Figure 7-3. Type **MECHANICAL** as the *Style Name*, as shown in the figure. Click on the *OK* button to close the dialog box.
- [ ] Check the *Text Style* dialog box to make sure all the options look like those shown in Figure 7-4. Click on the *Style Name* drop-down list to verify that both *Standard* and *Mechanical* styles exist. Click on the *Standard* style and then click the *Close* button.

Using the Mechanical Text Style in a Drawing

- [ ] Type **DT** and hit the *Enter* key.

Figure 7-3
Enter MECHANICAL as the *Style Name* in the *New Text Style* dialog box.

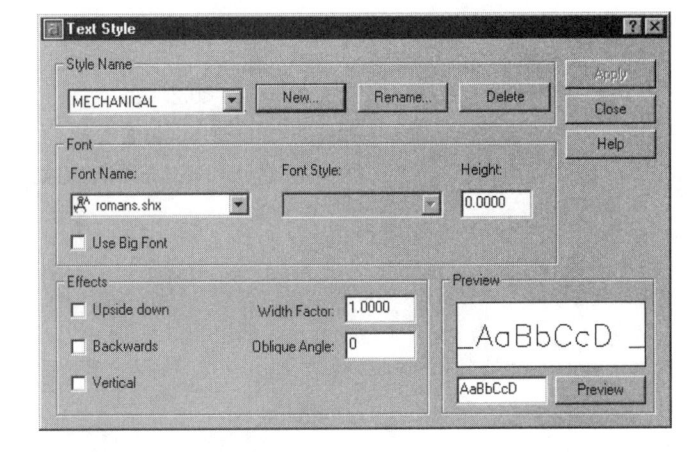

Figure 7-4
The *Text Style* dialog box set up for the new *Mechanical* text style

Command: DT
DTEXT
Current text style: "Standard" Text height: 0.2500

- [ ] Type **S** for the *Style* option and hit the *Enter* key.

Current text style: "Standard" Text height: 0.2500
Specify start point of text or [Justify/Style]: S
Enter style name or [?] <Standard>:

Note: Notice that "?" is one of the options. If you forget the name of a text style, you can type **?** on the command line, hit the *Enter* key twice, and the *Text* window will open to give you a complete list of all available text styles.

- [ ] Type **MECHANICAL** and hit the *Enter* key to make it the current text style.

Specify start point of text or [Justify/Style]: S
Enter style name or [?] <Standard>: MECHANICAL
Current text style: "MECHANICAL" Text height: 0.2500

- [ ] Use the crosshairs to pick a starting point on the left side of the drawing paper.

Enter style name or [?] <Standard>: MECHANICAL
Current text style: "MECHANICAL" Text height: 0.2500
Specify start point of text or [Justify/Style]:

- [ ] Hit *Enter* twice to accept the .25 text height and the 0 rotation angle.

Specify height <0.2500>:
Specify rotation angle of text <0>:
Enter text:

- [ ] Type **THIS IS MECHANICAL TEXT STYLE** from the keyboard.

Specify height <0.2500>:
Specify rotation angle of text <0>:
Enter text: THIS IS MECHANICAL TEXT STYLE

- [ ] Hit the *Enter* key twice to complete the dynamic text command. The line you just typed is in the *Mechanical* style with a text font of *romans*.

Enter text: THIS IS MECHANICAL TEXT STYLE
Enter text:
Command:

- [ ] Take some time to practice placing text using both the *Mechanical* and *Standard* text styles. You may also want to play with some of the other text options available in the *Text Style* dialog box.

- [ ] When you are done, exit AutoCAD and do not save the drawing.

Assignment
for Module 7 – Activity 1

The purpose of this assignment is to give you practice placing *Dynamic Text* on a drawing. In the first section, you will find step-by-step instructions on how to do this. Then, in the second section, you will be required to apply what you have learned to finish the assignment. After completing this assignment, you should be able to set up several different text styles, use the text styles when placing *Dynamic Text* on a drawing, and fill in the drawing's title block based on the standards in this book.

Procedure: ☑ Check each box as you complete that item.

- ☐ Start *AutoCAD 2002*.
- ☐ When the *AutoCAD 2002 Today* dialog box appears, open the drawing *M07A01-2.dwg* located in the *Module07* subdirectory on the CD.
- ☐ The drawing will open to paper space where you will be working.

Setting up the Mechanical Text Style

- ☐ Click on the *Format* pull-down menu and select *Text Style*. The *Text Style* dialog box will appear.
- ☐ Click on the *New* button and the *New Text Style* dialog box will open. Type **MECHANICAL** for the name and click *OK* to close the dialog box.
- ☐ Change the *Font Name* to "romans.shx" using the drop-down list. You will have to scroll up the list to find this font.
- ☐ Click the *Apply* button to apply this font to your new text style.
- ☐ Click the *Close* button to close the *Text Style* dialog box.

Completing the Drawing's Title Block

Now that you have learned how to add text to a drawing, you must completely fill in the title block on every drawing you create based on the standards listed below.

Text Style:	MECHANICAL
Font:	romans
Text Height:	1/8" (.125") for Name, Scale, Date, and Title
	1/4" (.250") for the Drawing Number
Text Rotation:	0°
Text Location:	Centered in each box

Remember, all text on a drawing must be in CAPITAL letters.

- ☐ Type **DT** on the *Command* line and press the *Enter* key.
- ☐ Verify that MECHANICAL is the current text style by looking on the command line. It should appear as shown below. If it does not, change it.

DTEXT
Current text style: "MECHANICAL" Text height: 0.2000
Specify start point of text or [Justify/Style]:

- [ ] Since the text must be centered in the white space of each box on the title block, it is easier to use justification to center it.
- [ ] Type **J** on the command line and hit the *Enter* key.
- [ ] Type **MC** (for middle center) and hit the *Enter* key. This enables you to pick the center of the white space in the box as a starting point and center the text top-to-bottom and left-to-right about this point.
- [ ] Place the crosshairs in the center of the open space in the *Drawn By* box and click the mouse button.
- [ ] Enter **.125** for the text height, hit *Enter*, and accept the default 0° rotation angle by hitting *Enter* on the next line.
- [ ] Type in your name in all caps on the command line. If you have a long name, you may have to use an initial for your first name. Hit the *Enter* key twice. Your name should appear centered in the box.
- [ ] If you are not happy with the location in the box or how your name appears, you can always erase it and try again.
- [ ] Use the same method to fill in the other boxes. You will have to set the MC justification each time you start a new line of text. The title block boxes should contain the following information for this drawing. Replace the italicized words with the appropriate information.

Scale:	NONE
Date:	*today's date*
Drawn By:	*your name*
Title:	DTEXT
Drawing Number:	M07A01-2 (Remember, this is 1/4" high.)

- [ ] After you have completed the title block, save your drawing to your removable disk with the name M07A01-2.

Practice Placing Different Text and Styles

In this section you will place several lines of DTEXT on the drawing using different text styles and fonts. The steps will walk you through placing the first line, but you will be required to set up and place the other lines. Make all text .150" high with the font and characteristics as listed in each line of text. For example, THIS IS ROMANC SLANTED RIGHT, will be placed using the romanc.shx font and the text will be slanted to the right. All text must always be inside the drawing border.

In this section you will place the following line of text centered near the top of the page.

THIS IS ROMANC SLANTED RIGHT

- [ ] Click on the *Format* pull-down menu and select *Text Style*. The *Text Style* dialog box will appear.
- [ ] Click on the New button and enter **ROMANC** for the name in the *New Text Style* box that appears. Click *OK* to close the *New Text Style* box. Remember that every time you need to change the font or the characteristics, you must make a new text style.

- ☐ Change the *Font Name* to "romanc.shx" using the drop-down list. You will have to scroll up the list to find this font.
- ☐ Change the *Oblique Angle*, located in the *Effects* part of the *Text Style* dialog box, to 15 so that the text will slant to the right at an angle of 15°. (To slant the text to the left, you would use −15.) Look in the *Preview* area to see how the text will look.
- ☐ Click the *Apply* button to apply this font to your new text style.
- ☐ Click the *Close* button to close the *Text Style* dialog box.
- ☐ Type **DT** on the *Command* line and press the *Enter* key.
- ☐ Verify that ROMANC is the current text style by looking on the command line. It should appear as shown below. If it does not, change it.

DTEXT
Current text style: "ROMANC" Text height: 0.1250
Specify start point of text or [Justify/Style]:

- ☐ Since the text must be centered, type **J** on the command line and hit the *Enter* key.
- ☐ Type **TC** (for top center) and hit the *Enter* key. This will allow you to pick the center of the drawing inside the border as a starting point, and the text will be centered below and centered left-to-right about this point.
- ☐ Place the crosshairs a short distance inside the top border centered left to right and click the mouse button.
- ☐ Enter **.150** for the text height, hit *Enter*, and accept the default 0° rotation angle by hitting *Enter* on the next line.
- ☐ Type in the line, as it appears at the start of this section, in all caps on the command line. Hit the *Enter* key twice. The line should appear centered about the point you picked.
- ☐ If you are not happy with the location, you can always erase the line and try again.
- ☐ Click the *Save* button on the *Standard* toolbar to save the work you just completed.

Place the following text on your drawing. You may place it anywhere you want as long as it is inside the drawing border and does not overlap any other text. If the text does not fit, erase it and try again. Make sure you are using the correct font and characteristics, as you did in the previous example. Remember, you must make a new text style for each line. If you change an existing style, it will change any text you already placed on your drawing with that style. You may want to save often so that you can back up if you forget to make a new style and the existing text on the drawing is incorrectly changed.

THIS IS SIMPLEX UPSIDE DOWN.

THIS IS ROMANT BACKWARDS.

THIS IS COMPLEX VERTICAL.

THIS IS SCRIPTS, WIDTH FACTOR 1.5.

THIS IS ITALIC ROTATED 90°.

THIS IS ROMAND OVER AND UNDER LINED.

- [ ] When you are satisfied with your work, save your drawing again.
- [ ] Print a copy of your drawing.

Activity 2

Multiline Text

Objectives: After completing this activity, you should be able to do the following:

- Place multiple lines of text on a drawing using the *Multiline Text* button on the *Draw* toolbar.
- Use the *Multiline Text Editor* dialog box to set the font, style, size, and justification of the text.
- Resize the multiline text boundary to fit text into specific areas of a drawing.
- Use the *Character Map* to import special characters into *Multiline Text*.
- Edit multiline text.

Procedure: ☑ Check each box as you complete that item.

- ☐ Start *AutoCAD 2002*.
- ☐ When the *AutoCAD 2002 Today* dialog box appears, open the drawing *M07A02-1.dwg* located in the *Module07* subdirectory on the CD.
- ☐ When the program has loaded, you will notice that the drawing has opened in *Paper Space*. Verify that only the *Paper* button on the *Status* bar is selected.

Inserting *Multiline Text* in a Drawing

Inserting *Multiline Text* in a drawing is similar to using a word processor. Text is typed and modified using an editor before it is placed in the drawing. And before any text is entered, the area where the text will appear is defined on the drawing.

- ☐ Use Figure 7-5 to locate and click on the *Multiline Text* button located at the bottom of the *Draw* toolbar.

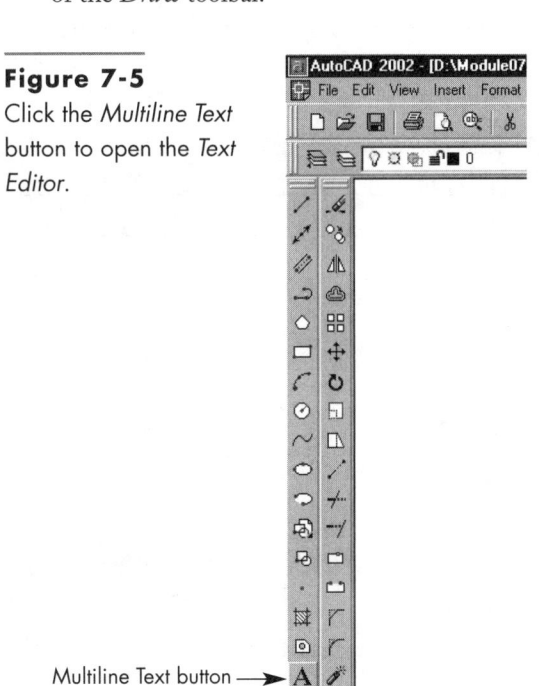

Figure 7-5
Click the *Multiline Text* button to open the *Text Editor*.

alternate method

There are two other methods of starting the *Multiline Text* command. You can click on the *Draw* pull-down menu, slide the pointer to the *Text* menu item, and select *Multiline Text* from the cascading menu that appears. Or you can type **MTEXT,** or just **T,** on the command line and hit the *Enter* key.

☐ A check of the command line shows that AutoCAD is asking you to specify the first corner of the box that will enclose the text on the drawing.

Command:
Command: _mtext Current text style: "Standard" Text height: 0.2000
Specify first corner:

☐ Place the crosshairs near the upper left corner of the drawing inside the border and click the mouse button to start the box.

Command: _mtext Current text style: "Standard" Text height: 0.2000
Specify first corner:
Specify opposite corner or [Height/Justify/Line spacing/Rotation/Style/Width]:

☐ Drag the cursor down and to the right to form the text box. The box will look similar to Figure 7-6. The arrow in the box indicates the direction of text flow in the box. When the box is approximately one-fourth the size of the white area, click the mouse button again.

☐ The *Multiline Text Editor*, shown in Figure 7-7, will open. The editor is in its own window, so you can move and resize it to make it easier to work in.

☐ Verify that the *Character* tab of the editor is selected. Click on the first drop-down list and select *RomanS* as the font. (See Figure 7-8.) Depending on the number of fonts on your computer, you may have to use the scroll bar to locate it.

☐ Place the cursor over the window of the second drop-down list and click the mouse button. The numbers will become highlighted, indicating that they are selected for editing. Hit the *Delete* key and the 0.2000 will disappear. Type **.125** from the keyboard and hit the *Enter* key. This sets the text size to 1/8 inch.

☐ You should now see a flashing vertical line in the large white area that indicates where the text will be entered. If not, place the mouse cursor anywhere in that area

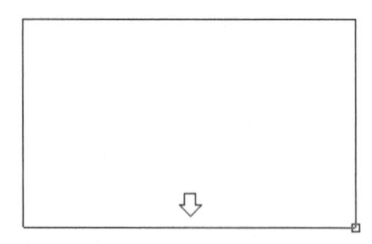

Figure 7-6
Text box

Figure 7-7
The *Multiline Text Editor* works like a word processor.

Figure 7-8
Set the font to 1/8" high *RomanS*.

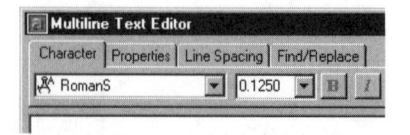

and click the mouse button. The flashing cursor will appear. Type the following, hitting the *Enter* key at the end of each line. (Some of the lines of text may wrap to the next line before you hit the *Enter* key for that line. This is not a problem and will be corrected in the next section.)

THIS IS MULTILINE TEXT.
UNLIKE DYNAMIC TEXT EACH LINE IS NOT SEPARATE.
IF I HIT ERASE, ALL THE TEXT WILL BE LOST.

☐ Click the *OK* button. The dialog box will close, and the text will appear on the drawing.

Resizing the Text Box

☐ Place the mouse cursor over one of the lines of text and click the mouse button. The multiline text will take on a strange dashed appearance, indicating that it has been selected, and four square boxes, called *grips,* will appear at the corners.

☐ Move the mouse pointer over the grip at the bottom right corner of the text. With the cursor over the grip, click the mouse button and that grip will turn red, indicating that it has been selected. A check of the command line indicates that you have actuated the *Stretch* mode. Move the mouse toward the left. This will make the text box, indicated by a rectangle on the screen, narrower and taller.

☐ When the text box appears to be about half its original width, click the mouse button again. This releases the grip and sets the new text box size. Hit the *Esc* key to deselect the text. Notice that the text has wrapped to fit inside the new text box size.

☐ Place the cursor over one of the lines of text and again click the mouse button to select the text. Place the cursor over the bottom right grip, click the mouse button to select the grip, and slide the mouse to the right until the text box is wide, but not very high.

☐ Click the mouse button again to release the grip, and hit the *Esc* key to deselect the text. Notice that the text now appears as the three lines that you had originally typed. By using the grip method, you can resize any text box to meet your needs.

Erasing

☐ Click on the *Erase* button and then click on the second line of text. What happened? Hit the *Enter* key to erase all the multiline text.

Other Options in the Text Editor

☐ Click on the *Multiline Text* button and draw a text box about one-fourth the size of the white area, as you did earlier in this activity. When the box is the proper size, click the mouse button to enter the *Multiline Text Editor.*

☐ This time select *Times New Roman* as the font and again use .125 for the height.

☐ Notice the three buttons located next to the height. They are *B* for bold, *I* for italic, and *U* for underline. Click on the *B* and *U* buttons to select them and type the following line.

THIS IS TIMES NEW ROMAN.

☐ The line of text appears bold and italic. Turn off the *B* and *U* buttons by clicking on each, and then hit *Enter* to move to the next text line.

☐ Special characters and symbols are added to multiline text using the *Symbol* button as shown in Figure 7-9. Clicking on this button gives you the three special characters

Figure 7-9

Special characters and symbols are obtained by clicking the *Symbol* button.

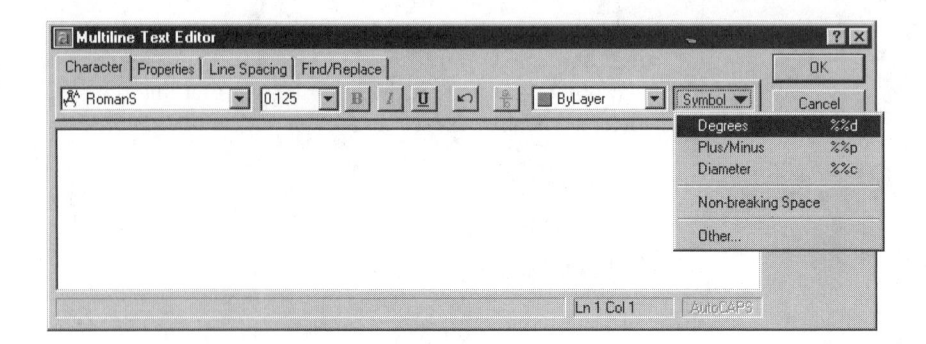

you learned in the last activity, a non-breaking space option that keeps two adjacent words together on the same line, and other characters and symbols to be covered shortly. If you clicked on this button, click in the white text area and the drop-down menu will close.

☐ Type **SPECIAL CHARACTERS** from the keyboard.

☐ Hit the *space bar*, click the *Symbol* button, and select *Degrees* from the list by clicking on it. The degree symbol appears in the line of text.

☐ Hit the *space bar* and select *Plus/Minus* from the *Symbol* list. The plus/minus sign appears.

☐ Hit the *space bar* and select *Diameter* from the *Symbol* menu. What appeared on the text line? Hit the *Enter* key to move to the next text line.

☐ The *Other* option in the *Symbol* menu gives you the greatest flexibility for adding special characters and symbols.

☐ Type **OTHER CHARACTERS**: and hit the *space bar* once.

☐ Click on the *Symbol* button and select *Other* by clicking on it. The *Character Map* dialog box will appear (see Figure 7-10). This box gives you access to all the characters from all the fonts on your computer.

☐ Verify that the font on the *Character Map* is *Symbol*. If it is not, click on the *Font* drop-down list and select *Symbol* from the list using the scroll bar. Click on the pi (π) symbol and its box will become larger, as shown in Figure 7-10, so that you can verify that you have selected the correct character. Click on the *Select* button and pi (π) will appear in the *Characters to copy* area at the bottom of the dialog box. Click on the *Copy* button, and finally on the *Close* button. You have just copied the pi (π) character to the Windows clipboard and you can now paste it into the text.

Figure 7-10

Character Map

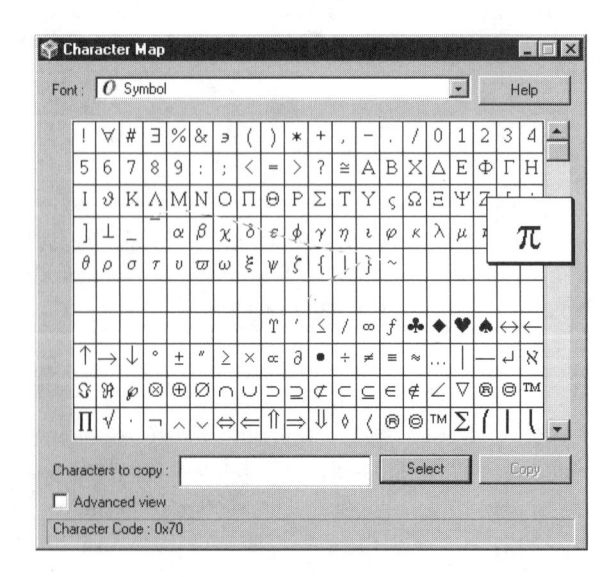

Putting Text on a Drawing 209

- [ ] Place the cursor in the text window to the right of the last line of text and click the mouse button. A flashing cursor will appear indicating where the character will be placed.
- [ ] To place the character you copied, click the right mouse button and select *Paste* from the menu that appears. The pi (π) symbol should now be at the end of the line.
- [ ] Type a comma (,) behind the pi character and then hit the *space bar* once.
- [ ] Select *Other* from the *Symbol* list, locate and click on the perpendicular symbol ($\perp$), and click the *Select* button. Note that the symbol appears in the *Characters to copy* area at the bottom of the dialog box.
- [ ] Locate and click on the angle symbol ($\angle$) and click the *Select* button. This symbol now appears next to the perpendicular symbol in the *Characters to copy* area. In the future you can place a number of characters in this area and copy them all at the same time.
- [ ] Click the *Copy* button and then the *Close* button.
- [ ] Place the cursor in the text window to the right of the last character you pasted, click the mouse button, and the flashing cursor will appear. Click the right mouse button and select *Paste* from the menu. The two characters will appear on the text line.
- [ ] Use the back arrow on the keyboard to place a comma and space between the perpendicular symbol and the angle symbol. Move the cursor back to the end of the line and hit the *Enter* key to move to the next line of text.
- [ ] Note that if you started typing right now, you would be in the *Symbol* font at a height of .150. Change the font back to *Times New Roman* and the height back to .125 by selecting each from its drop-down list.
- [ ] Type **THE END** and hit the *OK* button to place the text on the drawing.

Editing Text

- [ ] Place the cursor over one of the lines of text and click the mouse button. The text box will be selected.
- [ ] Click the *right* mouse button and a pop-up menu will appear. Select *Mtext Edit* (not *Repeat Multiline Text*) from the menu by clicking on it. The *Multiline Text Editor* will reopen with the selected text appearing in the window.
- [ ] Place the cursor just to the left of the pi symbol (π) and click the mouse button. The flashing line should appear at that location.
- [ ] With the cursor at that location, press and hold the mouse button and drag the cursor to the right until it is just right of the angle symbol ($\angle$). This is called selecting the text. The three symbols including commas and spaces should be highlighted.
- [ ] These symbols were pasted at a height of .150 and you will now change them so that they are the same size as the other text. Click on the height drop-down list and select .125 by clicking on it.
- [ ] Hit the *Enter* key and you should see the text change size.
- [ ] Using the same method to select text, select the entire first line and then click the *U* button to eliminate the underline.
- [ ] Click the *OK* button to close the dialog box and the changes will appear on the drawing.
- [ ] After you have had an opportunity to look at the text you placed on the drawing, erase it.

Working with Fractions and Stacked Text

Fractions are commonly found on engineering drawings. In this section you will learn different methods of making stacked fractions and stacking other text. Since there are several possible ways of stacking fractions, and some of them occur automatically, you will first learn how to stack non-numeric text so you have the opportunity to see the options. Then you will learn how to manually or automatically format numerical fractions.

☐ Click on the *Multiline Text* button and draw a text box about one-fourth the size of the white area, as you did earlier. When the box is the proper size, click the mouse button to enter the *Multiline Text Editor*.

☐ Change the font to RomanS and the text size to .375. This will make the text large enough so you can see the differences between each of the following options.

☐ Type the following in lowercase letters exactly as it appears. There is a space between each set of three characters. The ^ and # characters are found above the numbers 6 and 3, respectively.

a/b c^d e#f

☐ Place the cursor to the left of the "a", press and hold the mouse button, and slide the cursor to the right to highlight the "a/b" only.

☐ Locate and click on the *Stack fraction* button located to the right of the *Undo* button above the text area. The letters will be stacked in a fractional form.

☐ Place the cursor to the left of the "c", press and hold the mouse button, and slide the cursor to the right to highlight the "c^d" only.

☐ Click on the *Stack fraction* button to stack these letters.

☐ Place the cursor to the left of the "e", press and hold the mouse button, and slide the cursor to the right to highlight the "e#f" only.

☐ Click on the *Stack fraction* button to stack these letters.

☐ Click the *OK* button to close the editor and place the text on the drawing.

The following describes the three stacking arrangements you see on the drawing.

Horizontal Fraction—A horizontal fraction is produced when you place a forward slash (/) between the letters or numbers making the fraction. A short division line is placed between the numerator and denominator.

Tolerance Stack—A tolerance stack is formed when you place a caret (^) between the letters or numbers making the fraction. A tolerance stack has no line separating the numerator and denominator and both are left aligned. This format is commonly used when specifying a tolerance on a drawing.

Diagonal Fraction—A diagonal fraction is formed when you place a number sign (#) between the letters or numbers that make the fraction. A diagonal line is placed between the numerator and denominator.

☐ Place the cursor over one of the lines of text and click the mouse button. The text box will be selected.

☐ Click the *right* mouse button and a pop-up menu will appear. Select *Mtext Edit* from the menu by clicking on it. The *Multiline Text Editor* will reopen with the fractions appearing in the window.

☐ Place the cursor to the left of the *e-f* fraction, press and hold the mouse button, and slide the cursor to the right to highlight only the *e-f* fraction.

☐ Click on the *Stack fraction* button. The fraction will be unstacked. Click the *Stack fraction* button again to restack it.

☐ Highlight the *a-b* fraction using the method described above.

☐ Place the cursor anywhere in the white text editing area and click the right mouse button. A pop-up menu will appear, as shown in Figure 7-11. Select *Properties* from the menu by clicking on it. The *Stack Properties* dialog box will open.

Figure 7-11
Right-click in the white text editing area and select *Properties* from the pop-up menu.

Figure 7-12

The *Stack Properties* dialog box

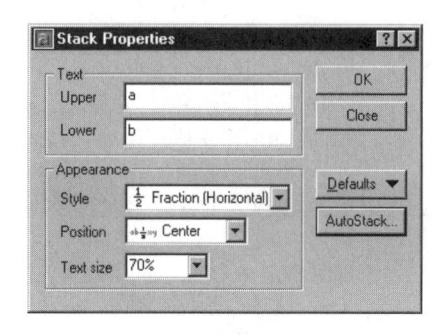

The *Stack Properties* dialog box, shown in Figure 7-12, allows you to modify the fraction you have selected and to set other options. The following gives you a brief description of each area in this dialog box.

Text—This area is used to revise the numerator's and denominator's text for the selected fraction.

- **Upper**—This type-in box allows you to change the existing text in the fraction's numerator.
- **Lower**—This type-in box allows you to change the existing text in the fraction's denominator.

Appearance—This area is used to define the appearance of the fraction on the drawing.

- **Style**—This drop-down list allows you to change to any of the three styles, Horizontal, Tolerance, or Diagonal, regardless of the character you placed between the numerator and denominator text.
- **Position**—This drop-down list allows you to specify where the fraction will align with the other text in the line. Center is the default, but you have the option of aligning the top of the fraction with the top of the line or the bottom of the fraction with the bottom of the line. Each option on the list shows a small example of how the fraction will appear in the line of text.
- **Text size**—This option lets you set the percentage size for the text in the fraction. 100% would make the numerator and denominator text the same size as the rest of the line. This makes the fraction quite large, so it usually is sized smaller. 70% is the default, but the drop-down list provides options from 50% to 100%.

Buttons—The following list describes the functions of the four buttons located along the right side of this dialog box.

- **OK**—The *OK* button applies the changes you made and closes the dialog box.
- **Cancel**—The *Cancel* button closes the dialog box without making any changes.
- **Defaults**—The *Defaults* button produces a menu that enables you either to reset the dialog box to AutoCAD's original default values, or to save the current settings so they will appear the next time you open this dialog box.
- **AutoStack**—The *AutoStack* button opens the *AutoStack* dialog box that will be described later in this activity.

☐ In the appropriate text box, change *a* to **15** and *b* to **16** and close the dialog box by clicking on the *OK* button. The changes will take effect in the text editor.

- ☐ Highlight the *e-f* fraction and open the *Stack Properties* dialog box by right-clicking in the white area of the text editor.
- ☐ Click on the *AutoStack* button and the *AutoStack Properties* dialog box will open. Make sure that the *Enable AutoStacking* check box and the *Don't show this dialog again* check box are NOT checked. Click the *OK* button to close the dialog box and return to the *Stack Properties* dialog box. (You will learn more about the *AutoStack Properties* dialog box later.)
- ☐ In the appropriate text box, change *e* to **5** and *f* to **8,** the *Style* to *Horizontal*, and the *Text size* to 100%. Close the dialog box by clicking on the *OK* button. The changes will take effect in the text editor.
- ☐ Place the cursor to the right of the 5/8 fraction and click the mouse button. Hit the space bar and type **FRACTIONS**. Click the *OK* button to return to the drawing. If necessary, resize the text box so that FRACTIONS appears on the same line as the other fractions. You can now see why 100% text size produces an overly large fraction.
- ☐ After you have had an opportunity to look at the text you placed on the drawing, erase it.

Using AutoStack

In this section you will learn how to automatically stack your fractions.

- ☐ Click on the *Multiline Text* button and draw a text box about one-fourth the size of the white area, as you did earlier. When the box is the proper size, click the mouse button to enter the *Multiline Text Editor*.
- ☐ Change the font to RomanS and the text size to .375.
- ☐ Type **1/2** from the keyboard and hit the *space bar*. As soon as you hit the *space bar*, the *AutoStack Properties* dialog box will open.

The *AutoStack Properties* dialog box shown in Figure 7-13 is used to specify how AutoCAD will treat your fractions in the future. Most companies have a standard way they want fractions to appear on drawings. This dialog box allows you to set the style, so you do not have to enter special characters or format every fraction you type. The following list gives brief descriptions of the features of this dialog box.

> **Enable AutoStacking**—This check box allows you to turn on the *AutoStacking* function. When checked, AutoCAD will apply the other options in this dialog box to the fractions you type.
>
> **Remove leading blank**—This check box is only available when *AutoStacking* is on. When checked, the space before the fraction will be removed. This allows the fraction to be placed directly behind a whole number. This would be set depending on a company's standards.

Figure 7-13

The *AutoStack Properties* dialog box

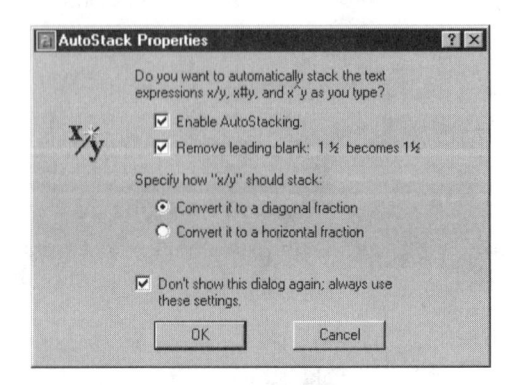

Putting Text on a Drawing 213

> **Specify how "x/y" should stack**—Two options are provided in this area. You can specify how you want the fraction to appear, either diagonal or horizontal. Since most people type / as the separator for fractions, this option allows you to specify which way the fraction will appear. By clicking the *Convert it to a diagonal fraction* button, you can type **1/2**, and not **1#2**, for example, to get diagonal fractions.
>
> **Don't show this dialog again**—When this box is checked, AutoCAD will automatically apply the above settings to fractions without opening the dialog box. This allows you to type in fractions and continue working without having to format each one individually.

- ☐ Select the following options from the dialog box by clicking on them.

    Enable AutoStacking
    Remove leading blank
    Convert it to a diagonal fraction
    Don't show this dialog again

- ☐ When done your dialog box should look like Figure 7-13. This will be the standard style for fractions in future activities.
- ☐ Click the OK button.
- ☐ Now type **3/4** and hit the space bar. The fraction will be automatically stacked.
- ☐ Type **5 3/16** (remember to put a space between the 5 and the 3) and hit the space bar. The fraction will be stacked and the space removed between the whole and fractional parts of the number.
- ☐ Click the *OK* button to return to the drawing.
- ☐ This completes this activity. You may want to spend some time practicing placing *Multiline Text* and examining the other word processing options available by selecting the *Properties, Line Spacing,* and *Find/Replace* tabs in the *Multiline Text Editor*.
- ☐ When you are done, close the AutoCAD program without saving the drawing.

Assignment
for Module 7 – Activity 2

The purpose of this assignment is to give you practice placing *Multiline Text* on a drawing. Most drawings contain notes about the units and precision that apply to the drawing and what manufacturing standards should be used. After completing this assignment, you should be able to place large blocks of text and general notes on a drawing.

Procedure: ☑ Check each box as you complete that item.

- ☐ Start *AutoCAD 2002*.
- ☐ When the *AutoCAD 2002 Today* dialog box appears, open the drawing M07A02-2.dwg located in the *Module07* subdirectory on the CD.
- ☐ The drawing will open to paper space where you will be working.
- ☐ Complete the drawing's title block based on the following information. You must set up the *MECHANICAL* text style before proceeding.

Text Standards for Title Blocks:

Text Style:	MECHANICAL
Font:	romans
Text Height:	1/8" (.125") for Name, Scale, Date, and Title
	1/4" (.250") for the Drawing Number
Text Rotation:	0°
Text Location:	Centered in the white space of each box

Title block information for this drawing:

Scale:	NONE
Date:	*today's date*
Drawn By:	*your name*
Title:	MTEXT
Drawing Number:	M07A02-2 (remember, this is 1/4" high)

☐ After you have completed the title block, save your drawing to your removable disk with the name M07A02-2.

Place the following block of text in the upper half of the drawing using *Multiline* text. The text is to be .20" high using the *Stylus BT* font.

I HAVE LEARNED THE IMPORTANCE OF MAKING NEAT, PROFESSIONAL CAD DRAWINGS. I KNOW HOW TO PROPERLY PLACE BOTH DYNAMIC AND MULTI-LINE TEXT ON A DRAWING, AND HOW TO COMPLETE THE DRAWING'S TITLE BLOCK BASED ON THE STANDARDS SET IN THIS BOOK. I ALSO KNOW HOW TO INSERT SPECIAL SYMBOLS LIKE ∅, ±, AND °, AND HOW TO INSERT SPECIAL CHARACTERS LIKE Ω, μ, AND π.

☐ Click the *Save* button on the *Standard* toolbar to save the work you just completed.

Place the following general notes in the lower half of the drawing using *Multiline* text. The text is to be 1/8" high using the **MECHANICAL** text style. Most companies place general notes near the bottom of the drawing, and they are numbered from bottom to top so that additional notes can be added the top of the list. Place the following notes starting in the lower left corner of the drawing.

5. WORKMANSHIP MUST CONFORM TO COMPANY'S ENGINEERING STANDARDS.

4. PAINT ALL NON-MACHINED SURFACES WITH STANDARD GRAY PRIMER.

3. REMOVE ALL BURRS AND SHARP EDGES.

2. UNLESS OTHERWISE SPECIFIED, ALL HOLES TO BE 9/16" ∅.

1. UNLESS OTHERWISE SPECIFIED, ALL DIMENSIONS ARE IN INCHES.

NOTES:

☐ When you are satisfied with your work, save your drawing.
☐ Print a copy of your drawing.

Applying the Concepts

Your boss has asked you to draw an organizational chart of upper management for your company. Your company's president will use it for an upcoming meeting with the board of directors. Your boss gave you a rough sketch of the organization with names. Since your name will appear in the title block of the drawing, this is an opportunity for you to display your AutoCAD skills not only to your boss, but also to the president and the board of directors.

You only have a hand drawn sketch (see Figure 7-14) and must determine how to lay out the chart so that it will fit on the drawing paper. Since you were given limited information about how to prepare the drawing, you must make decisions about size and location of the objects on the drawing. You must do a lot of preplanning before you even start putting lines on the drawing. The most important thing is that you make a very professional looking drawing. You should consider having uniform size and spacing for all boxes on the chart, i.e., rows and columns that line up, and making sure that the all the boxes are the same size and correctly connected. You are not permitted to deviate from the general layout that was given to you, i.e., you cannot move or reorder the boxes. Also, you must make sure that the names and titles fit inside the boxes you create. You may want to experiment to determine the length of the longest name or title, and the height of two lines of text before you set the box dimensions.

The only restriction on your drawing is that the text for the names and positions be in the *Mechanical* text style, .125" high, using both capital and lowercase letters.

Good luck. Your job may depend on how well you do on this assignment.

Figure 7-14
Company chart

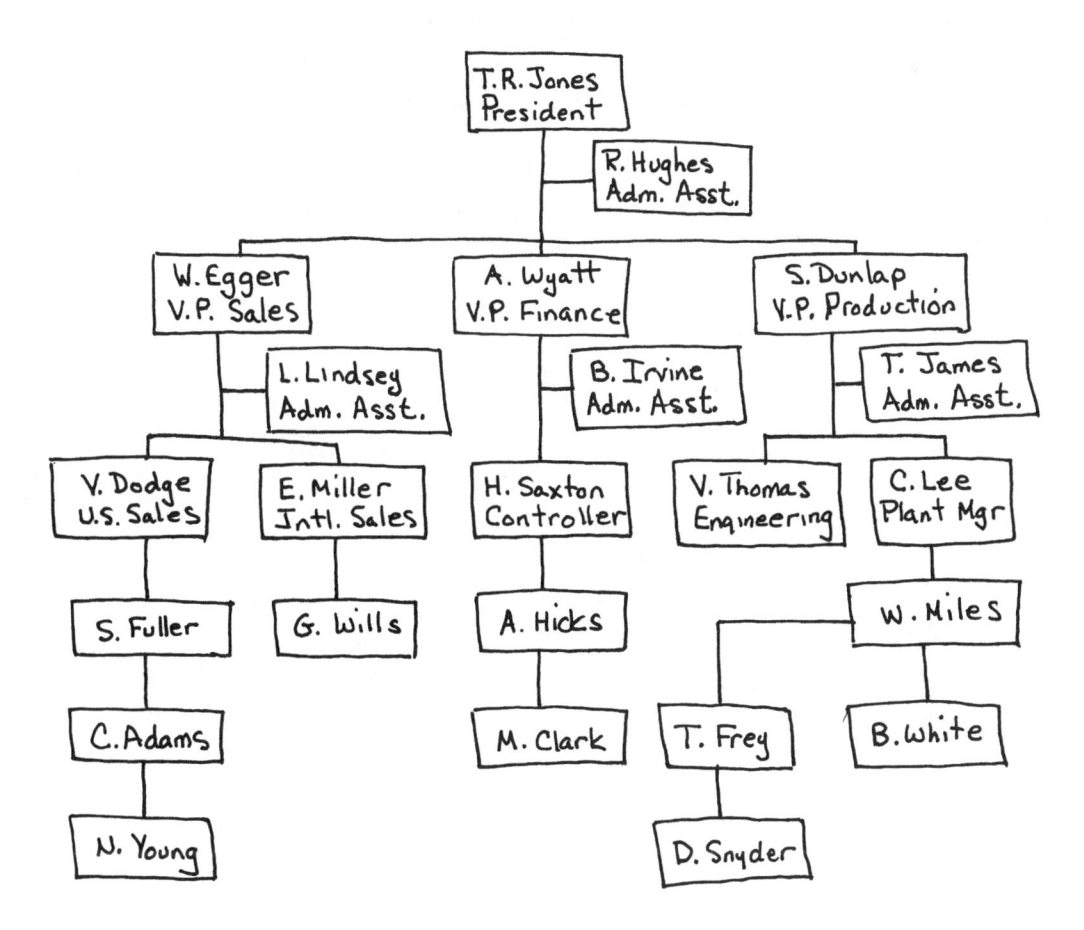

Procedure: ☑ Check each box as you complete that item.

- ☐ Start *AutoCAD 2002*.
- ☐ When the *AutoCAD 2002 Today* dialog box appears, open the drawing *M07APP.dwg* located in the *Module07* subdirectory on the CD.
- ☐ When the drawing opens, you will see a large rectangle on the screen. You must place the entire organizational chart inside this rectangle. The rectangle is provided as a reference to ensure that your chart will fit on the paper.
- ☐ Enter all the names and titles. Use *Mechanical* text style, .09″ high, using both capital and lowercase letters.
- ☐ When you finish the chart, click on the *A-size Sheet* tab. You will see the chart you drew inside the blue rectangle on the paper; however, it is probably not centered. The rectangle you used as a reference also appears with your chart, but it will not print on your final drawing, so you can ignore it when centering your chart.
- ☐ As you did in the previous activity, center the chart on the paper by changing to model space, using the *Pan* command, and then changing back to paper space. Do not use the *Zoom* command during this operation. If you are unsure of how to do this, refer to the Assignment for Module 6 – Activity 1.
- ☐ Complete the drawing's title block with the following information.

　　　Scale:　　　　　　NONE
　　　Date:　　　　　　*today's date*
　　　Drawn by:　　　　*your name*
　　　Title:　　　　　　COMPANY CHART
　　　Drawing Number:　M07APP

- ☐ Save the drawing to your removable disk with the name M07APP.
- ☐ Print a copy of your drawing using the methods you learned in previous activities.

Module 7 Review Questions

These questions are provided to help you review the topics and concepts covered in this module.

True or False

Determine whether the statement is true or false. Place your answer, either T or F, in the blank.

____   1. Any changes you make and save to an existing text style will change all the text on the drawing that was made with that text style.

____   2. It is impossible to have two lines of text on the same drawing with one line slanted to the left and the other line slanted to the right.

____   3. **%%C** is the special code for the diameter symbol (∅).

____   4. When drawing a text box for *Multiline* text, the text box must be the correct size and in the correct location, as it cannot be changed.

____   5. *Enable AutoStacking* allows you to standardize how AutoCAD will stack fractions.

____   6. **%%UO** is the special code used to make the text both underlined and overlined.

____   7. Using Multiline text allows you to have several fonts, character types, and sizes of characters within the same line of text.

____   8. When setting up a new text style using the *Text Style* dialog box, it is important to set the text height you want.

____   9. Importing characters from other fonts is easy when using *Dynamic* text.

____ 10. Each line of *Multiline* text is independent of all others and can be individually erased using the *Erase* command.

____ 11. *Justification* can be used with both *Dynamic* and *Multiline* text.

____ 12. The *Rotation* angle and the *Oblique* angle produce the same text effects when they are set to the same value.

Module 8

Using a Template and Setting a Drawing's Parameters

Activity 1

Starting a New Drawing Using a Template

Objectives: After completing this activity, you should be able to do the following:

- Describe the use of templates.
- Identify a template based on its file extension.
- Start a new drawing from a template using the *AutoCAD 2002 Today* dialog box.
- Start a new drawing from a template using the *New* button on the *Standard* toolbar.
- Make and save your own template.
- Start a new drawing using your template.

Templates are used to save time when starting a new drawing. In this activity you will learn how to use a template to start a new drawing, and how to make and save your own personalized template. This will save setup time in future drawing assignments. Templates are important because they let you develop and save a standard drawing that contains things you use every time you start a new drawing, such as your name, text styles, etc.

Procedure: ☑ Check each box as you complete that item.

- ☐ Open the *AutoCAD 2002* program.
- ☐ When the *AutoCAD 2002 Today* dialog box appears, click on the *Create Drawings* tab in the *My Drawings* area. (See Figure 8-1.) Verify that *Template* appears in the window following *Select how to begin*. If it does not, select it from the drop-down list.
- ☐ You will see a list of template groups. Each group is made up of all the templates having the same first letter in their name. Recently used templates appear at the top of the list and all other available templates are listed alphabetically below. Each list can be opened and closed by clicking the arrowhead next to the list's title. The names and number of recently used templates will vary based on what templates you and others have recently accessed. AutoCAD also provides a large number of templates

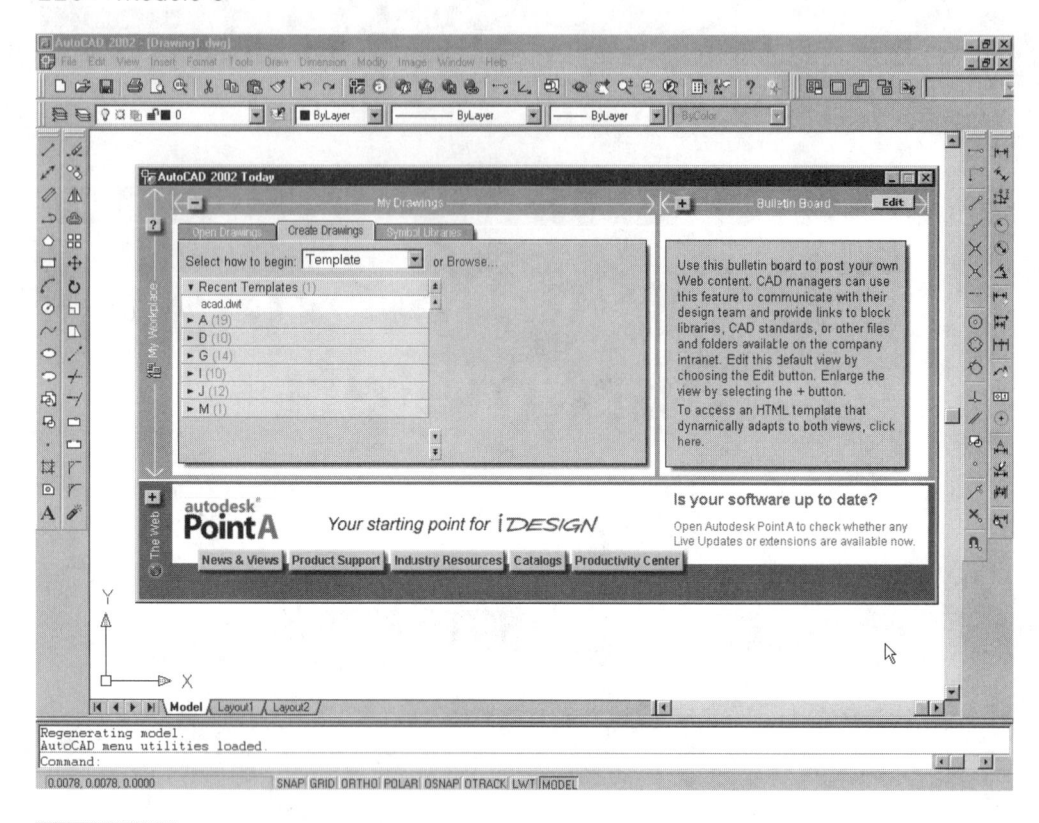

Figure 8-1
Select the *Create Drawings* tab in the *AutoCAD 2002 Today* dialog box.

based on different engineering standards. If you open the various lists you will see drawing templates based on ANSI, DIN, ISO, and other engineering standards.

> **Note:** Unlike other drawings you have opened, the file extension for this drawing is *.dwt* not *.dwg*. In AutoCAD, *.dwt* indicates a template drawing, and although it is a drawing like any other, the program treats it differently. The most important difference is that after it is opened, it automatically changes its name from *AnyNameTemplate.dwt* to *Drawing1.dwg* (or 2, 3, 4, etc.), a regular AutoCAD drawing. This prevents you from making changes and then accidentally saving them back to the template file. It takes a special procedure to save a drawing as a template and you will learn to do this later in this activity.

☐ Click on the *Browse* hyperlink as you have done when opening other drawings. As in past activities, the *Select File* dialog box will open, but this time it has opened to the *Template* subdirectory in the *AutoCAD 2002* directory. Templates are usually stored in this directory so that they can easily be located. Often when a company makes a new template it is placed here where everyone can find it.

☐ For this activity you will have to look elsewhere for the template you will open. Click on the *Look In* drop-down list, and locate and select the CD-ROM drive by clicking on it. Double-click on the *Template* subdirectory and you will find the *CAD Template.dwt* to be used in this activity.

☐ Double-click on the template's icon to open it. After the program has finished loading, observe the name of the open drawing in AutoCAD's title bar. It is *Drawing2.dwg*, not *CAD Template.dwt*.

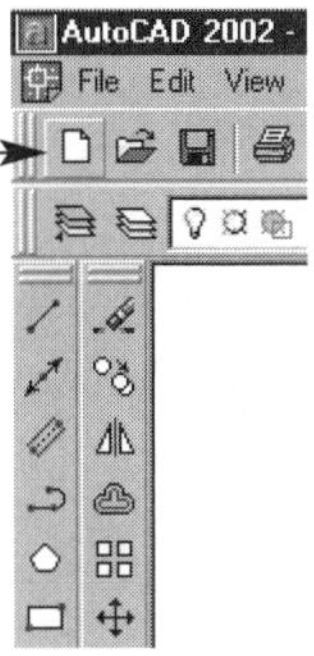

Figure 8-2
Click on the *New* button to create a new drawing.

- ☐ This template is set up to open to *Model* space since that is where you begin most drawing work.
- ☐ At the bottom of the drawing area are three tabs marked *A-*, *B-*, and *C-size Sheet*. These are the three standard paper sizes you will use to print your drawings in these activities. You can use the same template for all your drawing work regardless of the final print size. In a future activity you will learn how to add tabs for other drawing sizes or layouts.
- ☐ Click on the *A-size Sheet* tab. This drawing layout should be familiar to you since it is the one you have seen in several other activities. It is the standard 8.5″ × 11″ letter size sheet.
- ☐ Click on the *B-size Sheet* tab. This is the next standard paper size, 11″ × 17″, and usually requires printing on a larger device called a plotter.
- ☐ Click on the *C-size Sheet* tab. This is the next standard paper size, 17″ × 22″, and also requires printing on a plotter.
- ☐ Click on the *File* pull-down menu, slide the mouse pointer down the list, and select *Close* by clicking on it. AutoCAD's *Save Changes* warning will appear. Select *No* and the drawing will close.
- ☐ You can also start a new drawing using a template by clicking on the *New* button on the *Standard* toolbar, as shown in Figure 8-2. This enables you to start a new drawing while you are working in AutoCAD. Click on the *New* button now.
- ☐ The *AutoCAD 2002 Today* dialog box will appear. You should now see the *CAD Template.dwt* listed under *Recent Templates*. This is a hyperlink. Click on it and open the template.

Creating and Saving Your Own Template

You will use the *CAD Template* to make your own customized template and save it to your disk for future use. One thing that must be done on every drawing is to complete the title block. In the following sections you will set up the *Mechanical* text style and complete the title blocks for the three size drawings. You will then save this drawing as a template so you do not have to create the text style and fill in the title blocks each time you make a new drawing.

Creating the Mechanical Text Style

- ☐ Click on the *Format* pull-down menu, slide the mouse pointer down to the menu *Text Style*, and click the mouse button.
- ☐ For your *Mechanical* text style, you will use *romans*. Open the *Font Name* drop-down list, use the scroll bar to locate the *romans* font, and select it by clicking on it. Be careful as there are several roman fonts. Make sure that you have *romans*.
- ☐ Locate the *Height* box to the right of the *Font Name* box and make sure the value is zero. Remember that you never set this to any other value.
- ☐ Verify that all the check boxes in the *Effects* area are NOT checked, the *Width Factor* is set to 1.000, and the *Oblique Angle* is set to zero.
- ☐ Click on the *New* button that is located next to the *Style Name* box. The *New Text Style* dialog box will open. Type **MECHANICAL** as the *Style Name*, and click on the *OK* button to close the dialog box and return to the *Text Style* dialog box.
- ☐ Click on the *Style Name* drop-down list to verify that both *Standard* and *Mechanical* styles exist. Click on the *Mechanical* style to select it and then click the *Close* button.

Completing the Title Blocks

- ☐ Click on the *A-size Sheet* tab.

Figure 8-3
Select *TitleBlock* from the *Layer* drop-down list.

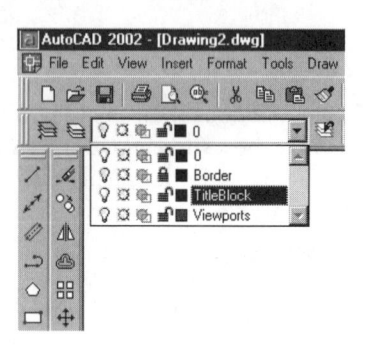

- Locate the *Layer* drop-down list on the *Object Properties* toolbar. Open the list by clicking on it, and slide the cursor down the list to highlight the *TitleBlock* layer, as shown in Figure 8-3. Click the mouse button and the list will close. *TitleBlock* will now appear as the active layer. Layers and their uses will be covered in a future activity.
- Type **DT** on the command line and hit *Enter*. You will notice that *Mechanical* is the current text style.
- Type **J** (for justify) on the command line and hit *Enter*.
- Type **MC** (for middle center) on the command line and hit *Enter*. This will center the text about the point you will choose in the next step.
- Place the crosshairs in the center of the *open space* in the *Drawn By* box and click the mouse button.

Make sure that your text does not touch or overlap any lines or any other text. If you confine your text in the title block to the areas indicated by the dashed rectangles in Figure 8-4, you will not have any problems. (The dashed rectangles appear only in the figure and not on the drawing. They are there to help you picture where the text must be.)

- Type **.125** on the command line and hit *Enter*.
- Hit *Enter* to select the default 0° rotation angle.

Since most of the information in the title block changes on every drawing, you will place generic text that can be easily changed in most of the blocks. To see how this works, in the next step you will assign generic text for your name and then modify it to your real name. When you use your template, you will use a simple method to modify the Date, Scale, Title, and Drawing Number without having to worry about font, text height, etc. It is very important that you get the text placed correctly now so that you will not have to move it every time you make a new drawing.

- Type **MYNAME** on the command and hit *Enter* twice. MYNAME should appear inside the block. If you are not happy with the placement, erase it and try again. Remember, you are making a template that will be used over and over, so it is important that you get it right this time so you won't have to correct it on future drawings.

Figure 8-4
Text must be located only in the open space indicated by the dashed boxes.

Using a Template and Setting a Drawing's Parameters   223

In the following steps you will change MYNAME to your real name.

☐ Place the mouse pointer over MYNAME and click the left mouse button. Blue squares will appear indicating that the text has been selected.

☐ Click the right mouse button and a pop-up menu will appear. Slide the pointer up the list and select *Text Edit* by clicking on it. The *Edit Text* dialog box will appear with MYNAME in the edit window. (See Figure 8-5.)

☐ Type in your real name (you may need to use initials for your first name so that it will fit), and click the *OK* button. Hit the *Enter* key to exit the modify mode. The last line in the command window should read *Command*.

☐ Using Dynamic Text as above, place the following in each of the other boxes of the title block. As you do this, check that you are using *Mechanical* text style and 1/8" (.125") high text, except for the Drawing Number, which should be 1/4" (.250") high text. It is also very important to use *MC* to center the text so that when you make changes in the future the new text will be centered about the point you choose.

Scale: X=X
Date: XX/XX/XX
Title: MYTITLE
Drawing Number: MXXAXX-X   (1/4" high text for this one)

☐ This completes the work on the *A-size Sheet*.

☐ Click on the *B-size Sheet* tab. Notice that the title block is sideways for this drawing size to provide more drawing area.

☐ Click on the *Zoom Window* button and draw a window around the title block. Do not include the logo portion of the title block in the window. This will enlarge the title block enough so that you can complete the following. (If you zoomed incorrectly, use the *Zoom Previous* button and try again.)

☐ Type **DT** on the command line and hit *Enter*. Notice that the current text style is *Mechanical*.

☐ Type **J** (for justify) on the command line and hit *Enter*.

☐ Type **MC** (for middle center) on the command line and hit *Enter*. This will center the text about the point you choose in the next step.

☐ Place the crosshairs in the center of the open space in the *Drawn By* box and click the mouse button.

☐ Type **.125** (MTC standard height) on the command line and hit *Enter*.

☐ Type **90** to change the text rotation angle to 90° and hit *Enter*.

☐ Type your name, as it should appear on the drawing, on the command line and hit *Enter* twice. It should appear in the proper orientation in the *Drawn By* box. If not, erase it and try again.

☐ Using Dynamic Text as above, place the following in each of the other boxes of the title block.

Figure 8-5
Edit Text dialog box

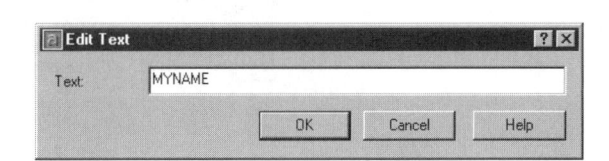

Scale: X=X
Date: XX/XX/XX
Title: MYTITLE
Drawing Number: MXXAXX-X   (1/4" high text for this one)

- [ ] Click on the *Zoom Previous* button to return to an overall view of the drawing paper.
- [ ] This completes the work on the *B-size Sheet*.
- [ ] Click on the *C-size Sheet* tab. Notice that the title block is back to horizontal for this drawing size.
- [ ] Click on the *Zoom Window* button and draw a window around the title block. This time you need to include the logo in the window. This will enlarge the title block enough so that you can complete the following. (If you zoomed incorrectly, use the *Zoom Previous* button and try again.)
- [ ] Type **DT** on the command line and hit *Enter*. Notice that the current text style is *Mechanical*.
- [ ] Type **J** (for justify) on the command line and hit *Enter*.
- [ ] Type **MC** (for middle center) on the command line and hit *Enter*. This will center the text about the point you choose in the next step.
- [ ] Place the crosshairs in the center of the open space in the *Drawn By* box and click the mouse button.
- [ ] Type **.125** (MTC standard height) on the command line and hit *Enter*.
- [ ] If necessary, type **0** to change the text rotation angle back to 0°. Hit the *Enter* key.
- [ ] Type your name, as it should appear on the drawing, on the command line and hit *Enter* twice. It should appear in the proper location in the *Drawn By* box. If not, erase it and try again.
- [ ] Using Dynamic Text as above, place the following in each of the other boxes of the title block.

Scale: X=X
Date: XX/XX/XX
Title: MYTITLE
Drawing Number: MXXAXX-X   (1/4" high text for this one)

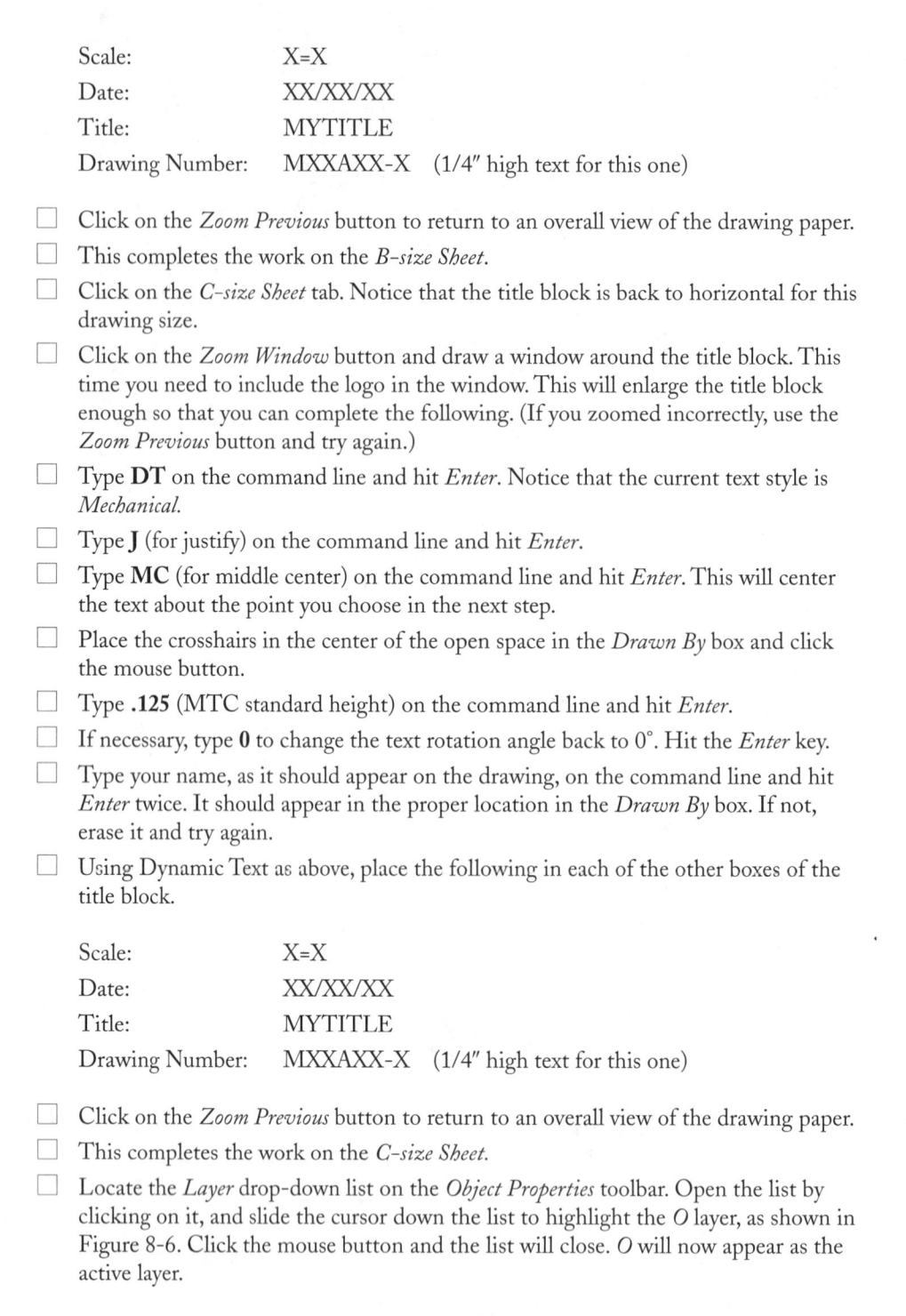

- [ ] Click on the *Zoom Previous* button to return to an overall view of the drawing paper.
- [ ] This completes the work on the *C-size Sheet*.
- [ ] Locate the *Layer* drop-down list on the *Object Properties* toolbar. Open the list by clicking on it, and slide the cursor down the list to highlight the *O* layer, as shown in Figure 8-6. Click the mouse button and the list will close. *O* will now appear as the active layer.

Figure 8-6
Select the *O* layer from the *Layer* drop-down list.

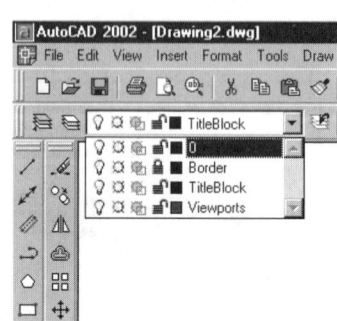

- ☐ Click on the *Model* tab to return to model space. You must be in model space when you save your template. Otherwise, when you select your template, it will open to the tab that was active when you saved it.

Saving Your Template

In this section you will save your new template to your disk.

- ☐ Click on the *File* pull-down menu, slide the mouse pointer down the list, and select *Save As* by clicking on it. The *Save Drawing As* dialog box will open.
- ☐ *You must save this drawing as a template.* Click on the *Files of type* drop-down list at the bottom of the dialog box to open it.
- ☐ Slide the pointer down the list to highlight *AutoCAD Drawing Template File (*.dwt)* and click the mouse button to select it. *AutoCAD Drawing Template File (*.dwt)* should now appear in the *Files of type* box.
- ☐ You will see that the Save in subdirectory has changed to *TEMPLATE*. This is on the hard drive and NOT where you want to save your template.
- ☐ Make sure that your disk is in the removable drive. Click on the *Save in* drop-down list and select *Removable Disk* by clicking on it.
- ☐ In the *File name* box type in XXX TEMPLATE, where XXX is your initials.
- ☐ Click the *Save* button. A *Template Description* box will appear. You can change the description if you want or leave it as is by clicking the *OK* button. Your new template will save to your disk.
- ☐ Click on the *File* pull-down menu, slide the mouse pointer down the list, and select *Close* by clicking on it. The drawing will close.

Using Your Template

The following procedure will show you how to use your template.

- ☐ Click on the *New* button to start a new drawing. The *AutoCAD 2002 Today* dialog box will open.
- ☐ Since your template is not stored on the computer's hard drive, click on the *Browse* hyperlink and the *Select a template file* dialog box will appear.
- ☐ Click on the *Look in* drop-down list and select *Removable Disk* by clicking on it. If you saved your template correctly in the previous section, you should now see your template listed.
- ☐ Click on the template's icon and click the *Open* button. If *AutoCAD 2002 Today* reopens, click the *Close* button to close it.
- ☐ Verify that this is your template by clicking on one of the *Sheet* tabs to see if your name is there.
- ☐ This completes this exercise. In the future, as you learn more of AutoCAD's features, you may want to add to your template or make new templates.
- ☐ Close the AutoCAD program. Do not save your drawing when asked.

Activity 2

Setting the Units and Limits of the Drawing Area

Objectives: After completing this activity, you should be able to do the following:

- Locate and use the *Units* menu selection to set the units for a new drawing.
- Locate and use the *Drawing Limits* menu selection to size the drawing area for a new drawing.
- Zoom to the extents of a new drawing area.
- Set up a drawing for metric units.

In this activity you will learn how to set up a new drawing using the *Units* and *Drawing Limits* commands. When you start a new drawing, you must first select the type of units to be used on the drawing. The units part of this activity was originally introduced in Module 2, and is being reviewed here because it is the first step in getting ready to draw. After setting the units, you then set up the size of the drawing area, called the limits, so that you have enough room to draw all the objects to be included on the drawing. The last part of the activity will introduce you to the differences between metric and US standard drawings, and the changes you must make to do a metric drawing.

Procedure: ☑ Check each box as you complete that item.

- ☐ Open the *AutoCAD 2002* program.
- ☐ When the *AutoCAD 2002 Today* dialog box opens, click on the *Create Drawings* tab (if it is not already selected), and use the *Browse* button to load your template from the *Removable Disk* drive. If you are unsure how to do this, review the last part of Module 8 – Activity 1.
- ☐ Move the graphics cursor around the drawing area and watch the coordinates display on the *Status* bar to make sure it is turned on. If it does not change and appears grayed out, click on it to activate it.

Setting the Units

Every time you start a new drawing you must determine what type of units you will use and then set the *Drawing Units* to match. The following describes that procedure.

- ☐ Click on the *Format* pull-down menu, slide the mouse pointer down the list, and select *Units* by clicking on it. The *Drawing Units* dialog box will appear.
- ☐ Click on the *Type* drop-down list and select *Fractional* by clicking on it. For the first part of the activity, you will use fractional units. Don't forget how to change units because you will be doing it several times in this activity.
- ☐ Click on the *Precision* drop-down list and select *0 1/32* by clicking on it.
- ☐ Click on the *OK* button to close the dialog box. Verify that you are in fractional units by checking the format of the coordinates on the *Status* bar.

Setting the Limits

Once the units are set, you must determine how much space is required to make the drawing. Remember that you always draw everything full size in AutoCAD, so you must have a drawing area that is sized large enough to hold everything you will be drawing. The following describes the procedure for setting up the drawing limits. Although it is possible to draw anywhere outside the set limits, the combination of setting limits and using the *Zoom All* command will help you manage your drawing layout.

☐ Move the graphics cursor to the upper right corner of the drawing area. The coordinates should be approximately 10 1/2, 7 1/2, 0. Your exact coordinates will vary depending on what toolbars are loaded and where they are located. As long as you are within an inch or two of these numbers, everything is fine.

☐ Click on the *Format* pull-down menu, slide the mouse pointer down the list, and select *Drawing Limits* by clicking on it. (See Figure 8-7.)

☐ It may appear that nothing happened, but look at the command line. It should look like the lines below. It is asking you what coordinates you want to use for the lower left corner of the drawing. The default value 0,0 is shown in the angle brackets. Most of the time you will use this value. Hit the *Enter* key to accept it.

Command: '_limits
Reset model space limits
Specify lower left corner or [ON/OFF] <0,0>:

☐ The command line is now asking you to specify the coordinates for the upper right corner of the drawing. The current default, shown inside the brackets, is 10,7.

Reset model space limits
Specify lower left corner or [ON/OFF] <0,0>:
Specify upper right corner <10,7>:

☐ Type **48,36** on the command line and hit the *Enter* key. It is very important that you include the comma (,) between the two numbers because you are specifying the ordered pair, x-coordinate and y-coordinate. If you forget the comma you will get an error message on the command line.

☐ Move the cursor around the screen and watch the coordinates display on the Status bar. There appears to be no change. The reason is that although the limits are set to 48,36 the zoom on the screen has remained at the original 10,7. The next step will correct this.

☐ Move the mouse pointer to the Zoom flyout, press and hold the left mouse button, and slide the pointer down the list to the *Zoom All* button. Release the mouse button when you are over the *Zoom All* button.

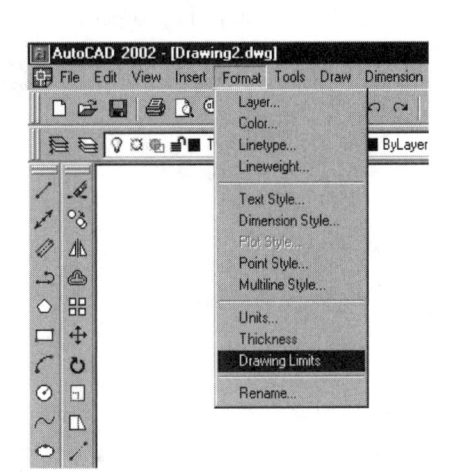

Figure 8-7
Select *Drawing Limits* from the *Format* pull-down menu.

- ☐ Now move the cursor around the screen and watch the coordinates display. You see that the coordinates of the upper right corner are around 48,36.
- ☐ The drawing is now set up for you to draw in fractional units on a 48″ × 36″ area.
- ☐ Suppose that after you start a drawing you find that 48″ × 36″ is not large enough to get everything on the drawing. AutoCAD allows you to reset the limits at any time. Repeat the above procedure and make the limits 72,54. Remember to *Zoom All* at the end to see the entire area.

To give you additional practice, set the units, precision, and limits to each of the values shown below. After you set each, *Zoom Extents* and move the cursor around the drawing area and observe the coordinates to verify that you have the correct settings. When entering the limits, type in the numbers exactly as they appear below. Note in the first two examples that there is a big difference between 96,72 and 96′,72′.

	Units	Precision	Limits
1.	Architectural	0′-0 1/2″	96,72
2.	Architectural	0′-0 1/8″	96′,72′
3.	Engineering	0′-0.00″	42,32
4.	Engineering	0′-0.0″	12′3.5,8′8
5.	Decimal	0.000	12,9

Setting up a Metric Drawing

All metric drawings are done using decimal units. When drawing in millimeters, the precision is usually set to "0" because a millimeter is slightly larger than 1/32″ and this provides sufficient precision for most applications. Only when machining operations are involved will you use decimals of a millimeter.

The major difference in using metric is setting the limits. When using decimal units in AutoCAD, the program does not distinguish between inches and millimeters. When you enter 1, it could be one millimeter, one inch, or even one mile. But to AutoCAD, it is just one unit. Since there are 25.4 millimeters to an inch, most metric drawings have limits set to values approximately 25 times larger than inch drawings. For example, limits set at 36 × 27 for an inch drawing would be around 900 × 675 for the same size part on a metric drawing.

To print a metric drawing on a standard paper size, you must scale it down using a 1/25.4 scale factor. This process will be covered in detail in a later module.

- ☐ This completes this activity. Close AutoCAD without saving the drawing.

Module 8 Review Questions

These questions are provided to help you review the topics and concepts covered in this module.

True or False

Determine whether the statement is true or false. Place your answer, either T or F, in the blank.

_____   1. Template drawings can be identified because they have a .dwg file extension.

_____   2. Setting a drawing's *Limits* prevents you from drawing anything larger than that size. You have to reset the limits if you must draw anything larger.

_____   3. Template drawings save time because they allow you to set up a standard drawing that can be used over and over.

_____   4. Entering **48,36** as the limits on a drawing set in *Architectural* units produces the same effect as setting the limits to 4',3'.

_____   5. The limits of a metric drawing are approximately 25 times larger than those of a similar US standard inch drawing.

_____   6. You have to be aware of the *Units* setting because it determines how you enter distances on the command line.

_____   7. Although most templates are stored in the same subdirectory in AutoCAD's directory on the hard drive, templates can be stored on any drive.

_____   8. It is not a problem if text touches the edges of the borders in the drawing's title block.

_____   9. Using *Edit Text* always opens the *Multiline Text Editor*.

_____   10. Clicking the *New* button starts a new drawing based on a template.

Module 9

Final Project

This module gives you an opportunity to use what you have learned in this book to complete a real-world engineering project.

One of the processing machines in the plant where you work broke down and is being rebuilt. Three of the machine's original gaskets were damaged during disassembly and new ones must be made before the machine can be put back together and returned to service. The maintenance department has the proper material to make the new gaskets, but needs an accurate drawing of each gasket to use as a template to cut the gasket material.

Your boss has asked you to go into the shop, measure and make sketches of the three gaskets, and then use the sketches to make an exact size drawing using AutoCAD. You have returned from the shop with the three sketches shown in Figures 9-1, 9-2, and 9-3. Now your job is to make a drawing of each of the gaskets. A three-dimensional picture of each gasket has been provided to help you visualize what the final gaskets will look like.

Flange Gasket

- ☐ Open the *AutoCAD 2002* program.
- ☐ When the *AutoCAD 2002 Today* dialog box opens, select the *Create Drawings* tab, and use the *Browse* button to locate and load your personal template, which you created in Module 8, from the *Removable Disk* drive.
- ☐ Use the sketch shown in Figure 9-1 to draw the flange gasket.
- ☐ As you have done in past activities, click on the *A-size Sheet* tab and center the figures in the middle of the blue rectangle. Do not use the *Zoom* command while you are centering the drawing.
- ☐ Using 1/8" high, mechanical style, dynamic text, place the following note somewhere in the drawing near the gasket.

MATERIAL: 0.150" THICK NEOPRENE RUBBER

- ☐ Complete the drawing's title block with the following information.

    Scale: FULL
    Date: *today's date*
    Drawn by: *your name*
    Title: FLANGE GASKET
    Drawing Number: M09APP-1

Figure 9-1
Flange gasket

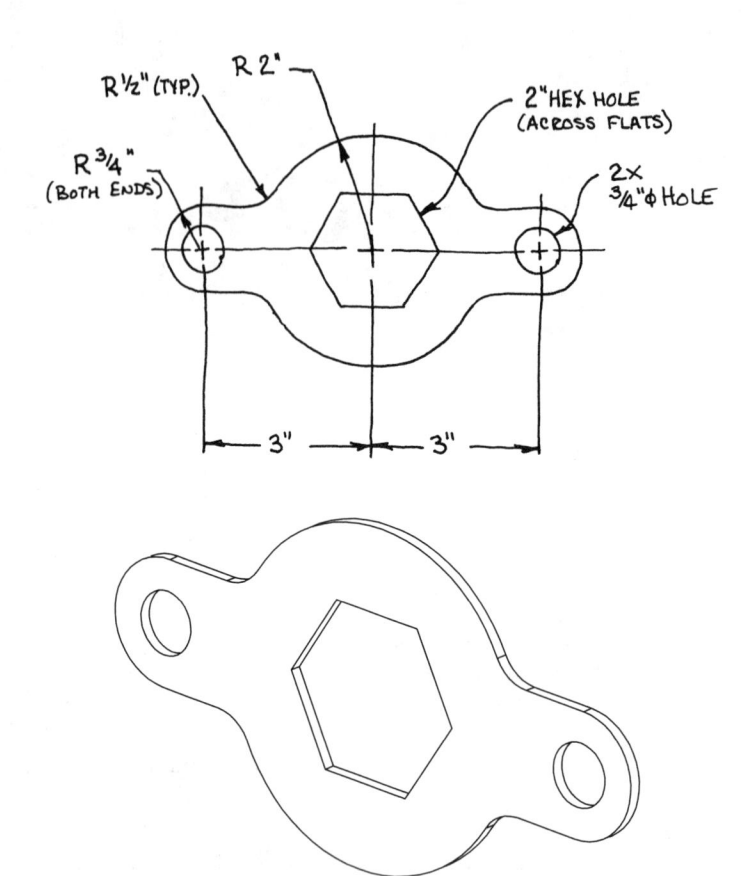

- ☐ Save your drawing to your removable disk with the name M09APP-1.
- ☐ Print a copy of your drawing.

Cover Gasket

- ☐ Open the *AutoCAD 2002* program.
- ☐ When the *AutoCAD 2002 Today* dialog box opens, select the *Create Drawings* tab, and use the *Browse* button to locate and load your personal template, which you created in Module 8, from the *Removable Disk* drive.
- ☐ Use the sketch shown in Figure 9-2 to draw the cover gasket.
- ☐ As you have done in past activities, click on the *A-size Sheet* tab and center the figures in the middle of the blue rectangle. Do not use the *Zoom* command while you are centering the drawing.
- ☐ Using 1/8" high, mechanical style, dynamic text, place the following note somewhere in the drawing near the gasket.

MATERIAL: 0.125" THICK CORK

- ☐ Complete the drawing's title block with the following information.

Scale:	FULL
Date:	*today's date*
Drawn by:	*your name*
Title:	COVER GASKET
Drawing Number:	M09APP-2

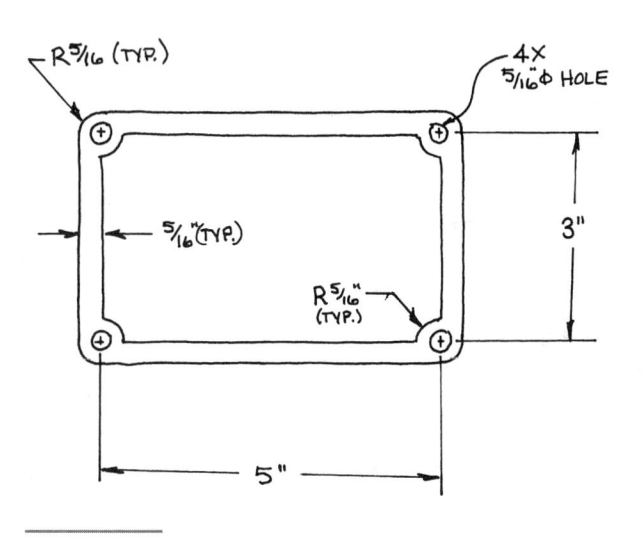

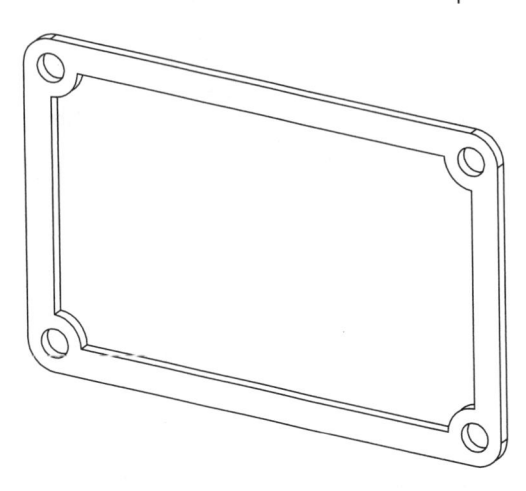

Figure 9-2
Cover gasket

☐ Save your drawing to your removable disk with the name M09APP-2.
☐ Print a copy of your drawing.

Head Gasket

☐ Open the *AutoCAD 2002* program.
☐ When the *AutoCAD 2002 Today* dialog box opens, select the *Create Drawings* tab, and use the *Browse* button to locate and load your personal template, which you created in Module 8, from the *Removable Disk* drive.
☐ Use the sketch shown in Figure 9-3 to draw the head gasket.
☐ As you have done in past activities, click on the *A-size Sheet* tab and center the figures in the middle of the blue rectangle. Do not use the *Zoom* command while you are centering the drawing.
☐ Using 1/8" high, mechanical style, dynamic text, place the following note somewhere in the drawing near the gasket.

MATERIAL: 0.05" THICK STAINLESS STEEL

☐ Complete the drawing's title block with the following information.

Scale:	FULL
Date:	*today's date*
Drawn by:	*your name*
Title:	HEAD GASKET
Drawing Number:	M09APP-3

☐ Save your drawing to your removable disk with the name M09APP-3.
☐ Print a copy of your drawing.

Figure 9-3
Head gasket

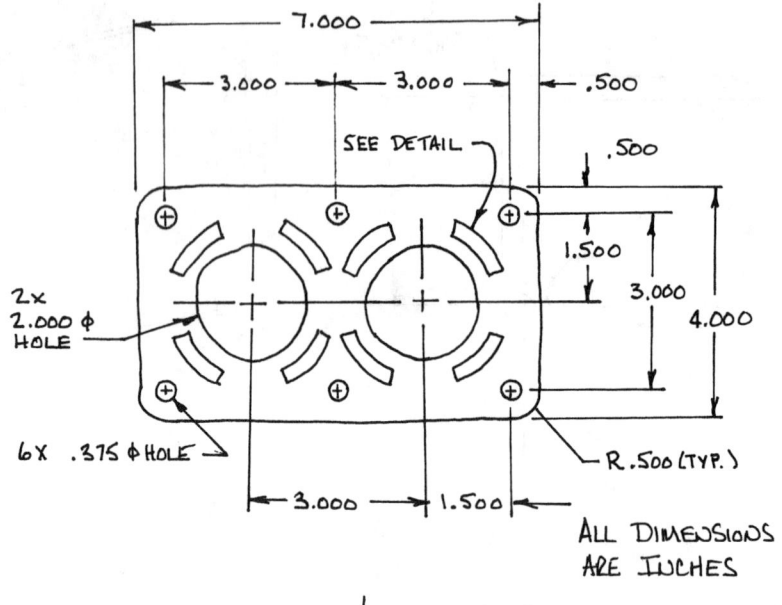

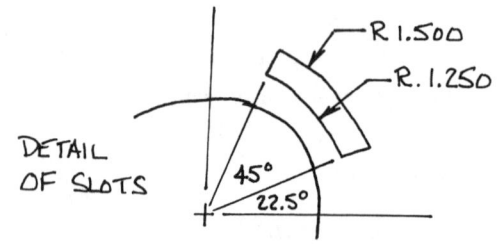

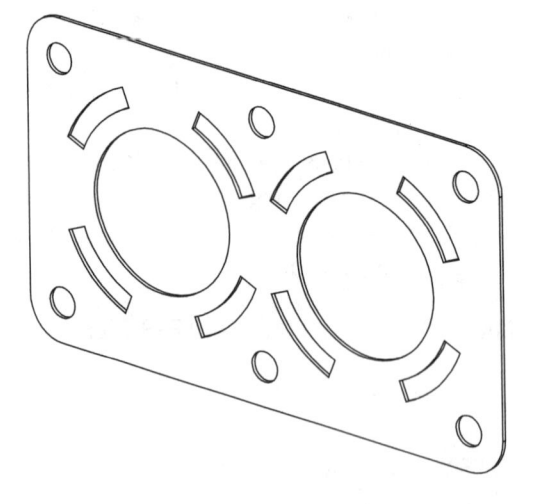

Appendix **A**

Using Engineering Scales

Activity 1

Using a Combination Scale

Objectives: After completing this activity, you should be able to use a combination scale to measure lines using the:

- Full scale (fractional) to 1/32" precision
- Full scale (decimal) to 0.01" precision
- ½ and ¼ size scale
- 1:10 (1:100) and 1:50 (1:500) scales
- Metric scale to 1 mm precision

In this activity you will learn how to use a *combination scale* to measure the scaled length of a line. As a student of CAD you should own and be able to read a combination scale. Because a scale is a reasonably precise measuring device, you need to be careful when using it. Do not drop it or bang it on a hard surface as nicks or chips in its edges will make it unusable.

Although all drawings you make in the AutoCAD program are drawn full size, it is impossible to print every drawing full size. You cannot design and draw a house and then expect to make a print of it full size. You have to print it in a smaller, proportional size so it will fit on a standard piece of paper. This resizing is called scaling. You also do not make it just any smaller size. You have to make it to a standard size so that others can measure distances directly from your print using a device called a *scale*. (It is not a ruler, so don't call it a ruler!) The engineering profession has a number of standard sizes that it uses for scaling. The scale you will use for this activity has a combination of full size and other scales; thus it is called a combination scale. Each of these will be described in detail in this activity.

It is very important that you learn to produce drawings that are properly sized (correctly scaled). Therefore, you must first learn to read a scale so that in the future you can use it to check every print you make to guarantee that it is to scale.

236 Appendix A

Procedure: ☑ Check each box as you complete that item.

☐ Double-click on the *AutoCAD 2002* icon to open the program.

☐ When the *AutoCAD 2002 Today* dialog box appears, select the *Open a Drawing* tab, and use the *Browse* hyperlink to locate and open the drawing *CScale-1.dwg* from the *Other* subdirectory on the CD.

☐ The drawing will open to *Paper* space. You will print and use this drawing to learn how to measure objects using the combination scale.

☐ Click on the *Print* button and the *Plot* dialog box will open.

☐ Select the *Plot Device* tab by clicking on it.

☐ Locate your printer in the *Name* drop-down list and select it by clicking on it.

☐ Select the *Plot Settings* tab by clicking on it.

☐ Set the *Paper Size* to *Letter 8 ½ x 11 in.* and then click the *OK* button to print the drawing.

☐ Close the *AutoCAD 2002* program by clicking on the *Close* button. You will not be using the program for the remainder of this activity.

Full Scale (Fractional)

Before you learn to use a combination scale to measure objects that have been resized, you should learn to make full size measurements. In this part you will use the fractional full scale.

☐ Use Figure A-1 to locate the fractional full scale on your combination scale. The number 32 indicates that for this scale an inch is divided into 32 parts, each 1/32" wide. You should be somewhat familiar with this scale as it is similar to that on a standard ruler. However, it has more divisions and is manufactured to a higher-quality standard.

☐ To make the scale easier to read, different length lines are used for the divisions. The longest marks indicate full inches, next longest are the 1/2" marks, followed by the 1/4", 1/8", 1/16", and finally the 1/32" marks.

☐ An enlarged view of this scale is shown in Figure A-2. Several markings are indicated to help you understand how this scale works. Although you could always count the number of 1/32" divisions and make a fraction from them, like 9/32", it is better that you learn to identify each division based on its length, like 1/4".

Figure A-1
Full scale (fractional)

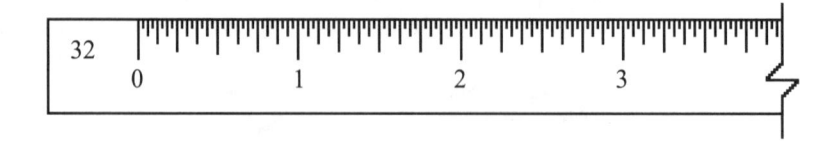

Figure A-2
Enlarged view of the full scale

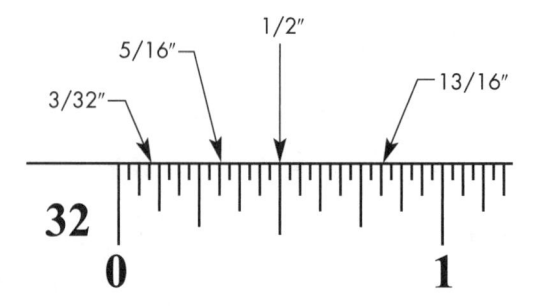

Figure A-3
Using the full scale (fractional) to measure distance

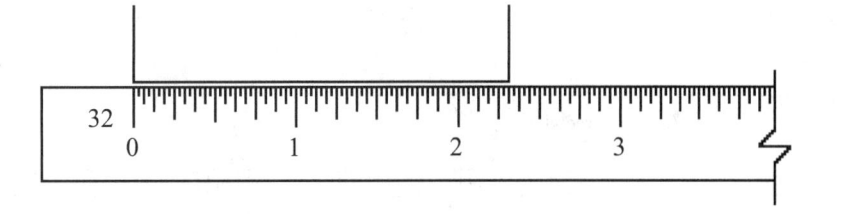

☐ Practice locating the following on the full scale.

5/8"   3/16"   31/32"   11/16"   5/32"

☐ Measurements with this scale are made by first placing the "0" mark at one end of the line or distance you want to measure. Place your scale on *View A* of the drawing you printed out and line up the "0" mark, as shown in Figure A-3.

☐ Look at the other end of the line and determine its relation to the scale. You should measure the line as being 2 5/16" long.

Note: Not all printers are created equally, so your results may vary. There may be a slight variation in the length of the lines in printed copies of drawing *M02A03-1.dwg*. You may not arrive at the exact same length given in this activity, but it should be close. The important point is that you learn to read the length based on the drawing you have.

☐ Practice measuring the length of the lines in the other views. They should measure: View B = 1 15/16", C = 1 11/16", D = 2 7/16", E = 2 3/16", F = 1 1/16", G = 1 5/8".

Full Scale (Decimal)

As you learned in a previous activity, drawings are done in both fractional and decimal units. In this section you will learn to use the decimal full scale.

☐ Use Figure A-4 to locate the decimal full scale on your combination scale. The number 50 indicates that for this scale an inch is divided into 50 parts, each .02" wide. The scale can be read left to right or right to left, so the inch marks have a dual numbering system. The 0" mark shown is also the 12" mark if you were measuring from the right end of the scale.

☐ The smaller numbers between "0" and "1" are decimals of an inch in tenths, i.e., 2 = .2 and 8 = .8. The longer, unmarked lines are the odd-numbered tenths, i.e., .1, .3, .5, etc.

☐ The other lines are .02" apart. To make the scale easier to read, two short and two longer lines are used between each tenths division. If a measurement falls halfway between these two lines it would be .01". You should be able to use this scale to measure to .01".

☐ An enlarged view of this scale is shown in Figure A-5. Several markings are indicated to help you understand how this scale works.

Figure A-4
Full scale (decimal)

Figure A-5
Enlarged view of the full scale

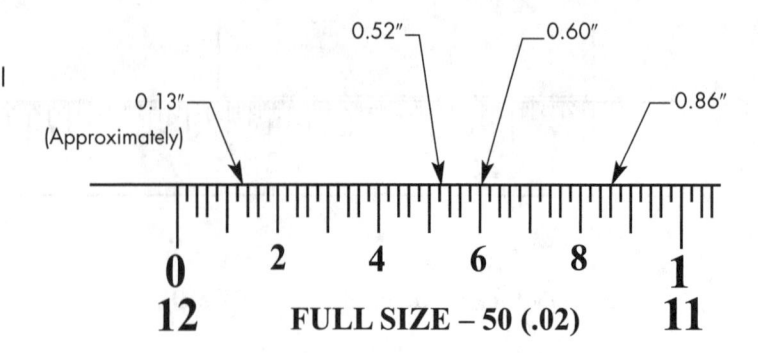

Figure A-6
Using the full scale (decimal) to measure distance

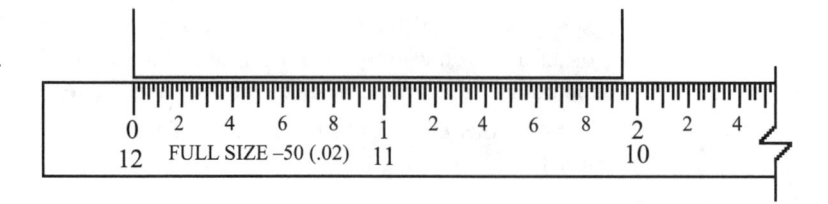

- [ ] Practice locating the following on the full decimal scale.

    1.62   3.18   6.06   10.40   4.88

- [ ] Measurements with this scale are made by first placing the "0" mark at one end of the line or distance you want to measure. Place your scale on *View B* of the drawing you printed out and line up the left end "0" mark as shown in Figure A-6.
- [ ] Look at the other end of the line and determine its relation to the scale. You should measure the line as being 1.94″ long.
- [ ] Practice measuring the length of the lines in the other views. They should measure: View A = 2.31″, C = 1.69″, D = 2.44″, E = 2.20″, F = 1.06″, G = 1.61″.

Half (1/2) Size Scale

The half size scale is used to make objects on a drawing one-half their original size. If you draw an object that is 15″ long, it will not fit on an 8 1/2 × 11 piece of paper. But if you scale it to half size (7 1/2″), it will fit. Then, when you make measurements from the drawing, everything would actually be twice as large. You could always use a full scale and multiply each distance by two, but it is easier and there is less chance of making a mistake if you use the half size scale and read the distance directly.

- [ ] Use Figure A-7 to locate the half (1/2) size scale on your combination scale. The half size scale may appear confusing at first because there are actually two different scales along the same side of the combination scale. The longer numbered lines are associated with the half size scale, and the shorter numbered lines are associated with the quarter (1/4) size scale that you will study next. When using the half size scale you must ignore the other scale markings.

Figure A-7
Half size scale

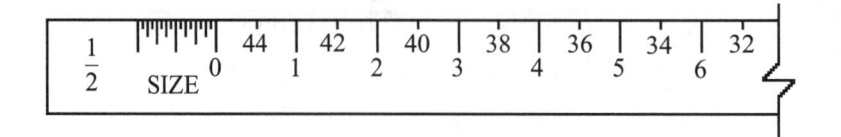

Figure A-8
Using the half size scale to measure distance: First step

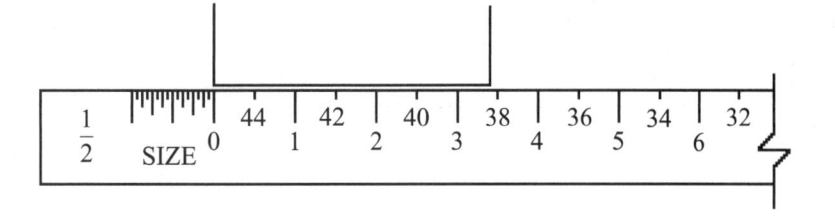

Figure A-9
Using the half size scale to measure distance: Second step

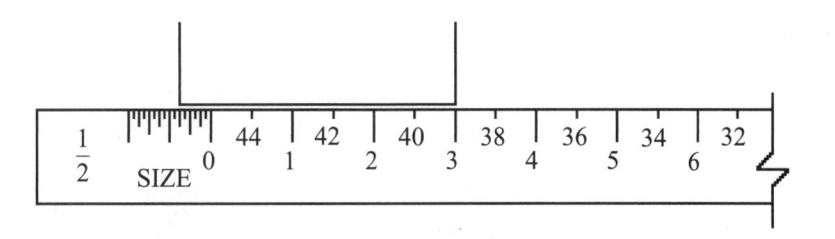

- When reading the half size scale, the whole inches are read to the right of zero and the fractional inches are read to the left of zero.
- Look at the fractional scale. Each mark represents 1/16″. You should be able to identify the various length marks as representing 1/2″, 1/4″, 1/8″, and 1/16″ units.
- Measurements with this scale are made by first placing the "0" mark at one end of the line or distance you want to measure. Place your scale on *View C* of the drawing you printed out and line up the "0" mark as shown in Figure A-8.
- Notice that the end of line you are measuring lies between the 3″ and 4″ marks. (Remember, you have to ignore the other size scale markings.)
- This section is very important, so follow the directions carefully. The line is longer than 3″ but smaller than 4″. You will always move the scale to the *smaller* whole dimension. Slide the scale to the RIGHT to line up the right end of the line with the 3″ mark as shown in Figure A-9.
- Now read the fractional part of the length from the part of the scale to the left of zero.

Note: If the left end of your line does not fall in the fractional part of the scale, you slid the scale the wrong direction. Go back and try again.

- You should measure the line as being 3 3/8″ long.
- Practice measuring the length of the lines in the other views. They should measure: View A = 4 5/8″, B = 3 7/8″, D = 4 7/8″, E = 4 13/32″, F = 2 1/8″, G = 3 1/4″.

Quarter (1/4) Size Scale

The quarter size scale is very similar to the half size scale. It allows objects to be printed one-fourth their original size and measured to their true size. Therefore, for the quarter size scale, an object that is actually 15″ long will be 3 3/4″ long on the printed drawing.

- Use Figure A-10 to locate the quarter (1/4) size scale on your combination scale. This scale is read from right to left. When using the half size scale you ignored the quarter size scale marking, but for the quarter size scale you must use the half size scale markings. The longer numbered lines associated with the half size scale are the odd-numbered whole numbers for the quarter size scale. Therefore, 22 = 1″ and 17 = 11″ on the quarter size scale.

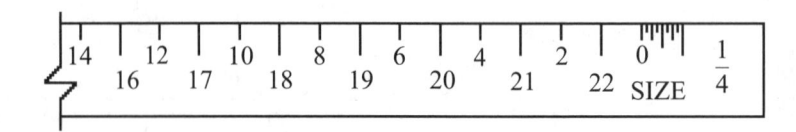

Figure A-10
Quarter size scale

Figure A-11
Using the quarter size scale to measure distance: First step

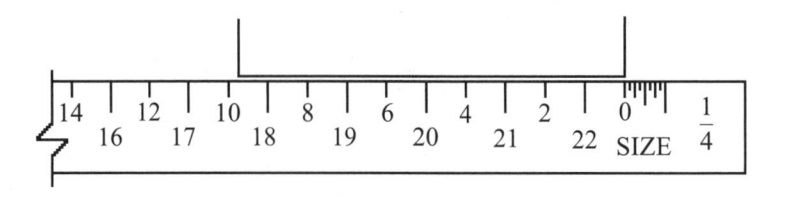

Figure A-12
Using the quarter size scale to measure distance: Second step

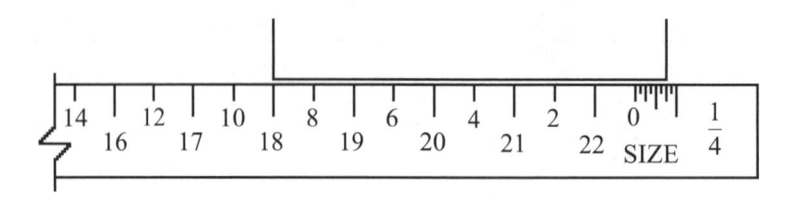

- [ ] When reading the quarter size scale, the whole inches are read to the left of zero and the fractional inches are read to the right of zero.
- [ ] Look at the fractional scale. Each mark represents 1/8″. You should be able to identify the various length marks as representing 1/2″, 1/4″, and 1/8″ units.
- [ ] Measurements with this scale are made by first placing the "0" mark at one end of the line or distance you want to measure. Place your scale on *View D* of the drawing you printed out and line up the "0" mark as shown in Figure A-11.
- [ ] Notice that the end of line you are measuring lies between the 9″ and 10″ marks. (Remember, the longer lines are the odd numbers and you are reading from right to left.)
- [ ] The line is longer than 9″ but shorter than 10″. You will always move the scale to the smaller whole dimension. Slide the scale to the LEFT to line the left end of the line up with the 9″ (18) mark as shown in Figure A-12.
- [ ] Now read the fractional part of the length from the part of the scale to the right of zero.

Note: If the right end of your line does not fall in the fractional part of the scale, you slid the scale in the wrong direction. Go back and try again.

- [ ] You should measure the line as being 9 3/4″ long.
- [ ] Practice measuring the length of the lines in the other views. They should measure: View A = 9 1/4″, B = 7 3/4″, C = 6 3/4″, E = 8 13/16″, F = 4 1/4″, G = 6 1/2″.

10 or 100 Scale

As with the other numbered scales, the number 10 indicates that every inch is divided into 10 equal parts.

- [ ] Use Figure A-13 to locate the 10 scale on your combination scale. This scale has a dual purpose. It can be used for objects scaled to 1/10 their original size, with the

Figure A-13
10 (or 100) scale

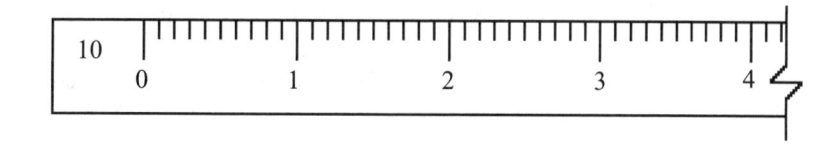

Figure A-14
Using the 10 scale to measure distance

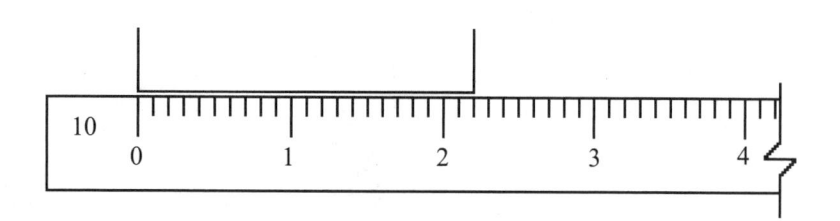

whole numbers on the scale being 10, 20, etc., and the smaller marks being 1, 2, etc., Or it can be used for objects scaled to 1/100 their original size, with the whole numbers then indicate 100, 200, etc., and the smaller marks 10, 20, etc. Since the marks are far apart, you may need to estimate when the distance is between two marks.

☐ Measurements with this scale are very easy. Place the "0" mark at one end of the line or distance you want to measure. Place your scale on *View E* of the drawing you printed out and line up the "0" mark as shown in Figure A-14.

☐ Look at the other end of the line and determine its relation to the scale. You should measure the line as being 22″ long (based on 10).

☐ Practice measuring the length of the lines in the other views. They should measure: View A = 23″, B = 19.25″, C = 17″, D = 24.25″, F = 10.5″, G = 16″.

50 or 500 Scale

This scale is similar to the 10 scale. Every inch is divided into 50 parts. It can be used to measure objects that are 1/50 their original size or 1/500 their original size.

☐ Use Figure A-15 to locate the 50 scale on your combination scale. This scale has a dual purpose. It can be used for objects scaled to 1/50 their original size, with the whole numbers on the scale being 20, 40, etc., and the smaller marks being 1, 2, etc. Or it can be used for objects scaled to 1/500 their original size. The whole numbers then indicate 200, 400, etc., and the smaller marks 10, 20, etc. Since the marks are close together, you must be careful reading this scale.

☐ Measurements with this scale are made by placing the "0" mark at one end of the line or distance you want to measure. Place your scale on *View F* of the drawing you printed out and line up the "0" mark as shown in Figure A-16.

Figure A-15
50 (or 500) scale

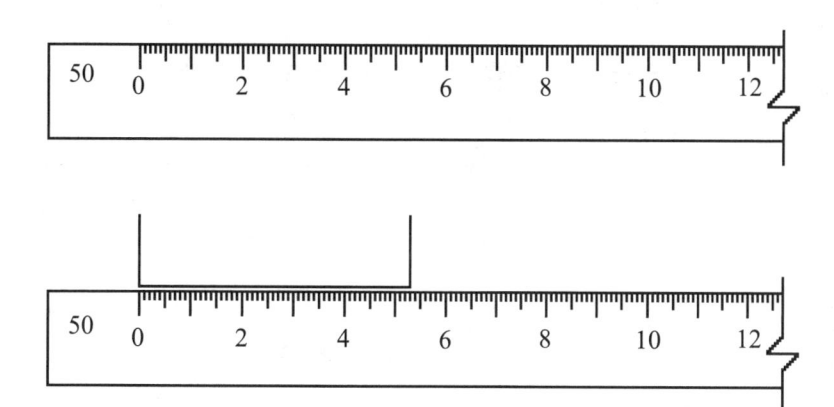

Figure A-16
Using the 50 scale to measure distance

☐ Look at the other end of the line and determine its relation to the scale. You should measure the line as being 53" long (based on 50).

☐ Practice measuring the length of the lines in the other views. They should measure: View A = 116", B = 97", C = 84", D = 122", E = 110", G = 81".

Metric Scale

Because of the international economy, and because most of the world uses the metric system of measure, many companies are now using the metric system when designing and manufacturing their products. The metric system is based on meters. A meter is approximately 39.37". The metric system is easier to use because it is based on multiples of 10. The meter can be divided into 100 parts, each called a centimeter, or 1000 parts, each called a millimeter. Unlike the US system, you never mix units (like feet and inches). For example, you will never see 2 cm 6 mm; it would be given only in millimeters (26 mm). Dimensions are given only in meters, in centimeters, or in millimeters depending on the smallest unit involved. Most metric drawings are in millimeters.

☐ Use Figure A-17 to locate the metric scale on your combination scale. The longer marks with numbers are centimeters. The shorter marks are millimeters.

☐ When using the scale to read millimeters, remember that each number represents 10 millimeters.

☐ Measurements with this scale are made by first placing the "0" mark at one end of the line or distance you want to measure. Place your scale on *View G* of the drawing you printed out and line up the "0" mark as shown in Figure A-18.

☐ Look at the other end of the line and determine its relation to the scale. You should measure the line as being 41 mm long.

☐ Practice measuring the length of the lines in the other views. They should measure: View A = 59 mm, B = 49 mm, C = 43 mm, D = 62 mm, E - 56 mm, F = 27 mm.

☐ This completes this activity. Practice using the combination scale as much as possible because it will often be used in these activities.

Figure A-17
Metric scale

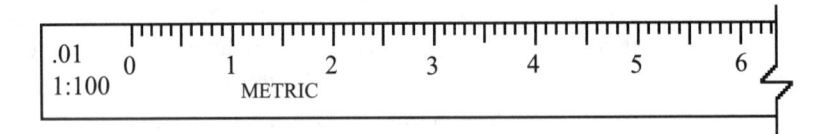

Figure A-18
Using the metric scale to measure distance

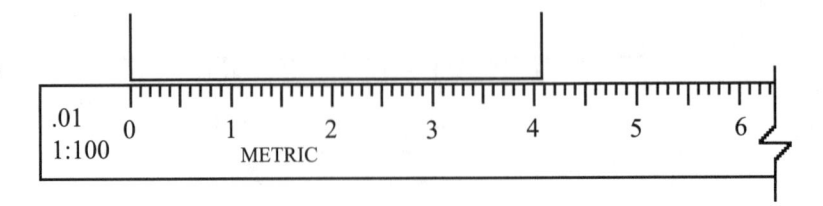

Assignment 1
for Appendix A – Activity 1

In this assignment you will print two drawings that have objects that are approximately the same size on the drawing but vary greatly in size in the real world. Use your combination scale to determine the actual size of these scaled objects.

- ☐ Double-click on the *AutoCAD 2002* icon to open the program.
- ☐ When the *AutoCAD 2002 Today* dialog box appears, select the *Open a Drawing* tab, and use the *Browse* hyperlink to locate and open the drawing *CScale-2.dwg* from the *Other* subdirectory on the CD.
- ☐ The drawing will open to Drawing 1, which shows a hex bolt, a wall switch plate, and a clevis bracket. Click on the *Print* button and the *Plot* dialog box will open.
- ☐ Select the *Plot Device* tab by clicking on it.
- ☐ Locate your printer in the *Name* drop-down list and select it by clicking on it.
- ☐ Select the *Plot Settings* tab by clicking on it.
- ☐ Set the *Paper Size* to *Letter 8 ½ x11 in.* and then click the *OK* button to print the drawing.
- ☐ Click on the tab labeled *Drawing 2* at the bottom of the drawing area. This is a drawing of a microwave oven and a truss. Use the methods above to make a print of this drawing.
- ☐ Close the *AutoCAD 2002* program by clicking on the *Close* button.

Use your combination scale to answer the following questions. The scale of each object is listed on the drawing.

Hex Head Bolt

Use the full scale (decimal) to determine the following dimensions.

1. _____ the bolt's length (a)
2. _____ the height of the bolt's head (b)
3. _____ the distance across the flats on the bolt's hex head (c)

Use the metric scale to determine the following dimensions.

4. _____ the bolt's length (a)
5. _____ the height of the bolt's head (b)
6. _____ the distance across the flats on the bolt's hex head (c)

Wall Plate

Use the appropriate scale to determine the following dimensions.

7. _____ the height of the plate (d)
8. _____ the width of the plate (e)
9. _____ the vertical distance between the screws (f)

10. ____ the distance from the top of the plate to the first set of screws (g)
11. ____ the distance from the right side of the plate to the first set of screws (h)
12. ____ the horizontal distance between the screws (j)

Clevis Bracket

Use the appropriate scale to determine the following dimensions.

13. ____ the width of the top of the clevis bracket (k)
14. ____ the distance from the top of the clevis bracket to its hole (m)
15. ____ the diameter of the hole in the clevis bracket (n)
16. ____ the radius at the end of the clevis bracket (p)

Microwave Oven

Use the appropriate scale to determine the following dimensions.

17. ____ the width of the microwave (q)
18. ____ the height of the microwave (r)
19. ____ the width of the microwave's window (s)
20. ____ the height of the microwave's window (t)

Truss

Use the appropriate scale to determine the following dimensions.

21. ____ the length of the bottom cord of the truss (u)
22. ____ the height of the truss (v)
23. ____ the length of the top cord of the truss (w)

Assignment 2
for Appendix A – Activity 1

- ☐ Double-click on the *AutoCAD 2002* icon to open the program.
- ☐ When the *AutoCAD 2002 Today* dialog box appears, select the *Open a Drawing* tab, and use the *Browse* hyperlink to locate and open the drawing *CScale-3.dwg* from the *Other* subdirectory on the CD.
- ☐ The drawing will open to paper space. Click on the *Print* button and the *Plot* dialog box will open.
- ☐ Select the *Plot Device* tab by clicking on it.
- ☐ Locate your printer in the *Name* drop-down list and select it by clicking on it.

☐ Select the *Plot Settings* tab by clicking on it.
☐ Set the *Paper Size* to *Letter 8 ½ x11 in.*, and then click the *OK* button to print the drawing.
☐ Close the *AutoCAD 2002* program by clicking on the *Close* button.

Use your combination scale to measure each line and complete the table on the right side of the drawing.

Activity 2

Using an Architect's Scale

Objectives: After completing this activity, you should be able to use an architect's scale to measure lines using:

- 3" and 1 1/2" = 1'- 0" scales
- 1" and 1/2" = 1'- 0" scales
- 3/4" and 3/8" = 1'- 0" scales
- 1/4" and 1/8" = 1'- 0" scales
- 3/16" and 3/32" = 1'- 0" scales

In this activity you will learn how to use an *architect's scale* to measure the scaled length of a line. As a student of CAD you should own and be able to read an architect's scale. Because a scale is a precise measuring device, you need to be careful when using it. Do not drop it or bang it on a hard surface as nicks or chips in its edges will make it unusable.

The architect's scale is similar to the combination scale you used in Activity 1. It is used for US Standard drawings because all the scales are based on feet and inch units. It is usually used for scaling larger objects like buildings, houses, bridges, and structures. It is most commonly used by architects, thus the name architect's scale. But it is important to understand that even though it is called an architect's scale, it is used in other areas of engineering.

There are 11 scales on an architect's scale. One is a full scale (fractional) with 16 divisions per inch. Since you studied full scales in Activity 1, this scale will not be covered here. The other 10 scales are all similar to each other and you use the same methods to read all of them. Therefore, only two of the scales, 1" and 1/2" = 1'- 0", will be covered in detail. You should apply the methods you learn to the other 8 scales.

Procedure: ☑ Check each box as you complete that item.

- ☐ Double-click on the *AutoCAD 2002* icon to open the program.
- ☐ When the *AutoCAD 2002 Today* dialog box appears, select the *Open a Drawing* tab, and use the *Browse* hyperlink to locate and open the drawing *AScale-1.dwg* from the *Other* subdirectory on the CD.
- ☐ The drawing will open to *Paper* space. You will print and use this drawing to learn how to measure objects using the combination scale.
- ☐ Click on the *Print* button and the *Plot* dialog box will open.
- ☐ Select the *Plot Device* tab by clicking on it.
- ☐ Locate your printer in the *Name* drop-down list and select it by clicking on it.
- ☐ Select the *Plot Settings* tab by clicking on it.
- ☐ Set the *Paper Size* to *Letter 8 ½ x11 in.* and then click the *OK* button to print the drawing.
- ☐ Close the *AutoCAD 2002* program by clicking on the *Close* button. You will not be using the program for the remainder of this activity.

1" = 1'- 0" Scale

The first scale you will learn to use is the 1" = 1'- 0" scale. This scale is used to make one inch on the drawing equal to twelve inches (one foot) in the real world.

Figure A-19
1" = 1'- 0" scale

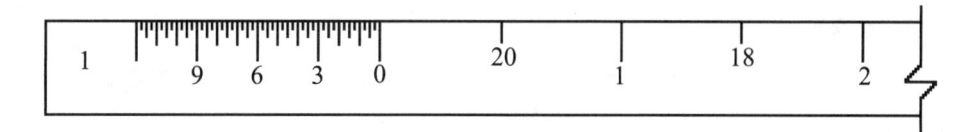

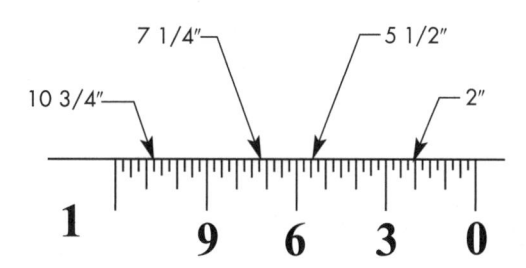

Figure A-20
Enlarged view of the
1" = 1'- 0" scale

- [ ] Use Figure A-19 to locate the 1" = 1'- 0" scale.
- [ ] This scale may look confusing because there are actually two different scales, the 1" = 1'- 0" scale and the 1/2" = 1'- 0" scale, along the same side. The 1" = 1'- 0" scale is read from left to right, and the 1/2" = 1'- 0" scale is read from right to left. To use the 1" = 1'- 0" scale, you ignore the shorter numbered lines, 20, 18, etc., as they belong to the other scale.
- [ ] You may recall that when using the 1/2 size and 1/4 size scales on the combination scale, you read the whole inches in one direction and the fractional part of an inch in the other direction from "0". The scales on the architect's scale are similar.
- [ ] Take a close look at the enlarged scale in Figure A-20 and its divisions left of "0". They are very different from what you used in the last activity. There are no 1/2, 1/4, or 1/8 markings; instead the numbers 3, 6, and 9 appear.
- [ ] Remember that the purpose of this scale is to make 1" equal to a foot. If you divide a foot into smaller units, you do not fractions of a foot, you use inches!
- [ ] The markings you are see to the left of the "0" are inches. If 1" equals a foot, then what does half an inch equal? It is 6". Look at the scale: What is the number of the marking at the midpoint of this part of the scale? 6 for 6".
- [ ] On this scale, inches are read from right to left starting at "0"; the 3" mark is to the right of the 6" mark, and the 9" mark is to the left of the 6" mark.
- [ ] The two longer marks between the numbered lines are also inches. You should be able to identify the 4" and 5" marks lying between the 3" and 6" marks. The next length lines are 1/2" and the smallest ones represent 1/4".
- [ ] Several markings are indicated in the enlarged view of the 1" = 1'- 0" scale to help you understand how this scale works.
- [ ] See if you can locate the following on your scale. You may have to read between the lines to find some of them.

    1 1/4"   4 1/2"   6 1/2"   8 3/8"   11 1/2"

- [ ] Measurements with this scale are made by first placing the "0" mark at one end of the line or distance you want to measure. Place your scale on *View A* of the drawing you printed out and line up the "0" mark as shown in Figure A-21.
- [ ] Notice that the end of the line you are measuring lies between the 1'- 0" and the 2'- 0" marks (yes, feet not inches; numbers to the right of "0" are feet). Also, remember to ignore the other size scale markings.

248 Appendix A

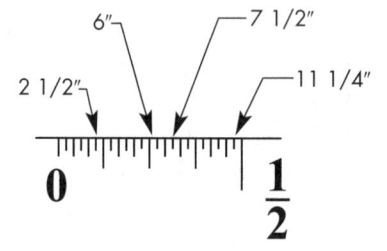

Figure A-21
Using the 1″ = 1′- 0″ scale to measure distance: First step

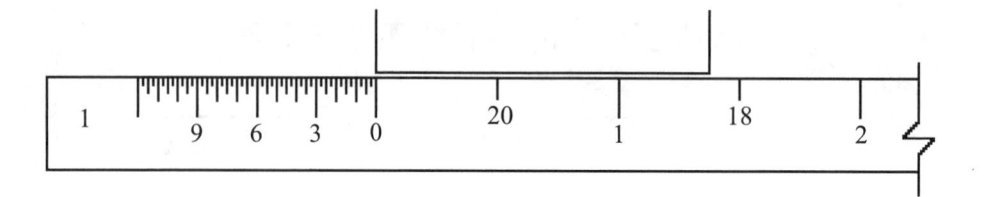

Figure A-22
Using the 1″ = 1′- 0″ scale to measure distance: Second step

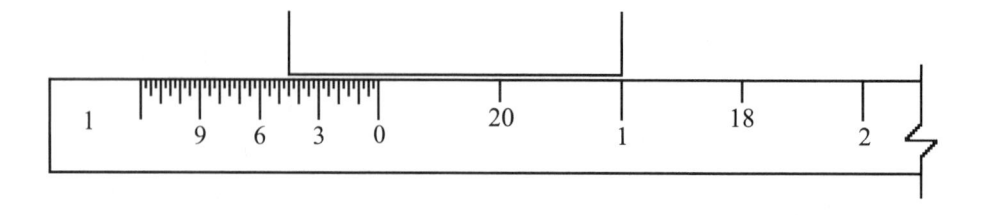

- [ ] The line you are measuring is longer than 1′- 0″ but shorter than 2′- 0″. Slide the scale to the RIGHT to line up the right end of the line with the 1′- 0″ mark as shown in Figure A-22. You will always move the scale to the *smaller* whole dimension.
- [ ] Now read the inches part of the length from the part of the scale to the left of zero.

Note: If the left end of your line does not fall in the inches part of the scale, you slid the scale in the wrong direction. Go back and try again.

- [ ] You should measure this line as being 1′- 4 1/2″ long.
- [ ] Practice measuring the length of the lines in the other views. They should measure: View B = 1′- 10″, C = 3′- 2 1/4″, D = 2′- 9″, E = 6′- 4 1/2″.

1/2″ = 1′- 0″ Scale

The second scale you will learn to use is the 1/2″ = 1′- 0″ scale. This scale is used to make one-half inch on the drawing equal to twelve inches (one foot) in the real world.

- [ ] Use Figure A-23 to locate the 1/2″ = 1′- 0″ scale on your architect's scale. This scale is read from right to left. When using the 1″ = 1′- 0″ scale, you ignored the 1/2″ = 1′- 0″ scale marking, but for this scale you will use the other scale's markings. The longer numbered lines associated with the 1″ = 1′- 0″ scale are the odd-numbered feet for the 1/2″ = 1′- 0″ scale. Therefore, the 10 = 1′- 0″ and the 8 = 5′- 0″ on this scale.

Figure A-23
1/2″ = 1′- 0″ scale

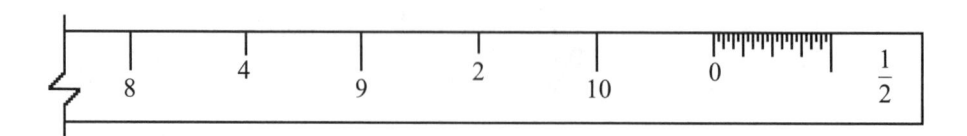

Figure A-24
Enlarged view of the 1/2″ = 1′- 0″ scale

Using Engineering Scales   249

- [ ] When reading this scale, the feet marks are to the left of zero and the inch marks are to the right of zero.
- [ ] Take a close look at the enlarged scale in Figure A-24 and its divisions right of "0". It is similar to the inch scale on the 1" = 1'- 0" scale except that some of the numbers are missing because there is not enough room for them. The three longer lines represent 3", 6", and 9", and the two lines between each of these are the other inch marks. The shortest lines represent 1/2" markings.
- [ ] Several markings are indicated in the enlarged view of the 1/2" = 1'- 0" scale to help you understand how this scale works. Again note that this part of the scale is read left to right.
- [ ] See if you can locate the following on your scale. You may have to read between the lines to find some of them.

    1 1/4"   4 1/2"   6 1/2"   8 3/4"   11"

- [ ] Measurements with this scale are made by first placing the "0" mark at one end of the line or distance you want to measure. Place your scale on *View B* of the drawing you printed out and line up the "0" mark as shown in Figure A-25.
- [ ] Notice that the end of line you are measuring lies between the 3'- 0" and 4'- 0" marks. (Remember, the longer lines are the odd numbers and you are reading from right to left.)
- [ ] The line is longer than 3'- 0" but smaller than 4'- 0". Slide the scale to the LEFT to line the left end of the line up with the line 3'- 0" line as shown in Figure A-26. You will always move the scale to the smaller whole dimension.
- [ ] Now read the inch part of the length from the part of the scale to the right of zero.

Note: If the right end of your line does not fall in the fractional part of the scale, you slid the scale in the wrong direction. Go back and try again.

- [ ] You should measure the line as being 3'- 8" long.
- [ ] Practice measuring the length of the lines in the other views. They should measure: View A = 2'- 9", C = 6'- 4 1/2", D = 5'- 6", E = 12'- 9".

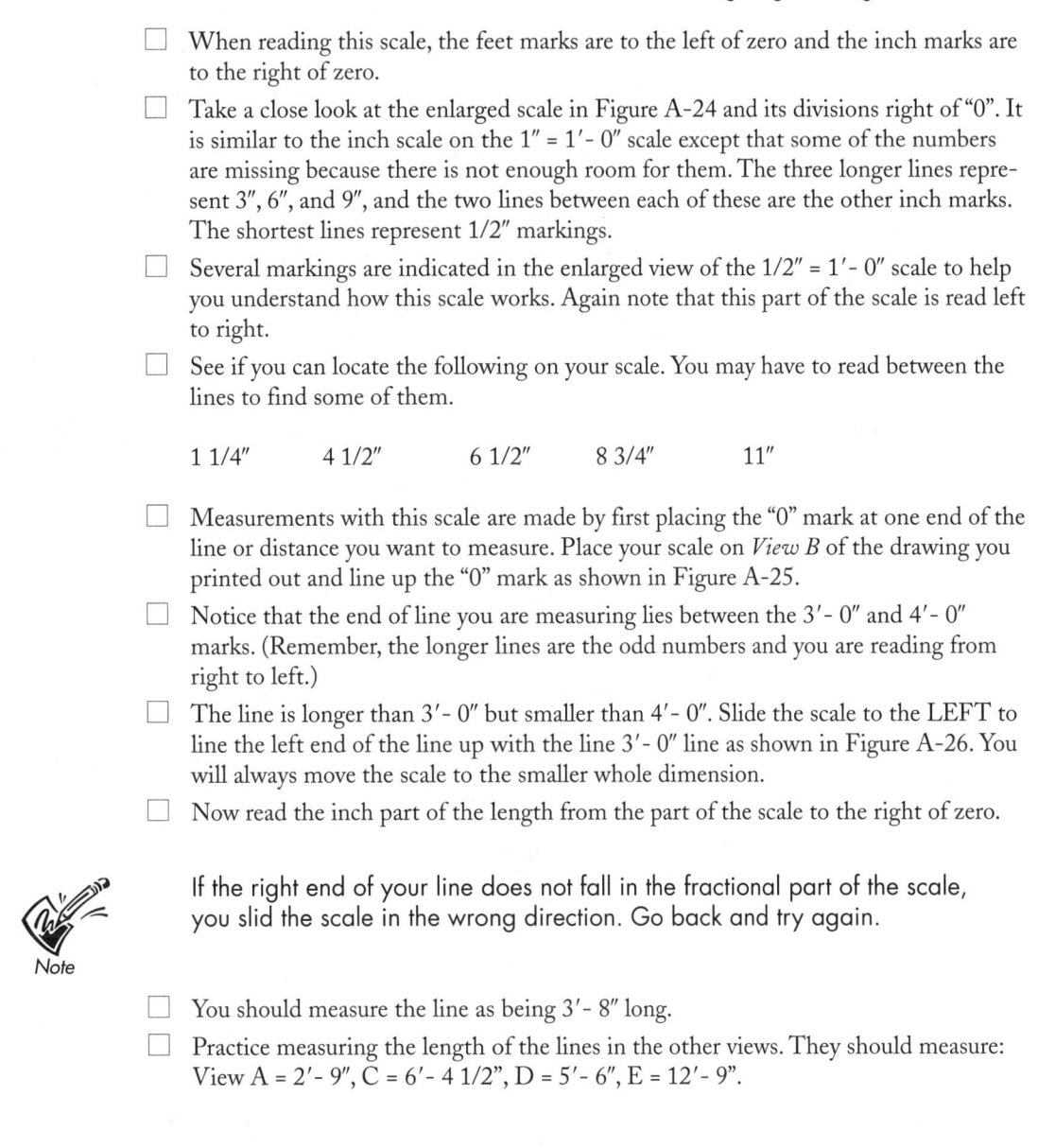

Figure A-25
Using the 1/2" = 1'- 0" scale to measure distance: First step

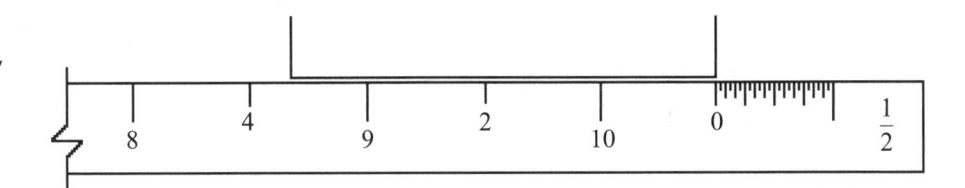

Figure A-26
Using the 1/2" = 1'- 0" scale to measure distance: Second step

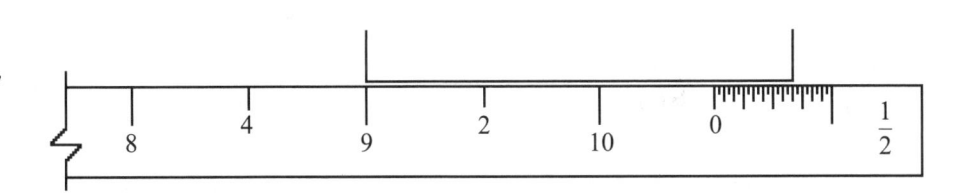

The Other Scales

The following section shows sketches of each of the other scales and the length you should obtain when you use that scale to measure the lines on the drawing you printed out. Each of the following sections contains two scales that share the same edge of the scale.

3″ and 1 1/2″ = 1′- 0″ Scales

3″ = 1′- 0″ Scale:

☐ Notice that the smaller divisions on the inch scale shown in Figure A-27 represent 1/8″. You should be able to read this scale to 1/16″.

☐ Notice that the shorter divisions (the smaller numbers 2 and 4) on the foot part of the scale belong to the 1 1/2″ = 1′- 0″ scale and are not used with this scale.

☐ Practice measuring the length of the lines in the views. They should measure: View A = 0′- 5 1/2″, B = 0′- 7 1/16″, C = 1′- 0 3/4″, D = 0′- 11″, E = 2′- 1 1/2″.

1 1/2″ = 1′- 0″ Scale:

☐ Notice that the smaller divisions on the inch scale shown in Figure A-28 represent 1/4″. You should be able to read this scale to 1/8″.

☐ Notice that the longer divisions (the larger numbers 1 and 2) on the foot part of the scale belong to the 3″ = 1′- 0″ scale and are used as the odd-numbered feet on this scale.

☐ Practice measuring the length of the lines in the views. They should measure: View A = 0′- 11″, B = 1′- 2 5/8″, C = 2′- 1 1/2″, D = 1′- 10″, E = 4′- 3″.

3/4″ and 3/8″ = 1′- 0″ Scales

3/4″ = 1′- 0″ Scale:

☐ Notice that the smaller divisions on the inch scale shown in Figure A-29 represent 1/2″. You should be able to read this scale to 1/4″.

☐ Notice that the shorter divisions (28, 26, etc.) on the foot part of the scale belong to the 3/8″ = 1′- 0″ scale and are not used on this scale.

☐ Practice measuring the length of the lines in the views. They should measure: View A = 1′- 10″, B = 2′- 5 1/4″, C = 4′- 3″, D = 3′- 8″, E = 8′- 6″.

Figure A-27
3″ = 1′- 0″ scale

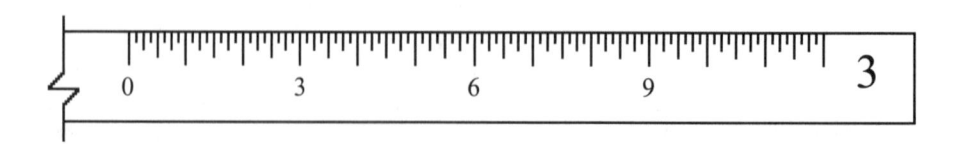

Figure A-28
1 1/2″ = 1′- 0″ scale

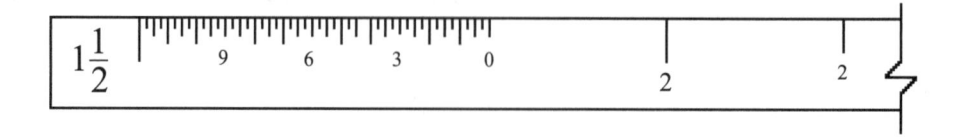

Figure A-29
3/4″ = 1′- 0″ scale

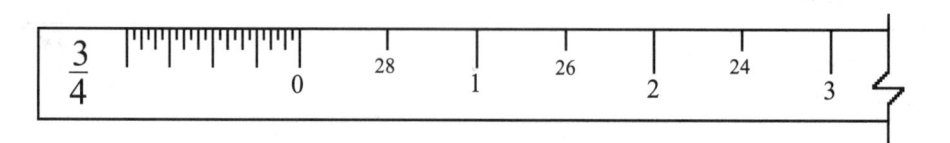

Figure A-30
3/8" = 1'- 0" scale

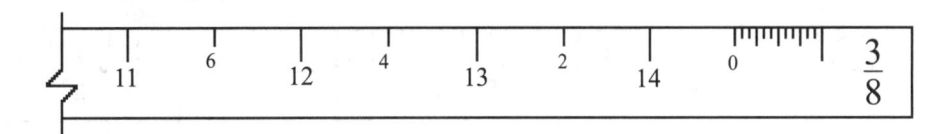

3/8" = 1'- 0" Scale:

☐ Notice that the smaller divisions on the inch scale shown in Figure A-30 represent 1". You should be able to read this scale to 1/2".

☐ Notice that the longer divisions (11, 12, etc.) on the foot part of the scale belong to the 3/4" = 1'- 0" scale and are used as the odd-numbered feet on this scale.

☐ Practice measuring the length of the lines in the views. They should measure: View A = 3'- 8", B = 4'- 10 1/2", C = 8'- 6", D = 7'- 4", E = 17'- 0".

1/4" and 1/8" = 1'- 0" Scales

1/4" = 1'- 0" Scale:

☐ Notice that the smaller divisions on the inch scale shown in Figure A-31 represent 1". You should be able to read this scale to 1/2".

☐ Notice that the shorter divisions (72, 76, etc.) on the foot part of the scale belong to the 1/8" = 1'- 0" scale and are not used on this scale. Also notice that not all of this scale's longer lines are numbered. The unmarked longer lines are the odd feet for this scale.

☐ Practice measuring the length of the lines in the views. They should measure: View A = 5'- 6", B = 7'- 4", C = 12'- 9", D = 11'- 0", E = 25'- 6".

1/8" = 1'- 0" Scale:

☐ Notice that the smaller divisions on the inch scale shown in Figure A-32 represent 2". You should be able to read this scale to 1".

☐ Notice that the longer divisions (46, 44, etc.) on the foot part of the scale belong to the 1/4" = 1'- 0" scale and are used as part of this scale. Also, notice that not every division is numbered, so you have to be careful to read this scale correctly.

☐ Practice measuring the length of the lines in the views. They should measure: View A = 11'- 0", B = 14'- 8", C = 25'- 6", D = 22'- 0", E = 51'- 0".

Figure A-31
1/4" = 1'- 0" scale

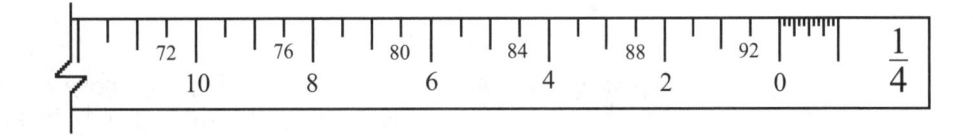

Figure A-32
1/8" = 1'- 0" scale

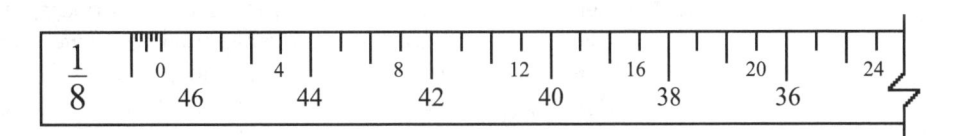

Figure A-33
3/16" = 1'- 0" scale

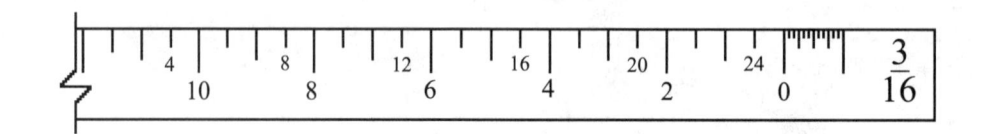

Figure A-34
3/32" = 1'- 0" scale

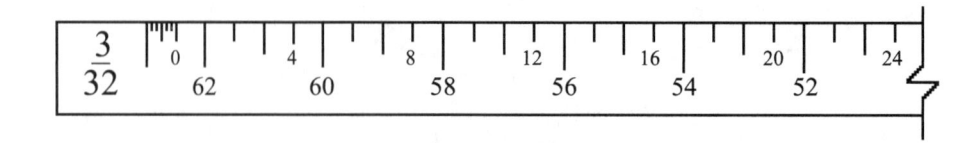

3/16" and 3/32" = 1'- 0" Scales

3/16" = 1'- 0" Scale:

☐ Notice that the smaller divisions on the inch scale shown in Figure A-33 represent 1". You should be able to read this scale to 1/2".

☐ Note that the shorter divisions (4, 8, etc.) on the foot part of the scale belong to the 3/32" = 1'- 0" scale and are not used on this scale. Also, notice that not all of this scale's longer lines are numbered. The unmarked longer lines are the odd feet for this scale.

☐ Practice measuring the length of the lines in the views. They should measure: View A = 7'- 4", B = 9'- 9 1/2", C = 17'- 0", D = 14'- 8", E = 34'- 0".

3/32" = 1'- 0" Scale:

☐ Note that the smaller divisions on the inch scale shown in Figure A-34 represent 2". You should be able to read this scale to 1".

☐ Notice that the longer divisions (62, 60, etc.) on the foot part of the scale belong to the 3/16" = 1'- 0" scale and are used as part of this scale. Also notice that not every division is numbered, so you must be careful to read this scale correctly.

☐ Practice measuring the length of the lines in the views. They should measure: View A = 14'- 8", B = 19'- 7", C = 34'- 0", D = 29'- 4", E = 68'- 0".

☐ This completes this activity. Practice using an architect's scale as much as possible because it will often be used in these activities.

Assignment 1
for Appendix A – Activity 2

In this assignment you will print two drawings that have objects that are approximately the same size on the drawing, but vary greatly in size in the real world. Use your architect's scale to determine the actual size of these scaled objects.

☐ Double-click on the *AutoCAD 2002* icon to open the program.

☐ When the *AutoCAD 2002 Today* dialog box appears, select the *Open a Drawing* tab, and use the *Browse* hyperlink to locate and open the drawing *AScale-2.dwg* from the *Other* subdirectory on the CD.

☐ The drawing will open to Drawing 1, which shows a clevis bracket and a microwave oven. Click on the *Print* button and the *Plot* dialog box will open.

- ☐ Select the *Plot Device* tab by clicking on it.
- ☐ Locate your printer in the *Name* drop-down list and select it by clicking on it.
- ☐ Select the *Plot Settings* tab by clicking on it.
- ☐ Set the *Paper Size* to Letter 8 ½ x11 in., and then click the *OK* button to print the drawing.
- ☐ Click on the tab labeled *Drawing 2* at the bottom of the drawing area. This is a drawing of a stop sign and a truss. Use the methods above to make a print of this drawing.
- ☐ Close the *AutoCAD 2002* program by clicking on the *Close* button.

Use your architect's scale to answer the following questions. The scale of each object is listed on the drawing.

Clevis Bracket

Use the appropriate scale to determine the following dimensions.

1. ____ the width of the clevis bracket (a)
2. ____ the distance from the top to the hole in the clevis bracket (b)
3. ____ the thickness of the top of the clevis bracket (c)
4. ____ the diameter of the hole in the clevis bracket (d)
5. ____ the radius of the end of the clevis bracket (e)

Microwave Oven

Use the appropriate scale to determine the following dimensions.

6. ____ the width of the microwave oven (f)
7. ____ the height of the microwave oven (g)
8. ____ the width of the glass in the microwave oven (h)
9. ____ the height of the glass in the microwave oven (j)

Stop Sign

Use the appropriate scale to determine the following dimensions.

10. ____ the height of the stop sign (k)
11. ____ the width of the stop sign (m)
12. ____ the width of the stop sign's post (n)
13. ____ the height of the letters on the stop sign (p)

Truss

Use the appropriate scale to determine the following dimensions.

14. ____ the length of the bottom member of the truss (q)
15. ____ the height of the truss (r)
16. ____ the length of the top member of the truss (s)
17. ____ the length of the angled member of the truss (t)

Assignment 2

for Appendix A – Activity 2

- ☐ Double-click on the *AutoCAD 2002* icon to open the program.
- ☐ When the *AutoCAD 2002 Today* dialog box appears, select the *Open a Drawing* tab, and use the *Browse* hyperlink to locate and open the drawing *AScale-3.dwg* from the *Other* subdirectory on the CD.
- ☐ The drawing will open to *Paper space*. Click on the *Print* button and the *Plot* dialog box will open.
- ☐ Select the *Plot Device* tab by clicking on it.
- ☐ Locate your printer in the *Name* drop-down list and select it by clicking on it.
- ☐ Select the *Plot Settings* tab by clicking on it.
- ☐ Set the *Paper Size* to *Letter* 8 1/2 x11 in., and then click the *OK* button to print the drawing.
- ☐ Close the *AutoCAD 2002* program by clicking on the *Close* button.

Use your combination scale to measure each line and complete the table on the right side of the drawing.

Appendix A Review Questions

These questions are provided to help you review the topics and concepts covered in this module.

True or False

Determine whether the statement is true or false. Place your answer, either T or F, in the blank.

____   1. Decimal units are commonly used for metric units.
____   2. 3/32″ = 1′ - 0″ is a standard engineering scale.
____   3. Architectural units are only used for drawing buildings and structures.
____   4. All scales are read from left to right.
____   5. An architect's scale is only used by architects.

Multiple-choice

Place the letter of the best answer in the blank.

1. 2′- 8.5″ is an example of ____ linear units.
    a. Decimal
    b. Fractional
    c. Engineering
    d. Architectural

2. 37d15′36″ is an example of ____ angular units.
    a. Decimal
    b. Deg/Min/Sec
    c. Radians
    d. Surveyor's

3. .877r is an example of ____ angular units.
    a. Decimal
    b. Deg/Min/Sec
    c. Radians
    d. Surveyor's

4. 24.325 is an example of ____ linear units.
    a. Decimal
    b. Fractional
    c. Engineering
    d. Architectural

5. 45 is an example of ____ angular units.
    a. Decimal
    b. Deg/Min/Sec
    c. Gradients
    d. Surveyor's

6. 12′- 2 15/16 is an example of ____ linear units.
    a. Decimal
    b. Fractional
    c. Engineering
    d. Architectural

7. 2 5/8 is an example of ____ linear units.
    a. Decimal
    b. Fractional
    c. Engineering
    d. Architectural
8. S 15d30" W is an example of ____ angular units.
    a. Decimal
    b. Deg/Min/Sec
    c. Gradients
    d. Surveyor's
9. 17g is an example of ____ angular units.
    a. Decimal
    b. Deg/Min/Sec
    c. Gradients
    d. Surveyor's
10. ____ is the only true example of surveyor's units listed below.
    a. N16d05"E
    b. W14d15'17"S
    c. N30d15'S
    d. E22s14'N

Appendix B

Answers to End-of-Module Questions

Module 1

True or False:
1. T, 2. T, 3. F, 4. F, 5. T, 6. T, 7. F, 8. F, 9. T, 10. F, 11. T, 12. T, 13. F, 14. T, 15. F, 16. T

Multiple-choice:
1. b, 2. d, 3. b, 4. d, 5. a, 6. c, 7. c

Matching:
1. e, 2. h, 3. j, 4. l, 5. a, 6. c, 7. f, 8. g, 9. i, 10. m, 11. k, 12. d, 13. b

Module 2

True or False:
1. F, 2. F, 3. T, 4. F, 5. T, 6. T, 7. F, 8. F, 9. T, 10. F, 11. T, 12. F, 13. F

Multiple-choice:
1. c, 2. b, 3. c, 4. a, 5. a, 6. d, 7. b, 8. d, 9. c, 10. a, 11. c, 12. a, 13. b, 14. c, 15. a, 16. b, 17. a, 18. c

Module 3

True or False:
1. F, 2. F, 3. T, 4. F, 5. T, 6. T, 7. T, 8. F, 9. T, 10. F, 11. F, 12. T, 13. F, 14. T, 15. F, 16. T

Multiple-choice:
1. d, 2. b, 3. c, 4. a, 5. c

Module 4

True or False:
1. T, 2. F, 3. F, 4. F, 5. F, 6. F, 7. F, 8. F, 9. T, 10. F

Multiple-choice:
1. c, 2. c, 3. d, 4. a, 5. b

Module 5

True or False:
1. F, 2. T, 3. T, 4. F, 5. T, 6. F, 7. T, 8. F, 9. T, 10. F

Multiple-choice:
1. b, 2. c, 3. a, 4. b, 5. d, 6. c, 7. a, 8. b, 9. c, 10. d, 11. b

Module 6

True or False:
1. T, 2. T, 3. T, 4. T, 5. T, 6. F, 7. F, 8. F, 9. T, 10. F, 11. F, 12. T, 13. F, 14. F, 15. T

Multiple-choice:
1. b, 2. a, 3. c, 4. a, 5. d, 6. d, 7. b

Module 7

True or False:
1. T, 2. F, 3. T, 4. F, 5. T, 6. T, 7. T, 8. F, 9. F, 10. F, 11. T, 12. F

Module 8
True or False:
1. F, 2. F, 3. T, 4. T, 5. T, 6. T, 7. T, 8. F, 9. F, 10. T

Appendix A

True or False:
1. T, 2. T, 3. F, 4. F, 5. F

Multiple-choice:
1. c, 2. b, 3. c, 4. a, 5. a, 6. d, 7. b, 8. d, 9. c, 10. a

Index

A

Absolute coordinates, 61
Angular units. *See* Units
Arc, 153
   button, 154
   drawing:
      using start-center-angle, 157
      using start-center-chord length, 158
      using start-center-end, 155
      using start-end-radius, 160
      using 3-point, 154
   elliptical. *See* Ellipse arc
Architect's scale, 246
AutoCAD 2002 Today dialog box, 16, 21, 219

C

Cartesian coordinate system, 45-47
Center object snap, 149
Chamfer, 116
   angle, 120
   button, 117
   distance, setting, 120
   trim option, 117
   unequal distances, 119
Character Map dialog box, 208
Circle, 141
   button, 142
   diameter option, 143
   drawing:
      tangent to a circle, 143
      tangent to a line, 143
      using three-point option, 147
      using two-point option, 147
   solid circle. *See* Donut
Combination scale, 235

Commands, typed-in:
   ARC, 163
   CHAMFER, 119
   CIRCLE, 143
   COPY, 95
   DONUT, 177
   DTEXT, 192
   ELLIPSE, 168
   ERASE. 78
   EXPLODE, 109
   EXTEND, 89
   FILL, 175
   FILLET, 182
   LINE, 57
   MOVE, 92
   MTEXT, 206
   OPEN, 18
   POLYGON, 113
   QUIT, 5
   RECTANGLE, 102
   SAVE, 28
   TOOLTIPS, 13
   TRIM, 87
   ZOOM, 134
Command window, 10-11
Coordinate system, 45-47
Copy, 94
   button, 94
   multiple, 95
   using polar coordinates, 96
   using relative coordinate, 96

D

Donut, 175
   solid, 177
Drafting Settings dialog box, 48

Drafting Settings dialog box, *continued*
   Snap and Grid tab, 48-50
Drawings:
   opening, 16, 21
   printing, 29
   saving, 26
Drawing Units dialog box, 36, 41
Dynamic text, 191
   justification, 194
   rotation angle, 193
   special characters, 196
   underscoring and overscoring, 197

E

Ellipse, 165
   button, 166
   drawing:
      using axis endpoints and rotation, 168
      using center and axis endpoints, 167
      using three axis endpoints, 166
Ellipse arc, 171
   button, 171
Endpoint object snap, 58
Erase, 77
   all, 79
   button, 55, 78
   crossing box, 81
   crossing polygon, 84
   fence, 84
   window, 80
   window polygon, 83
Explode, 108
   button, 108
Extend, 88
   button, 89

F

FILL, 175
Fillet, 180
   button, 180
   radius, setting, 183
   trim option, 181
Fractions, 209
   AutoStack, 212
   AutoStack Properties dialog box, 212-13
   stacking, 209-10
   Stack Properties dialog box, 211

G

Grid, 47
   button, 47
   settings. *See* Drafting Settings dialog box

I

Intersection object snap, 69

L

Limits, setting drawing, 226
Line, 54
   button, 54
   drawing, 54
      tangent to a circle, 149
      using absolute coordinates, 56
      using polar coordinates, 66
      using relative coordinates, 61
   undo option, 57
Linear units. *See* Units

M

Mechanical text style, 199
   setting up, 201
Metric drawings, setting up, 228
Midpoint object snap, 63
Model space, 29
Move, 91
   button, 91
   using polar coordinates, 93
   using relative coordinates, 93
Multiline text, 205
   button, 205
   editing, 209
Multiline Text Editor, 206

N

New, button, 221

O

Object snaps:
   center, 149
   endpoint, 58
   intersection, 69
   midpoint, 63
   quadrant, 150
   tangent, 149
Open, button, 17
Ortho, 91
   button, 91

P

Pan, 135
   point, 136
   realtime, 137

using scroll bars, 135
Paper space, 29
Plot dialog box:
    Plot Device tab, 30
    Plot Settings tab, 31
Polar coordinates, 66
Polygon, 111
    button, 111
    circumscribed, 111
    inscribed, 111
Print, 29
    button, 30

Q

Quadrant object snap, 150

R

Rectangle, 101
    button, 101
    chamfer option, 107
    fillet option, 105
    width option, 104
Relative coordinates, 61

S

Save, 26
    button, 27
    save as, 26
Save Drawing As dialog box, 27
Scales:
    architect's, 246
    combination, 235
Screen layout, 6-9
Scroll bars, 135
Select File dialog box, 18
Snap, 47
    button, 47
    settings. *See* Drafting Settings dialog box
Snaps. *See* Object snaps
Stack Properties dialog box, 211

T

Tangent object snap, 149
Templates, 219
    creating, 221
    saving, 225
    using, 225

Text:
    dynamic. *See* Dynamic text
    multiline. *See* Multiline text
Text style, setting a new, 197
Text Style dialog box, 197-98
Text window, 12
Title block, completing the drawing's, 201, 221
Toolbars:
    docking, 13
    hiding, 14
    moving, 13
    showing, 14
    standard layout, 14-15T
Tooltips, 18
Trim, 85
    button, 86

U

UCS Icon dialog box, 51
Undo, button, 79
Units:
    angular, 41-44
        decimal degrees, 41
        degrees/minutes/seconds, 42
        gradients, 43
        radians, 43
        surveyor's, 44
    linear, 35-40
        architectural, 39
        decimal, 36
        engineering, 38
        fractional, 37
        metric, 37
    setting the drawing's, 226
User Coordinate System (UCS), 50

Z

Zoom, 129
    all, 131
    center, 133
    dynamic, 132
    extents, 131
    in, 134
    out, 134
    previous, 131
    realtime, 132
    scale, 133
    window, 130